Lord Minto, A Memoir

By

John Buchan

Copyright © 2013 Read Books Ltd.
This book is copyright and may not be
reproduced or copied in any way without
the express permission of the publisher in writing

British Library Cataloguing-in-Publication Data
A catalogue record for this book is available from the
British Library

John Buchan

John Buchan, first Baron Tweedsmuir of Elsfield, was born in Perth, Scotland in 1875. In his youth, his father immersed him in the history, legends and myths of Scotland, and he was an avid reader, stating some years later that John Bunyan's *The Pilgrim's Progress* was a "constant companion" to him. Buchan's education was uneven, but at the age of seventeen he obtained a scholarship to study classics at Glasgow University, where he began to write poetry. His first work, *The Essays and Apothegms of Francis Lord Bacon*, was published in 1894, and a year later he enrolled at Oxford University to study law.

In 1900, Buchan moved to London, and two years later accepted a civil service post in South Africa. In the years leading up to World War I, he worked at a publishers, and also wrote *Prester John* (1910) – which later became a school reader, translated into many languages – as well as a number of biographies. In 1915, Buchan become a war correspondent for *The Times*, and published his most well-known book, the thriller *The Thirty-Nine Steps*. After the war he became a director of the news agency Reuters.

Over the course of his life, Buchan would eventually publish some one hundred books, forty or so of which were novels, mostly wartime thrillers. In the latter part of his life he worked in politics, serving as Conservative MP for the Scottish universities and Lord High Commissioner of the Church of Scotland (1933-34). In 1935, Buchan moved to Canada, where he became the thirty-fifth Governor General of Canada. He died in 1940, aged 64.

*Gilbert John, 4th Earl of Minto, K.G., P.O., G.O.S.I., etc.
(From a sketch by P. A. Laszlo, 1912)*

PREFACE

In writing this Memoir I have had access to the journal and the private papers of Lord Minto, as well as to the official records of his administration in India and Canada, and I have had the further advantage of talks and consultations with many of his friends. To these I would offer my sincere thanks, and I would gratefully acknowledge the kindness of Lady Hutton, who lent me some of the papers of her husband, the late Lieutenant-General Sir Edward Hutton, and the generosity of the executors of the late Lord Morley and Messrs. Macmillan & Co., who have permitted me to quote extracts from Lord Morley's letters, both published and unpublished.

The book owes a special debt to two collaborators. It was undertaken at the request of Lady Minto, who has given me such constant and invaluable help that in a real sense the book is her own. She not only arranged and analysed for me a formidable mass of documents, but from her intimate association with her husband's work she was able to cast light on many obscure matters, and to reproduce for me the atmosphere of events, which cannot be recovered from the written or printed page. I have had, too, the use of her delightful Indian diary, which I wish could be given intact to the world, for in light and colour those words of an eye-witness are far superior to any Chronicle at second hand.

The other is the late Arthur Elliot. He was my friend for many years, and only those who had the privilege of knowing that wise and gracious character can realize how much better this book would have been if he had lived to give it his kindly criticism. Throughout their lives the two brothers shared each other's full confidence. Minto's letters to him are the most revealing in the correspondence, and from him I received most of the material for the early chapters. My hope is that the Memoir in its final form may be such as he would have approved.

    J. B. ELSFIELD MANOR, OXON.

CONTENTS

INTRODUCTORY........ Page 13

BOOK ONE

1. BOYHOOD: ETON AND CAMBRIDGE........ Page 26

2. STRENUOUS IDLENESS........ Page 53

3. APPRENTICESHIP........ Page 87

4. CANADA: 1883-85........ Page 124

5. SOLDIERING AND POLITICS AT HOME........ Page 143

BOOK TWO

6. GOVERNOR-GENERAL OF CANADA, 1898-1904........ Page 187

7. GOVERNOR-GENERAL OF CANADA (continued)........ Page 246

8. GOVERNOR-GENERAL OF CANADA (continued)........ Page 279

BOOK THREE

9. VICEROY OF INDIA, 1905-6........ Page 316

10. VICEROY OF INDIA 1907-8........ Page 370

11. VICEROY OF INDIA 1909-10........ Page 421

12. VICEROY OF INDIA: DEPARTURE........ Page 469

13. CONCLUSION........ Page 492

INDEX........ Page 512

ILLUSTRATIONS

Gilbert John, 4th Earl of Minto, K.G., P.O., G.O.S.I., etc. (From a sketch by P. A. Laszlo, 1912)........Frontispiece

Gilbert John Elliot, at the age of thirteen (From a miniature at Minto House)........ Page 28

"Mr. Rolly"........ Page 64

Lord Melgund in the Uniform of the Border Mounted Rifles, 1883......... Page 98

Lord Melgund in 1890 (Photo by Chancellor)........
Page 158

Lord Minto as Governor-General of Canada, 1899........
Page 229

Lord Minto and "Dandy," 1900. (Photo by Topley, Ottawa) .... Page 274

Lady Minto, 1907........ Page 374

Lord Minto addressing the First Meeting of the new Legislative Council, Government House, Calcutta, 1910........ Page 446

INTRODUCTORY

THE BORDER ELLIOTS

Scottish Borderland in its widest sense embraces the country from the Ken to Berwick, and from the Solway and the Cheviots to the backbone of mountain which runs from Merrick to the Lammermoors and cradles all the streams of the Lowlands. In that broad region the Britons of Strathclyde, the Northmen from the sea, and the later immigrants have so mixed their blood as to produce a certain uniformity of type, akin to and yet something different from other Lowland stocks. The history of each valley has been the same tale of poor soil, inclement seasons, stunted cattle and niggardly crops, a hard life varied by constant bickering among neighbours and raids into England; these valleys lay, too, in the track of the marching armies, whenever there was war between Stuart and Plantagenet and Tudor, and, save for the religious houses and the stone castles of the nobles, there could be few enduring marks of human occupation. It was a gipsy land, where life could not settle on its lees, since any night the thatch might be flaring to heaven, and the plenishing of a farm moving southward under the prick of the raiders' spears. There the hand must keep the head, and a tough, watchful race was the consequence, hardy as the black cattle of their hills, tenacious of a certain rude honour, loyal to their leaders, staunch friends, and most patient and pestilent foes. Rough as the life was, it had its codes and graces. The Borderer was quarrelsome, but he was also merciful, and was curiously averse to the shedding of blood. He was hospitable to a fault, scrupulously faithful to his word, and in giving and taking hard knocks preserved a certain humour and mirthfulness. "The men are lyght of harte," wrote Bartholemew the Englishman in the thirteenth century, "fiers and couragious on theyre enemies." And Bishop Lesley, writing in the sixteenth century, noted that they were skilful musicians and "lovers of eloquence and poetry." Mr. Andrew Boorde, an English physician, who visited them about that date, bore witness to the same qualities, and had little fault to find except with "their develysh dysposicion not to love nor favour an Englyshman," their extreme clannishness, and their boastful pride of race. "Many," he wrote, "wyll make strong lyes." Among their green glens harpers and violers wove some of the loveliest of Scottish airs, and the gift of imagination had other issue than mere vaunting, since it gave birth to the noblest ballads that ever graced a literature.

Of the Borderland in the wider sense the Marches were the heart and citadel, and no part was in more constant unsettlement than that western area from the upper waters of Liddel to the Solway. There dwelt the Armstrongs and the Elliots, and lesser septs like the Nixons and the Croziers. It is hard to take the view of the old pedigree-makers that the Elliots as a clan were transplanted bodily from the village of Alyth, in Forfarshire, by the first Earl of Angus, when the Douglas interest became powerful on the Border. For this view historical and philological proofs are alike wanting, and it is more probable that the Ellwalds, Elwoods, or Ellets were of the same race as the other septs of Liddesdale, autochthonous in a true sense, deriving their descent from some ancient admixture of the blood of Norse rovers with that of the British of Strathclyde. The earliest records show them holding the upper glens of Liddel, as the Armstrongs held its middle course.

The piety of lettered descendants-for few Scottish family histories have been so carefully written as that of the Elliots--has preserved what is known of the rude March life before the Union of the Crowns took the heart out of Border war. The Elliots of Liddesdale lived for three centuries the life of the camp. Their little massy stone towers could not be altogether destroyed, but rooftree and thatch and wooden outbuildings were perpetually blazing to heaven. They had occasional quarrels with Scots neighbours, and standing feuds with Musgraves and Fenwicks and Grahams across the English line. Sometimes they were bridled by the Scottish Warden of the Marches and their warlike ardour made to serve the national cause, but more often it was a war of kites and crows, wild rides on moonlit nights, desperate affrays in moorland hollows, the "hot-trod" down Tyne or Tees when men died for a half-dozen lean cattle. The name of Liddesdale was feared as far as Yorkshire; it is recorded that in the year 1541 the English Warden tried to induce reprisals, but Tynedale and Redesdale "refused to commit slaughter of any of the notable surnames of Liddesdale for fear of deadly feud," and preferred to harry their less dangerous neighbours of

Teviotside. Sometimes the Church took a hand, and the Archbishop of Glasgow was prompted by Cardinal Wolsey to lay on the Borderers a most terrible curse, concluding with "I condemn them perpetually to the deep pit of hell to remain with Lucifer and all his fellows, and their bodies to the gallows on the Burrow Mure, first to be hangit, syne revin and ruggit with dogs, swine, and other wild beasts abominable to all the world." But to hang an Elliot you had first to catch him--no easy matter, and for the empty thunder of the Church he and his kind cared not a straw. As for the Douglas lords of Liddesdale, they could threaten, and occasionally hang, but they could not restrain. "Dark Elliot's Border spear" might be kept at home for a little by burdensome bonds and hostages, but presently would come a harvest moon and it would be taken down again from the thatch. Hangings and homings availed little, and it was to do justice on the Elliots that Bothwell marched into Liddesdale in 1556, whereby he nearly lost his life and brought Queen Mary galloping through the mosses from Jedburgh to Hermitage. Let it be said to their credit that they were stubbornly national, and rarely paltered with the English enemy. Hence their long friendship with the "rough clan" of Buccleuch, who were of the same way of thinking.

This wild life of the Marches ended early in the seventeenth century, when the governments of Scotland and England combined to crush the lawless clans. The process which James V. had begun with the hanging of Johnnie Armstrong was carried to an effective conclusion. In Stevenson's words "the rusty blunderbuss of Scots criminal justice, which usually hurt nobody but jurymen, became a weapon of precision for the Nicksons, the Ellwalds, and the Croziers." The lairds were compelled to give security for good behaviour, the old merry days of hunting in the Cheviots and raiding Northumberland were over, and, since their occupation was gone, poverty closed in on them. Men drifted to other parts of Scotland or went abroad to the wars; in the sixteenth century the Elliots had been able to muster 450 mounted men, which meant a clan numbering at least 1500; by the middle of the eighteenth century the latter figure represented the total population of Liddesdale. Soon, as Nicol Burne the Violer sang, "many a place stood in hard case where blithe folk kent nae sorrow," and Scot of Satchels in the seventeenth century thus deplored in his rough doggerel the Elliot fortunes:--

"For the Elliots, brave and worthy men, Have been as much oppressed as any name I ken, For in my own time I have known so much odds, No Elliot enjoyed any heritage but Dunlibyre, Fanash, and Stobs."

It is with the last-named remaining heritage that we are now concerned. As Mangerton had the headship of the Armstrongs, so the chief of the Elliots was the laird of Redheugh, which stood near the foot of the Hermitage Water. But as time went on the Redheugh family became more identified with the peel of Lariston, higher up the Liddel valley. Stobs, across the hills on the Slitrig Water, a tributary of Teviot, became an Elliot property in 1580,* and in the second decade of the seventeenth century passed into the hands of one Gilbert Elliot, a cadet of Lariston, whose mother was a Scott of Buccleuch. This Gilbert, known as "Gibbie wi' the Gowden Garters," married another Scott, the "Flower of Yarrow," a daughter of "Auld Wat of Harden," and, judging from his place in ballad literature, must have been of a character to impress the imagination of the countryside. Of the Stobs family several represented the county of Roxburgh in Parliament, both before and after the Union, and from it sprung the famous soldier, Lord Heathfield, the defender of Gibraltar; but we must turn aside from its main line and follow that of Gilbert's fourth son, Gavin of Midlem Mill, who by his marriage with Margaret Hay of the ancient Tweeddale house of Haystoun was the father of two sons, Robert and Gilbert. This latter was the first Elliot of Minto.

* Weir of Hermiston.

Born the younger son of a younger son, Gilbert had to carve out his own career. Though barely three generations removed from the moss-troopers, he possessed that compound of worldly sagacity and religion, that ability both to watch and to pray, which is characteristic of one Scottish type. He began as a writer (Anglice solicitor) in Edinburgh, and in the strife of Covenant and Crown took the side of the former. A mission to London to save the life of the well-known minister, William Veitch, brought him under the notice of the leaders of the Opposition, and presently he was mixed up in the affairs of Argyll, and joined the group which included Baillie of Jerviswood, Hume of Polwarth, and William Carstares. In January 1685 he was compelled to fly the land, and returned from Holland in May with Argyll and his friends to start the futile rising which brought its leader's head to the block. There was some of the old riding blood left in the Whig lawyer, for Gilbert Elliot was with Sir John Cochran in the skirmish at Muirdykes, and gave a good account of himself. Thereafter he led a hunted life, though by some accident his name was omitted from the Government proclamation. Presently he left the country, and in his absence was sentenced to death and forfeiture, which sentence was remitted in 1687 in consideration of the earlier services of his father to the Royalist cause. He returned to Edinburgh, was admitted as an advocate to the higher branch of his profession, and when the Revolution brought his friends into power advanced swiftly at the Bar. Knighted in 1692, a baronet in 1700, member of Parliament for the county of Roxburgh in 1703, he was now of a fortune to entitle him to purchase an estate, and in this last year he bought the lands of Minto. Two years later he went to the bench under the title of Lord Minto, becoming a judge of the very court which twenty years before had condemned him to death. He died in 1718 at the age of sixty-seven, having won out of the disorders of the Revolution a modest fortune and estate. His portrait shows a long, heavy-jowled, mellow face, with humorous and sagacious eyes. He was the essential moderate, who managed to steer a middle course even in the stormy waters of the Union controversy, but who, when occasion required, could show himself a devoted friend and imperil his career in a doomed cause. Wodrow describes him as a man of "unshaken probity, integrity, and boldness against all unrighteousness and vice"--a tribute which showed how far the race had advanced in decorum since the ancient days of Lariston.

His eldest son, Gilbert, the second baronet, sat like his father for Roxburgh, like him and under the same title became a Lord of Session, and for forty years adorned the Scots bench, becoming eventually Lord Justice Clerk in succession to Erskine of Tinewald. There is scarcely an incident which stands out in his placid life except that he was visited by Prince Charlie's army on its march to Derby, and had to take refuge in Minto Craigs. But he created the bones of the house as we know it to-day, laid the foundations of the fine library, planted the avenues, made the pond, and turned the glen from a wilderness into a pleasaunce. With his son, the third Sir Gilbert, the family embarked on the tides of British politics. Brought up at the colleges of Edinburgh and Leyden, he married the heiress of the Melgund lands in Forfar and the Kynnynmond property in Fife, and, partly owing to his friendship with Charles Townshend (who had married Lady Dalkeith), abandoned a promising career at the Scots Bar for London and Parliament. In him the astuteness of his grandfather and his power of steering a middle course were abnormally developed. He held various Government posts--Lordships of the Admiralty and Treasury and such-like--

and would have undoubtedly gone farther but for his nationality, for he was a good man of business and a brilliant debater. But he managed to remain in office, like a permanent civil servant, when Ministers fell, for he conciliated antagonisms and united oppositions; a close friend of Bute, he was also a follower of the elder Pitt; professing himself a consistent Whig, he became one of the most noted of the "King's Friends," and was a vigorous opponent of the Americans. A temper so supple and accommodating is not the soil in which to look for a sturdy growth of principles; but his friends, who were numerous and devoted, believed that he was always prepared "to take a stand on the supreme authority of Parliament."

His eldest son, Gilbert the fourth, was destined during the sixty-three years of his life to convert the title of the old "paper-lords" of Minto into a lordship of Parliament and an earldom. In his generation of Elliots there was not only a high level of talent, but a strain of something fantastic and adventurous. The third son, Alexander, was the friend and agent in India of Warren Hastings, who erected a monument to him on his early death. The second, Hugh, was one of the most brilliant of British diplomatists in a brilliant age; a creature of strange moods and impulses, who as a boy fought with the Russians against the Turks, called out his man in a duel, held his own with Frederick the Great, and was the author of bons mots at which all Europe laughed. It was he who, when the King of Prussia commented tartly on the expression of gratitude to God which accompanied the official account of Sir Eyre Coote's victory over Hyder Ali, "Je ne savais pas que la Providence fut de vos allies," replied "Le seul, Sire, que nous ne payons pas." Gilbert, the eldest son, began life with a resounding success at the English Bar, but presently entered Parliament, and, as the friend of Burke and Fox and Windham, rose high in the favour of the Whigs. He was one of the managers of the Warren Hastings trial, and took his part in that debauch of frigid rhetoric. When the Revolution broke out in France he inclined to the views of Burke, and presently was sent on various continental missions, in returning from one of which he had the good fortune to be an eye-witness of the battle of Cape St. Vincent. At fortysix he was made a peer on his return from the viceroyalty of Corsica; then followed the embassy at Vienna; and then in 1806, after having been President of the Board of Control in the "Ministry of all the Talents," the Governorship of India. There he had the difficult task seeing and providing against Napoleon's Asiatic ambitions, and his chief problems were those of external policy, the relations with Persia and Afghanistan and the great Sikh Power at Lahore. In the space of his viceroyalty he saw the menace of France disappear, and largely by his own exertions Java and the Moluccas added to the possessions of Britain. An attractive figure he seems to us, who could win and retain the affection of men so different as Burke and Nelson, and who in all the whirl of public duties found his chief refreshment in the letters of his family, in the recollection of "home-felt pleasures and gentle scenes," and in plans for beautifying his Border home. He was not fated to see Minto again, for when he returned after seven years' rule in India with an earldom and a great name, he died on the first stage of that happy northward journey of which for seven years he had dreamed.

With the second Earl and fifth Baronet the house of Minto had become established in that character which attaches as clearly to families as to individuals, though it is slower to develop. The descendants of the riding Elliots were now decorous and public-spirited citizens, Whigs who cherished a belief in the People combined with a strong conviction that only a few families were fit to govern. The old devil-may-care spirit of Lariston had revived for a moment in Hugh the ambassador, but in the first half of the nineteenth century it slumbered. The second Earl was successively ambassador to Berlin, First Lord of the Admiralty and Lord Privy Seal, and by the marriage of his daughter, Frances, to Lord John Russell, was connected with the inner counsels of his party. In the days of the Lords of Session Minto had been a plain Scots country house, and the company that visited it an occasional judge on circuit, or a vacation party of Edinburgh lawyers, with a stray historian or philosopher from the university. But the last Sir Gilbert and first Earl had widened the bounds, great men like Burke journeyed thither, and soon the house, enlarged and adorned, was one of the chain of lodgings by means of which the leaders of politics and society made their northern tours--a stage between Dalkeith and Alnwick. As in duty bound its dwellers kept touch with the latest books, music, gossip, and learned speculation; but, having that union of far-wandering impulses with the love of home which characterizes their countrymen, they were never mere Londoners taking the rural air, but country folk, thirled to the soil, and loving every rood of it. He who would seek an account of the full and vigorous life of Border gentlefolk a hundred years ago will find it portrayed for all time in the pages of Lockhart.

The third Earl--a William and not a Gilbert--chose the fallentis semita vita. He sat for many years in Parliament, but never held office, and much of his time was given to the management of his estate, county business, country sports, and long periods of foreign travel. His wife's father was Lieutenant-General Sir Thomas Hislop, and her mother a daughter of Hugh Elliot, so she was a distant cousin of her husband's. Never strong in body, she had the spirit of a soldier, and wherever she went radiated an atmosphere of gentleness and mirth and courage. Like many who are not robust in health, she had an insatiable zest for life, and had, perhaps from her sufferings, keener perceptions than other people, and a quicker sense of joy. Each new experience and interest was adopted with gusto, and few quiet lives have been more fully lived. The list of the books she was reading at the age of twenty-three might shame many professed scholars; but she had nothing of the blue-stocking in her, and her learning was a small thing compared to her wit, her sense of fun, her startling acumen, and her broad tolerant wisdom. She is a figure that may be commended to the acquaintance of those who, in Lady Louisa Stuart's phrase, have "an old-fashioned partiality for a gentlewoman," and one could wish that Mr. Arthur Elliot's privately printed volume of extracts from her letters and journals could be made accessible to the world. For as a letter writer she ranks with Lady Louisa. She was also an accomplished historian and biographer, as her memoir of Hugh Elliot and her four volumes on the first lord minto prove, and her Border Sketches show how deep she had drunk of the traditions of her ancestral countryside. But it is in her diaries and letters that she most reveals herself, and whether she is trying to probe the secret of some rare landscape, or discoursing gravely on politics and metaphysics--till she breaks off with a laugh, or gossiping about manners and people, or formulating from a rich experience a mellow philosophy of life, she leaves on the reader an impression of a soul rich in the best endowments of humanity, a spirit at once sane and adventurous, securely anchored and yet reaching out delightedly to the cyclic changes of the world. If there were two strains in the Elliot blood--the venturesomeness and speed of Liddesdale, and the sagacious centrality of the Whig lairds--in her they were mixed in right proportion, and she bequeathed something of this just equipoise to her sons.

BOOK ONE

CHAPTER 1

BOYHOOD: ETON AND CAMBRIDGE

The subject of this Memoir was born in London on July 9, 1845, at 36 Wilton Crescent, the house of his grandmother, Lady Hislop. He was given the family name of Gilbert, and the second name of John after his uncle and godfather, Lord John Russell. Two months later his father. Lord Melgund, who was then out of Parliament, carried off his wife and child on one of those protracted continental visits which were the fashion in that generation. The Melgunds took with them their carriage--in which a shelf had been fitted to serve as the baby's crib--a courier, a nurse, and a lady's maid, and made a leisurely progress up the Rhine to Switzerland, and then over the St. Gothard into Italy. The winter was spent chiefly in Rome and Turin with the British Minister, Sir Ralph Abercromby,* who had married Lady Mary Elliot. Country house visits filled the rest of that year, and at Cambridge Gilbert John took his first wavering steps on the lawn in front of the lodge at Trinity. It was not until the early spring of 1847 that the Melgunds returned to Scotland and the child saw the home of his ancestors.

*Afterwards Lord Dunfermline.

Most of Gilbert John's boyhood was spent at Minto, and it would be hard to find a happier environment for a child than the roomy old Border house set among its lawns and glens and woodlands. All accounts agree on the sunniness of his temper, the vigour of his body, and his uncommon good looks. He had his mother's deep blue eyes, which Mrs. Norton praised in the style of the period.* Presently brothers came to keep him company: Arthur, born in 1846; Hugh in 1848; Fitzwilliam in 1849; and the four little boys formed a stalwart clan, sufficiently near in age to be true playmates.

* The following verses were written as a postscript to a letter from "Miss Letitia Bellamy" in London to Miss Fanny Law of Clare, Northumberland, describing Lady Melgund's children among others at a children's party given by the Duchess of Argyll. They were published in Fisher's Drawing Room Scrap Book, edited by Mrs. Norton:--

"The prizes have been given--but no time can be lost, I must hurry lightly through them if I wish to save the post: For the loveliest sleeping infant, to the Duchess of Argyll (It was like a little rosebud, if a rosebud could but smile), The prettiest two-year-old who walked the distance from the door Being carried in his nurse's arms and set down on the floor, And the loveliest little three-year-old that ever yet was seen, In a glittering ducal palace or a daisied village green, With eyelashes like shadows and eyes like summer stars, A little stately, graceful thing no imperfection mars: Both were won by

Lady Melgund, I don't know who had gained The ones before I entered, these were all that then remained"

Gilbert John Elliot, at the age of thirteen (From a miniature at Minto House)

The love of horses was Gilbert's absorbing passion, and during his continental visits at the age of one he was reported by his father to have shown a precocious knowledge of horseflesh at the various posting-houses. Before he was four he rode a bay Shetland pony, "Mazeppa," under the tuition of the old groom, Robert Donald, and barely a year later commenced his hunting career with the Duke of Buccleuch's hounds, of which hunt he was one day to become a noted figure. It was a recognized practice on the days he was going to hunt not to send up his porridge, as he was far too excited to eat any breakfast.

Few children can have had more engaging ways. The love of his home was deep in him, and before he was five, when driving with his mother to inspect the havoc caused among the Minto trees by a gale, he revealed his anxious affection. She writes: "Berty invariably shuts his eyes not to see the injured silver. 'No, I can't bear to look at it, it makes my heart too sad,' and occasionally he sighs out a most mournful 'Alas' when we pass any grievous wrecks. His sentiment about everything surpasses anything I ever heard, and in some things he certainly shows considerateness beyond his years; he always offers to go out with me, and often insists on doing so, though I know he would rather have his pony. Once he said to the nurse, 'Well, I would rather ride, but I promised Papa to take care of Mama, and so I had better go with her;' and it is perfectly true that William did tell him so, but I was not at all aware how seriously he was impressed with the charge. However, he certainly keeps his promises, for he watches me as a cat does a mouse."

Lady Minto often breaks off her letters to chronicle the return of the boys and dogs, far too dirty to be allowed to come beyond the door. There were many sports in that happy place: rabbit-hunting in the Lamblairs, fishing in the Teviot and the hill burns, house-building with fir branches on the side of the Big Glen below the Green Walk, tree-climbing in the great beeches and sycamores whence the upper windows of the house could be spied on, walking--in emulation of certain feats of a previous generation--along the stone ledge which runs round the top of the house, skating and glissading in the bitter winters which now seem to be unknown in the land. They were even allowed to keep a lamb under the turret stairs, which their long-suffering mother did not evict until it became a sheep.

Usually Minto was filled with a big family party, but there came times when Lord Melgund was attending the House of Commons, and mother and children were left in comparative solitude. Such seasons were devoted by her to the beginning of their education. The family did not believe in private schools, and certainly with such a mother no seminary for youth could compare with home. Her strong good sense on these matters is witnessed by a hundred passages in her letters: "Minds, like bodies, should have good solid meals, and leisure for digestion, and time to stretch! Beef makes bone, and les études fortes nourish the mind; but it will not do to let it gnaw every merry-thought, nor refine itself into spun sugar" In her room the boys read poetry and history and fairy tales, and we hear of Gilbert declaiming with passion Pope's version of Diomede's speech in the 9th Iliad. But the chief formative influence was the atmosphere of good talk in which they lived, talk about books and politics and the events of a larger world, which stimulates a child's interest. Gilbert was, in his mother's view, a little slower to quicken than the others, for he had a certain placidity and contentment which lived happily in the day and might foretell a lack of mental enterprise.

On his seventh birthday she writes in her journal:--

"He is not as advanced in learning as many of his contemporaries, but he learns easily and bids fair to possess more than average intelligence. He has a good memory, is very observing, and extremely obedient and docile. He has a natural turn for poetry, and certainly admires the beauty of numbers even when he can scarce understand the words. He is very fond of fairy tales, and indeed of any description of story I will read to him, unless it is very dry or he suspects me of an intention to instruct him. . . . I don't think he has as much curiosity to learn about the things round him as his brothers have." (Those earnest inquirers, be it remembered, were of ages varying from two to five.) "He has a most amiable disposition, and not a spark of malice, sulkiness, or envy in his character. He is very sweet-tempered and yielding, always gay, never put out. . . . I don't think him a child gifted with deep sensibilities or enthusiastic feelings of any kind, neither has he the perseverance or love of overcoming obstacles of some children, but he is sensitive to blame, and has little sentimentalities about localities and past days, is very open to impressions of fine weather, scenery, and pleasant ideas of all kinds. He is very courageous and high-spirited."

And the candid mother concludes that "energy and perseverance" are the qualities at present most to seek, qualities which were assuredly not absent in his subsequent career.

In 1853 the children joined their grandparents at Nervi, on the Riviera, returning by the Lake of Geneva, where Gilbert had his first sight of the snow mountains which later were to throw their glamour over his fancy. His military instincts were early apparent, and the Crimean War gave him something to talk about; he used to present himself daily at the luncheon table after the newspapers had arrived with the breathless question, "Does Silistria still hold out?"

It is a delightful group of boys that is portrayed in Lady Minto's letters, portrayed by one who understood all the subtleties of childhood. "The people who really enjoy life in this house are the boys," she writes; "nevertheless, I suppose they have their grievances, for Fitz told me one day he could never remember the time when he had been happy! Hughie, on being asked what he thought of things in general, answered, 'Oh, weary! weary! no change, the same thing every day; I think we must go to Africa.' And the next day he repeated his

African intentions to me, adding, 'And if we did go I suppose they would put taxes on everything directly--tax the date trees.' I made out afterwards that his horror of taxation arose from a difficulty about keeping another dog which he had been wanting to have."*

* There is a story of one of the little boys who bore with difficulty the visit of several girl cousins. On their departure he was heard condoling with his dog: "Poor old man, poor old fellow, did those horrid little girls give you fleas?"

II

Gilbert went to Eton in the summer half of 1859, to Mr. Balstone's house, which next year became Mr. Warre's. In July his grandfather died, and by his father's accession to the earldom he became Lord Melgund. He was no classical scholar, though, like Kinglake, he had "learned the Iliad through Pope in his mother's dressing-room," and the Eton of his day did not offer much in the way of a general education. His mother writes:--

"Berty has already taken his first flight from home. He left us for Eton last May, and has now returned to spend his second holiday with us. Gentle, gentlemanlike and loving, manly, intelligent and sincere, his character promises well for future goodness. His learning will never be deep nor his energy great, nor is he remarkable either for originality or quickness, but he is sensible, easily interested, likes history, poetry, and drawing, and will, I think, as I have always thought, learn more when his learning is of a kind more to his mind. . . . He is impressible, and not without a desire of doing well. His chief characteristic has ever been his strong moral sense."

Melgund speedily found his feet at Eton: he was supremely happy, and flung the full vigour of his strong young body into every form of sport. His mother records his cheery letters: during the first summer half he wrote that he had started in the school tub race and had come in seventy-second, which, he adds, was not so bad for a first attempt. His optimism was fully justified, as before leaving Eton he had pulled up seventy-one places, finishing second in the School Sculling. He also made a name for himself in the running field, was just beaten in the mile race, and ran the "Long Walk" (three miles) in fifteen and a half minutes.

The journal which he began to keep in 1861 is as scrappy as other schoolboy chronicles. It records famous days with the beagles, steeplechases, and games of football in which he was a demon at shinning, but the river was his chief joy. He rowed in the Defiance and the Victory, and in his last summer half was first choice out of the Eight, winning the Silver Sculls. Corkran (Captain of the Boats) and he were both hoisted after the race. The determination to keep fit prevented any indulgence at the sock shop. The Elliots were a hardy race, and Melgund remembered his indignation at being given a greatcoat when he first went to Eton, driving from

Hawick to Carlisle, a distance of nearly fifty miles, on the top of the stage coach.

A few characteristic entries may be quoted from the journal. He writes on February 1863:--

"The Prince of Wales came through here to-day: he had been out with the harriers. I thought he looked a very decent sort of chap, but I didn't see what sort of a horse he had."

The marriage of the Prince and Princess of Wales in March gave the Eton boys a holiday.

"At 10:30 the whole school assembled in the School Yard and walked up arm-in-arm to the Castle. We had a very good place inside the upper gates of the Castle. There was an awful crowd, which I got jolly well into once and had roaring fun. We went, down to the College for dinner, and went up to the Castle again afterwards to see the Prince and Princess of Wales depart for Osborne. Directly their carriage had passed all the Eton fellows rushed through the crowd and regularly forced their way down to the corner of the street near Layton's, where a body of police were drawn up, but they were quickly dispersed, and we rushed down to the station, broke through the barrier, and got on to the platform and squealed like mad. I had a better view of the Princess than I ever had before, as she stood bolt upright in the railway carriage as it went slowly out of the station. It was about the greatest lark I ever had, bowling over the crowd, which was a thundering tight one, and smashing through the police!"

In the summer half of 1863 Melgund was elected to "Pop," and made his maiden speech in favour of "instantaneously going to war with America." Under 2nd June the journal has this entry:--

"Jersey,* Hope major,** Phipps, and I made up a nice little party to go to Ascot. We all of us wore whiskers except Jersey, who wore a loose overcoat and a blue veil. I wore a flexible moabite sort of hat and my great-coat. Hope looked about the handsomest fellow I ever saw: he had on a light-coloured overcoat and black whiskers. We all had light ties We went to Bachelor's Acre, where we got into an open fly which we had ordered beforehand and drove in it. We got to Ascot about twenty minutes past four. When we got to the course we all took off our false whiskers except Phipps, but he got so bothered by the Gypsies, who asked him whose hair he had got on, etc., that he finally had to follow our example. Hope and I somehow or other got separated from Jersey and Phipps; we caught sight of Parker and a lot of fellows who had a drag; they gave us some champagne and let us stand on the top of the drag. Phipps and Jersey walked right up to 'Parva Dies'* and were nailed. We saw one race--the Prince of Wales' Stakes: 'Avenger' won. I thought the race itself an awfully pretty sight and very exciting. We started from Ascot about five, and got back in loads of time. We got out of our fly at the footbarracks, where 'Sambo' (the raft man) met us and took our clothes. Day* complained of Jersey and Phipps, and they were both swished. There was great excitement about it, and the space round the swishing-room door was crowded."

* The seventh Earl of Jersey. The late Sir Edward Hope, K.C.B., registrar of the Privy Council, known among his friends as "Blackie" Hope.

* Mr. Day, one of the masters.

After this performance the quartette had the effrontery to be photographed in their costumes at Hills and Saunders'. There was a later escapade:--

"June 25th.--Went up town to make purchases in the shape of a disguise to go to Henley. After dinner I stayed out and started for Henley by a train which leaves Windsor at about 3:30. We drove from Twyford to Henley, a distance of about five miles. I had a round hat on and a thin overcoat, a moustache, no whiskers, and a couple of bits of sticking plaster on my face. Sherbrooke had nothing but a thin overcoat and a pair of blue spectacles. Very few fellows knew us. Snowe (a master) went and came back with us in the same train, and I think if it had not been for Hubbard's and Freeling's good nature (they had left school) we should have been nailed.

"Hope lent me a key which would open all the doors of the carriages on the Great Western Line, which proved very useful. I was in a horrid funk when I first saw Snowe on the platform at Slough. I met him again at Henley once when I was walking on the bank, on which occasion we took advantage of our acquaintance with Heave, who is rowing for Trinity Hahl, and hung on to him and passed Snowe all right. The next time I met him was on the Bridge^ and I lounged by him without taking any notice, I met the Eight coming over the Bridge, just before they got into their boat. Sheepwood was one of the few fellows who recognized us: he set up a howl in the middle of the Bridge and swore he would have known us anywhere: he was very nearly getting us nailed, for Warre was close behind him, but luckily stopped just at the moment to say how-d'ye-do to Freeling.

"Snowe was on the station at Henley, but Hubbard and Freeling kept a lookout for us. We came back second class, and at Slough got out on the wrong side of the carriage. We got into a fly and drove up to Serle's, where we were the first to publish the news of the race. It was Eton 1st, Trinity Hall 2nd, and Radley 3rd. It is glorious our licking a Cambridge crew which is second boat on the river at Cambridge. We won by about a length and a half.

"When we came back I found that I had not been nailed, and Snowe called Sherbrooke in the evening and told him about the race. I felt rather guilty when my tutor came to tell me about it. He told the fellows in the Eight that he knew I should be as anxious to hear about it as any one.

"June 27th.--After lock-up my tutor sent for me and told me that my name was mixed up in the row about Henley, and after Prayers he came up to my room and began again. He was justgoing out of the room when he said, 'Then I am to understand that you were in the house?' I said, 'No, sir, I was not in the house.' He said, 'Where were you?' to which I answered, 'I was at Henley, sir.' He stood for some time without saying anything. At last he said that of course he would say nothing as I has told him in confidence, but that the thing was not yet finished. He was in an awful way about it, and declared that he would never go to Henley again as he had found out that he could not trust his fellows. The worst of him is that he expects you to treat him exactly as any of your friends, but I don't think tutor and pupil ought to be on the same footing.

"June 30th.--Yesterday my tutor sent for me and said that I had escaped out of the Henley row; that I was the luckiest fellow in creation; that I had been within an ace of being nailed; that inquiries had been made at the house, and that owing to some mistake of Mrs. Digby's (the matron) I had got off. He said there was only one link wanting in the evidence against me. This evening he came up to my room again and told me that there was a report that I had gone to Henley disguised as a Methodist Parson. At this I nearly had a fit of hysterics: of course the Methodist Parson was Lamb, who has been swished and turned down. My tutor says that the worst of this row is that if it happened again next year it might put a stop to our Eight going to Henley altogether. The only thing I care particularly about is that my tutor has taken it to heart."

On 17th July he writes in his journal:--

"Upper Eights were rowed to-day. I suppose this is the last long boat race I shall ever row in, and I am sorry for it. I do not believe there can be anything much jollier than rowing a good race: it is awfully stunning to come up with a boat and then go by and row past the Brocas in triumph. Even though you don't win the race, yet you know that you have done your best, and after all perhaps there is more honour in rowing a good stern race than in winning an easy one. . . . Sam Corkran wanted me to start with him in the pulling. I would have given worlds to start with Sam, but I did not see how I could get off Pope."

To refuse to row with the Captain of the Boats because he was pledged to another boy was proof of a stiff sense of honour. He stuck to Pope, and Corkran and Richards won the pulling.

Melgund was automatically moving up in the school; but his parents, fearing that sport was occupying the major part of his time, decided to take him away from these alluring surroundings and send him to a tutor. He regretfully bade farewell to Eton at the end of the summer half of 1863, just after his eighteenth birthday. He had become one of the most popular and distinguished figures in the school, and carried away with him sixty-four leaving books. Although he had frequently transgressed the rules from sheer devilry and love of excitement there had been no shadow of meanness or untruth on his career. With his tutor, Mr. Warre, he had formed a close friendship, for the latter, in spite of his strict standards of conduct, had much tolerance for youthful extravagances so long as they were honest and clean and did not offend against the canons of sportsmanship. To Lady Minto he wrote that "Melgund was unspoilt and unspoilable," while the journal records that "Warre certainly is a very jolly fellow, not the least like a master when he is not acting as one."

But the most delightful days in the retrospect of all the brothers were those spent at Minto, hunting and shooting, curling and skating in the winters, fishing and swimming in the long summer days. Hunting was the serious family pursuit--"A' Elliots can ride," said the old Buccleuch huntsman at a time when the two families were in opposite political camps and he was not prepared to allow them any other virtue. It was a Spartan business in those days, and we have a picture of the boys on bleak mornings shivering at covert side, in everyday little short jackets and waistcoats, a linen shirt (no under-flannels or drawers), trousers and riding-straps, no overcoats and no gloves. There was rarely a meet nearer than six or seven miles; ten miles was not considered distant, and fifteen nothing to complain of. The party would leave the house long before it was light, and hack the long roads in any weather^on the off-chance of hunting. In summer there was fishing in the Teviot, standing in the river all day up to their waists without waders; but the chief game was navigating a boat called a "trows," used for "burning the water," and consisting of two troughs joined together at an angle. In this venerable craft the boys shot the rapids of the Teviot, but the end came when Melgund and his brother Hugh embarked in it in a high spate, barely escaped shipwreck at Rulefoot, and in the end scrambled perilously ashore, while their Argo was whirled down towards Tweed. We hear of them in winter daring each other to swim the river in spate, and finishing stark naked in the open haugh with the sleet whipping their small bodies. There were days with the otter hounds, too, on Ale and Teviot, beginning long before sunrise; and there was shooting with old Stoddart, the head keeper, shooting with muzzle-loaders and later with pin-fire breech-loaders, pottering in the woods and boggy pastures, and long autumn days after grouse on the Langhope moors. There was no desire at Minto for record bags, and shooting always played second fiddle to hunting; but it was an enchanted country for boys to wander over with a gun.

School is a chief formative element, no doubt, in every life, but at that period still more depends upon the background of holidays, when young thoughts range adventurously before they find their inevitable grooves; and Eton in Melgund's case was only an interlude in the full and happy course of a Border boyhood. The hereditary feeling for his home, found in every Elliot, was strengthened by his mother's deep passion. She could write thus of the Craigs:--

"The White Rock this afternoon was much more like a holy place to me. Nothing could be more peaceful, and we all sat there for some time listening to the wood pigeons, and watching some boys wading in the river, probably following a salmon. I think sometimes if we would let God draw us to Him by means of the natural agencies with which He has surrounded us, instead of insisting upon it that we can only get at Him by violent and distasteful efforts of our own, by singing without voices and preaching without brains, we should be more religious people. And certainly no sermon I ever heard can speak to one's heart so forcibly as do the scenes and associations of an old family house like this, where tender memories are in every room, like dried flowers between the leaves of a book."

III

The autumn and winter of 1863 was spent by Melgund with a tutor in Dresden, and part of the summer of 1864 with a coach in the Isle of Wight. In February 1864 he went to hear the Queen's Speech in the House of Lords. The Elliot clan had for generations produced diplomats and lawgivers, but Melgund had scant respect for politicians, whose ways, he considered, lacked candour. While still at Eton his father had taken him to hear a debate in the House of Commons, and in the journal he describes the legislators as "about the noisiest set of old coves I have ever seen." It was an aversion of temperament which to some degree remained with him through life.

In October 1864 he and his brother Arthur went up to Cambridge together as fellow commoners of Trinity.* As a peer's son, according to the rule of those days, he had the privilege of taking his degree in seven terms instead of nine. The journal of his undergraduate life does not reflect any great desire for learning, but it reveals untiring enthusiasm for every form of sport. He naturally became a member of the Third Trinity Boat Club, and, though other arenas soon proved more attractive than the river, we find him a competitor for the ^olquhoun Sculls. He was distinguished on the running track, winning the Third Trinity Mile though heavily handicapped by having his arm strapped to his side owing to a fall with the Drag, and he came in second at the London Amateur Athletic Club. He was earnestly exhorted to continue that career by his friend, Dick Webster, the future Lord Chief Justice of England, who wrote him disconsolate letters from London complaining of the utter boredom of the study of law. The journal records "a match with Trickett for two miles, giving him a hundred yards start, and I backed myself £5 to a postage stamp to beat him. At first I thought I should hardly catch him, but very soon got up to him, and he shut up almost directly after I passed him." But soon all other sports gave way to his passion for riding and horses, not as an idle spectator but for the physical accomplishment of horsemanship. He never missed a good race meeting, if within reasonable distance, or a chance of riding in it. He hunted with the true Elliot industry, as witness this entry: "I went out with the Fitzwilliam to-day They met at Ashton Wold. I had about 32 miles to ride to cover . . . we had a pretty good day, and I had about 32 miles to ride home as we left off very near where we began." He had the good fortune to be out with the Pytchley the day of the famous "Waterloo Run." Captain Anstruther Thomson, the Master, was on his fifth horse, and Melgund on his hireling saw about a third of it. He was constantly at Newmarket, and rode frequently in local steeplechases, but he had then, as he always had, a dislike of the gambling fashion which tends to degrade a famous sport, and he never betted. In the jottings in his journal, and the correspondence which remains from those days, there is none of that dreary chatter about cash lost and won which makes the conversation of some honest sportsmen like the gossip of a bucket shop.

* Dr. Montagu Butler, Master of Trinity, wrote in 1914: "My memory goes back to 1865, when Melgund had but lately left Eton as confessedly one of the best loved that even that great school of friendship had produced."

There are records in the journal of balls and amateur theatricals and undergraduate high jinks which do not differ greatly from the undergraduate doings of to-day. He lived at the start with his brother Arthur in Rose Crescent, but when the latter went into college he migrated to a famous set of apartments called "French's," a resort of riding men, which remained his headquarters, except when he was careering about the country to race meetings, and contenting himself, if no better accommodation could be found, with a shake-down in a brush shop or the back room of a wine merchant.

There was little time left for study during those strenuous days. That the pace must have been furious is evident from the entries in his journal recording wonderful gallops, serious falls, and hairbreadth escapes. In reading old letters of this period from Queensberry, Aberdour,* Jersey, Horace Seymour, "Cat" Richardson, and others, one is struck by the deep affection in which Melgund was held by his friends. He brought from Eton the nickname of "Rolly" (apparently from his slightly rolling gait), and there must have been something curiously engaging in his manner, a kind of serious jollity, without a trace of the arrogant or the selfish or the peevish. But he did not win his popularity by any slackness of standards, for he had a very strict notion of what he considered right and wrong. He burned out a gambling set at French's with hot cayenne pepper, and when he first came up took a strong line about the snobbishness of some of the clubs. Snobbery, indeed, and all the minor vices which attend society, he cordially disliked. At the time his mother wrote of him: "Don't be alarmed about Berty; the ballroom will have no chance in his affection for many a day against the hunting field and the river: but his Dresden life has done him good by making him more ready to talk, and more anxious to understand what people are talking about. I must say, though I perhaps ought not, that he is a very satisfactory chip of a very good old block (I don't speak of his father only, but of his race); perfectly natural and unassuming, and as spirited and energetic as a boy can be." And again: "The boys' Cambridge talk is very amusing and thoroughly satisfactory--I mean as to the moral effect of their residence there. I can't say I see any evidence of intellectual training whatever; but it is impossible to listen to Berty's frank and full revelations of himself and his habits and companions without feeling thoroughly happy about him; he is not intellectual, but he has plenty of good sense, a singularly fair and candid mind, and a will strong enough to be unconscious of itself, by which I mean that there is no effort in his independence of mind. He sees what seems to him to be right, and as a matter of course does it."

* Afterwards twentieth Earl of Morton

Of his studies there are few records. The journal contains occasional entries such as:--

"Had a trigonometry paper this morning, which, of course, I did not attempt to do a word of. In the afternoon we had a Livy translation paper. I think I could have managed most of it with the help of the man next me, but unluckily I got throwing pens about, one of which cut over one of the examiners. . . . Hudson, the other examiner, got in a great rage: he found out that Montgomerie, among others, had been throwing pens about, and has gated him at 8 o'clock for the rest of the term. Luckily the term is just at an end. . . . Before I left Cambridge to-day I wrote a note to Hudson to tell him that it was I who had hit the examiner with the pen during the examination and not Montgomerie."

It may be mentioned that, in spite of a notable economy of effort Melgund never failed to pass the requisite examinations either at Eton or Cambridge.

His Cambridge vacations, like his Eton holidays, were pleasantly varied. Christmas of 1864 was spent with his family in Rome, as we learn from his mother's letters:--

"Berty, with all his spirits and idleness (which perhaps I exaggerate) is as good as it is possible to be. He has really not a wish or a taste or a habit which we would rather see away. He leads a very lively life, hunting twice a week, and going out constantly in the evenings to dinners, operas, balls, parties, and private theatricals. His dinners are frequently to meet Lord and Lady Grey, or some Monsignori, or some other persons equally old and dignified; but he always finds them 'awfully jolly,' is quite without shyness, and among foreigners or English has always the same perfectly easy well-bred manner."

Elsewhere she writes:--

"Berty, I fear, has no honourable intentions towards any of the many young ladies to whom he offers his hand in the cotillon. He dances six times in one evening with the prettiest, and blushes about her next day; and he dances most nights, and therefore blushes most mornings; but the first of pleasures to him is a good gallop across country, and no young lady would have the slightest chance of attracting his attention on hunting days. . . . His Sunday best costume includes a waistcoat with the buttons of a Cambridge Club-the 'Quare Haec'--and a breastpin in his cravat with a note of interrogation in dark blue enamel on a gold ground! I say that no one but Socrates has the right to go about in the guise of a perpetual question."

There were seasons at Minto when balls and race meetings were attractions which now took the place of the old voyaging in the "trows," and parties of Cambridge and Eton companions were added to the clan of relations. During two summer vacations Melgund went to Switzerland, once with his friend Maclean,* with whom he made the third ascent of the Schreckhorn; the journal records sleeping out on a ledge of rock in the snow from which the top was reached in seven and a half hours. They also climbed the Wetterhorn and Monte Rosa, and traversed the Jungfrau with the famous mountaineer, Mr. Horace Walker, and his daughter, leaving Zermatt just before Mr. Whymper's first ascent of the Matterhorn, when Queensberry's brother was killed. High mountains were with the Elliots a hereditary passion, and as an Eton boy Melgund had begun his mountaineering career by ascending the Breithorn, the peak which his father had, thirty years earlier as an Eton boy, ascended with his father long before there was an inn at Zermatt, or the Alpine Club had been dreamed of. He came of age on July 9, 1866, on the top of the Lyskamm. It is significant that the only extracts copied into his early journals are a poem by the Rev. Arthur G. Butler defending the assault on the Matterhorn when Lord Francis Douglas was killed:--

"We were not what we are Without that other fiery element-- The love, the thirst for venture, and the scorn That aught should be too great for mortal powers";

and the great speech of Claverhouse to Morton in Old Mortality:--

"When I think of death as a thing worth thinking of, it is in the hope of pressing one day some well-fought and hard-won field of battle, and dying with the shout of victory in my ear--that would be worth dying for; and more, it would be worth having lived for!"

* Later Chief Justice of Calcutta, when Minto was Viceroy of India.

His love of mountains never left him, and his last climbing adventure was in 1900, when he delayed his journey through the Rockies at Glacier in order to ascend Mount Avalanche--to the amazement of the imported Swiss guides, who could not believe that the Governor-General would get out of his train after a prolonged official tour and spend eleven arduous hours climbing a mountain. He wrote in his journal: "Ascended Mount Avalanche: two guides. Started 6:30 a.m., reached the summit 12:30. Left again 1:30 p.m. and arrived Glacier House 4:40. Very hard climb. We came down roped together, and glissading down a severe slope came to grief and finished the glissade on our backs, but no damage done." He had taken the precaution of inscribing his name on a card which was placed inside a bottle and laid in the snow on the summit, on the chance of its coming to light as "the last message of the Governor-General" should anything untoward happen.

In November 1866 Melgund passed the final examination at Cambridge, and on 13th December took his degree and bade farewell to the University in characteristic fashion. Steeplechasing had been forbidden by the authorities till the men had gone down, so it happened that the race for the Fitzwilliam Whip and the bestowal of degrees took place on the same day. "The Whip" had been twice won by Cecil Legard, who expected to carry it off for the third time and therefore retain possession of the trophy. Melgund determined to bring off the double event. He duly appeared in cap and gown, but under his academical dress he wore boots and breeches, and his spurs were in his pocket. A cob was waiting outside the hall, and as soon as the ceremony was over he was in the saddle and galloping for Cottenham. He reached the course not a moment too soon; rushed to the weighing room as the bell for the race was ringing and the horses were leaving the paddock; mounted his horse "Rival" and galloped to the starting-post, getting into line just as the flag fell. It was a desperate race, neck and neck the whole way; a breathless second of silence; then shouts of excitement from Melgund's backers--Legard had been beaten by a head.

Melgund's next appearance in the Cambridge Senate House was forty-four years later, when he was given an honorary doctor's degree.

CHAPTER TWO

STRENUOUS IDLENESS

Having done with tutors and preceptors, Melgund had the world before him, but to one in his position the exact road to travel was not immediately clear. He was destined for the Army, but the Army in the late 'Sixties was not a profession to absorb all the energies of a young man gifted with perfect health, untiring vitality, and a desperate love of enterprise. His education had been drawn less from books than from life, and his taste was more for action than for argument, for adventure of the body rather than of the mind. He could concentrate fiercely on what had captured his interest, and he was prepared to run any risk; indeed, the greater the risk in any business the more ardently he followed it. Supremely honest with himself and with all men, he had the courage which is a matter of instinct and inclination rather than of duty, and he pursued the "bright eyes of danger" for their own sake. Such a one must make a cast in many directions before he finds his true line. Life seems very good to him, and he warms both hands joyfully at its fire. It was this abounding appetite and unquenchable high spirits that marked him out from the other young men of his year who came down from Cambridge. He had no trace of laziness or indifference in his composition, but time must elapse before the flow of energy could be effectively canalized.

In the spring of 1867 he was gazetted to the Scots Guards (then called the Scots Fusilier Guards). It was rather a dead time in the Army, those years between the Crimean War and the Cardwell reforms, and it was hard for Melgund to acquire much interest in home soldiering in London, or at Aldershot or Windsor, though many of his Eton and Cambridge friends were in the Guards or the Household Cavalry. But there were interesting links with the past. He notes in his journal in July 1868 that he dined with the old Field-Marshal, Sir Alexander Woodford: "He is really a wonderful old man: he told me all about the ball at the Duchess of Richmond's at Brussels, just before Waterloo, and says he remembers four Highlanders of the 42nd being brought into the ballroom and dancing a reel, and that three of them were killed next day at Quatre Bras. Sir Alexander himself left the Duchess's ball post-haste for the field, and remained four days campaigning in his dancing pumps. He commanded a battalion of the Coldstream at Waterloo, and he looks as fit as a fiddle now."

Melgund found the routine of duty with his regiment at the Tower, Chelsea, or Wellington Barracks too monotonous for an active man, and the journal contains few professional incidents beyond the "review" held in Windsor Park in June 1869 for the Khedive of Egypt. He had never in his life a taste for gambling, and play in the Guards in those days was high, for he records that a poverty-stricken friend of his lost £3000 in one night, and that bets of £5000 and £7000 would be laid on a rubber of whist. Nor did orgies of meat and drink amuse him, as when sixty gentlemen in barracks consumed at dinner one hundred bottles of champagne in addition to other wine. He tells his mother darkly that the woods at Minto will have to be cut down to pay his mess bills.

The boredom of his profession did not prevent him from enjoying a variety of social life. Old letters which have been preserved are full of chaff and gossip--stories of boxing and fencing at Angelo's, boisterous evenings at "Billy Shaw's" or "Evans'," and now and then a stately function such as the Queen's Ball on July 2, 1868, after which, in company with Lord Lansdowne and Lord Charles Beresford, and with the help of the Fitzwilliams' terriers he indulged in a cat hunt--a picture for the historical artist of three future most eminenl servants of the Crown, all in gala clothes, whooping and careering among the sober shades of Berkeley Square. He describes a breakfast at the Palace in the following to which he went in "a blue evening coat and brass buttons with a thistle on them, light trousers and a white waistcoat, being the costume the Prince of Wales wished people to wear." In his letters to his mother, delightful letters full of badinage and affection, he tells of the pretty girls he met, and the races he rode, and the utter ennui of the hours spent on duty. Here is an extract: "I was driven over (to Ascot) every day on some kind friend's drag, which, as I daresay you know, is a vehicle drawn by four horses, which generally have never been together before, and driven by an individual who considers himself a coachman, but is without any idea of holding horses together. The smashes in the first day's racing were really without end--my coachman drove me over an iron railing, luckily without upsetting me, and on the way home, though quite unable to drive myself, I had to take the reins and stop the horses by main force . . . One coach which left barracks arrived on the course with no leaders, and another with its roof bathed in blood, which, the driver said, was owing to the horses having been all over the top of the coach." Those were lighthearted days, as witness the bitter complaint of his brother Hugh: "The Oxford and Cambridge match commenced yesterday at Lord's. I met Berty in the Pavilion of the M.C.C., a place set apart specially for members, neither of us being members. The brute had the impudence to try and have me turned out as a nonmember! . . . I must say Berty is devoid of all principle."

The serious business of those years was horses. Melgund kept up his rowing and running for some time after leaving Cambridge, but it was in riding that he found his true interest. Whenever he could get leave from his regiment he was off hunting or steeplechasing. In 1868 we find him riding "The Begum" second in the race for the Household Brigade Cup, and winning the Hunters' Handicap at Aylesbury on "Darkness." In October of that year he paid his first visit to Limber Magna the home of his friend Mr. John Maunsell Richardson, and so began that association with Lincolnshire which was to be one of the happiest episodes of his life. "Cat" Richardson had been one of the old group at French's, and the friendship which Melgund began at Cambridge ended only with his death. No greater gentleman-rider lived during the last half-century than the man who won the Grand National on "Disturbance" in 1873, and on "Reugny" in 1874. A visitor to his Cambridge rooms once asked for a book to pass the time of waiting, and was told by his servant that Mr. Richardson did not possess a book of any sort; but so strong was the "Cat's" character that he could shut himself up and read for a solid year in order to pass his examinations.

At first Melgund went to Limber principally for the hunting, which to him and the "Cat" meant conjugating all the moods and tenses of that verb. On off days there was racing, which consisted in riding one of the Limber stable chasers, or getting a mount wherever one was available, no matter whether bad or good, for the possibility of broken bones was not considered. The fascination of the Limber life decided Melgund to send in his papers. Brother officers like "Bar" Campbell and Lord Abinger begged him not to "make a damned fool of himself," and assumed that there was some woman at the bottom of it, and that he wanted to get married. Nothing was further from his mind. Melgund was very susceptible to a pretty face if possessed by what he termed "a good sort"; and he would spend a whole evening in the society of a favourite partner. In those stiff days of etiquette his behaviour horrified the chaperones; when taken to task for his conduct in making a lady conspicuous he would laughingly declare that he was "a friend of the family"; and next day she would be forgotten in the excitement of those breathless matches round the Limber race-course, schooling the best blood on the turf over hurdles. He sought a life which would give outlet to his restless energies, and he believed he had found it in that career of peripatetic jockeydom of which Richardson was already a brilliant exponent. Throughout that spring he was posting about to race meetings all over the country, having adopted the serious business of a gentleman jockey.

II

Melgund's racing life began when he settled at Limber with the Richardsons in 1870, and practically closed in '76 with his mishap at the Grand National, though he continued to ride occasionally for some time. The four years in the Lincolnshire country house form a curious and strenuous interlude in a life which never lacked variety. To begin with, when the "Cat" was still at the height of his racing success, Melgund toured the land, riding whenever he could get a mount, but chiefly at north-country meetings, so that Mr. John Corlett, of pious memory, was moved to observe in the Sporting Times that "Mr. Roly has taken to riding like the devil." After the "Cat" gave up riding in 1874 Melgund rode almost entirely for the Limber stables, Lord Downe, Captain Machell, and Sir J. Astley being among the owners who had their horses trained there. The whole episode was characteristic of his serious simplicity in the pursuits which attracted him. Whatever he did he was determined to do in a workmanlike way: he hated the slipshod amateur, and had no love for half-heartedness in any walk of life, since it seemed to him that if a thing was worth doing at all it was worth doing well. It may be hard to explain why an education in horses is also an education in human nature, but it is the truth; and those years of mixing with all classes on a common ground were for him an invaluable training in the understanding and management of men. He was quite aware that many people looked askance at the jockey, but he was never prepared to accept conventional views for which he saw no valid defence. He writes to his mother: "I could not help smiling at your remarks on my 'jockeyship.' I believe the word 'jockey' conveys some horrible meaning to non-racing people. As long as one rides badly and sticks to country races I suppose it does not matter how much one rides; but directly one rides in the great races one is considered a jockey, which is a dreadful thing! My reasons against riding are that it takes too much time and is certainly not a thing to make a career of. Otherwise it is the finest game I know, requiring more head and more energy than other games. No doubt there is much blackguardism connected with it, but I should like to know one single profession in which there is not blackguardism. Certainly politics will not bear looking into." This was written when he had turned his back upon steeple-chasing, but there were still longing looks behind, and years after, when Viceroy of India, he told Francis Grenfell with a sigh that he wished he had been a trainer.

But the Limber days were marred by no looking before or after. He had found a task which absorbed all his energies, and he was supremely happy. The four years were spent in a discipline almost as rigid as that of a religious order. Old Mrs. Maunsell, Mr. Richardson's grandmother, used to say, "I pity the girls when he looks at them with those beautiful eyes of his." But the handsome young man cared only for horses. There were neighbours of the hard-riding persuasion, like the Yarboroughs and the Listowels, and the Rev. H. G. Southwell, who was Mr. Richardson's stepfather, and with whom Melgund formed an enduring friendship. On Sundays church was attended with exemplary regularity. Visitors came occasionally, famous racing men like Captain Machell and Captain "Bay" Middleton, and old Cambridge friends like Cecil Legard, now a sporting parson, and Aberdour and Wodehouse. But the party as a rule consisted of Melgund, the "Cat," his brother and sister, a very happy and well-agreed quartette. Miss Richardson in her biography of her brother has drawn a charming picture of the life: the long days in the open, the hungry party at dinner living over again the day's run, the sleepy evenings thereafter, each nodding in his chair. Nobody played cards or gambled; "drinks would come in, but they would go out again untasted night after night, for there were no drinkers." The "Cat" and Melgund did not smoke: never was seen a more blameless and healthy existence. But high spirits and hard conditions were sometimes too much for decorum and there would be bear fights, when the panes in the book-cases would be shattered and good dress-coats rent from collar to tail.

One episode deserves recording. Melgund and Richardson had a friend, a lady, whom they used alternately TO pilot out hunting. They each urged her to buy a favourite hunter. One evening a demand was received for the horse to be sent on trial, and an argument arose as to which horse should be sent. So serious became the dispute that their friends declared that the only way to settle the business was to fight it out. "Accordingly the combatants stripped to the waist and in a neighbouring wood had six rounds of the best. Both were severely punished; but Richardson, who was the bigger man of the two, remained the victor. Peter Flower was Melgund's second, Hugh Lowther* acted for the 'Cat,' and Colonel Machell witnessed this desperate and absurd encounter. An hour later the combatants, with their wounds bandaged, met at dinner on the best of terms, drank each other's health, and spent a merry evening."

* Now Earl of Lonsdale.

A chronicle of old races is apt to make dull reading for the uninitiated, but some of Melgund's performances must be noted. In 1874, when Richardson won the Grand National for the second time, Melgund was fourth on "Defence." The same year he won the French Grand National at Auteuil on his own Limber mare "Miss Hungerford," being the only gentleman rider in the race with seventeen professional starters. Melgund rode the Liverpool course altogether nine times, and competed four times in the Grand National. The Limber stable began the year 1875 very well at the Lincoln Spring Meeting: the five horses competing all won in the hands of "Mr. Rolly." He rode "Miss Hungerford" in the Grand National: "I always think she would have won," he wrote afterwards to Finch Mason, "if I had not been knocked over the second time round. I was quite by myself on the left-hand side of the course to keep out of the crowd, and an Irish jockey on 'Sailor' deliberately jumped into my quarters."

In the Grand National of 1876 he very nearly came by his end. He was riding "Zero," a Limber bay with magnificent shoulders, much fancied by the public. Here is his own account: "The horse was going splendidly and coming to Valentine's Brook I got a real good steadier at him--'Shifnal' and 'Jackal' were leading, and I was next to them. 'Zero' got the fence exactly in his stride and never touched it, and, as far as I know, tumbled head over heels on landing.* I jumped the fence almost touching the left-hand flag. I got up directly and found tom Cannon standing by me, who walked back to the weighing room with me. On our way we heard that Joe Cannon had won on 'Royal,' at which I was very pleased, for besides his fine horsemanship he was an excellent fellow." Melgund thought he had only lacerated internally a large muscle, but Sir James Paget, who was telegraphed for, confirmed the view of the other doctors that he had literally broken his neck. "You are one of those extraordinary people," said the great surgeon afterwards, "who have broken their necks and recovered. Your backbone should be very valuable." Melgund offered to leave it to him in his will. "Oh," said Sir James, "I shall be dead long before you, but the College of Surgeons will be very glad to have it." After being practically a cripple for months Melgund consulted Mr, Wharton Hood, the bone-setter, who advised exercise, and his own will power and the coming of the hunting season revived him. "I rode 'Weathercock' at Sandown Park in November, which I ought never to have done as I was still weak and ill and in pain from the fall in March, and tumbled head over heels at the fence going down the hill, 'Zero,' strange to say, falling by my side with Marcus Beresford on him." It was a crazy escapade, but a miraculous proof of nerve.

* Mr. John Osborne maintained that the horse put his foot, on landing, inttt an under-drain, which for some obscure reason had been overlooked by the authorities of the course.

Though this incident may be said to have ended Melgund's career as a jockey his interest in sport and horses never abated. At the farewell banquet given in his honour by the Turf Club at Calcutta at the close of his term of office as Viceroy he breathed again the atmosphere of comradeship among racing men, and in returning thanks for the toast of his health he said:--

"I cannot tell you how touched I am-I can find no other expression-by your invitation to this great gathering. I cannot but feel that it is your welcome and your farewell to a fellow-sportsman--that I am not here to-night as Viceroy, soldier, or statesman

"Mr. Rolly"

but--may I say so?-as the 'Mr. Rolly' of old days. I do not regret my racing days, gentlemen; very far from it. I learned a great deal from them which has been useful to me in later life. I mixed with all classes of men, I believe I got much insight into human character. You may think it strange, but I never used to bet, though I was on intimate terms with the ring--and as far as riding went I became absolutely callous as to public opinion. If I won, there was often no name good enough for me, and when I got beaten on the favourite it was Mr. Rolly, of course, who threw the race away.

"But talking of a jockey's popularity I must tell you a story which I am sure will appeal to the heart of gentlemen riders, and teach them not to be over sanguine even on the best of mounts. I was once riding in the big steeplechase at Croydon, which in those days was second only to the Grand National in importance. I had won several races on the horse I was riding, and we thought if he did well at Croydon he ought to have a chance for the Liverpool. He was very heavily backed, but he was an uncertain horse; one could never quite depend on his trying. However, the money was piled on, and it was considered that, if he was going well at the brook, opposite the Stand, the second time round, he could be relied upon, and if I thought it all right I was to make a signal on jumping the water and further sums were to be dashed down in the ring. When we got to the brook the horse was going splendidly, raced up to it, jumped it magnificently, couldn't have been running better. I made the signal and on went the money. But after the brook we had to turn away from the crowd, and he put his ears back and never tried another yard--never went into his bridle again. I was not popular that time when I rode back to weigh in! . . .

"And so, in the ups and downs of racing, I learned to keep my head, to sit still, to watch what other jockeys were doing, and to be a good judge of pace. The orders I liked best were 'Get off well' and 'Wait in front.'

"I suppose no one here is old enough to remember poor George Ede, who rode under the name of Mr. Edwards, one of the finest horsemen the world has ever seen. He won the Grand National on 'The Lamb,' and was afterwards killed, riding a horse called 'Chippenham,' in the Sefton Handicap at Liverpool, and a poem dedicated to him was published in Bailey's Magazine. If you will allow me I will quote two verses. To my mind they are very fine lines, expressive of what a really good rider should be:--

"'A horseman's gifts: the perfect hand And graceful seat of confidence; The head to reckon and command When danger stills the coward's sense;

"'The nerve unshaken by mischance, The care unlessened by success, And modest bearing to enhance The natural charm of manliness.'"

"You have surrounded me with the old atmosphere again and have got me to talk racing. You have brought back to me happy old memories and stories which I could go on telling by the hour. Seriously, the lessons of the turf need not be thrown away in after life. The lines to George Ede, and the old racing instruction ' Wait in front,' mean much in this world's struggles. Don't force the pace, lie up with your field, keep a winning place, watch your opportunity, and when the moment comes go in and win."

III

Had young officers in those days been encouraged to see something of foreign wars, as they were under a later regime, it is likely that Melgund would not have left the Guards, and that there would have been no turf career for Mr. Rolly. That he was still eager for service of a more active kind than Windsor and Aldershot afforded, and that he was not wholly content with a life of hunting and racing is shown by two wild adventures abroad which he managed to interpolate between his riding engagements. The first was his visit to Paris during the Commune. When the Franco-German War broke out in 1870 he was shooting grouse at Minto. A month later his journal records the death of his friend Colonel Pemberton, who, while acting as Times correspondent with the Prussians, fell at Sedan. "I am awfully sorry. I saw him just before he started, and afterwards laughed at his being cut up when he wished us good-bye, as I thought he had no chance of being shot. I had wanted to go with him, and he had promised to do all he could for me, but I gave it up for many reasons--chiefly from being hard-up, and also from not being able to speak German. He was a very clever fellow, and the news of his death has made me melancholy." But next year his chance came. In January 1871 Paris surrendered after a four months' siege, but the treaty of peace which followed did not end the war, and for months France was torn with internal strife. The Communists took possession of the capital, and it was only after a nine weeks' siege and much bitter fighting that the French National Army forced an entry and suppressed the revolt. It was known in London on 22nd May that French troops from Versailles had broken through the defences on the St. Cloud side, but that the Communists were still resisting fiercely at many points inside the city. That evening Melgund, with his brothers Hugh and Fitzwilliam, and his friend Captain Hartopp, left England to endeavour to make their way into Paris.

The adventure is described in Melgund's journal, and more fully in a letter which Hugh Elliot published in the Scotsman on 1st June of that year. The party arrived at St. Denis on the morning of 23rd May, where they found that all communications with Paris were cut. They took a cab to St. Germains, which was under French control where they hoped to find General Galliffet, as they had an introduction to an officer on his staff. But Gaihffet had left, so they decided to go on to Versailles. Before they left St. Germains they had seen that firing continued at Montmartre and in the neighbourhood of the Arc de Triomphe, and next morning they heard that Paris was in flames. At Versailles they called on the British Ambassador, Lord Lyons, who discouraged their project, but ultimately gave them a letter to the Prefect of Paris, asking for a laissez passer into the city. Thus equipped, they drove without difficulty through the gate at Sèvres, though the sentry warned them that it would be hard to get out again. They found rooms in an hotel in the Faubourg St. Honorûe, almost opposite the British Embassy, where a barricade had been erected which was defended by a band of Communists headed by a woman. Having deposited their luggage and ordered dinner for seven o'clock, the four sallied forth to see the sights.

For what followed I quote from Hugh's letter:--

"After passing a very large barricade at the entrance to the Rue de Rivoli we made our way into the Gardens of the Tuileries. The whole of the street seemed to be on fire: as far as we could see it was a continuous mass of smoke and flames. Almost immediately we were impressed to work at the pumps, which we did very readily, not knowing what was to come. Partly by cajoling, partly by arguing, we managed to escape after half an hour's labour, hoping to return to our dinner. As ill-luck would have it, while crossing the Place de la Concorde on the way home, we were seized by another large guard of soldiers, and in spite of all our expostulations were carried off to quench the same fire, only from a different side. I believe the building burning was that of the Administration de Finance, and occupied a large space in the Rue de Rivoli. . . . Sentinels were placed at the ends of all the streets so as to prevent the possibility of our escape. We were then ordered to pass buckets down the street to fill the pump. After working hard at this for some time our new taskmasters came up to ask for six volunteers to man the pump. One of us volunteered, and as we did not wish to separate we all declared our readiness to go to the pump in a body. However, as the wall was beginning to bulge out and a certain stack of chimneys to look remarkably off the perpendicular, I could not in my heart help thinking that the French might have shown some higher spirit of hospitality than to permit four out of six of the men sent to the front to be foreigners. Our work now became really very disagreeable. Our pump was placed exactly under the wall, the fall of which appeared imminent; the chimney too tottered just over our heads. After we had laboured for about half an hour, part of the wall fell in with a crash, though not near enough to injure us.

"From that moment it was almost impossible to get the men to pass up buckets to the pump, and I saw one of my brothers carrying the empty pails for many yards before he was relieved by the next man in the chain, so much they dreaded approaching the fire. When the pumping seemed to be coming to a standstill, as for a few minutes we had suspended our efforts, the people commenced to cry out 'Les Anglais! Les Anglais!' so we had to begin again. We were highly consoled, too, by hearing a voice from a safe position behind exclaim, 'Courage! c'est pour la France que nous travaillons!'

"As may be believed, we took the first opportunity of sneaking to the rear, as the salvation of France was not of very great importance to us. It was now very late at night, and the sentinels having apparently been withdrawn from one of the streets, we crept down the side of the houses, and were already congratulating ourselves on our luck, when a loud 'Qui vive?' was heard from under the shadow of the big barricade in the Rivoli. The answer not being satisfactory the sentinel advanced upon us at the double, and looked as if he were going to demolish us on the spot He threatened to shoot us if we did not retire, which accordingly we did, feeling very uncomfortable till we had got round the first corner.

"Tired as we were, there was nothing for it but to return to the pumps; and certainly the sight of the great conflagration was not a thing to be lost For some distance the street looked like a furnace the flames leaping high above the buildings; Occasionally there was a crash as some chimney or roof fell to the ground; and in the distance we heard the perpetual banging of cannon as the troops advanced upon the retreating Communists. A sight not to be missed, and, I hope, never to be repeated. Looking about me I noticed one of the soldiers bandaging a poor cat that had been injured by the fire, and it appeared strange to me at the time that men who were acting hourly with such marvellous brutality to their fellowmen should thus occupy themselves about an animal. We were now entirely in the clutches of the Pompiers, who each had a very tall brass helmet and wore a loose pair of brown holland trousers. These men stood over us, did no work, and whilst we were streaming with perspiration, contented themselves with shouting at intervals, 'Pompez donc, Messieurs! Pompez donc!'"

Their release came about 3 a.m. "We should never have got back at all," writes Melgund, "had it not been for a good-natured Breton soldier who talked a little English, despised the French, and managed to get us past all the sentries." After eight hours' work at the pumps the party of four regained their hotel in safety. They found that the front of the house opposite had been shot away by a shell, and the gutters were full of blood, but the hotel was not damaged.

They spent the next three days in Paris, for it was hopeless to think of getting out. "Paris," says the journal, "is quite the most insecure place I ever was in. The shells are not at all the most dangerous part of it; the soldiers and people are so excited that they don't care whom they arrest, or what they do." On the Saturday they secured a pass from the Embassy, and, carrying a dummy dispatch to Lord Granville, they finally, and none too easily, managed to depart by the Clichy gate. Although armed with their pass, they were held up for some time at the gate: Melgund at length produced his visiting card, which so impressed the sentry that he exclaimed, "Ah! Monsieur est Vicomte! Passez donc." At St. Denis the Germans were very civil to them, and their passes from Count Bernstorff, the German Ambassador in London, enabled them to go wherever they liked. They finally arrived home on Sunday, 28th May, after a remarkable five days' interlude in a London season.

The second adventure began in the August of 1874, when Melgund went out to the headquarters of the Carlist Army in North Spain. Fred Burnaby, who had been there as a special correspondent, had drawn glowing pictures of the Carlist spirit, and when Sir Algernon Borthwick asked Melgund to act as correspondent to the Morning Post he determined to try his luck. He left London on the 8th August, the farewells of his friends being coupled with "What a fool you are; you're sure to be shot." Of his experiences in Spain Melgund wrote a long and fascinating account which can only be briefly summarized here. He went first to Bayonne, where he fell in with a young French soldier, the Vicomte de Baume, and with him crossed the frontier and adopted the boina, a cap like a Kilmarnock bonnet, which was the Carlist headgear. They made their way to Tolosa, visited the Carlist arms factory, and then proceeded to the Quartier Royal, where they had an interview with Don Carlos, with whom they were not greatly impressed. Their next stage was General Dorregarray's headquarters at Estella, which was within reasonable distance of the front line. Melgund liked the Carlist officers, some of whom wore swords which came from Nathan, the London costumier. He has left an amusing description of his stay there, his earnest and fruitless efforts to see a battle, and the extreme boredom of the life in a baking little Spanish town where food and drink were vile, and the only relaxation was a bathe in the river or a game of billiards. On 30th August the journal records the movement of troops, and constant rumours that an attack was about to take place. The night was made hideous by artillery rattling over the street, every bugler was blowing his heart out, the dogs were howling, and sleep was impossible. The ritual of the extreme Catholic legitimists seemed strange to his Scottish soul. "I got up and went on to the balcony and saw the Host carried past, a ceremony which, when it takes place in the middle of the night, has to me something uncanny about it. I do not know why. In the daytime it may seem an absurd performance, but at night, when one hears the tinkling of the little bell and notes the superstitious awe which surrounds the procession, and remembers that it may mean a battle in the morning, it is apt to impress one more than at other times." No battle, however, came his way, and ne returned home in September much struck by the enthusiasm which had produced 80,000 men for the Carlist Army in two years, but seeing very little future for the cause. He records his gratitude to the officers for their courtesy and hospitality, and considers that their treatment of prisoners was exceptionally humane--a tribute which assuredly could not be paid to their opponents.

IV

The engagements of "Mr. Rolly" and the escapades abroad did not fill up the whole of those years, for there were many weeks in London, and long visits to his Border home. We hear of him in the summer of 1871, when he had just returned from the Commune, borrowing his brother Arthur's wig and gown and going to hear the Tichborne trial, feeling very nervous lest he should be offered a brief. One of his main interests--for though he had left the Guards he had not ceased to be a soldier--was the formation of a Border Mounted Volunteer Corps. The subject seems to have been first raised at the Caledonian Hunt Dinner in October 1871, and presently an offer to raise such a corps was made to the Secretary of State for War signed by most of the Roxburghshire gentry. Such was the origin of the Border Mounted Rifles, into which Melgund flung all his energies. It was recruited from the lairds and farmers, most of them zealous followers of the Duke of Buccleuch's hounds, and Melgund was given the first command, which he held for nearly twenty years. The history of its honourable existence, till it was killed by agricultural depression, may be read in General Sir James Grierson's Records of the Scottish Volunteer Force, 1859-1908.* It began in February 1872 as the "1st Roxburgh Mounted Rifles," and in January 1880 became the "Border Mounted Rifles," with a uniform of slate grey, grey helmets with silver star, and the Elliot motto: "Wha daur meddle wi' me?" It speedily won fame in marksmanship, and in 1884 its team was first and fifth, and in 1885 first and second in the Loyd-Lindsay competition at Wimbledon. Melgund was very proud of his corps, and a firm believer in mounted infantry, the value of which he expounded later in speeches and review articles. He was somewhat of a pioneer in his views, which did not become accepted doctrine till the end of the century and the South African War.

* Edinburgh: W. Blaekwood and Sons, 1909.

The work with the Border Mounted Rifles satisfied one side of Melgund's mind, but he was always on the lookout for other interests, and especially for that disciplined and continuous work which is involved in the term "service." In November 1873 he had a chance of standing for Parliament for North Lincolnshire in the Liberal interest, and at first, under Lord Yarborough's persuasion, he agreed. But presently, after reflection, he withdrew, having come to the conclusion that the House of Commons would not suit either his tastes or his talents. There is a small bundle of political notes extant, which he had prepared for his guidance in the event of a contest--modest little proposals on such matters as land, tenant right, education, and the suffrage, which enable one to realize that sober and conservative creed which was the elder Liberalism. The journal is full of entries which show how much his mind was beginning to hanker for full occupation. Opinions on war and foreign affairs gathered from any one in authority are carefully set down. In the autumn of 1876 Sir Garnet Wolseley stayed at Minto, and showed a flattering interest in the Border Rifles. "He said one thing which seems to me very evident," the journal records, "but which a great many honest people would not admit, viz., that the press (speaking of correspondents with an army) has become a power which a man should try to manage for himself; that it is an influence which one cannot deny, and therefore should try to make one's own."

This question of the press was one which touched Melgund closely, for at the moment it was only as a correspondent that he had a chance of seeing something of war. When the Russo-Turkish War broke out in 1877 he was permitted to go to Turkey as a representative of the Morning Post. He set forth in April, speeded by a letter To Lincolnshire friend, the Rev. H. G. Southwell, who kept for his use a fund of bracing wisdom and a special Din of champagne. "I am really pleased," he wrote, "to hear you are gomg to do something worthy of last. I cannot but think it is a pitiful ambition to have no higher aspiration than to win a steeplechase. . . . I hope you will take the Bible, Robertson's (of Brighton) Sermons, and Gibbon's Rome with you. The first contains the truest account of life; the second does one good, as you know; and the third will show you the origin of the Turkish Empire, and prepare the way for all its modern history."

Whether or not he was accompanied by these aids to reflection, Melgund had a strenuous and varied summer. "You may or may not be surprised to hear," he writes to his mother, "that I am on the point of leaving my native country. I shall probably start for Constantinople at the beginning of the week after next, viz., about the 1st May. I am by way of going as correspondent to the Morning Post with the Turkish Army, but by the present understanding I am only making use of the Post in order to give me a position of some sort, and can please myself about writing to them. Besides this there is a chance of my getting something to do which will suit me much better--something for the Intelligence Department. I went to-day to see Colonel Home, the head of the Department. He seems a capital fellow, and he wants me to go to a place on the Black Sea a little north of Varna to find out all I can about the country there and to let him know about it, which he says would be most useful to them, as they are thoroughly acquainted with all the country that lies directly between the Danube and Constantinople, whereas the piece of country they want me to go to they know nothing of. I shall probably do this, but I should think it would be in the shape of a separate expedition, and that after that I should be attached to some staff. Uncle Henry * seems to think I shall go with every advantage, and that I am sure to get on like a house on fire; in fact, I am delighted with it all."

* Sir Henry Elliot, P.C., K.C.B., Ambassador at Constantinople.

The journal describes the itinerary. On 2nd May he wrote:--

"Arrived in Venice about 8 p.m. this evening. Lovely view of the Alps this morning after leaving Turin: made out Monte Rosa and the Lyskamm distinctly and got a glimpse of the Matterhorn. I love the mountains, and this morning, when I first found myself among them before arriving at Turin, it gave me an indescribable feeling of excitement. I suppose it is the recollection of the adventures I have had amongst them, and when I look back now I look upon them and the guides as old friends. There is no better man than a good Swiss guide, and Peter Bohren and Melchior Anderegg and the Lancriers keep jumping up in my memory.

"I am delighted with the first appearance of Venice; it seems to me enchanting, and makes me wish to live here, and, like all places of the sort, makes one wish for some one else to see it with. However, that is all the twaddle of one's existence--the realities are the thing after all."

Melgund was in close touch with the Intelligence Department at the War Office, and was associated with Colonel Lennox, the British Military Attache at Cairo. In Constantinople he was impressed, like other people, by the scandals of the Turkish Government. Thence he went to Adrianople, Rustchuk, and Turtukai, meeting Osman Pasha. He then joined Lennox at Shumla, where he had a chance of studying Turkish military arrangements.

The following are extracts from his letters to his mother:--

"May 28.--Got back here (Shumla) this morning after a most interesting expedition to Rustchuk and Turtukai. We spent the whole of Friday going over the forts there: pretty strong! The bombardment of the town was expected to begin at any moment, and we could see the Russian batteries on the opposite side from the

Turkish forts above the town. We spent the evening at Mr. Reid's (the English Consul) house, where all the consuls were gathered together in a tolerable state of excitement. The extraordinary thing is that the Turks should have allowed the Russians to throw up these batteries under their very noses, occupying, as they do, much the stronger position. But they have done nothing to annoy them, and not a Turk dare show his face, and there were we, the General, the Chief of the Staff, and myself, all hiding behind trees, when really, looking at the positions of the two combatants, it is the Russians who should have been afraid of showing themselves!

"June 20th.--(Varna.) Lennox, Chermside, and I came on here from Rustchuk yesterday. I have seen an immense lot, and come in for all the fighting-- but before writing more I send you a copy of a letter which I got this morning from Sir Collingwood Dickson which I think will please you. Perhaps it is lucky that I should have had to report on the very line of road on which the Russians have since landed.

"'THERAPIA, June 28, 1877.

"'DEAR LORD MELGUND,--Mr. Layard is so very busy that he has not time to write to you himself, but he has requested me to thank you for your kind contributions to the public service in your reports on the Turkish Cavalry and Horse Artillery at Shumla, and in that lately received upon the road travelled by you between Rustchuk, Sistova, and Nicopoli. Both these reports were perused with much interest by the Ambassador and myself, and the latter I think so highly of that I requested Mr. Layard in sending it to mark that it should be forwarded to the Intelligence Department as an itinerary well worthy their attention.'

"On 26th June Lennox woke me up by telling me that the game had begun. I went out to the ridge of hills facing the Danube close to the Turkish batteries and stayed there till the firing was nearly over. The Russian practice was very good, shells pitching constantly on top of batteries and on the edge of infantry trenches.

"That evening I shall never forget. We went out to a cliff close to the town: the town itself is in a valley between a clock tower and the Fortress. All the Russian batteries were firing. I watched the flash from the Russian guns and took the time. While all this was going on there was the most magnificent sunset you ever saw! Try and imagine a dark stormy evening with a brilliant red sky, distant lightning, and the smoke from the guns rolling over the valley. It was a wonderful sight, and then, suddenly, a Russian signal blazed up, and another, and another; probably they had something to do with the crossing that took place early next morning.

"On the 27th we left Nicopoli for Sistova, and, on getting near, found that the Russians had crossed about 1 a.m. and were still crossing. Six battalions of Turks were entirely defeated this side. I could not, owing to the lie of the ground, see the exact spot where the Russians were crossing, but I saw their troops on this side, and the Turks in retreat. It was a beautiful moonlight night, and the roads were crowded with people flying from the enemy--Turkish troops straggling for miles.

"The next day Lennox sent Chermside and me to Rustchuk to try to get some letters which were supposed to be lying at the Consulate. Rustchuk was terribly knocked about, and the Kanak, which had been turned into a hospital, was almost entirely burned out. How on earth they got any one out alive I can't make out. As it was, they got all their sick away, none being killed, though I believe seventeen were wounded, and the two men on duty at the door were killed.

"When Chermside and I arrived at the Consulate we naturally found it locked up, Mr. Reid (the Consul) having left when that part of the town became impossible to stay in: we went all round the house but failed to find any way into it. At last, by the help of a Turkish officer, I got over the garden wall and in at a back window into Mr. Reid's study, and from there into the room where the letters were supposed to be. At first I found nothing but a few old newspapers, and was going to give it up as a bad job when I happened to look into a cupboard full of all sorts of rubbish, and there, to my delight, I found all the letters. One of them, addressed to Lennox, was open, and Mr. Reid had written on the back of it "Torn open by a Russian shell." I believe the letters had rather a narrow squeak of being demolished. I got back again over the garden wall with my spoil, and we returned to Rustchuk. . . . I have just come back from an evening visit to Mrs. Nejib Pasha. She has nearly smoked and drunk me under the table. Before dinner she dosed me with vermouth, she sitting cross-legged on her divan, and after dinner primed me with bitters. . . .

"July 11th.--I arrived at Osmanbazar on the 13th. The town, being chiefly Bulgarian, was nearly deserted by the Turkish inhabitants, who had fled for fear of the Bulgarians, while the Bulgarians themselves were very much frightened of the few Turks who remained in the town, as they were armed to the teeth. Said Pasha was there, though he was to leave at once for Shumla. He appeared very nervous about the state of affairs, and much incensed at reports of atrocities by Bulgarians.

"I am afraid I shall not come home a great Turk! Unless Suliman's lately arrived force wins a great battle in front of Adrianople there is nothing on earth to prevent the Russians going to Constantinople, and it seems to me only natural that a victorious army, such as they are, will expect to enter the capital. I doubt the Czar, should he wish to do so, having the power to stop such an entrance, and still more doubt the wish or the power he may have, if once there, of ordering the army out again. We are too late to stop it now."

In July Melgund, whose health was suffering from the effects of the climate, was compelled to return home. With his Turkish journey closed the stage of his life when he was content to seize the interest of the flying hour, whether it came in the shape of sport or adventure. He had long been far from contentment, and Mr. Southwell, from his country rectory, made it his business to fan the dissatisfaction and urged a political career. "I do not see," he wrote in September 1877, "why you should hold, so to speak, an amphibious position. You say you cannot go in for politics, but can find work if the war continues. Now if you were a younger son I could understand your embracing war, but being the elder, and likely to be a permanent fixture, surely you must want work that does not depend on an 'if.' You have industry and pluck. Industry may not make you an orator, but it can make you a very tolerable speaker, and pluck will give you cheek in time. Life is short, and you will fritter it away, and will have nothing to do as you grow older but eat and sleep and be weary of life." The writer returned to the charge a month later, and besought his friend to "set his head for Parliament." "I hope to hear from henceforth that you are a changed man; that hunting, steeplechasing, and horses generally are regarded by you as instruments of recreation after severe work; in short, that you have woken from sleep and have put away childish things."

But the matter was more complex than the honest hunting parson realized. "You have a noble soul," he told Melgund, "one of the noblest, but a short-sighted, material-interest mind." In this last phrase Mr. Southwell's acumen failed him. It was precisely because he cared so little for worldly wisdom that Melgund's problem was hard. A man more worldly-wise would have used the advantages given him by his birth, connections, and wide popularity to build up one of those undistinguished parliamentary careers which are possible even for the dullest, and which lead so many mediocrities to high office. Being singularly honest with himself, he believed that he had no real talent for political life, and if he could not make a true success, he would not be content with a sham one. In life, as in sport, he insisted upon the first-rate. He believed--with justice--that he had a gift for soldiering, but he had dropped out of the running, and it was hard for one who was now half an amateur to make his way back to a professional career. The kind of work, such as imperial administration, which was to draw out all his qualities and combine the interests of both politics and the Army, was still only dimly realized. Honestly and rightly he sought at this stage the sphere in which he believed he could best be used--the business of war. By the close of 1977 his mind was set upon this path, and the "childish things" of Mr. Southwell's letter had been relegated to their proper place. But the decade of strenuous idleness had not been wasted. He had behind him a youth active and honourable, which is the best foundation for the structure of maturer years. In body he was hard-trained and untiring; his mind was fresh and vigorous, if still not fully developed; no cynicism or satiety weakened his ardour for life. He had made in his sporting career those close and enduring friendships which belong to no other human pursuit in the same degree.* From sport, too, he brought standards of a strict faithfulness and a scrupulous truth, and in mixing with men of all classes and types he had acquired a broad and genial humanity.

* We need not accept the explanation of this fact given by Harriet Lady Ashburnham to Lord Houghton: "If I were to begin life again," she said, "I should go on the Turf merely to get friends. They seem to me the only people who really hold together. I do not know why. It may be that each man knows something that would hang the other, but the effect is delightful and most peculiar."

CHAPTER THREE

APPRENTICESHIP

The close of the 'seventies was for Britain an era of little wars. There was trouble brewing in South Africa, but the main anxiety lay on the north-west frontier of India, since the check to Russia at Constantinople had turned her thoughts to Central Asian expansion, and the uneasy politics of Afghanistan had begun to reflect her ambitions. The Second Afghan War began in November 1878, when Shere Ali, having received a Russian envoy at Kabul, had declined to receive a British. Sir Donald Stewart marched from Baluchistan through the Bolan Pass and occupied Kandahar, another force went through the Khyber to Jalalabad, and Sir Frederick Roberts moved from the Kurrum valley through the high passes, defeated the Amir at Peiwar Kotal, and occupied the Shutargardan Pass, which gave direct access to Kabul. Shere Ali fled northwards and presently died, and for six months it seemed hard to know how to bring the campaign to an end. A successor to Shere Ali must be found with whom Britain could treat, for it was idle to push British armies farther into a difficult and dangerous country with no strategic objective at the end of the advance.

While the war was thus stagnant on the frontier, Melgund set off from England to take his chance of seeing something of the campaign. He had no official position, or promise of one, but he had many friends at the front, and he trusted to the luck which had never deserted him on his expeditions. He arrived in Bombay in January 1879, and went on to Calcutta, to stay with the Lyttons at Government House. There he saw and admired the portrait of his great-grandfather, the first Earl of Minto, in the Council Room.

Though anxious to hurry on to the front, Melgund was delayed some days in Calcutta making the necessary preparations. "I am still here," he writes, "and have been enjoying myself very much. This is a very fine town, and Government House is quite magnificent. Altogether I am enchanted with what I have seen--everything beautiful, luxurious, and warm: every one is more than civil to me, and Bill Beresford, who is away steeplechasing somewhere, has left word that I am to ride his horses, and am also to have two which are already at Kohat. Last Sunday I went to Barrackpore with Colonel Baker, one of the Viceroy's military advisers, and a firstrate fellow. It is about twelve miles up the river from here, and is a country place of the Viceroy's. I think it is the prettiest place I ever saw anywhere. It is a large house in the middle of what might be a beautiful English park, with magnificent trees. The Staff have bungalows of their own which are dotted about in the park, and one breakfasts and lunches under an enormous banyan tree which is a small wood in itself."

Then he started for the Punjab to join General Roberts's column, seeing as much as he could of the sights on the way. The romance of the frontier caught his imagination as soon as he began to talk to frontier officers, and he was struck with a type of public servant very different from that which he had met at home. He sketched it for the benefit of Lady Minto, whom he suspected of being whiggishly inclined:--

"I assure you the stories one might tell of these frontier wars are without end, and the Englishmen we have on the frontier are a race to be very proud of. I believe there are dozens of men who have scarcely been heard of in England, but who have shown out here that they were first-rate leaders, first-rate soldiers, and excellent all round, and who have died like heroes one after another in these frontier fights. The churchyard here* and the church itself are both worth going to see as a history of frontier life. I counted in the church the names of about fifty officers who have died or been killed about here since the force was started, some thirty years ago. By the Frontier Force I mean the force which is separate from the rest of the army, and directly under the command of the Punjab Government. . . . Then, again, commissioners of districts must of necessity be rulers, and on the frontier at any rate the stronger they are the better. The goody-goody benevolent people could be of no use here except to get their own throats cut: the men who do rule are not of the English politician style, pasty-faced wretches who do nothing but talk; in fact, not at all the type of the young M.P. of the present day, but a hard-riding, steeplechasing, sporting lot of fellows. They are the sort of men that I hope we shall always have lots of, but they are not the type that a well-informed village meeting at home would choose to occupy the important positions they do."

* Kohat.

He went to Kohat, Peshawar, and Jalalabad, and formed the worst impressions of the playful homicidal habits of the border tribes. He was for a time with Sir Sam Browne's force, where he met Sir Louis Cavagnari, but he hankered after Roberts's column, which he believed was destined to advance to Kabul. This column he succeeded in joining in March. The staff comprised many congenial companions--Pretyman, Neville Chamberlain, George Villiers, Brabazon, and Padre Adams. The future still hung in the balance. He saw that the new scientific frontier, if it came into being, would have to be seriously held, and he doubted the ability of the British Government--for which at this time he professed small respect--to carry out such a policy.

"I do not think the people in England at all realize the state of this frontier, or the extreme danger of an insecure frontier line, that is, of one whose chief strength depends upon the goodwill of the Amir, or of the frontier tribes. Of course, have as many friends as you can, but be perfectly independent of them, and feel that the strength of your frontier does not rest on their goodwill alone. Neither do I think people understand the great danger of giving up an inch of ground. All retreat is looked upon as weakness by those frontier tribes, and directly you retire you will have them all about your ears. The only thing they respect is power: kindness I don't believe they care tuppence for. Unless you had been here you could not imagine the state of the country. One thinks very little of a few shots at night. I have seen a good deal myself. The other day I rode with one of the political officers almost fifteen miles down the road to Banu, most of which runs through the Waziri country, which does not belong to us. We found that fourteen camels had been looted out of a convoy of two hundred, and that only one had been recovered. We went through a very wild country, some of it simply a collection of conical hills. We met a native escort with a camel caravan armed to the teeth and carrying shields, the first I have seen carried. The people in this valley are very friendly, but I think the best definition of a friendly native is a man who only shoots you at night, whereas a hostile one shoots in the daytime as well."

When not employed in reconnoitring the country his time was passed in organizing sports, paper-chases, horse shows, and speculating on the probable news from Kabul. Melgund was keenly alive to beautiful scenery and his letters are full of vivid pictures. Nestling in a valley between Kurrum and Haleb Ketla, below the long range of the snow-covered Safed Koh, lies Shalozan, a village famed for the beauty of its women: Melgund describes the chenab trees, a ruined tomb, and the picturesque appearance of a troop of native cavalry, with their red puggarees, halting on the village green. Thirty years later, when Viceroy of India, he visited Peiwar Kotal, motoring sixty miles from Kohat over a specially prepared road to revive the memories of his campaigning days. From his camp at Parachinar he rode to Shalozan, the beauty of which, amid its desolate environment, had never faded from his memory. While riding through the village he met a tall bearded Pathan about whose appearance there was something familiar, and he observed to Mr. Merk, the Commissioner, that this man reminded him of the boy who had run messages for Sir Frederick Roberts in 1879, and who, as he ran, had a trick of brushing his ankles together till they bled. The man was stopped and questioned, his sandals were instantly flung off to disclose the old scars, and in wild excitement he prostrated himself at the feet of the great Lat Sahib who deigned to remember his unworthy errand boy.

In his long delightful letters to his mother, which for this year took the place of his journal, Melgund gives the gossip of the camp, vivid little sketches of places and personages, and much half-chaffing abuse of the follies of the stay-at-home politicians. "I long to encamp the British public in a place like Ali Kheyl for one night, with Gladstone, Chamberlain, Dilke, and a few others on outpost duty. I would join the Mongols for the night, and I think there would be some fun! I dare say it wouldn't do old Peter (his brother Arthur) any harm to do sentry-go for the public for an hour or two. I expect he's got a few 'humane' ideas in his head too!"

He expounds at length his views on the frontier question, which are interesting in the light of his later problems as Viceroy:--

"The more I see of this country, the more difficult the new frontier line appears to organize. I was always for a new frontier, and for occupying advanced posts at the other side of the passes leading into India, and I am still sure that this is right, though the difficulties in the way are far greater than I supposed. The fact is, we want to have a stronger frontier in case of a Russian invasion or demonstration against India, such as they certainly meant to make if we had fought them in Europe, and it is very short-sighted to say that they will not attack us for years. Neither do I think it should be allowed to stand over for future years, when we might be very hard pressed in Europe and unable to alter our frontier even if we wished it. It is nonsense shutting our eyes to the fact that it is Russia that one is afraid of, and justly so, though I think the day the Russian and English outposts touch the more chance there will be of a permanent peace. The scientific soldiers ought to be able to decide on the frontier line, and we ought to take it and have done with it, and not scream and howl every time Russia advances in Central Asia. With the old frontier we should have fought an invading army as they debouched from the passes, i.e., we should have been fighting inside our own doors, and on a powder magazine, which the slightest reverse would have set in a blaze; besides which we should have been fighting with the Indus behind us and a scarcity of bridges over which to retreat. One is bound to consider a retreat as on the cards, though when I said this to some one at dinner at Government House at Calcutta I was told that we here could never think of a retreat.

"If we are not to advance to strengthen our frontiers we could do so by retiring behind the Indus, so as not to massacre armies with the river behind us, simply keeping advanced posts to watch the mouths of the passes. This, I think, would be an immensely strong frontier, but it would be retiring, and goodness knows what the effect would be in India as to loss of prestige. I have no doubt that the right thing to do is to occupy places like Kandahar, Kurrum, and Jalalabad. You then have two lines of defence, and if beaten at the first you fall back upon the second--the southern mouths of the passes; but your first fight would be outside your own door instead of inside, which, in a country like this, must be of the greatest importance.

"There is, however, an immense difficulty regarding these new advance posts--their lines of communication, which must run through a country inhabited by wild, uncivilized races. Therefore, to make the advance posts really safe, we should have to be able thoroughly to depend on the tribes in no case molesting our communications. This is the great difficulty I see in the new frontier, and I am afraid the English public will not realize until too late its value, and will not be willing to supply the men and money that would be necessary to secure the roads to the advance posts. The thing will probably be done by halves; we shall occupy the places we want, and leave the country behind them altogether unreliable, and let the matter drop. Then some day the attack we have always been fearing and preaching about will come, we shall fight under frightful disadvantages, lose no end of men and money, and when we are utterly at our last gasp pull ourselves together and win, as we always have done."

The monotonous waiting came to an end in the latter part of May, when Yakub Khan, one of Shere Ali's sons, was recognized as Amir and concluded the treaty of Gandamak, which conceded the establishment of a British agent at Kabul and placed the foreign affairs of Afghanistan under the control of Britain. Melgund left the frontier and hastened home to his Border Mounted Rifles: he was anxious to be back in time for the summer inspection. His passion for active service, however, was wholly unsatisfied. He decided against going to the Zulu War, for he was weary of scratch campaigns. "A good European War," he wrote, "would be the thing, if there was a chance of our army existing over a fortnight." But his journey had not been fruitless, he had made many friendships, and had developed a profound admiration for Sir Frederick Roberts, from whom he learned much of the detailed business of war; and though he was for the moment inclined to take the high-handed Bismarckian view in foreign politics, he had learned invaluable lessons--the difficulties of the "man on the spot" and the need of sympathy and imagination in harmonizing his urgent needs with the preconceptions of the public at home. He loved to flutter the Whig dovecotes of his family by talking at random, but his matured opinions were full of wary good sense.

On his way home he spent a few days at Simla, and there an offer was made him which caused him acute perturbation. Cavagnari, the British envoy-designate to Kabul, asked him to accompany him, and the Viceroy pressed him to accept. The proposal was that he should go to Kabul, and then go on with Yakub Khan to the Uxus; from there he would carry a dummy dispatch from the Amir to the Russians, and somehow or other get to Samarkand. The notion fired his imagination: he liked and believed in Cavagnari, he wanted to see Kabul, and in journeying thence to Samarkand through the Russian outposts he would be undertaking not only a daring exploit but an important piece of public service. In the end he declined, principally because there was a chance of the Mission being shut up in Kabul for some time, and since he would have no official status he felt that it was too much in the nature of an escapade, and that duty called him home to his Volunteers. Cavagnari acquiesced in this view: probably he felt that the way was very dark before him and did not want to involve more lives than were necessary in a desperate venture, for he told Lady Roberts, "I feel I am going amongst the most treacherous people under the sun, but if anything happens to me it will make the course the Government ought to pursue very much easier, and I feel great satisfaction in that." "When I left him," Melgund records in his journal, "I said 'good-bye, and good luck to you,' and it came across my mind at the moment that he thanked me as if he thought there was need for the good luck."

When Melgund was back in Roxburghshire, busy with his Volunteers, there came the news that the treaty of Gandamak was waste paper, and that once more the fires of war blazed on the frontier. In September Cavagnari and his staff and escort were murdered in Kabul, and it was a solemn reflection for Melgund that he had come within an ace of sharing their fate. It is possible that, even had he gone, he might have escaped, for the man who carried the message from Yakub to Balkh got through, and that was to have been his job, though it is questionable whether a European in the same task would have succeeded. Reviewing the incident in his journal he writes: "The chief reason that I settled not to go with Cavagnari was that it appeared to me that I should be doing better by going home and looking after my Volunteer corps, which was a thing I had taken up and wanted to succeed, than by starting on a mission the success of which seemed doubtful. I thought that the corps might deteriorate, and that an expedition through Central Asia might be looked upon as flighty while the alternative was sticking to business. I also wanted to get to know more people in England, and to do some reading. I have had many doubts about it, but still think that even if I had succeeded in getting through I did better by giving it up." Twenty-seven years later, as Viceroy of India, he visited the Guides at Mardan, and saw the obelisk erected in memory of the Kabul victims on which his own name might so easily have been inscribed.

Lord Melgund in the Uniform of the Border Mounted Rifles, 1883.

He was very unsettled that autumn and winter, and his letters and journals contain little beyond speculations on frontier policy and the Afghanistan campaign. Sir Frederick Roberts sent him a postcard, written in the train near Loodiana, inviting him to rejoin his Kabul column. "Pretyman and I are now on our way back to Kurrum, accompanied by Baker, Brab, Hugh Gough, 'Polly' Carew, and a few more of the right sort." He could not go, and even if he could it is hard to see how he would have caught up with the active British commander. Roberts entered Kabul in October, and in December came the rising of the tribes, and he and his force were cut off from the world, till Sir Donald Stewart arrived from Kandahar. Next year came the settlement with Abdur Rahman; but in the summer the battle of Maiwand was lost by the British, and Roberts had to march in haste the three hundred miles from Kabul to Kandahar to take order with the pretender Ayub Khan. Not till September 1881 was Abdur Rahman able to assert his kingship and give his country peace, and meantime a new frontier policy had been adopted by Simla and Whitehall.

During the whole of 1880 Melgund was at home, and it is clear from his journal and his letters that he was restless. His thoughts were on the frontiers of India, his reading chiefly in Indian history, his correspondence mainly with soldiers. The care of his Border Rifles was not enough to fill his mind, and his eye was roaming the world in quest of active service. One piece of useful work he was able to perform early in the year.

There had been a good deal of trouble in both the Afghan and Zulu Wars with press correspondents, for the vicious system of employing serving soldiers for the purpose had not been abandoned, and there had been much partisanship shown, newspapers ranging themselves for or against particular generals. As a remedy for such abuses the military authorities framed a set of rules to regulate the work of the press, and these were strongly criticized in the January number of the Nineteenth Century by Mr. Archibald Forbes, the most distinguished living war correspondent. Melgund replied to him in the March number of the review in an article which was his first excursion in literature. He put the common sense of the matter very clearly and trenchantly. He sympathized with both sides, for he had been himself a war correspondent, and had been invited to write for the Times and Daily Telegraph while in Afghanistan. He believed that the journalist in a campaign was necessary, not only to the public at home but to the army in the field; but he saw that the delicate mission of war correspondents, unless it was to become a public danger, must be under certain reasonable restrictions. It may fairly be said that to-day his views would be accepted as they stand by both journalists and soldiers. In this, his first literary effort, Melgund revealed not only a judicial mind, but a real vigour of style:--

"The next war may not give us quite so much pleasant reading. We may miss a little of the seasoning of bygone days. We shall not suffer by it. About a year ago a British force was crossing one of our Indian rivers on its way to the front. With it was the usual representative of the press, and he had written his usual letter. He tells how crocodiles and palm trees people the water and adorn the banks, and hands the eloquent production to a prosaic English officer, who remarks that neither crocodiles nor palm trees are within many miles. Matter-of-fact man! The correspondent is describing India, and he replies-the best answer ever made, and the secret of much of the discussion, the essence of what our soldiers have long known to be true--'What does that matter? The British public must have its crocodile, and it must have its palm tree.'" The Nineteenth Century article brought him many congratulations--from Lord Chelmsford, who had suffered from an unfair press; from Admiral Sir Charles Elliot; and notably from his old Lincolnshire friend, the hunting parson, Mr. Southwell. "I suppose I may regard you as dead to the witcheries of women," added that mentor, "and that the rest of your mortal life is to be devoted to the interests of your country. 'Sporting with Amaryllis in the shade,' etc., has given place to the more laudable desire for fame. Now for Parliament. Suppress your thirst for adventure and excitement and go into the House. You'll soon be getting old--I mean too old to care about or indeed be capable of active life, and in Parliament as long as your head is clear it matters little if your legs are slow." But Melgund was at the moment very little in love with

Parliament and politics. His journal of 1880 records, indeed, his pleasure at his brother Arthur's success in Roxburghshire, where he was returned by the narrow majority of ten; but his political comments are acrid and he had small regard for the Prime Minister. "Arthur arrived to-day, having been sailing about on the West Coast of Scotland with Gladstone! Oh dear! Oh dear!" Some months later he and that eminent man met at dinner with the Fitzwilliams. "He has a wild look in his eye, and his appearance would never inspire me with confidence," says the journal.

As for Amaryllis, it would seem that for the moment Mr. Southwell's guess was right. "Lots of pretty people, but don't care for balls," is a common entry. One name begins to appear occasionally--that of Mary Grey, whom he was constantly meeting. But though he hunted and visited about the land, and took his full share in social life, he was profoundly dissatisfied. His note on some famous party is only of a talk with Sir Garnet Wolseley, who "promised me a knife and fork with him in the next war. . . . He thinks we may have a blow-up in Europe any day, and he says he will take me with him to the German manoeuvres in September if our authorities will allow me to go." He is more interested in discussing Afghanistan with Lady Lawrence than in dancing with the reigning beauty: the kind of country house he likes is Crabbett, where he could inspect Wilfred Blunt's Arabs; when he sits up at night it is to read confidential papers on the Greek frontier lent him by Sir John Ardagh. He goes to the most brilliant ball of the season--"I am almost ashamed to say I never danced once, but met Knox, the gunner, looked on with him for some time, and then went down to supper with him instead of a lady, and fought the actions of Ali Musjid and Peiwar Kotal over again. I am sure we sat through I don't know how many dances, and drank I don't know how much champagne, and agreed we were both longing to be off somewhere, and came away together. He has seen more service perhaps than any young soldier: viz., Abyssinia, Ashanti, Afghanistan, and Zululand, and also seen much fighting with the Turks in the Russo-Turkish War. *I do wish I were off somewhere!*"

The cri du coeur of the last sentence is the index to his frame of mind, a frame of mind which made him curiously intolerant of all sedentary life at home. At the age of thirty-five he had a violent fit of that fever which commonly takes a man at an earlier stage, a desire for a rough life in wild places and an impatience of a cosseted civilization. His natural inclination was for the hard-riding, forthright type of man he had known in his Lincolnshire days, and his experience on the Indian frontier had taught him that the same qualities could be conjoined with excellent brains and used for high public duties. Hence he moved in London drawing-rooms like Marius among the ruins of Carthage: vehemently critical, tantalized by ambitions which seemed infinitely far from realization. Occasionally in the journal he permits himself an outburst which the reader must take as an undress expression of a mood and not as a considered verdict:--

"Dined with the Derbys: took in the daughter of the house, a very nice girl. A regular London society dinner: i.e., every one on their p's and q's. The politicals seemingly oppressed with their own importance; the Duke of . . . trying to wind a fox all the evening in the neighbourhood of the ceiling, at least I'll do him the credit to hope it was a fox--head up, stern down! Why is it that these sportsmen in London (upon my word the men are almost as bad as the women) cannot be natural? They are never their bona fide selves, if they possess such a thing. From the time you enter before dinner till the time you come away it is all manière. When you get with first-rate soldiers it is different. Sir Garnet Wolseley is natural the instant he speaks to you: the men on the turf are natural: men who have gone in for riding, or soldiering, or any manly amusement are natural: they talk to the point and are unaffected, but I'm damned if these London sportsmen are! And when you see young men reared in London society, when it has been their only world, when they haven't been knocked about and made to feel what's what, but have been traditionally brought up as lawgivers, what can you expect of them except that society manners should become their second nature, and that their politics in after life will, as a rule, be unpractical? At least their foreign ones are likely to be so, for as regards home politics they will be much steered by the common sense of the nation, which is very great, and has time to collect itself over any home question of importance. But in foreign politics or in military affairs, when we are required to act quickly and to show common sense at once, preserve me from the politicals! There is not one of them fit to take a horse to a second-class metropolitan meeting and look after him. He would do something silly if he mingled on an equality with his fellow-men! . . .

"Have been reading this evening the Life of Brigadier-General Nicholson. What a splendid fellow he was! Yet I believe India could produce many such men. It is our school for great administrators, and as such alone is worth millions to this country; but many of our home-staying, book-taught, theoretical politicians are incapable of realizing this. I don't suppose they would be able to appreciate a good frontier officer."

During the summer he thought he saw a chance of work abroad. He heard from Lord Lansdowne that Charles Gordon, afterwards the defender of Khartum and then private secretary to Lord Ripon, the Viceroy of India, had resigned, and he was advised to become a candidate for the post. Having been a supporter of Lord Lytton's frontier policy, he was in doubt whether he could work under a successor who was pledged to its reversal, but his Indian friends were anxious that he should apply, and he allowed his name to be put forward. A day or two later he learned that Mr. Henry Primrose of the Treasury had been chosen. The comment in the journal is: "Am sorry I did not get it in some ways; not the sort of work I should like, but still a first-rate appointment, and under a good Viceroy a very fine position. But I doubt this man, and do not expect anything great of him. In fact, I think as regards Afghanistan the first object for the Government at home will be to get out of anything that costs money, and probably Lord Eipon will work to orders." That autumn, too, he received an invitation from Colonel Chermside to go with him to Central Asia, and by way of Meshed and Herat to Kandahar. He put the seductive proposal behind him; he wanted service and not adventure. The close of the year saw the end of the Afghanistan operations. Roberts was welcomed home early in 1881, and Melgund was present when he was given the freedom of the City of London and at the banquet at the Mansion House. "It was a magnificent sight," he wrote. "At the close of the dinner the Loving Cup was passed round: an official told us to 'charge our glasses' as each toast was proposed, and claimed 'silence' in a voice of thunder for whoever was about to speak. Young Childers is reported to have said that he appeared to be educated for the last trump! Roberts's speech was the best I ever heard, though in his entire condemnation of Cardwell's system, which has really never been given a fair chance, I should not agree with him. Perhaps it is hardly fair to say he condemned it, as he spoke only of the shortservice system as in existence, which is no doubt very faulty; but I do not agree with him as an opponent to the theory of short service. He spoke without the slightest hesitation, and thoroughly from his heart, as if he felt he was doing a duty in speaking out: he has a very taking voice, and from being a little below par it may have been even more sympathetic than usual. He was very muc^ cheered. The speech has been received with rapture by nearly every soldier."

Melgund was hunting a good deal with different packs during the winter months, but the notes of runs in the journal are scanty, and the reflections on public affairs voluminous. For in January 1881 tragic news had come from South Africa, of Sir George Colley's repulse at Laing's Nek and the Ingogo River, and then of his death at Majuba Hill. Melgund had known Colley and believed in him, and the tidings of the disaster made him move heaven and earth to get out to South Africa. His chance came unexpectedly. The entry in the journal for Saturday, 5th March, is written on board the Balmoral Castle: "I have never had such a time of it as the last few days. I think it was last Monday I dined with Polly Carew at White's, when we suspected that Bobs would be ordered to the Transvaal, and next morning Polly came into my room before I was up with a telegram from the General saying he was appointed to the Transvaal and wished to see me. I saw him at the War Office, and he asked me to come out as his private secretary. Since that moment I have been hunted to distraction. What with 'duns' and preparations, life has been purgatory!"

He had an interesting voyage, visiting St. Helena on the way, and struggling to inform his mind by means of blue books on South African questions. "My impression," he wrote, "is that the Government at home will probably square things, though how they can do so with decency I cannot see." His journal records the fiasco.

"31st March.-We arrived at Capetown at about 8:30 on Monday evening: the Calabria with the 7th Hussars cheering us loudly as we steamed up the Bay, the men answering from our ship. A boat, however, soon came off from the town, and before she came alongside the people in her were shouting 'Peace.' We soon heard that Peace had been proclaimed, and that the General was to return home at once. Every one was disgusted. We got passages in the Trojan next morning. We seem to have made peace with a hostile force sitting down in our own territory of Natal, after having given us three lickings under poor Colley, besides other reverses. . . . The behaviour of the home Government is impossible to understand. We sailed yesterday afternoon, i.e., Wednesday 30th. As we stood on deck the crowd on the quay cheered the General loudly and groaned for Gladstone. One feels ashamed of one's country, or rather of the wretched Government at the head of it. I believe thoroughly in England all the same. . . .

"1st April.--April Fool's Day! We really ought to have arrived at Capetown to-day to make a proper ending of the farce the Government at home have staged!"

There was a proposal that Melgund should remain in South Africa and go to the Transvaal with the Military Commission as Sir Hercules Robinson's guest in order to prepare some kind of history of the whole proceedings. This he declined for good reasons, and likewise an offer of service in Basutoland. He was out of temper with the country and the policy, for he considered that Roberts had been badly treated, and that the conduct of the British Government was a mere sowing of dragons' teeth--a view on which, in the light of after events, disagreement is unfortunately impossible. He returned forthwith to England, very clear that he did right to come home, since if he stayed out on the chance of picking up odd jobs he "ran the risk of gaining the character of a loafer and adventurer." The reason is characteristic of the man; he did not love the role of eager amateur, and longed in everything for professional status.

The winter of 1881-82 was occupied with hunting, and, to judge from the journal, with anxious reflections and discussions on public affairs, in which he did not see eye to eye with Her Majesty's Ministers. Here are a few extracts:--

"9th January.--I used for a long time to keep a journal for every day of my life. After I got that fall at Liverpool in '76 I gave it up for a bit, as I was so knocked up I fancied it tried me writing it in the evening. I have been so much behind the scenes lately in the two last campaigns, Afghanistan and the Transvaal, that I have heard many things which I regret not having written down, and I have also been thrown very much with men, particularly soldiers, of whom I might have written much. I therefore mean in future to try and put down more of interest than I have hitherto done in my journals. Besides the usefulness of making notes of anything worth remembering, a journal gives practice in getting one into the habit of writing one's experiences quickly, and if one can write them in fairly respectable English, which I shall endeavour for the sake of practice to do, it will help one elsewhere."

"5th February.-Aston Clinton. Had a long conversation with Sir Garnet this evening on Egyptian affairs. We agreed that the Power who should have befriended us there is Turkey, and that we have lost her friendship, though Sir Garnet thinks that she may send a force to Egypt for the sake of asserting her suzerainty, which may be on the wane. I don't think so. We have snubbed Turkey too much to expect her to do our dirty work, and she is now friends with Bismarck. If I was a Turk I would be damned if I would send troops to Egypt to help Gladstone out of a hole.

"Sir Garnet very agreeable and talking thoroughly practical sense, which so few people do. I like Lady Wolseley very much too. She is more cautious than he is, but very taking and clever--the sort of cleverness which comes from knowledge of the world and other people. I will not call it 'cleverness' as I am beginning to hate clever people, they are so damnably silly--I mean unpractical. The more I see the more I look down upon the learning obtained from books alone. The ordinarily accepted clever men and women of the world have drawn most of their knowledge from reading. Goodness knows, I know well enough the help, even the necessity, of information only to be obtained from books. At the same time those whose character is formed by such means alone can bear no comparison to the man who is naturally first-rate, has no book learning, but has gained all his experience in the school of a world of many sets, societies, and adventures. Combine the book learning and the experience of the world and you get something very rare. Sir Garnet is the best example I have seen of such a man. The book-taught man or woman is enthusiastic, brilliant, unpractical, and perfectly sickening. Then again there is the entirely untaught, uneducated, clever, conversational, full-of-repartee creature of London society, generally recognized as 'so clever,' but with no experience except that of his own society world. Horrible people!"

Meantime the Egyptian problem was growing more confused, and there were the first mutterings of Mr. Gladstone's Irish Home Rule. But towards the end of March politics were for a moment driven out of his head, when Lord Manners won the Grand National on his own horse "Seaman" by a head from Mr. Besley's "Cyrus." It was the kind of thing to fire Melgund's imagination. Here was an amateur who had bought the horse on purpose to win the great race, who had ridden very little before, who was by no means fancied by the public, and who won by sheer grit and skill. Melgund's feelings were a little like those of Lord George Bentinck, when, after he had given up racing for the public service, he saw "Surplice," which had once been his, win the Derby.

"It was a very great performance, and he deserves all credit. I do not know Manners at all, and I have never seen the horse either. It does seem strange that some of the best men over a country, who have been riding all their lives, such as 'Doggy' Smith, E. P. Wilson, and Bob L'Anson, should never have won the Liverpool, and that Manners, who had no experience and made no reputation in first-class company, should come and win a fine race by a head. I would have given anything to have won it at one time, but it is plainer than ever that one might toil away all one's life and never win that particular race. Of the steeplechase riders I have seen I shall always put 'Pussy' Richardson first either amongst gentlemen or professionals; Bob L'Anson facile princeps amongst the latter. He is a really fine horseman which so few of the professionals are; at least don't understand riding over a country; they put their hands down and go from end to end, as in a hurdle race; but they have no idea of putting a horse properly at a fence, or of correcting him if he has got it out of his stride; and then they wonder horses fall! Perfect horsemen are scarce, and in riding, and particularly in steeplechase riding, the public are very often gulled into thinking certain riders good by their hardness and dash, which may probably give them a run of luck for a bit. Immense practice is necessary to put a fine horseman at the top of the tree in race riding, and when I talk of the top of the tree I don't mean the men who have won most races, but the men who combine horsemanship, good hands, good seat, knowledge of the right way to put a horse at a fence, with the necessary qualities of the jockey; first and foremost knowledge of pace, then dash and a cool head, and the power of seeing what every other horse in the race is doing. And when one is talking of these really first-rate riders I don't admit them as perfectly excellent unless they are also first-rate to hounds. 'Pussy' Richardson has all the qualities--as good to hounds as he was on a racecourse, and he was a finished artist on the flat against the best professionals, and the best steeplechase rider of his day. When one hears society talk of so and so, and so and so, and so and so as the best rider in England, what bosh it is! Probably they only know the one trade, viz., hunting, or the other trade, perhaps race riding. Amongst the best men to hounds you find young men who are riding the best horses that money can buy--how can they lay claim to the horsemanship of men who have passed through every stage of schooling young horses of every sort? Horsemanship is not learned in a day or in a few seasons' hunting. Hard riding is a different thing."

In April of this year Melgund was suddenly summoned to his parents at Bournemouth, and on 21st April his mother died. She was fifty-seven years old, but no shadow of middle age had fallen upon her spirit. To the end her letters had the gaiety and the eager interest of youth. Melgund had not altered since his boyish days when she had analysed his character and professed her complete trust in it, and no mother and son were ever in more frank and intimate accord. He made fun of her staunch Liberalism and her fidelity to the political traditions of her youth, and posed now and then as a ruthless Cromwellian in order to elicit her gentle expostulations. It is not easy to overestimate the influence which her gay wisdom and fortitude exercised over one who was still in process of finding himself. It provided a perpetual incentive to honourable ambition, and an undogmatic and unostentatious idealism. Such a man as Melgund was too robust to be dominated by mere emotion, and at the same time too deeply affectionate and generous to be ruled solely through his reason. His mother's combination of a keen critical mind with the happy glow of romance and the warmth of love made her influence supreme, and her personality when alive, and after death her memory, were the chief shaping forces in his life.

During the early summer of 1882 Irish affairs seemed to be marching to dire confusion, and in May came the tragic news of the murder in Phoenix Park of Lord Frederick Cavendish, the new Chief Secretary for Ireland, and Mr. Burke, the Permanent Under-Secretary. Melgund at once wrote to Sir Garnet Wolseley offering himself for service in that country should the occasion arise. Talking with old Lord Strathnairn of this appalling tragedy, the latter said that he could soon put Ireland to rights: "it only wanted a little determination, and of course he would avoid unnecessary bloodshed!" At that time Melgund saw a good deal of this old warrior, who was renowned for his blunt speech and his many idiosyncrasies. Once, arriving for dinner, he found the table laid for sixteen, but they dined tete-a-tete, all the other invitations having somehow miscarried!

In July he celebrated his thirty-seventh birthday amid the stir of preparation for an Egyptian campaign. When war was declared Sir Garnet Wolseley was appointed to the command, and he applied for Melgund as private secretary, but there was some difficulty about employing an officer not on the active list. Wolseley therefore wrote to him officially regretting that he could not make the appointment, but at the bottom of the page there was a "P.T.O." and on the other side "Come along, Rolly." Privately he was advised to procure a couple of horses and present himself in Egypt. He left London on 4th August, travelling from Brindisi in the dispatch boat with Sir John Adye, Neville Lyttelton, and some of Sir Garnet's staff. On the 11th he was reconnoitring Arabi's position with Lord Methuen, and in the next few days he was feverishly scouring Alexandria for horses. Then Wolseley arrived, and on the 17th Melgund was gazetted as captain in the Mounted Infantry, a force the strength of which was 4 officers and 73 men. After some delay and much uncertainty they were sent to Ismailia, and landed on the 22nd August, proceeding to the cavalry lines. Of the action on the 24th an account may be transcribed from the journal:--

"29th August.--On Wednesday we received orders to parade at 4 a.m. Accordingly we fell in on Thursday morning in the dark. The Household Cavalry and some guns were to have come with us, but the guns were late and delayed the Cavalry, so we accordingly marched off alone: the Cavalry caught us up at daylight, but not the guns. About 5:30 we came across some Bedouins on foot who fired at us. The Mounted Infantry were ordered to attack them, which we did, driving them off and taking eight prisoners. We galloped a considerable distance after them. The country here was chiefly hard sand and very good going, but in some parts there was grazing ground, intersected by wet ditches. During part of our chase I galloped towards what I supposed to be a line of men about to fire, but on getting close found that they were a line of long-legged birds!

"After chasing the Bedouins and taking prisoners we thought the morning's work was over till we saw, rather to the left of the point to which we had pursued some skirmishers on a low ridge of hills. The enemy was now advancing in earnest. I saw little of what went on on our left, we being wholly on the right of our line. The action commenced with the Household Cavalry. The enemy advanced with large bodies of troops--infantry, and cavalry behind them, who remained on the high ground. I wondered at the time why our guns did not at once begin and play upon the enemy masses which offered such a rare mark for artillery. It turns out that the guns were not there: they had got stuck somewhere, and though they came up before long, we never got more than two guns in action. The first order given was about 6 a.m. for the Mounted Infantry to engage the enemy on our right flank. As it happened, the Corps only mustered forty-three men that morning, and we could only dismount half at a time. Throughout the morning we were always under fire, generally from our front, very often from our right flank, and sometimes from our right rear. We were required to draw out and keep in check the whole of the enemy's left flank with twenty dismounted men. In front of us the enemy was in considerable strength. I hear now that he had ten battalions of infantry on the ground, besides cavalry, and, I think, twelve guns, which were employed entirely against our left flank, where our two guns were.

"The enemy was constantly working round the rising ground and firing on our right flank, and at one time we were so far separated from the cavalry that we were in a fair way to be cut off. The cavalry gave us no support except the moral support of their presence in the rear of us. The enemy advanced in a long line of skirmishers dressed in white; they generally fired at about 1,200 or 1,000 yards, and never came within 700, as at that distance our fire began to tell, and they would not come on. Later the 84th Regiment and Marine Artillery came into action; then the guns; then a certain space without troops; then the cavalry; then ourselves. This was the largest number of troops we had in action. The Mounted Infantry had certainly a warm time under a nasty fire the whole morning. At about 11 a.m. Parr, who was in command, was shot through the right leg. I was standing close to him; we were both dismounted at the time and with our firing line. Piggott then took command. About an hour later I was hit in the hand.

We had run very short of ammunition, and I had just been round the troop of the 60th to see what remained, and was dismounted, talking to Sergeant Riarden on the flank of the Corps, when a shot hit me a little below the wrist, in the fleshy part between the thumb and forefinger. It bled a good deal at first, but Sergeant Riarden tied it up tightly and more or less stopped it, and I went to the rear, where I found the 1st Life Guards, and Hamilton, their doctor, tied me up. I afterwards rode to Ismailia, and went to the Khedive's Palace there, which has been turned into a hospital.

"Sir Garnet, who was out on the morning the engagement started, is said to have ordered breakfast at 10 o'clock, and I cannot think that at the outside more than a reconnaissance was intended. As it was, we became committed with a very small force against a very large one."

Melgund was to see no more fighting, but was left to contemplate the badness of the medical arrangements and listen to a hundred contradictory rumours, till on 13th September came the news of the battle of Tel-el-Kebir, followed the next day by the surrender of Arabi. On the 15th he was in Cairo hunting up what remained of the Mounted Infantry, and was much disquieted by the quarters he found them in.

"The infernal regions could hardly be worse! Mosquitoes! I never saw such mosquitoes! Stinks in abundance, and poor devils of loose horses which had been left here by the Egyptian Cavalry running about all night screaming! There have been all sorts of excitements: the railway station caught fire full of stored ammunition, and I shall never forget seeing Havelock Allan walk quietly towards the burning buildings to see if there was a possibility of removing the ammunition. There was a crowd of soldiers round the station, all standing back a long way from the flames, and no one apparently capable of taking the lead till he appeared on the scene. He is a very gallant fellow. He joined us during the fight at Magfar, borrowed a rifle from one of the Mounted Infantry and blazed away at the Egyptians, and amused me by shouting out, 'The Elliots will be proud of you to-day!' I assumed command of the Corps on 22nd September.

"The Khedive entered Cairo on Monday, 25th September; the troops lined the streets, the Mounted Infantry taking the Bel-el-Soug. On Saturday, the 30th, the 'march past' took place. Those who were looking on say it was a fine sight. The following Monday there was a grand function in the evening at the Palace given by the Khedive to all the officers of the force. Magnificent illuminations, native bands of different sorts, rope dancing, and a splendid supper, to which about a thousand must have sat down. Pope congratulated me on being mentioned in General Orders, of which I was quite ignorant."

In General Orders issued by Sir Garnet Wolseley at Cairo, October 1882, the following appeared:--

"The General Commanding-in-Chief wishes to take this opportunity of thanking Captain Lord Melgund and the officers and men of this Corps for the admirable services they have rendered during the campaign. On more than one occasion Sir Garnet Wolseley has had the pleasure of bringing to notice the gallantry of the Corps and of making special mention of its Commanding Officer, its officers, and its men."

In the Gazette of 17th November Melgund received the 4th Class of the Medjidie and promotion to the rank of honorary major. By the end of October he was back in England. In reading the careful summary in his journal of the campaign it is impossible not to be impressed with his grasp of the operations and his shrewd judgment of individual achievement. The officers whom he commended were without exception destined to justify his opinion in later and greater wars.

During the winter of 1882-83 Melgund kept horses at Aston Clinton, the Cyril Flowers' house, and hunted regularly with the Bicester, the Grafton, and Mr. Selby Lowndes. He saw Lord Wolseley often and corresponded with Sir Frederick Roberts in India, but his strenuous interest in public affairs was a little abated. For a new factor had entered his life. Seven years before, in the library at Minto, his mother had introduced him to the youngest daughter of General Charles Grey,* who had been private secretary both to the Prince Consort and to Queen Victoria. The two families had been friends and political allies for generations; some wit once called the Elliots "the Scots Greys," for in the days of political patronage the loaves and the fishes that were left by the one were snapped up by the other. Presently Mary Grey makes her appearance in Melgund's journal as a neighbour at dinner and a partner at tails. He had a host of women friends, for his chivalry and high spirits were extraordinarily attractive, but his mind seemed to be set on other things than marriage, and his men friends regarded him as the eternal adventurer who shakes his bridle reins and rides away. Something of the sort he believed himself, and was accustomed to scoff at domesticity and lay heavy odds in favour of consistent bachelordom. But that spring sealed his fate. Melgund and Mary Grey met during Whitsuntide at Panshanger, the Cowpers' place in Hertfordshire, a paradise of green lawns and blue-bell woods, and a week later the engagement was announced. Melgund was fortunate in many things, but his marriage was the crowning felicity of his life. He won a wife'who was to be a comrade and helpmate as perfect as ever fell to the lot of man.

* Second son of the second Earl Gray, who, as Prime Minister, introduced the Reform Bill of 1832.

The marriage took place on the 28th July at St. Margaret's, Westminster, and the honeymoon was spent at Lady Sarah Spencer's house at Berkhamstead, and at Minto. The bride's toother, in a letter to Queen Victoria has described it:--

"Mary was deeply touched by your Majesty's telegram, received just as we were starting for church. She really looked her best in white satin trimmed with dear Lady Minto's lace and veil. The service was beautifully performed by Canon Farrar. Six little bridesmaids--the eldest was seven--Sybil M'Donnell (Louisa's little girl), Albert's Victoria, Beatrix Herbert's child, Lady Clarendon's, Lady Zetland's, and Lady Grosvenor's pretty little girls; Albert's little Charlie, Victoria's boy, and Louisa's Dunluce, as pages. A large assemblage of mutual friends attended. Your Majesty's beautiful shawl and Princess Beatrice's brooch were much prized. . . . On occasions of this kind the loss of their dear father's blessing must be deeply felt, but I know he would have fully approved of their union. They have been attracted to one another for years. He is a thorough soldier, devoted to his profession, and full of merit."*

* This letter was found amongst Queen Victoria's papers and sent to Lady Minto in 1916 by the desire of King George V.

Of the many letters of congratulation which Melgund received, one may be quoted from Lord Wolseley which was characteristic of their friendship:--

"I am very glad to hear you are about to marry, for I think as an eldest son you ought to do so. I can therefore congratulate you with all my heart, and wish you every joy and blessing this world can afford. You may be quite certain that, if ever I again command troops in the field, I shall be very glad to have you with me. I wish you could take into the field with you five or six hundred mounted riflemen from the Volunteer Forces. In the event of war, you would be just the man to raise such a corps, and with your position and the prestige of your having been in the Army and wounded when in command of Mounted Infantry, I am sure you would be able to pick and choose from all the corps in the Volunteer service and the Yeomanry--the term of service to be for the war and two months, if necessary, after the declaration of peace. I wish you would think of this and work out the details, especially as to the course to be pursued to establish the corps. This is a ridiculous letter to write to a man just about to be married, but you began the subject of fighting first, as children say when they are quarrelling. Again I wish you every happiness, and wish it you with all my heart."

CHAPTER FOUR

CANADA: 1883-85

SHORTLY before Melgund's marriage Lord Lansdowne was appointed Governor-General of Canada, and Melgund, an old schoolfellow and friend, was offered the post of military secretary. The offer was at once accepted, for it was a chance of service, and service overseas, and under conditions where he could be accompanied by his young wife. In his journal in September 1883 Melgund wrote: "I am at a loss how to recommence this journal, and am sadly interrupted by Mary. The world has altogether changed for me, and my humble establishment, 'Pepper' (his dog) and Harrington (his valet), has been transformed. I am very happy, and with Mary now lying on the sofa before me am vainly attempting to sum up this journal to the present date." The revolution was complete, for the change from bachelordom was to be attended by the transference of his energies from sport and occasional soldiering to the grooves of official duties. The appointment was both military and civil: it was gazetted through the Colonial Office, accepted by the War Office, and published in the Army List, so that, as he told his brother Hugh, he went out as "recognized military secretary cocked hat and whole bag of tricks." The honeymoon ended in a wild bustle of preparation, and at the end of September 1883 the Melgunds sailed for Canada. Family history was repeating itself. In 1837 Lady Melgund's father, then Colonel Charles Grey, commanding the 71st Regiment, embarked at Cork with his bride in a sailing vessel bound for Montreal, and after a fair weather voyage reached his destination in fourteen days, making a quicker passage than his brother-in-law, Lord Durham, the newly appointed Governor-General, who was a passenger in one of the first steamships to cross the Atlantic.

The change to new scenes came at a fortunate time for Melgund, for not only did it give his active mind an occupation, but it removed him from the unwelcome proximity of home politics. The Gladstone administration was becoming to him, as to many others of his type, a dark obsession. His letters to his mother in the year before her death are clouded with forebodings and solemn with execration. "The Turf is purest gold compared with politics, and the extraordinary thing is that gentlemen with heads on their shoulders should become so utterly warped." Sometimes he made merry over it: "I write a line in the greatest haste, but I feel that you should instantly be made aware of the frantic excitement in political circles occasioned by yesterday's news in the press--that there is strong reason to suspect that Gladstone and Dizzy were changed at nurse, and that Dizzy is Gladstone and Gladstone Dizzy." But usually he was too depressed to joke.

Before he sailed he stayed at Howick with old Lord Grey. "He is a capital old fellow, and it is refreshing to find some one calling himself a Liberal who is not afraid to own that England has great imperial interests abroad which she is bound to look after if she wants to keep up her position. We literally shrieked over Gladstone." And from Canada--regarding from a distance the confusion in Ireland and Egypt--he wrote to Hugh: "I would not have thought any one could have disgraced his country as Gladstone has done. I wouldn't be seen frequenting such an unpatriotic, disreputable coffee-house as the House of Commons for a fortune. I suppose when one gets out of England one is more prone to remember that one is an Englishman."

To such a mood Canada was a welcome sedative. It was more; it was an essential stage in his political education. Hitherto his political views had been of the light-horseman type, acquired often second-hand from the company into which he found himself thrown, not based, as were his views on military questions, on personal thought and study. At the back of them were sound instincts, a generous humanity, and a certain largeness of vision, but they had not been adjusted to the needs of common life. He was to see at closer quarters the business of government and to learn to make allowance for fallible politicians. For years the glory of the British Empire and the infinite possibilities of its future had fired his imagination^ but he had feared that democracy and imperialism might be incompatible. He was now, in a strenuous young democracy, to come to some understanding of the root problems of the Empire, and to learn that upon the vigour and freedom of the parts depended the organic strength and unity of the whole. Above all he was to realize that the problems of statecraft were not to be solved by summary methods, but only by a slow and patient adjustment.

He was fortunate in serving under a chief, like Lord Lansdowne, of notable tact and judgment. He was fortunate, too, in going to Canada at a most interesting stage in her history. Five years before all British possessions in North America, except Newfoundland, had been constituted into one Dominion. In 1878 Sir John Macdonald had entered upon that long tenure of power which endured till his death in 1891, and the "national" policy of the Conservatives, based upon the creation of a high tariff wall against the United States and a bold development of Canada behind its shelter, had the assent of the great mass of the people. The province of Quebec held the balance between the two parties, and in it the new Governor-General's French connections gave him a unique popularity. Meanwhile the Canadian Pacific Railway was slowly moving to completion through occasional scandals and constant difficulties. The final arrangement with the Dominion Government had been made in 1881, but the undertaking was still on the razor edge of fortune' and the year after Melgund's arrival saw its most acute financial crisis. It was an era of vigorous national life and far-reaching national ambitions, and it was a time, too, when some of the greatest men of modern Canadian history were at the height of their powers. Sir John Macdonald, in especial, was the type of statesman whom Melgund could study with sympathy and profit. He was an incomparable manager of men, and contrived by his dominating personality and his keen eye for the essential in every problem to drive as difficult a team of jealous factions as ever Minister had in charge. He had, too, that largeness of outlook which is fitted to inspire a young man at the threshold of his career. He had been the main architect of Canadian union; he had fostered the nationalism of his country, realizing that without national pride on the part of the units the Empire would be a feeble thing; it was his vision and faith, more than the money of the capitalists, that carried the Canadian Pacific Railway to brilliant success; and he never wavered from the first days of his political life in insisting on the truth that the prosperity of Canada depended upon its close and permanent connection with Britain. As Lord Rosebery said in unveiling his monument in the crypt of St. Paul's Cathedral, "he grasped the central idea that the British Empire was the greatest secular agency for good now known to mankind; he determined to die under it, and strove that Canada should live under it."

The Melgunds arrived in Canada a week before the Lansdownes, and were welcomed by Lord Lorne, the retiring Governor-General, and Princess Louise. They took up then* quarters at Government House, Ottawa, till Rideau Cottage was made ready for them, and in December were settled in their own home. They were received with extraordinary kindness by the people of Canada, for to their personal charm they added ancestral credentials. Lady Melgund's family had many claims on Canada's gratitude, and among a people where Scottish blood predominated a Border Elliot bore an honoured name. It was an ideal way in which to begin married life, for the honeymoon atmosphere was not marred by the weight of a too onerous household, and the young people were free to move about and see the world. They visited many parts of Eastern Canada, and in the summer of 1884 a trip to the United States took them to Albany, Newport, New York, and Boston. There was endless sport, too--skating in winter, at which both became experts, and fishing in those noble Canadian rivers, which had not yet become the preserves of millionaires. On the Cascapedia, which flows into the Bay of Chaleur, three blissful weeks were spent, for Melgund, like his chief, was a devoted fisherman. The modest angler of to-day will read with envy the casual jottings which record their baskets. In five consecutive June days, when there was supposed to be no great run of fish, Lord Lansdowne had twenty-six salmon to his own rod, averaging over 25 lbs., including one of 43 lbs.

The day-to-day duties of a military secretary are prosaic enough, but Melgund speedily found tasks more important than the ordering of the Governor-General's household and the oversight of his stables. Affairs in Egypt were marching to calamity. In January 1884 General Gordon had proceeded to Khartum at the request of the British Government to carry out the evacuation. By March it was clear that there could be no peaceful withdrawal of the Egyptian garrisons in the Sudan, and by May Khartum was cut off from the world. It was not till August that the British Government decided to send a relief expedition under the command of Lord Wolseley. One of Wolseley's first steps was to cable through the Colonial Secretary to Lord Lansdowne to inquire if Canada could provided 300 voyageurs (whose value he had learned in the old Red River campaign) to act as steersmen in the Nile boats. He also asked if Melgund could be permitted to go to Egypt in command of the party. The Governor-General was willing, but Melgund, after much searching of heart, felt himself bound to decline; his wife was soon to be confined, and he dared not leave her. There was no time to be lost, so Sir John Macdonald agreed to the request of the British Government, and Melgund set off tor Ottawa to recruit the force, while Lord Lansdowne remained at Quebec. It was not an easy task to enlist so many picked men in a few weeks. The Militia Department had to be tactfully handled, and Mr. Caronf the Minister of Militia, co-operated loyally. The voyageur class of the Red River days had virtually disappeared, and the men who had served with that expedition, and whom Wolseley specially asked for, were now for the most part sedentary folk and growing old. Melgund had recourse to the lumbermen, who in the winter were quartered in shanties, felling timber in the woods, but in the spring were engaged in rafting logs down the rivers and in working their "scows" upstream with provisions. Wolseley stipulated that Indians should be included, particularly the Iroquois of Caughnawaga. The War Office required that the party, which was presently increased to 500, should arrive in European waters by 1st October.

The contingent ultimately numbered 367--collected from Ottawa, Three Rivers, Caughnawaga, and Manitoba. The Manitoba draft included thirty Indians, the Ottawa party was divided equally between Canadians and French Canadians, and the Three Rivers men were all French Canadians. Major Frederick Denison, who had been Wolseley's orderly in the Red River campaign, was appointed to the command. The Abbé Bouchard, a missionary in Egypt, who had visited Khartum and happened to be home on leave, went out as chaplain, and Colonel Kennedy was added as an unpaid foreman, because the Manitoba Indians would not go without him.

Melgund spent a hectic month, and his task was not facilitated by the British Government, who, after he had made all arrangements with the Allan and Dominion lines, suddenly announced that they had chartered a special ship to take the men straight to Alexandria. It was not easy to impress upon the authorities that Canadian boatmen had voracious appetites, and could not support life on army rations. But all difficulties were surmounted, and on Sunday, 14th September, the party embarked at Montreal on the Ocean King. Next day Lord Lansdowne inspected them at Quebec, and they began their journey towards that desert town where Gordon was waiting upon death. It was Canada's first participation as a Dominion in an imperial war, and it was Melgund's first important administrative task performed on his own responsibility, for Lord Lansdowne left all the details in his hands. From the correspondence and reports the reader gathers a strong impression of the good sense, tact, energy, and business capacity of the military secretary.

Three months later, on 13th December, his daughter Eileen was born at Ottawa. Sir John Macdonald happened to be dining that night at Government House, and proposed the toast of "La Petite Canadienne."

Wolseley, through no fault of his own, was too late; Khartum fell on January 25, 1885, and Gordon died on the Dervish spears; the British expedition retraced its steps, and the Sudan was in the Mahdi's hands. Shame and anxiety were universal throughout the Empire, and from the black clouds which overhung the Egyptian frontier might at any moment come the thunderbolt of a barbarian invasion. The possibility of military aid from the Dominions was mooted, and the Dominions themselves began to inquire into their military assets. As early as March 1884 Mr. Goldwin Smith had written to Melgund: "It looks almost as if your military service might be required on the other side of the water. A war, though terrible, would not be an unmixed calamity if it put a stop to the work of those wretched factions in England. But it would sadly undeceive the English people as to the armaments and military disposition of Canada, about which enormous falsehoods have been told them. One of our public men* did not shrink from assuring them that we had a force of 400,000 men, organized and ready for the field. He meant the 'enrolled

Militia,' which can hardly be said to exist, even on paper."

* Apparently Sir John Macdonald.

The dispatch of the voyageur contingent was followed by duties of a different type which gave Melgund a valuable insight into the problems of imperial defence. A committee was appointed in 1884, consisting of the Minister of Militia, Mr. Caron, the Deputy-Minister, Lieut.-Colonel Panet, Major-General Middleton commanding the Canadian Militia, and Melgund himself, with Mr. Colin Campbell as secretary, to go through the papers in the archives on the subject of Canadian defence, and report on their use. The committee confined itself to coast defence, and considered a vast mass of documents--reports of royal commissions, dispatches from Secretaries of State and Governor-Generals, official and private letters of admirals and generals, memoranda by all sorts and conditions of experts. In the voluminous correspondence on the subject we find Melgund sorting and arranging documents with the industry of a Record Office official. He had also an immediate and practical defence problem to face. In the spring of 1885 there were rumours of a Fenian raid from the United States across the Manitoba frontier to be directed against Winnipeg. The Clan-na-Gael saw in the troubles then threatening in the Canadian North-West a chance for their peculiar brand of patriotism, and the Canadian Government had before them the dossiers of the various firebrands who were believed to be implicated. Nothing came of the enterprise, but Canada was well prepared, and had the raiders marched they would have found a stern reception. Melgund's memorandum on the subject works out in minute detail the nature of the welcome which awaited the invasion.

But the most interesting of the questions which during these months he had to consider was the possibility of Canada assisting the British Army in the Egyptian campaign. The whole earth was full of the rumours of war, no man knew where the Sudan entanglement might end, and the old suspicion of Russia on the Indian frontier had grown into active fear. Australia had sent troops to Egypt, and it was felt that Canada could not be eclipsed by New South Wales. The Egyptian campaign came to a close before active steps were taken, but it was fortunate for Melgund that he had to look into the matter, since the insight and knowledge which he thereby acquired were to be of the utmost value to him when fifteen years later, in a position of greater authority, he had to face the same question. On one point he was clear from the start. Any Canadian force must be enrolled for Imperial service and not as Canadian militia, and the selection must lie with the Imperial authorities. This was also the view of Sir John Macdonald, and of Colonel Otter, one of the chief militia officers. The latter believed that no militia regiment could take the field as it stood, or indeed could furnish more than twenty per cent, of its officers and men as fit for foreign service. But he also believed that it would be perfectly easy to recruit a force--say a brigade of three battalions--for a term of not less than a year's service abroad, from Canadians and from Britons in the United States, and that such a force could be trained and got ready in less than a fourth of the time required for ordinary recruits. Proposals poured in for the undertaking. Major-General Winburn Laurie, an officer still on the British active list but resident in Nova Scotia, proffered a scheme for a force which he was willing to command; General Middleton had another; Mr. Goldwin Smith suggested the sending of a Canadian battery of field artillery, to which Melgund replied that no single Canadian battery was fit to take the field and that a composite battery would take too long to create. Early in 1885, while the Imperial need still seemed urgent, he wrote to his brother Fitzwilliam Elliot setting forth his views, and the letter was shown to Lord Wolseley. His brother, who had himself served in Canada, approved, and concluded with some gloomy prognostications of trouble in the Canadian North-West. That may have been done to make sure that the stormy petrel would not grow restless in a too pacific clime. "Don't be in an infernal hurry to get out," he wrote. "Every man ought to stick to his post now, where he knows the ropes, and he may be perfectly certain that he will have his work cut out for him."

The fraternal prophecy was right. Fifteen years earlier the Red River rebellion under the half-breed Louis Riel had been broken by Wolseley's expedition to Fort Garry, and Riel had fled to the United States and suffered sentence of outlawry. Since then things had changed; Fort Garry was now the rising city of Winnipeg, and the three months from Toronto to the Red River by boat and portage were now five days by the Canadian Pacific Railway. But the discontent of the half-breeds and the Indians remained; only the problem had shifted five hundred miles into the wilds. It was the story of the Great Trek in South Africa repeated; the half-breeds fell back before the advance of officialdom and discovered grievances when officialdom overtook them-- land laws which offended their notion of justice, new regulations which they did not understand. It may fairly be said that there was nothing in the policy of the Canadian Government to give them ground for complaint, but they did not easily appreciate the complexities or the delays of the administrative machine, and they had the old dislike of a conservative people to any novelty. Moreover, there were white settlers to fan the discontent, men who had taken up land in the Edmonton, Battleford, and Prince Albert districts in the expectation that the new railway would follow them, and who, when the route chosen lay far to the south, found themselves en Vair. Also the Indians--the Cree nation-- were out of temper. They had seen their hunting grounds broken up, and the buffalo, which was the backbone of their livelihood, exterminated. In 1883, 150,000 buffalo robes were sold in St. Paul, and next year only 300. The wonder is not that trouble broke out, but that, with so much inflammable material to hand, it proved such a flash in the pan.

The outbreak began in the fork of the North and South Saskatchewan Rivers, where lay a Cree reserve, nearly three hundred miles from the nearest point on the Canadian Pacific Railway. On March 22, 1885, news reached Ottawa that Riel, who had long ago been free to return to Canada, had seized the mail bags and cut the telegraph wires at a place called Duck Lake in the fork. General Middleton, commanding the Canadian Militia, left at once for Winnipeg in the hope that the rising might be quelled without bloodshed. The situation was sufficiently grave, for in that spacious North-West there were white women and children in the farms along the river banks dispersed among 30,000 Indians, with no protection except the scattered posts of the 500 Mounted Police. On the 28th came news of a fight between a detachment of Police and Riel's rebels, in which the Police had over a dozen killed and were forced to retire to Fort Carlton on the North Saskatchewan. There they were joined next day by Colonel Irvine, commanding the Police, and after burning the fort they retired downstream to Prince Albert. This meant that all the white settlements were directly threatened, and the Militia were at once put in motion and a call sent out for volunteers. The 90th battalion at Winnipeg were the nearest troops; the rest must travel the better part of two thousand miles from Eastern Canada.

Melgund left Ottawa on the 26th, and was in Winnipeg on the 30th. Middleton had asked for him, and the Governor-General assented, with many injunctions to remember that he was a married man and not to run into needless danger. They left Qu'appelle station, the nearest on the Canadian Pacific line to the scene of hostilities, on 2nd April, having only between 300 and 400 men, mostly from the 90th regiment. On the 6th Melgund was appointed Chief of the Staff and the march began in earnest. It was the worst season of the year for campaigning, for the winter was breaking up, the snow was turning into slush, and the trails were quagmires. Rain, blizzards, and a perpetual high wind attended them, and their boots froze to the stirrup irons; yet the force did its twenty miles a day, and the Hudson Bay Company laboured manfully at transport and supplies.

On the 13th they were at Humboldt, and the next step was to secure Clarke's Crossing on the Saskatchewan. This was done on the 17th, and the force, now increased to some 800, began its descent of the river, moving on both banks. News had come of Riel, who was at Batoche, thirty-three miles away, with one Gabriel Dumont, a famous rifle shot and buffalo-hunter, directing operations. On the 24th they came in touch with the enemy, who was strongly posted in a ravine called Fish Creek on the right bank of the stream. Melgund, who was on the left bank at the time, brought the troops across, and all day long the half-breeds in their rifle pits hung up the advance. The force engaged was barely 1,000 strong, and the losses that day amounted to 10 killed and 45 wounded. Middleton himself had a narrow escape with a bullet through his cap, while both his aides-decamp were wounded. The position was grave, and he decided not to expose his small volunteer force to needless losses. In pouring rain camp was made, and there the troops waited till 7th May, when considerable reinforcements arrived. Meantime the enemy had fallen back from Fish Creek to Batoche. Suspense prevailed at Ottawa as to the fate of that small force, composed as it was mainly of volunteers. To Melgund fell the duty of selecting each camping ground, of posting the sentries, and riding round the patrols, while the Indians from their rifle pits and hiding-places showed discrimination in trying to pick off the officers. A rumour which circulated in Ottawa that Melgund had been shot did not tend to allay the anxiety.

The advance on Batoche began very early on 9th May, with the steamer Northcote in attendance. By 8 a.m. it had reached the township, and found the rebels strongly ensconced in rifle pits and a thick belt of bush. Middleton, personally most gallant but very careful of his men, hesitated to rush the place, and all day futile skirmishing continued. In the afternoon, Melgund to his disgust was sent off to the telegraph station at Humboldt with dispatches, and so missed the last stage of the campaign. For on the morning of the 11th the General was persuaded by his officers to allow them to carry the position by storm, and in an hour or two the rebellion was over. Dumont escaped across the frontier, and Riel was captured four days later, and was eventually tried and hanged.

It was a curious little war, one of the smallest in recent history, for there were never as much as 2,000 men in action on both sides. But its importance was not to be measured by its size. It was the first campaign in which a purely civilian and volunteer force was in action, and so must be read as the opening page of a famous chapter. The transport difficulties, which were the core of the problem, were brilliantly surmounted. All the troops, except the 90th battalion and some of the mounted scouts, were brought from Lower Canada, and the feat was a commentary upon the progress of Canadian communications. To quote Melgund: "From Ottawa to Qu'appelle is 1,685 miles. From Qu'appelle to Batoche is a march of 243 miles. Wolseley left Toronto on the 21st May 1870, and arrived at Fort Garry on the 24th August--three months. In 1885 the last troops ordered out left Montreal for the front on the 11th of May, and arrived at Winnipeg on the 20th of May--nine days. So much had fifteen years of civilization and a railway done for Canada." The expedition was a first-rate advertisement to the world of the agricultural riches of the North-West, and, by making immigrants safe, it hastened its settlement. Also it compelled an inquiry into the grievances of the Indians and the half-breeds, and the whole system of administering the new provinces. The rebels were in revolt against the Dominion Government but not against Britain, and at their feasts drank the health of Queen Victoria before that of Riel.

One part of the system which needed overhauling was the Mounted Police. Lord Lansdowne, in a letter to Melgund during the expedition, stated some of the reforms which he thought essential: an increase in numbers, and a first-class man in command who could himself undertake the direction of a "little war." The Government of Canada was of the same opinion, and in the summer the post of commandant of the North-West Police was offered by Sir John Macdonald to Melgund. It was a high compliment, as was shown by the later refusal of Canada to consider a British officer for the post, and it proved that Melgund had the confidence of the Dominion. It offered him the active open-air life which he loved, and a problem of first-rate military importance to solve, and he was sorely tempted to accept. In the end he declined, and one of his chief reasons was his wife. He would have been compelled to leave her for weeks at a time alone in the prairie at Regina while he visited his outland stations.

General Middleton returned home to be officially thanked for his work, and to receive the K.C.B. which he well deserved, and in his report he laid stress upon Melgund's services and asked that they should be recognized. In the following year Queen Victoria invited Melgund to Windsor, and proposed to decorate him with the C.B. for his work in the North-West. The recommendation had, however, to go through the Colonial Office, and, since the Dominion authorities considered that jealousy might be created by the special honouring of a British officer in a campaign which

Canada regarded as peculiarly her own, the matter was dropped.

By the autumn of 1885 Melgund had resolved to return to England, several private reasons contributing to his decision; so early in January 1886 he was home again with his small household, taking with him the memory of many friendships and a warm interest in Canada's future. How keen was this interest may be seen from his correspondence after his return with Lord Lansdowne and many Canadian friends, and his efforts to induce the Times to give more attention to Canadian news. What Canada thought of him may be gathered from Sir John Macdonald's farewell. "I shall not live to see it" said the Prime Minister; "but some day Canada will welcome you back as Governor-General."

CHAPTER FIVE

SOLDIERING AND POLITICS AT HOME

FOR twelve years after his return from Canada Melgund was content to cease from foreign wanderings. His whole attitude of mind had changed; he was no longer restless, but eager to fling his whole energies into the task which came first to his hand. Canada had accustomed him to service, and he was now in the mood to forgo glittering and adventurous enterprises and work hard and soberly at what appeared to be his immediate vocation. He found that vocation awaiting him. Having long been an enthusiast for the Volunteer auxiliary forces, he had now an opportunity of pushing their cause and perfecting their organization. Those twelve years were strictly a period of professional soldiering. He toiled at the work of his command, he preached the gospel of the Volunteer with voice and pen, and his laborious activities brought him no reward except the approval of other soldiers and the satisfaction of his own mind. He had reached that stage when the ambitions of youth are not forgotten, but the impatience of youth is curbed, and a man schools himself to tasks which may not kindle the fancy but approve themselves to the reason.

He arrived in England to find the country in a political turmoil. In June 1885 the Liberal Ministry had been beaten on the Budget, and the general election in November had put Lord Salisbury in power with a precarious majority of Parnellites and Tories. While

Melgund was crossing the Atlantic Mr. Gladstone had announced his conversion to Irish Home Rule, and early in 1886 the provisional Government was defeated and the Liberals were again in power. Then began the break up of the Liberal party, a Liberal-Unionist group came into being, and Mr. Gladstone's Home Rule bill was, on its second reading, defeated by thirty votes. The general election which followed was one of the most famous in recent history, and Melgund, feeling that it was the duty of every man in such a crisis to play a part, appeared, very much to his own surprise, as a candidate for that institution which he had aforetime described as a "disreputable coffee-house." He was invited to stand for Peebles and Selkirk against Sir Charles Tennant, and for Berwickshire against Edward Marjoribanks (the late Lord Tweedmouth), but he chose the Hexham division of Northumberland, chiefly on the advice of his brother-in-law Albert Grey, who was himself standing against Mr. Wentworth Beaumont in the Tyneside division. Melgund stood as a Liberal-Unionist, and in his election address dealt only with the Irish question, "the surrender to an organized rebellion repeatedly denounced by your present Ministers." The constituency was one of the largest in the kingdom, and, as he started late, he had only a fortnight for his campaign. He put every ounce of weight into the contest, and might well have beaten the Home Rule candidate, who was something of a trimmer, but for the abstention of Tory voters. The alliance between Tory and Unionist was still a loose one, and stalwart Conservatives objected to vote for a man who called himself any sort of a Liberal. The result was that he polled 440 votes less than the Conservative at the election in the year before, and, though the Liberal poll fell by over a thousand, it was enough to give the Home Ruler a majority of 967. Melgund heartily enjoyed the fight, and was not greatly depressed by the result. In seconding the vote of thanks to the sheriff after the declaration of the poll at Hexham, he said "that the Unionists could at any rate congratulate themselves that their army was winning from one end of England to the other, and that though they had lost in the Hexham division they must recollect that no great battle was ever won without a few losses."

Albert Gray was defeated at Tyneside, but Arthur Elliot held Roxburghshire, and Sir Charles Tennant went down at Peebles. Had Melgund chosen to take this constituency when the offer was made to him his whole career might have shaped itself on different lines.

He was happier about public affairs. "Now that Mr. Gladstone is finally disposed of," he wrote to Lord Wolseley in July of that year, "we may start on new lines in Ireland, and I can't help thinking that possibly some opportunity may crop up of getting something to do." But that something did not turn up, so he flung himself into his Volunteer work. The Border Mounted Rifles were that year at the height of their strength, with two troops, one at Hawick and one at Kelso, and their commanding officer was busy throughout the summer and autumn with shooting competitions, summer camps, and manoeuvres. Parliament was suggested again in 1887 by his brother Arthur--a division of Edinburgh--and was categorically declined. He had made up his mind for good and all upon that point. "The slavery to a constituency and the unhealthy life of an M.P. are not enticing, and to assume a profession one ought to foresee success, which I should not. In any case it would be accepting a line of life which would be peculiarly uncongenial, and not in itself likely to be very beneficial from either a patriotic or selfish view. Opportunity is the thing to wish for, and I doubt a seat in Parliament being an opportunity to me." So he stuck to his military work and began seriously to study the literature of his subject. His journal records his admiration for Napier's Peninsular War--

"A delightful book, the very essence of soldiering--only wish I had been up in it before. While going into details, every line he writes brings out clearly the incalculable value of individual character, the power to take a correct view in an emergency and act on it. The Duke of Wellington is the personification of common sense, possessing the qualities of certain success--courage, prudence, determination, patience, the gift of acting at once, and with them all--though not necessary to success--honesty. I have been reading some of his dispatches to-night, clear and straight to the point, and bringing in small details in a way which a less experienced man would almost certainly have thought unnecessary."

In July 1887 he stayed at the Staff College for the Aldershot Review, when the 2nd Army Corps was entirely composed of Volunteer battalions. He was enthusiastic at the performance of the Volunteers: "the finest sight I ever saw . . . and of immense significance." In June of the following year the scheme of brigading the Volunteers took effect, and Melgund was offered and accepted the command of the Scottish Lowland Brigade with the rank of brigadier-general. It was an infantry brigade of six battalions, with one regiment of Yeomanry attached. The journal records: "Though I always believed that by sticking to soldiering one might, with the way the Auxiliary Forces are coming to the front, make something of it, I did not expect to be promoted so soon; and now, looking ahead with one's position recognized, there is room to rise--with the opportunity."

The journal throughout 1888 is full of speculations on military and foreign affairs, in which the name of Kitchener begins to appear. The following is a typical entry:--

"December.--Have just finished A Nation in Arms by von der Goltz, a bad translation from the German. Purely a professional book, but the best handbook to bona fide soldiering that I know: goes much into the moral qualities required of officers and men, and the qualities required of chiefs. A knowledge of these things is what makes a good soldier and a good leader, far more than any learning acquired from books alone. It is rare to get book learning combined with the greater qualities--

insight into character, ability to lead, and the instinct as to what other men may do in certain circumstances. This last is, I think, only acquired by experience. If these greater qualities are combined with actual learning the result is a very first-rate man, but the combination must be rare, and I believe our greatest leaders have, as a rule, perfected themselves more by experience of life and close observation of other men than by study and research. I expect it is in their leisure hours--which in an active man's life must largely be in the autumn of his career-- that they have had time to reap much knowledge from books."

It was his favourite doctrine that knowledge of human nature ranked first, second, and third in any human pursuit. Wolseley was his constant mentor, and he has a story of him worth repeating. "When Sandhurst was at the War Office he wanted to get Wolseley's opinion of two candidates for official posts to lay before Campbell Bannerman, so he asked Wolseley if he could let him have some written opinion which he could show to the Prime Minister. Wolseley gave him the following letter: 'A. is very clever but a damned thief. B. is very honest but a damned fool,' and signed it officially as Adjutant-General."

In the summer of 1889 we find the first mention of a figure which was to play a great part in the next decade. "Albert Grey came in this morning wanting to know if I could recommend any man suitable to take charge of the affairs of a company, on the Zambesi, of which he is a

Director, the idea being to open out Central Africa, working from the south. Rhodes seems to be the moving spirit (brother of the man in the Royals*). I believe he has made a fortune in South Africa." Melgund thought the whole affair a very doubtful business, and his opinion was confirmed when, at the banquet to Mr. Arthur Balfour given in Edinburgh in December of that year, the chairman, the Duke of Fife, raised the question again, told him that the new British South Africa Company meant to send out an expedition next year, and asked Melgund if he would like to command it. "In the meantime the Company have sent out some black bulls, escorted by four Blues. The object is to propitiate Lobangula (or whatever he calls himself), the native chief, and it is said the Blues are to appear before him in full fig, tin bellies and all, and are to leave their tin bellies as well as the bulls as an offering. At any rate bulls and escort have gone, and it sounds to me one of the strangest performances I ever heard of." Already Melgund had his doubts about the "brother of the man in the Royals," doubts which on a better acquaintance it pleased Providence to increase.

* Frankie Rhodes.

In the autumn of 1889 Melgund was compelled by pressure of work to hand over the command of the Border Mounted Rifles to Lord Dalkeith. It was a hard severance. On 31st December he wrote in his journal:--

"The old year has been a fairly busy one for me on account of Brigade work. I resigned the command of the Border Mounted Rifles in the autumn. Giving them up was a pang, for I had commanded them ever since they were raised in '72. Sir George Douglas asked me if I would take command of such a corps if it was raised, and he practically secured the names of those first joining. I took command, and retained it till I resigned the other day, as I felt it was not satisfactory to attempt to go on with it together with the command of the Brigade. But it is impossible to tell how devoted I have been to the corps: it has been such an interest to me, and I have been so anxious to make it a bona fide soldiers' corps with good discipline, and none of the lax ideas which some seem to think are justifiable in a Volunteer corps. The consequence was it became exceptionally smart and workmanlike, and has earned a reputation to be proud of. I have worn its uniform in India and in Africa and in the Russo-Turkish campaign, and have had letters from New Zealand and Trinidad asking for information as to its organization for the guidance of corps there. Dalkeith has succeeded me: he was officially junior to Cunningham, but the latter has always behaved most generously, and entirely put himself aside in deference to Dalkeith's great local position. As to Charlie Cunningham, I have never anywhere seen a better officer to command irregular cavalry in the field, full of leading qualities and a great power over men. I can't help feeling that my resignation of the command of the Border Mounted Rifles has separated me from what has hitherto been a great part of my life; however, they remain in my Brigade. . . .

"I have much to look back upon during the last seven years--the Egyptian Campaign, Canada, the Riel Rebellion, and have been married, and now I am a Brigadier-General. It has been a very eventful time, and one likes to think of it all. And now we will look ahead for another year and what it brings."

The journal during the late 'eighties records much beside soldiering--dinners, visits, conversations, days with hounds, and the thousand and one interests of a full life. An entry may be quoted:--

"Dined with Jersey at his annual dinner of old Oxford and Cambridge men. Dick Webster (Solicitor-General), 'Bunny' Pelham, 'Friday' Thornton, 'The Professor'--Lawes, Spencer Lyttelton, Bob Follett, etc., etc. Webster's has been a remarkable rise. He was at Cambridge with me, though my senior, and was a wonderful runner, especially for two miles. I ran fourth in the University two miles when he won. If I had been third, which I think I ought to have been, I should have run for Cambridge against Oxford in the inter-University races, and, as I represented the University in the steeplechase at Aylesbury, would have been a sort of double blue, which at that time I should have greatly valued; but I used to ride so much that I was not half trained for running.

"Women's rage for matchmaking is a marvel, and the cold-blooded way in which they decide that an idiot or an effeminate ass, or a perjured debauchee, 'will do very nicely,' provided, of course, he is possessed of means, for some charming girl who is only blinded by the flattery of being proposed to, and who ought by her kind friends to be enlightened instead of being helped into the pit, I--well, I shouldn't like to say what it is!"

Every winter the Melgunds rented a small hunting box in the Grafton, Bicester, or Pytchley country. Melgund had never been able to afford to buy made hunters; he invariably rode young horses, schooled them, and, if all went well, sold them at a profit. He was very proud one year, with six horses in the stable, to find that his hunting expenses had been £19.

"Received a cheque this morning for £300 for 'Stockdale.' Very sorry to part with him. The best-tempered horse I ever had. However, it can't be helped, as I can't afford to keep such expensive luxuries. Jumped a highish gate on him in a wire fence off the high road the other day. Sinclair told me that if I rode like that I should break my neck! The greatest compliment I have had paid me for some time!"

He had a wealth of hunting stories. He remembered during a run when the fox crossed the Ale seeing one of the hounds in hot pursuit emerge from the water with a salmon in its mouth. Another day he watched the fox jump over the White Rock on the Minto Craigs, a drop of a hundred feet. There was a moment of anxiety lest the hounds should follow, but the huntsman succeeded in calling them off in time. The rest of the pack were waiting below, and on breaking up the fox one of the hounds swallowed the brush whole lengthways. The whip made frantic endeavours to pull it out, but although his arm was half-way down the hound's throat he only succeeded in retrieving a few hairs!

While hunting with the Quorn in March 1890 Melgund recorded "about the maddest performance I have ever seen--a moonlight steeplechase. I suppose the old prints of such a race started the idea; at any rate we were told that competitors would meet at Lady Gussy Fane's at 11:30 p.m. The night was pitch dark, and it seemed ridiculous to think of going. However, my host and hostess were bent on it, and off we went, driving to Melton, where another trap had been ordered to take us to the course. We went first to Lady Gussy's, and there found most of the competitors assembled, beautifully got up in boots and breeches, with their night-shirts over all. The latter were so much frilled that I suspected Lady Gussy had issued a supply.

"We then drove over to the course near Melton Spinney; a dark, cloudy night, though there was a moon which made a feeble attempt to show itself The race was to be run over some small fences which I believe are used for a schooling course. Over the fences of the country it would have been an impossibility. I could only just see what the first fence was like by looking close into it. It appeared to be an old fence, cut over and weak, but pretty high, quite five feet, with a very small shallow ditch on the far side. A lantern was placed at each end of the fence, and the other fences were marked with lanterns, and a lantern in a tree for the turningpoint. They were to finish over the first fence, and the first over was to be the winner. There were, I think, ten runners there--Burnaby and Wilson (in the Blues), Warner (the Master of the Quorn), Zobrowski, M'Neil, a new man to me, a mad Irishman, Gerald and Sidney Paget.

"The performance began by M'Neil taking a preliminary canter over the first fence, over which he tumbled head over heels, and then they started. I stood at the first fence, and the crowd of nightshirts rushed desperately by me with a crash over, or rather through it, and as far as I could see without a fall; the only two who went slowly at it being the two Pagets, who walked through the hole made by the rest. So they all disappeared in the darkness till one heard them tearing back again to win. All I could see was two night-shirts racing for the last fence, over which one landed with a lead of half a length, the other falling. The winner turned out to be Burnaby, the second, who fell, being Zobrowski. I only saw one loose horse come in-Zobrowski had remounted at once. They tell me Zobrowski was leading up to the last fence, and it was very confusing owing to the number of lights where it was to be jumped, but Burnaby managed to get first run at it. I do not fancy the fences were much, but all the same it was a strange and marvellous performance. What extreme youth and champagne can do!

"The course was crowded with spectators and foot people. The competitors, I believe, adjourned to Lady Gussy's afterwards for supper, where no doubt there was a cheery evening! We drove home to Somerly, the moon coming out so bright that lamps would have been unnecessary if the race had been run an hour later."

The last time Melgund rode in a point-to-point race was this year. There were twelve competitors, all members of the Buccleuch Hunt. They started from Horslihill, and went round the Minto hills to Teviot Bank, a distance of about seven miles. Melgund won the race easily on "Polecat."

Horses did not absorb Melgund's entire affections, for he was never happy without a dog, always chosen from that sporting breed of Dandy Dinmonts peculiar to the Borders. "Pepper," "Dandy," and "Dehra" all in turn shadowed their master, and each received that measure of devotion which their adoring fidelity deserved.

"Poor old 'Pepper' died this morning. He has been the truest of the true, and never cared for any one but me; the hardest and gamest I ever saw. I got him as a puppy from the keeper at Branxholm, and he must be over sixteen years old. He was with me through all the most eventful years of my life. I never took him campaigning, but the old dog was always the same to me when I came back, however long I was away from him. My best friend for many years is gone. I shall always remember what an honest, thoroughly true model of a friend he was. I miss the old fellow so!"

Melgund was also an ardent fisherman, putting fishing as a sport next to hunting. He was constantly on the Tweed, on the Floors, or Makerstoun, or Bemerside waters. He chronicles the talk of George Wright, the fisherman, who considered that "London maun b'e a gran' place for leddies--Hyde Park will be then: best cast, and they'll use verra fine tackle there."

The Melgunds, having both passed their tests, became members of the London and the Wimbledon Skating Clubs. Mr. Algy Grosvenor, himself a finished skater, first instructed Lady Melgund in the art of combined hand-in-hand figure skating. A few years later the artificial ice rink, called "Niagara," at Westminster, organized by Mr. Hwfa Williams, gave them endless amusement and exercise. It became the daily resort of skating friends, while a periodical fancy dress or masked carnival produced amazing costumes and baffling incognitos. Melgund was one of the few hunting men who welcomed an occasional frost, if not too protracted: it gave his hunters a rest, and he and his wife would skate all day long as well as by moonlight. A spectator, after watching Lady Melgund's rapid and dashing turns, said that he considered her style was "abandoned," while an old Scots minister, in a subdued religious voice, spoke of it as "unear-r-thly."

The year 1890 was remarkable for its literary activity, and Melgund wrote several articles and papers dealing with the mounted rifleman, of whom he had become the chief prophet. He took part in a symposium in the United Service Magazine, where he championed the cause of mounted infantry as against cyclists and ordinary yeomanry, and secured Wolseley's assent to his views. September was taken up with the Army Manoeuvres, on which he wrote a detailed report, full of shrewdness and good sense:--

"The regiment leaders in our Brigade were good; French of the 19th a first-rate soldier, excellent in all I saw him do, decided and full of dash. Of the commanding officers on the other side I had little opportunity of forming an opinion, with the exception of Hutton of the Mounted Infantry. He thoroughly knows his work and appreciates the role of Mounted Infantry, and he placed his men capitally. He is one of those of whom there are not enough, who try to see things without prejudice and who take a big view. Of the gunner officers I saw little. The general result has been to show how much we are in want of opportunities for giving officers instruction in the leading of anything like large masses of men. The scouting was extremely well done--a branch of the work to which officers accustomed to hunting will always readily take. Evelyn Wood was the heart and soul of the whole thing. The manoeuvres are entirely due to him, and the cavalry officers I have spoken to as to the position he has held during the manoeuvres heartily acknowledge the good turn he has done them."

On 4th November Mrs. Grey,* Lady Melgund's mother, died.

Lord Melgund in 1890 (Photo by Chancellor)

"If ever any one was perfect she was," her son-inlaw wrote, "never thinking of herself, so good and kind to every one. It is a great break-up at St. James's. She had lived there for forty years, and it has been a very happy gathering place for all of us. The old house is full of associations. We were married from there, and Ruby and Violet were both born there."

* Daughter of Sir Thomas Farquhar, Bart.

Queen Victoria gave Lady Melgund permission to stay on at St. James's Palace in view of her approaching confinement:--

BALMORAL CASTLE, November 16, 1890.

"DEAR MARY,--I must write you a line to thank you for your two kind letters, and to say how truly pleased I am to feel that my offer to you to remain for the expected event at St. James's Palace is a convenience and comfort to you. But what a trying time it will be to you without your beloved mother, one of the kindest and most unselfish of parents!

"I hope I may see you soon some morning at Windsor.

"Ever yours affectionately,

"VICTORIA, R.I."

On February 12, 1891, a son was born. The Queen stood godmother, and one of the godfathers was Lord Wolseley, who wrote that he would be proud to undertake the duty, and hoped that the boy "may be as good and as brave a soldier as his father." The child was christened in the Chapel Royal on 25th March with the names Victor Gilbert Lariston Garnet-Lariston after the old Liddesdale home of the Elliots.

On the coming of the new generation followed the departure of the old, for on 17th March Lord Minto died. While leading a quiet country life, he had always taken an alert interest in public affairs. His nature was rare and fine; his extreme modesty, his complete indifference to his own advancement, and his dread of ostentation inclined him to conceal, even from those nearest to him, his public and private services. It was only those who actually worked with him who knew his quality. One of these was the late Lord Moncreiff, who wrote thus of him: "His temperament was unassuming, as his manners were courteous and unobtrusive, but he was eminently and essentially a man having a pervading interest and influence in public affairs. . . . There were, during the many years Lord Minto was a member of the House of Commons, few public questions affecting Scotland on which he had not left the mark of his vigorous thought. . . . He never laid himself out as a candidate for place or for self-seeking of any kind. He preferred independence and unostentatious usefulness. These he cultivated to the end in his household and in his circle of friends, as well as in such more public duties as his position prompted him to discharge." Like the rest of his family he was a firstrate rider to hounds; and he appeared on horseback almost on the eve of his death.

II

On succeeding to the peerage Minto was asked to bring forward in the House of Lords the grievances of "purchase officers" and press for a Royal Commission on the subject, but he was too busy with his Volunteer work to take his seat yet awhile. To his deep regret it was found necessary to disband the Border Rifles, but his own Brigade was increased by two battalions. In his journal at this time he tells a story which proves that the discipline of these Borderers was not equally good off and on parade: "Met a volunteer sauntering in the plantation with his arm round the neck of a very pretty girl, which he never attempted to remove, but saluted gravely with the other hand, both looking me full in the face and neither seeing anything in the least odd in it. I felt it would have been brutal to interfere, the thing was so gravely ridiculous."

In August 1892 Minto, with Colonel Wardrop of the 12th Lancers, attended the French Cavalry Manoeuvres at Tarbes and filled a note-book with comments, which show how acute and ardent was his study of his profession. He was especially interested in the details of equipment, the distribution of weight on the saddle, and the handling of the horses. He thought the horses good and the men a fine, sturdy lot, but the leadership poor. There seemed to be little speed and initiative, and the faults were all on the slow side. One comment has been fully justified in recent years: "To a great extent I believe we are wrong in our estimate of the French character. I think there is much more moderation and common sense, and far less flightiness than we are accustomed to give them credit for. We judge too much by Paris, and Paris probably does take the lead, but the average Frenchman is no scatter-brain."

Early in 1893 Lord Roberts returned from India. The journal comments:--

"A large gathering to receive him, nearly all Indian soldiers, and a great many old friends were there, amongst them Sir Hugh Gough, whom I don't think I have met since Afghanistan in 1879. Seeing them all reminded me of a party at the India Office in the summer of '80. I had just taken off my coat when I met one of the Plowdens. It was before Roberts's march to Kandahar, and Donald Stewart had just got the chief command at Kabul, going over Roberts's head. Plowden said to me, 'I am so glad to see Stewart has the command at Kabul; people have found out: now what Roberts is-- we never thought much of him in India.' I rather shut him up and went upstairs. The first person I met was Wolseley. He said, 'I am so sorry to see Donald Stewart has gone over Roberts's head at Kabul.' I answered, 'But I suppose, Sir, he is his senior officer.' 'I don't care about senior officer,' said Wolseley, 'I have watched Roberts's career now for a long time, and I'll tell you what it is, he is a very fine fellow.'

"Roberts has, I believe, expressed a wish to make Wolseley's acquaintance, as apparently they don't know each other. I am, I suppose, among the very few who are friends with both. It will do much good it they show that there is room in the world for two great men, and that though they may differ in opinion they are at any rate above petty jealousies. Both men are very much to be admired; Wolseley, I should say, the better read of the two, very agreeable and the best of friends; but with all his good fellowship I never think he inspires the individual love of every one as Roberts does. Charming man as he is, he has not the same personal influence. The men worship Roberts. I doubt if they care much for Wolseley personally, though they know he is a leader they can rely on. Myself, I was surprised, when reading his Life of Marlborough, at his power of description and the poetry and romance of his nature. I should not have given him credit for appreciating the picturesque side of life as much as he evidently does. He sets great value upon the sympathetic nature so important for a great leader, and this is always the quality I have doubted his possessing. He has it very markedly as regards his friends, for no one has drawn more sincere admirers towards him than he has, but I have always thought him lacking in the magnetism which captivates the masses. It is a remarkable book, and the country can be proud of the man who wrote it, for it is refreshing to see all through it the admiration of the writer for patriotism, high spirit and heroism, and his contempt for the party politician and the time-server, and for the tendency which exists now in certain circles of sneering at the Volunteer, who is ready to expose himself more than his duty requires. But indeed I believe that, owing to Wolseley and those who think like him, much of this sneering tendency is already dying out. One likes to know that we are at least possessed of one distinguished man who has the courage to say what many feel as to the pettiness and time-serving of men in high places, and their apparent inability to realize that those who form our public life can never be deemed great unless they lead, and are not led about themselves by every whim of the multitude."

Minto's life in 1893 was a busy one, for, apart from work in connection with his estate, he had his duties as a Brigadier, and was much in request to umpire at manoeuvres and attend military discussions, while he was constantly being asked to write on army subjects. In June he made his maiden speech in the House of Lords on the employment of discharged soldiers, a matter on which he was constantly bombarding the War Office. His speech, which was carefully prepared and well received, urged that "situations in Government Offices should be open preferentially for the employment of such discharged non-commissioned officers and soldiers of good character as may be able to pass the requisite examination." He pointed out that in an army raised by voluntary recruiting there must be some inducement to enlist; that it was impossible to expect from the Treasury a rate of pay high enough to be an attraction as compared with the rates of pay in civilian life; but that much might be done in ensuring for a soldier a career after his discharge, and fitting him for it by education while still serving in the ranks.

Home Rule was once more the question of the hour, and though Minto was inclined to leave ordinary politics alone and stick to his own subject, the journal is full of comments on the events of the moment:--

"Just back from the House of Commons after hearing the closing debate on the Home Rule bill, the remaining clauses of which have been passed without discussion according to closure rule. A most disgraceful scene occurred arising out of a speech of Chamberlain's, during which one of the Irish members shouted at him as 'Judas': a free fight ensued and many blows were struck, the Speaker was sent for, and after much heated discussion the matter dropped. I should think at least some forty or fifty members were engaged in a violent melee in which it was difficult to say who actually took the lead. One felt utterly ashamed for one's country: nothing could have been more disgraceful, and one wonders if we shall go on for ever under the rule of such an assembly. The Speaker was very dignified and was listened to with respect. . . .

"Hartington at his meetings at Dalkeith and Edinburgh a little while ago referred most strongly to Ulster's right to resist, alluding to our rebellion against James II. and to the possibility of civil strife in England as well as in Ireland, and instancing the action of our ancestors against James as an example to us of what we might be bound to do for the sake of the country. Such words from a man certainly not given to romance, and carefully weighing what he says, should bring the position of affairs home to everybody. We are, I believe, on the verge of very great danger. The leading men on our side consider Ulster justified in armed resistance should any attempt be made to enforce Home Rule, and such resistance might not be confined to Ireland, for passions would be roused in England too which would appeal to force. I cannot believe that the dangers in the air are fully known to the Government. Only the other day Antrim wrote to me for advice as to the organization and drilling of men (I sent him the Mounted Infantry organization as best suited for hastily raised infantry), and Saunderson last year spoke to me more than once as to my serving in Ulster should matters come to a climax.

"Within the last few days Lewis Dawnay has issued a circular in Yorkshire (backed by a letter of Saunderson's) asking for names of those willing to enroll themselves in a corps of gentlemen, should occasion arise to assist the people of Ulster. Though I think this ill-judged and premature, it shows the way the wind blows and the feeling that is already stirring, and as such may perhaps do good."

In the beginning of 1894 we find Minto re-reading his old journal of the Turkish War and reflecting on the changes of time. "I couldn't be happier than I am now, and there is much to do here to occupy me--but still the active life and the insight into great events have as much charm as ever, and I hope they always will have." He lamented that as a country gentleman he had no leisure for reading, the days being filled with an endless routine of small duties. "I don't waste time, but looking into everything myself really fills most of the day. I suppose it is good work--in fact it is a profession, and, with Brigade work, gives me plenty to do, but it leads nowhere, and, well--right or wrong, I long to be in the stream of the world of history again." He adds Loyally, "All the same home here is perfection."

It was a year full of great interest:--

"March 6th.--Gladstone has resigned, and yesterday it was announced that Rosebery had accepted the Premiership. I hope now we may consider that Gladstone has finally given up the reins of Government. He has done his country an immensity of harm at home and abroad, and I hope his countrymen will never be tempted by the recollection of his brilliant oratory to forget this. Certainly the power he wielded at one time was enormous, not only at home but amongst many European races. I always remember, when crossing the Balkans and sleeping in a small place called Kasan at the summit of the pass, a deputation of Bulgarians coming to see me to talk over Mr. Gladstone's speeches, he having then taken up the cause of Bulgaria. As I had not seen the papers for weeks I could say little, but the Bulgarian villagers seemed well up in them. Rosebery, who succeeds him, I used to know well in old racing days; he was very amusing and sarcastic, but I never see him now. He has always impressed me as very ambitious, very able, and capable of playing a game he does not quite believe in himself."

During the summer came an unexpected chance of service abroad:--

"June 5th.--The last few days have been very interesting and puzzling ones for me. Last Wednesday we dined at the old Duchess of Marlborough's. I took Lady Loch in to dinner. I had not known her or him before, but after the ladies left the room he said to me, 'Will you come with me to South Africa on Saturday?' I said I could certainly not come as a loafer, in no position, to which he answered he would take me as military secretary. He spoke to me again about it before we left and asked me to think it over. I thought the matter well over, and wrote to him next day that I had been a great deal away from home in connection with different expeditions and campaigns, and now that I had succeeded my father I felt rather a fear of getting too much of a roving reputation, and believed that possibly, though it was very humdrum here, I might perhaps eventually be the better for remaining in England, for a time at any rate. But I must say I am just as eager to be off as ever I was. . . .

"On Thursday evening I met him again at a party at the Fifes', and he pressed me very strongly to come and to send him a telegram next morning. I, however, determined not to go, and on Saturday morning wrote to thank him before he started. It has been a most difficult question to decide for many reasons, but the chief ones I considered for and against going were those I have named, and every time I thought it over I came to the conclusion that so far as ambition was concerned it was better not to go; but the temptation to be employed again, and in the sort of work I like, was great. Of course, leaving home, and the bitter break it must be, was a heavy consideration, the pain one may give, the home duties one must leave: it is bound always to be a difficult question which way real duty leads, but no great country was ever made by those who feared sacrifice. It has all rather put me in mind of Cavagnari asking me to go with him to Kabul in 1879."

Only for a moment had he hesitated. Had he gone he might, like his brother-in-law Albert Grey, have fallen under the spell of the Rhodesian dream.

In October, at the age of ninety-two, old Lord Grey died. He had been Lord John Russell's Colonial Secretary. "There is an excellent account of Lord Grey's career in the Times" the journal notes, "the last words of which aptly sum up what he was: 'Men more brilliant and more original our days have seen. They have seen none more steadfast or more honourable.' The Greys are a wonderfully hard, long-lived race. John, a brother and a parson, is 82, wiry, and with an eye like a hawk. The other day, to amuse himself, he came down a canvas fire-escape from the top window, and, as he forgot to stick out his elbows to moderate the pace of his descent, he came down like a catapult, and nearly demolished the butler and servants waiting his arrival below!"

When the general election in June 1895 restored the Conservatives to power there was a chance of Minto becoming Under-Secretary for War, but it was necessary that the occupant of the post should be in the Commons, so Mr. St. John Brodrick was appointed.

Minto had now passed his fiftieth birthday, a solemn moment, or, as he put it, "a nasty fence with a big ditch on both sides. Except for the sake of those one leaves behind the best death for a soldier is to be killed in action before he gets too old. Evelyn Wood told me the other day that Wolseley wants to be killed this year. He (Evelyn Wood) thinks he had better see his term of office out."

That year ended with many dark clouds on the horizon of public affairs--the difficulties with America over Venezuela, the eternal trouble with Turkey, and the threatening situation in the Transvaal. "I do hope," Minto wrote, "that we shall at any rate go on the lines of honour as regards the country, and have no mean trimming for the sake of peace, notwithstanding the awful horrors of a great war." The following are notes in the journal:--

"May 11th.--I have not followed closely the campaign (the war between China and Japan). I believe the result of it to be one of the greatest revolutions in history that has occurred for centuries. It is the ratification of the rise of another Power in the East, and that an Eastern Power which has shown itself capable, not, I think, of superficially skimming the products of European civilization, but of solidly grasping and understanding the spirit of that civilization. The intervention of Russia, France, and Germany in the peace negotiations was on the part of the first Power very natural, for she has great interests in the Far East. France, too, restless, and with advisedly Russian sympathies, one can also understand; but the intervention of Germany is, to my mind, simply another ill-judged performance of the autocratic lunatic who rules that country. The Japanese have acted with much self-restraint, probably after their great successes the strongest card they could play. I am very glad we have kept clear of official intervention in the peace negotiations."

"October 12th.--In the East the Armenian atrocities are the centre of all interest. It looks very critical for the peace of Europe. We have mismanaged the Turks, the finest fighting material in the world, when with common sense and a little friendliness we could have greatly benefited them and their subjects and have had an immensely strong ally in the East. I can't help thinking that much of the Armenian discontent is organized in London. Things look bad, and I keep on wondering what it may mean, not only for Europe, but perhaps for me."

One other entry is worth quoting, for it chronicles a dinner of a delectable club, now, alas! no more:--

"To Edinburgh and dined at the 'In Loco Club,'* a creation of Rosebery's. . . . Thirteen at dinner--Rosebery, Robertson (the Lord President), Balfour (ex-Lord Advocate), Darling, George Baird, Ronald Ferguson, Sir H. Dalrymple, Andy Wauchope, Professor Butcher, Lamington, Donald Crawford, Sinclair (I think the Radical brother of Sinclair of Grahamslaw), and myself. A pleasant dinner. As honorary members several defunct historical personages were proposed, amongst them John Knox. I voted against him, but he was elected."

* "Dulce est desipere in loco."

III

The year 1896 opened with the astounding news of the Jameson Raid. At first Minto sympathized with it, and disapproved of Mr. Chamberlain's repudiation. "I must say it delights me to see the red tape of home officials utterly ignored by a good man on the spot." He was furious, too, at the German Emperor's telegram to President Kruger. Then he began to wonder, as many others did. He could not believe that Dr. Jameson had acted independently of Mr. Rhodes: he was soon inclined to think that Mr. Chamberlain was right, and his military soul was shocked by the muddle of the whole business. His brother-in-law, Albert Grey, was appointed in Jameson's place as administrator of Rhodesia, and in February the Raid prisoners arrived, to be received with, as he thought, unseemly ovations. He considered their performance "a muddle from the first, an unjustifiable raid and bad soldiering, though the participants are no doubt a firstrate lot of fellows." A little later he met Dr. Jameson at dinner and liked him-"sensible and modest, but nothing has altered my opinion that it has all been simply a plot to upset the Transvaal Government, money playing a very large part in the game." The journal has an interesting record of soldiers' views: Wolseley thought the invasion well organized, Redvers Buller that it had been both badly conceived and badly executed. "Personally," Minto wrote, "the iniquity of the expedition is patent, but any good young fellow would have gone with it, and those who went are worth a hundred of those who hung back. . . . All the same I would lock up the whole blooming lot!"

Later events increased his distaste. He thought that President Kruger was being unfairly hustled by Mr. Chamberlain, and he in no way shared Albert Grey's admiration for Mr. Rhodes. He could not see behind the scenes to the strange strife of racial destinies, and it seemed to him that the Chartered Company, led by "the brother of the man in the Royals," was engaged in a disreputable attempt to lay hands on the wealth of the Rand under the pretence of patriotism, and he was inclined to subscribe to Buller's opinion that "Rhodes was a damned blackguard." "To my mind the recent South African story, with all its dirty speculation, is abominable, and one which the Government of our country should have disowned with scorn, which they have not done." He thoroughly approved of the verdict on the raiders, and even of the sentence on the Johannesburg Reformers, and he longed to see Mr. Rhodes laid by the heels.

The episode sheds a light on Minto's solid independence of mind. He may have judged wrongly in the light of history, but he judged honestly on the data he possessed. He was himself an imperialist of an advanced type, and no lover of official pedantries, but he refused to believe that an ideal could be furthered by dubious methods, and romance and enterprise could not atone in his eyes for a lack of common sense.

In March 1897 came the official inquiry, as to which his comments in the journal reveal his stiff sense of equity.

"An undignified performance. He (Rhodes) with a very strong face, but peevish, and yet sometimes a bullying manner. . . . Strongly opposed as I have always been to Rhodes's South African recent policy, one could not help feeling that a strong man was being bully-ragged by a collection of professional politicians, which, in my opinion, is about the worst class of animal that exists. . . .

"Met Rhodes at dinner the other night at Ferdy Rothschild's: was not introduced to him and did not want to be: Mary introduced herself to him on the grounds of being Albert's sister. "C"* told me after dinner that Rhodes certainly ought to have five years, in which I thoroughly agree. The idea seems to be gaining ground that, in connection with the recent Raid, he was not influenced by money motives, but had in view imperial objects only. It may be so, but the fact cannot be got over that he deceived the High Commissioner and his colleagues in the Cape Government, that he falsified the date of a telegram, and that he drew upon, or allowed to be drawn upon, the funds of a Company in which he was largely interested in order to assist a revolution in a friendly neighbouring state. If this sort of thing is winked at, all I can say is that the standard of political morality is even lower than I thought it was. . . . The worst feature of the whole thing to my mind is the very lukewarm condemnation of Rhodes in high places, the evident wish to palliate what he has done, and the one-sidedness of the press on his behalf. No doubt in London society money interests in South Africa have much influenced public opinion, and money, one must suspect, has done the same thing with the press. But we might have expected some display of common decency from the British public."

* The late Marquis of Londonderry.

In November of 1896 Minto had had a bad smash out hunting which laid him up for most of the winter.

His horse hit a stiff rail and fell on the top of him, breaking a rib and severely lacerating the muscles of his back and thighs. At the end of the year a characteristic entry in the journal mentions the incident. "Seven weeks yesterday since my fall. Quite unjustifiable of a rail in this country not to break. Every one has been so kind it is almost worth tumbling for."

Throughout these years he had been indefatigable in working for the efficiency of his Brigade, and the entries in his journal are in the main details of training and military gossip. Commenting on the bad feeling and behaviour of the Guards on their being sent abroad he writes:--

"It is not soldiering for a number of officers to go about talking in the way the Guards officers have been doing as to the iniquity of sending them abroad. It may be a mistake on the part of the authorities, but the first duty of a soldier is to do his best without cavil, and I must say the Guards, in my opinion, in this matter have displayed a regrettable strain of 'chalk' in their constitution."

Again:--

"Meeting of Volunteer officers at the Institute, and in the evening the annual dinner at the Grand Hotel. Lord Wolseley in the chair, self on his left. I proposed his health, and in returning thankswell--all I can say is that he referred to me as a good comrade and a good soldier."

At the Diamond Jubilee Minto was appointed to command all the Scottish Volunteer troops assembled in London for the occasion when twenty-seven detachments, 700 of all ranks, lined both sides of the Mall. Minto was proud of the command and of the important position allotted to the Volunteers.

"On thinking it over it seems to me wonderfully creditable that Volunteer troops that had never been together before should have assembled from all parts of Scotland punctually at their rendezvous, more especially as we did not get our orders from the officer commanding the Auxiliary Troops till Monday at 12 noon, therefore I could not issue my final orders till Monday evening" (the day before the Jubilee).

"In May a Galloway team from my Brigade won the Cycling Cup at Bisley. There were four teams of eight men and an officer and N.C.O.: they cycled some 45 miles, firing 20 rounds at 500 and 600 yards. And in July the Border Team won the Lucas Cup for Volunteer Brigades.

"Shooting for my Cup at Melrose. Jack Napier and I walked the whole way with the teams. The starting-point was about two miles this side of Stow, and from there to the ranges I made it 10£ miles. My object in presenting the Cup is to establish a practical kind of competition and to enable Volunteers and Regulars to see something of each other. In Scotland they are not nearly so much thrown together as in England. The conditions of the competition are the same as at Bisley.

"The Galloway Team won, followed by Hawick, Galashiels, and Jedburgh, then the Gordons and the Black Watch. It was a great triumph for my Brigade beating the Regulars: I believe it is the first time the Regulars have been beaten by Volunteers in this sort of competition, the average shooting of the Regulars being far above that of the Volunteers. The winning score was 161. The umpires deducted points for bad volleys, and though the volleys of the Regulars seemed quite excellent, they each lost points for them; the extraordinary thing being that the Hawick Team, which was second, did not lose a single point for volleys.

"I think the competition will do a great deal of good. General Chapman gave a Cup for beaten competitors which was won by a Hawick man!"*

* The following year the Border Volunteer Teams distinguished themselves, again beating the Regulars. Fourteen of the nineteen teams competing were from Minto's Brigade. The Border Rifles won, followed by Galashiels, Galloway, and Jedburgh.

The alarums and excursions of politics did not interfere with crowded seasons. There were visits to Taplow, Panshanger, Castle Ashby, Waddesdon, and elsewhere, and Minto was not insensible of the delights of London in an age when standards of wit and beauty were at their highest. He summarized the charms of a season thus: "A great deal of rot, a great deal one likes, and a great deal to learn: interesting people to meet, and the centre of everything, charity and devilry, soldiering and politics." During a week-end with the Harry Whites Minto met the Chamberlains, by whom he was greatly impressed:--

"He interested in all foreign questions, and very sound on them: she full of information, ready to talk about anything, and delightfully free from the usual talk and jargon. . . . The social events lately have been a large and delightful dinner and dance at the Londonderrys' and the masked ball at Holland House, which was most amusing. Mary and Lady de Trafford went in similar dominoes. I danced with Mary, not quite certain of her identity."

Throughout the autumns the Mintos kept open house The visitors' book records amongst their friends many notable names--Sir William Harcourt, George Curzon, Alfred Lyttelton the Devonshires, Portlands, Brodricks, Poynders, Grenfells, Granbys; and in October 1896 Mr. Asquith stayed at Minto. "I like him very much" writes Minto in his journal; "he gives one the idea of a strong man, and I should say a fair-minded one too." Now and then he felt that the part of playing host was too much of a tax on his time:--

"We are now alone: a relief after the constant coming and going of visitors. They come with a rush on their way north, then there is a lull while they are gadding this side of the Border, and then another rush when they go south. They are by way of shooting deer and catching salmon, but shooting has become so much more luxurious nowadays: they want all the game to play round them, and my own idea is that few of them would do a good day's walking, and certainly would not remain in the river all day without waders, as I used to do."

No picture of Minto would be complete without a glimpse of his domestic life. The atmosphere of his home radiated happiness. The family now consisted of three girls, Eileen, Ruby, and Violet, and two boys, Larry and Esmond. They all inherited the love of horses of their father, who with the utmost care taught in turn each child to ride. Together they shared all pursuits, and the younger generation learned from him to appreciate the tales of Border chivalry. Love of home was a tradition in the family, and the affection of past generations still seemed to cling like an atmosphere to the old house.

On succeeding his father Minto set himself, with the assistance of his wife, to beautify the house and gardens. The entrance hall was enlarged and panelled with oak that had adorned the walls of the old Law Courts in London. Terraces and balustrades were built: a rose garden was planned: an addition was made to the Church Garden, which was encircled with yew hedges in a battlement design. Minto was an expert landscape gardener; he and his wife would spend hours in marking out the ground, adjusting the curve of a path, and removing offending railings "to enable the eye to roam." The old castle, situated on the summit of the Craigs, described in Sir Walter Scott's Lay of the Last Minstrel, was restored, and turned into a museum for objects of historical interest brought from foreign parts by the different generations. To Minto's love of order is due the present systematic arrangement of the Paper Room and the cataloguing of the family archives. "It has been a very long and tiresome job," he mentions in the journal, "and sometimes I have wondered if I was justified in giving so much time to it, but I think I was. There is a great deal that is interesting, and will grow more so as years go on." Historical documents were sorted out from among old estate papers and accounts; a Spanish flag was brought to light which had been taken from the captain of the St. Josef by Nelson at the battle of St. Vincent in 1775 and given to Sir Gilbert Elliot, who was present at the engagement, and which had been lost sight of for a hundred and twenty years.

When bicycling first came into vogue, the family took to it with enthusiasm. Immense expeditions were undertaken, and Minto once cycled over the Border to Newcastle, sixty-four miles, before luncheon. Forty-two miles with his wife in pouring rain along the Caledonian Canal to Inverness was not considered excessive, and the Mintos even took their bicycles abroad, going by train to the summit of the St. Gothard, and bicycling down the pass and along the Italian Lakes to Baveno and Orta. Every spring they had a month's holiday on the Continent. One year they went to Florence and Venice, first driving by way of the Upper Corniche road to Portofino: another year they went to Spain, saw the pictures of the Prado, and stayed during the Easter revels of bull-fights and fairs in the beautiful palaces of the Due d'Alba in Madrid and Seville.

Generations of Elliots had been nurtured in the Presbyterian faith, and the family invariably attended the kirk at Minto. Fifty years ago two sermons were preached at the morning service, each lasting for about fifty minutes; but times were changing, and one sermon of thirty minutes was now considered adequate. The harmonium had taken the place of the tuning fork, and in later days this had been superseded by an organ--a prelatic innovation--and the younger generation were gradually abandoning the old Presbyterian austerity. But the stiffness of the ancient regime was not wholly gone. At one of the farm dances Minto noticed that the oldest employee of the estate, the shepherd Aitchison (with a game leg and seventy-five years of age) was not, as usual, opening the ball with Lady Minto. On making inquiries he was reassured as to Aitchison's health; "but," added one of the farm hands, "has your Lordship no' heard? Aitchison is an elder, and he was had up afore the kirk session and tell't that he must either gie up dancin' with her leddyship, or stop bein' an elder of the Kirk!"

The following are extracts from the journal:--

"I was asked the other day by a lady to sign a petition protesting against the cruel prosecution of the

Bishop of . . . for certain malpractices in forms of worship, as to which I knew nothing. I noticed that there were only three signatures to the document, one being that of a well-known drunkard. I was at my wits' end how to get out of it when it flashed across me that, of course, I am a Presbyterian! and as I had been brought up as such I could have nothing to say to Bishops!"

. . . .

"Went to church alone last week. It was communion Sunday. Old Watson (a farmer), who was taking the collection at the door, earnestly pressed me to stay with the congregation: 'They're a' wrang, thae sections in the Kirk: we're a' gaun to one place.' I said I hoped we were, but I did not stay, much as I felt inclined to do so; I hadn't strength of mind enough, I suppose, to break through the old custom, for I never recollect any of my people doing so. I remained for the service, however, until just before the giving of the sacrament. There is much that is to me more solemn and impressive about the Scots ceremony in a village church than about the ordinary English celebration. Old Watson and Ainslie (who used to be the smith) are the elders, and to see these handsome old men standing at the Communion Table waiting for the commencement of the ceremony had a reality and sternness about it that made me think of the old Covenanters, and brought home to me the honest true religion which plays such a deep part in Scots character."

. . . .

"The other day the Duke of Argyll, speaking in the House of Lords on religious teaching in the schools, said, 'There is a God, there has been a Christ, and there will be a future state.' In this age of scepticism it is refreshing to hear words of simple faith and strong belief from a learned and brilliant man, when philosophers are inclined to believe in nothing, and the pigmies of the world follow suit for the want of a logical proof to which they consider their Lilliputian brains entitled."

IV

Minto thought 1897 "a very happy year"; it was to be the last year of his peaceful life as a private gentleman. In March 1898, while he was busy working at Army Estimates, came the news of Mahmud's advance to the Atbara, the prelude to Kitchener's triumphant campaign, and once more Minto's thoughts began to turn towards what he had once called "the way of ambition." The Governor-Generalship of Canada would be vacant that autumn; Wolseley had always urged that he was well suited for the office, and he now told Wolseley privately how greatly the post appealed to him. Nothing, however, happened for several months. He had no claim on the politicians, for, while he liked and admired Mr. Chamberlain, he had not hesitated to criticize him, and he had never held even the humblest office in the political hierarchy. His work had been military, and his friends, who trusted and admired him, were soldiers.

However, forces were at work on his behalf, and in his journal he writes: "My Canadian negotiations are still proceeding. I have done nothing directly myself; friends, however, have done a great deal: Lord Salisbury, the Duke of Devonshire, Mr. Chamberlain, Arthur Balfour, have all been approached, and whether I go or not it is pleasant to think one has so many warm supporters."

The likelihood of his appointment was talked of that summer, though Lord Lansdowne warned him privately that there were strong candidates against him. India was also vacant, and his soldier friends had visions of sending Minto there, so the time passed in a maze of rumours and hopes. Then on the 21st July he received a letter from Mr. Chamberlain informing him that he proposed to submit his name to the Queen as the successor to Lord Aberdeen in Canada, and five days later the papers announced the appointment.

In such fashion did one who had small political purchase, who had never canvassed or schemed for preferment and who had been content to perform his duties far from the limelight, attain one of the highest posts in the gift of the British Crown. Minto's nature was too sanely balanced to be upset by either success or failure; in the hunting phrase he could "take his corn," and the journal to which he confided his thoughts sets out very modestly what he considered to be his qualifications, and descants on the loyalty of his friends:-
-

"I am pleased, and so is Mary-and-well--I suppose, writing in the privacy of one's own journal, I may say that I feel proud. Anyhow it is a position to be proud of. I can't help looking back over my past career and feeling that it has not been the path that usually leads to great appointments. With me it has been as a boy athletics, then steeplechase riding, then soldiering, till the love of a military career became all-absorbing. But through it all I have gathered a good deal of experience of other men in many countries, and the older I grow the stiffer has become my rule of doing what I thought right in the line I had taken up as soldier and country gentleman. This, with a certain amount of reading, a little writing occasionally for reviews, and a good deal of intercourse with those people who are helping to make, or are interested in, the world's history, both men and women, has helped me to where I am. It does not seem much, and yet it has often meant hard work, and the sacrifice of many social engagements and other things which to the society world may often have seemed inexplicable, as there was little to show for it. I am thinking chiefly of my Volunteer commands: the work they have given me has frequently been very heavy, and always very thankless, the military authorities alone knowing the value of what I was doing. . . . My present appointment I know I owe largely to the firm support of friends, and the furtherance of my career to Lord Wolseley more than any one else: on service and at home he has helped me more than I can say. . . . I have had shoals of telegrams of congratulation all day. Certainly till the last few months I never knew I had so many friends."

BOOK TWO

CHAPTER SIX

GOVERNOR-GENERAL OF CANADA, 1898-1904

The Problem of Defence

The hot summer of 1898 was filled with great events; death removed two men of the first rank from the arena of politics--Gladstone and Bismarck; in the first week of September the battle of Omdurman gave the Sudan to our hands; and presently came the difficulties with France over Fashoda. Minto spent his time in a whirl of interviews with Cabinet Ministers and with men like Lord Strathcona, who could talk to him of Canada. Then he repaired to the Borders to bid good-bye to his old friends and to receive the freedom of the town of Hawick.

"Kissed hands at Balmoral. . . . The Queen, as she always seems to be, quite charming, full of conversation and in good spirits. On my alluding to the appearance of a rapprochement between the United States and ourselves, she said she could see none. . . . Mary was then sent for. The Queen told her she felt sure she would uphold the position, and above all she must never give her name to any scheme that might be criticized, but only to those above suspicion, adding:--

'Your father advised me to make this rule nearly forty years ago, and I have never deviated from it.'"

In the series of farewell dinners in October one stood out especially, that given by Etonians to Minto, Mr. George Curzon, and the Reverend J. E. C. Welldon, who were leaving for the Governor-Generalship of Canada, the Viceroyalty of India, and the Bishopric of Calcutta. Lord Rosebery was in the chair, and made one of his happiest speeches. He pointed out that of the last six Governor-Generals of Canada all but one had been Etonians, and he spoke thus about his old school contemporary:--

"To most of us he is better known as 'Melgund,' to some of us as 'Rolly.' Lord Minto's position raises in my mind a controversy which has never ceased to rage in it since I was thirteen years old. I have never been able to make out which has the greater share in the government of this Empire--Scotland or Eton. I am quite prepared to give up our fighting powers to Ireland, because when we have from Ireland Wolseley and Kitchener and Roberts I am sure that Scotland cannot claim to compete. But when, as in Lord Minto's case, Scotland and Eton are combined, you have something so irresistible that it hardly is within the powers of human eloquence to describe it. Lord Minto comes of a governing family -- indeed at one time it was thought to be too governing a family. Under former auspices it was felt that the Elliots perhaps bulked too largely in the administration of the nation. At any rate, whether it was so or not, it was achieved by their merits, and there has been a Viceroy Lord Minto already. There have been innumerable distinguished members of the family in the last century, and there has also been a person, I think, distinguished above all others--that Hugh Elliot who defeated Frederick the Great in repartee at the very summit of his reputation, and went through every adventure that a diplomatist can experience. And now Lord Minto goes to Canada. I am quite certain, from his experience, from his character and knowledge, from his popularity, that he is destined to make an abiding mark."

Attended by felicitations and goodwill in which there was no note of dissent, Minto, accompanied by his wife and children, left England on 3rd November, and on Saturday, 12th November, arrived at Quebec, where he was met by the outgoing Governor-General, Lord Aberdeen, and sworn in. The Mayor of Quebec presented an address, in which there were graceful references to Lady Minto's family connections with Canada and to Lady Eileen as Canadian-born.

A word must be said on the position of Canadian affairs at the moment when Minto assumed office. Sir John Macdonald's great public career of over forty years had ended only with his death in 1891. Thereafter followed dissensions and difficulties for the Conservatives, culminating in their defeat at the polls in 1896, when the Liberal party under Sir Wilfrid Laurier entered upon a term of power which was to endure for thirteen years. The change of party did not involve a change of policy, for the old Liberal free-trade dogmatism was dropped, and Sir Wilfrid Laurier carried on the protective system of his predecessor, which by fostering her native industries aimed at making Canada economically independent of the United States. He maintained the close connection with Britain, indeed he drew it tighter, for it was under his auspices that a preference was granted to the products of the mothercountry. There was thus no violent divergence of political views within the country, and the old racial difficulties between French and British were quiescent under a Prime Minister of French-Canadian blood. There were many questions outstanding with the United States, chiefly with regard to the coast fisheries, questions which were to give trouble in the future, but at the moment none were urgent. It was a season of political inertia.

But with the ordinary life of the citizen it was otherwise. There was a stirring on the face of the waters, the beginnings of an immense change in economic conditions and in the outlook of the Canadian people. In 1870 the development of Canada appeared to have come to a standstill, and it seemed as if all that was worth reclaiming from the wilds had been reclaimed. In the 'eighties, in spite of a protective tariff, the completion of the Canadian Pacific Railway, and a modest boom in the North-West, the country still halted. But about 1896 the veil began to lift. The settlement of America's virgin lands was almost complete, and the American pioneer began to turn his attention to Canada's hinterland. The minerals of the East and the corn-lands of the West were developed more swiftly, and lumbering, which had been a decaying trade, was revived in the form of the wood-pulp industry in papermaking. A new activity in railroad building began, and the revenues of the Canadian Pacific rose by leaps and bounds. Little townships in the prairies suddenly expanded into cities, and towns appeared where before there had been only a shanty. Both Federal and Provincial Governments instituted a vigorous immigration policy, and the proportion of the immigrants which came from the British Isles largely increased. A wave of hope and confidence passed over the land, and men looked with a correcter judgment at the immense assets which before they had forgotten or undervalued.

Joined with this pride in their own possessions was another kind of pride, which marked a further stage in Canada's progress to self-conscious nationhood. The advent of Mr. Chamberlain at the Colonial Office had wrought a miracle in imperial administration. He had determined to understand for himself the mind of the overseas dominions, and make it understood by every home official. The vision of imperial development, to which Cecil Rhodes had given a captivating power, was being changed into a reasoned policy, which yet did not lack the glamour of a dream. The effect was remarkable in Britain, where the colonies became a fashionable interest, and lost that atmosphere of dreariness which had repelled earlier generations. It was still more notable in the Dominions themselves, where politics suddenly ceased to be parochial, and the imperial tie was transformed from a platitude into an inspiration. The Canadian, proud of his own land and newly awake to its possibilities, found his efforts stimulated by the consciousness that that land was a part of the greatest confederation known to history, which too, like Canada, was but at the outset of its triumphant journey. To an economic revival was added a spiritual enlargement.

Minto thus entered upon office at a most critical and fascinating epoch in Canadian life. The Prime Minister with whom he had to work was the most notable figure in Canadian politics since Sir John Macdonald. Sir Wilfrid Laurier, now fifty-seven years of age, had already won a reputation which might well be called international. He had visited England the year before during the Queen's Diamond Jubilee, and had attended the first Imperial Conference ever held, and by his eloquence and breadth of vision had impressed both the British and the French peoples. He seemed to combine what was best in both cultures, and to understand both traditions; his devotion to his own race and Church was free from particularism and clericalism, and he could mellow the bustling matter-of-factness of British Canada with sympathy and imagination. Though the Liberal leader in his own country, his temperament was naturally conservative--cautious, loving precedents, sensitive to tradition, strongly rooted in the past.

In such a man Minto had a like-minded and sympathetic colleague, whom he could regard with both admiration and affection. But it was a colleague and not a dictator. In the nature of things, with imperial and Canadian affairs closely interwoven, and with Mr. Chamberlain at the Colonial Office, it was impossible for the new Governor-General to be merely a spectacular figure, opening and dissolving parliaments and giving automatic assent to ordinances. He was a representative of a new school of imperial thought which Canada could not ignore; and with this new spirit abroad his office took on a greater significance. While he must rely often on Laurier, he brought much to the partnership. Sir Wilfrid was a statesman, but he was above all things a consummate politician, whose first business it was to harmonize conflicting races and parties and interests. It is a primary duty and a necessary task, but in it a man is apt to lose simplicity. The devotion and integrity of the Prime Minister were beyond question, but in the honourable opportunism which his work required there might sometimes be a lack of perspective and a want of vigour. To the manipulator of a political machine a risk may seem greater, a set-back more final, than is the fact. It was Minto's supreme merit that he saw things clearly and simply, without the irrelevant subtleties with which the practice of law or politics clogs the most honest minds, and that his broad humanity enabled him sometimes to read more correctly the heart of the plain man than the plain man's official exponents.

A Governor-General in an autonomous Dominion walks inevitably on a razor edge. His powers are like those of a constitutional monarch, brittle if too heavily pressed, a shadow if tactlessly advertised, substantial only when exercised discreetly in the background. Once in conversation Sir Wilfrid Laurier gave his view of the position: "The Canadian Governor-General," he said, "long ago ceased to determine policy, but he is by no means, or need not be, the mere figurehead the public imagine. He has the privilege of advising his advisers, and, if he is a man of sense and experience, his advice is often taken. Much of his time may be consumed in laying corner-stones and listening to boring addresses, but corner-stones must be laid, and people like a touch of colour and ceremony in life." Sir Wilfrid Laurier was too shrewd a man to underrate the ceremonial side of the duties of His Majesty's representatives ("Let not Ambition mock their useful toil"); and he put his finger on one vital function, that of advising their official advisers, the custody of the custodians. But a second function, not less vital, he omitted--their task of interpreting to Britain the ideals and aims of the Dominion, and, conversely, of expounding to the Dominion the intricate problems of the mother-country. These two functions--often obscured for the ordinary citizen by the fog of ceremonial--are of the first importance in our imperial system, and of a high degree of delicacy and difficulty. Advice to Ministers in their administrative work, and a constant effort to make sure that Britain and the Dominion see with the same eyes and speak the same language--these are duties which make far greater demands upon character and brain than the easy work of a dictator. There have been many failures among those sent abroad to represent the British Crown, due largely to the narrowly circumscribed area from which they are chosen; but that does not derogate from the tremendous importance of the office or belittle the success of the rare few who have succeeded. For the first task-advice--the main qualification is experience and native shrewdness; for the second-interpretation--an alert sympathy and an open mind. In the conversation which has been quoted Sir Wilfrid had something to say of the Governor-Generals he had known. Minto he held remarkable for his sound sense and "a stronger man than was thought"--a high compliment, for no Governor-General should have a popular repute for strength: it breeds suspicion in a young nation. "When he came to Canada first, he was absolutely untrained in constitutional practice . . . but he took his duties to heart, and became an effective Governor, if sometimes very stiff."* The first sentence is the truth; Minto had no training in methods of government, and had all his experience to acquire. In his function of adviser, consequently, he had to bide his time till he learned his business. But on one subject, that of armed defence, he was already an expert, and, as it chanced, this subject came to the forefront in the earliest months of his term of office, and he played a part in advising, controlling, and stimulating his Ministers which was new in the annals of the Dominion. It was in this connection, no doubt, that he earned with them the reputation of being "very stiff." In considering Minto's Canadian record it will be well to deal first with this group of military questions; they were the subjects of all others to which his interest was pledged, and in which he could speak from the first with clearness and authority.

* Life and Letters of Sir Wilfrid Laurier, by O. D. Skelton, II., page 86, note.

II

Under the Act which brought the Dominion of Canada into being the British Government had assumed full responsibility for the defence of the Canadian frontier. The old Canadian levy, including a large proportion of men of French blood, had distinguished itself in the war of 1812 with the United States, and Lord Wolseley, when on the staff in Canada in the early 'sixties, had prepared an admirable framework of a militia system which had been bequeathed to Canada with the grant of self-government. In 1872 the British troops, approximately 10,000 in number, had been withdrawn with the exception of the garrison at Halifax, and when Minto came into office there remained of British Regulars only the small detachments at Halifax and Esquimault under a British Lieutenant-General, while the main defence was in the hands of the Canadian Militia. This Militia was a purely Canadian force, under the charge of the Minister of Militia and Defence, but commanded by a British officer, who was paid from Canadian funds. It consisted of a small permanent nucleus, which in 1898 was only 850 strong, quartered in various schools, and used chiefly for the training of the volunteer Militia, which mustered in the same year about 35,000. Its efficiency had been allowed to decline, for the Government of the Dominion, with Britain to lean on, was not inclined to interest itself unduly in what seemed the academic question of defence. This was true of whatever party was in power; Sir John Macdonald and Sir Charles Tupper had been no less supine than Sir Wilfrid Laurier. The business of the Militia was left in the hands of a few enthusiasts, who were regarded by the politicians at the best with a good-natured toleration, as strange people who wanted to play at soldiers; and Parliament, whether Liberal or Conservative, voted supplies from year to year with scarcely disguised reluctance. A sum of £300,000 was considered enough for the purpose, the equivalent of one shilling and fourpence per head of the population, by far the smallest contribution in the British Empire. Under such circumstances it would have been a miracle if the Militia had preserved any high standard of competence. Its training was poor, its administrative services were rudimentary, it had nothing of what the Germans call the intendantur side. It was the Cinderella of the public services, a concession to the fussiness of Britain, and useful chiefly to provide a modest patronage for politicians.

But the Venezuela difficulty in the winter of 1895-96 had stirred the better kind of Canadian opinion to a juster view. War with America, however much it might be regarded as both a blunder and a crime, was seen to be within the bounds of possibility. General Nelson Miles, the Commander-in-Chief of the Army of the United States, had declared that any troops which the British Navy could transport would be wholly inadequate for the defence of Canada against the force which his country could put into the field. "By the time these vessels could go back for reinforcements and return there would probably be no British troops in Canada to be reinforced . . . Canada would fall into our hands as a matter of course."* And Mr. Henrichson, President Cleveland's Secretary of State, had announced that he thought a war with England would be "a very good thing. Our country needs a war about once in a generation. It serves to keep alive the American spirit; opens the field for the expenditure of a great deal of superfluous energy, enthusiasm, and patriotism; gives employment to a large number of people who would rather fight than work, and deadens the bitterness between political parties." These were foolish utterances, but they came from responsible men, and thinking Canadians could not but regard with anxiety Canada's land frontier of 3,800 miles, where, in place of the three routes of attack open from the south in 1812, there were now at least ten owing to the railway development of her southern neighbour. The problem of Canadian defence was not insoluble, but it demanded an energy and intelligence which had so far been conspicuously lacking in her Government.

* San Francisco Examiner, December 23, 1895.

At the same time the question was being raised from the other side of the Atlantic. In view of the growing menace of Germany, British soldiers, and an occasional British statesman, were turning their thoughts to the matter of Britain's imperial liabilities, and attempting to work out a system of local defence for each part of the Empire, and a co-operative scheme for the defence of the Empire as a whole. This involved no tampering with colonial autonomy. Its aim was by advice and assistance to enable each unit to place its own defence on a sound basis, and at the same time so to arrange the lines of such local defence that, in the event of Britain being engaged in war, a dominion would be able, if it so decided, to render prompt and effective assistance. The younger school of soldiers, under the inspiration of Lord Wolseley, set to work vigorously on the problem. The Colonial Defence Committee induced the Canadian Government to ask for a Defence Commission of three eminent soldiers to go to Canada in July 1898 and report on Canada's problem. In August Major-General Edward Hutton (afterwards Lieut.-General Sir Edward Hutton) left England to take command of the Canadian Militia. He had already done good work in New South Wales, where the principle of his "cooperative defence" had been accepted by the different Australian Governments, he was one of the best known of Wolseley's younger disciples, and his appointment seemed to herald an era of reform and construction in Canada's neglected defences. Moreover, he had been at Eton with Minto, had been a brother officer of his in Egypt and a fellow-worker in the cause of the mounted infantry. If Canada was in earnest in the matter, it looked as if she had found the right man to carry out the work.

General Hutton was a soldier of high character, of real military talent, and of unsparing energy. He had already had experience of working with a Dominion government, and he realized that his task must be a delicate one; he was the servant of Canada, not of Britain; he could not dictate, but must persuade and advise, and in all things carry the Ministers with him. On certain matters like internal discipline he must clearly be supreme, but in all others he was the subordinate of the Militia's Cabinet representative. But he was an enthusiast, and an enthusiast was the last thing that Sir Wilfrid Laurier's Cabinet wanted in a domain in which they were something less than half-hearted. A Liberal Government is always in a difficult position as regards questions of armed defence, for the word has an ugly Conservative sound. Moreover, the Prime Minister owed much of his power to the French-Canadians in Quebec, who had shown a marked hostility to the whole business, and, being a most wary politician, he was averse to the expenditure of money or time on matters which, though he was prepared to admit their importance as an abstract proposition, had small electioneering value. The Minister of Militia, Dr. (afterwards Sir) Frederick Borden, was a country banker and physician from Nova Scotia, who held indeed a surgeon's commission in the Militia, but had no serious knowledge of military affairs. He had many amiable qualities; but he was neither a courageous man nor an able man, and he conceived his duties chiefly as a balancing of party interests and a judicious exercise of party patronage. Among the other members of the Cabinet one of the strongest, Mr. F. W. Scott, the Secretary of State, was an irascible Irishman, who had not wholly shaken off the anti-British prepossessions of his youth; and Mr. Israel Tarte, the Minister of Public Works, was of so cross-bench a temper that it was hard to foretell what line he would take on any subject or by what fantastic reasons he would justify it. To the Laurier Government the advent of General Hutton was far from welcome. This ardent being, with a clear purpose and boundless vitality, might commit his masters against their will, and force them into a road where they saw no profit. Accordingly their apathy on matters of defence hardened into distaste, almost into hostility. The report of the Defence Committee was pigeon-holed; Minto could only get access to it after repeated demands, Hutton was never shown it at all. The new commander of the Militia was coldly received, and for long was denied an interview with his official superiors.

Flectere si nequeo superos, Acheronta movebo. A man in such circumstances might have yielded to a foolish temptation to turn to the political Opposition; but Hutton was too much in earnest to give way to pique, so he flung himself without further words into the duties of his office. These duties, as he saw them, were fourfold. As an expert he must rouse Canadian opinion to the reality of the need of a proper defence; by awakening the enthusiasm of its members and of young men throughout the Dominion he must make the Militia a force of the highest order of competence and discipline, must aggrandize its prestige and pluck Cinderella from the ashes; he must resist any political interference with questions of discipline, and so make it a national army, as clearly outside party influence as the army of Britain; and, finally, he must endeavour to put the force in such a position that, in the event of a war in which Canada decided to take part, her assistance should be prompt and effective. All of these four purposes lay strictly within the four corners of his official duties. He was there to exalt his office; he was there to secure the efficiency of his command; political interference had admittedly done mischief in the past, but it was repudiated as a policy by responsible Ministers. As for the question of bringing the Canadian force into line with the other forces of the Empire, there was sufficient warrant in Sir Wilfrid Laurier's eloquent speech the year before at the Diamond Jubilee. "England has proved at all times that she can fight her own battles, but if a day were ever to come when England was in danger, let the bugle sound, let the fires be lit on the hills, and in all parts of the Colonies, though we may not be able to do much, whatever we can do will be done by the Colonies to help her."* If such a generous policy was in the Prime Minister's contemplation, it was surely right to prepare in advance the ways and means.

* June 18,1897. See Sandford Evans: The Canadian Contingents and Canadian Imperialism

Accordingly General Hutton set himself with confidence and ardour to his task. He got into touch at once with his command. He inspected the Militia divisions and visited in turn each military district; he made the acquaintance of the officers, and had soon won their confidence and stirred their enthusiasm. He took an early opportunity, in a speech on October 14,1898, at Toronto, of expounding his ideal of a national army complete in all arms, which was received by the press and the public with general approval. His first annual report, in which he set forth in detail his proposed reforms, was apparently accepted without demur by the Government and met with no criticism in Parliament. Early in 1899 he had, indeed, a brush with his Minister over a disciplinary question, where party influence was used to prevent the retirement of an incompetent man, but he gained his point, though only after considerable opposition in the Cabinet. Finally, in June, a general order instituting a Militia Medical Service was accepted by the Government and published in the Gazette--a most significant step, for by that order the principle of a national militia army was first officially recognized. It may fairly be said that during his first nine months of office he had won for his scheme a wide popular acceptance and awakened in Canada a new military fervour. The trouble was that he was too successful, and with Ministers his stock sank daily lower. He was a propagandist, a missionary fired with an apostolic zeal, and apostles do not think greatly of tact. His frequent speeches, the constant interviews with him published by the newspapers, the pains he took to manipulate the press--with no other motive than to get technical matters correctly stated--it all looked to the Government like the whirlwind campaign of a man who was determined to carry the ministerial fortress by storm. No one of his doings was a breach of official etiquette; cumulatively, they left on Ministers the impression of a subordinate too masterful for safety.

With Hutton's policy Minto was in full agreement. It was a matter to wllich he brought an expert judgment, and in the multitude of novel duties he rejoiced to find one that was familiar. Hutton behaved as regards the Governor-General with a rare discretion. He saw that nothing but mischief would ensue if it appeared that he and His Majesty's representative were in too close alliance, so he did not press the claims of an old friendship, and let Minto take the first steps. Minto was of the same opinion; "it is better," he wrote, "that I myself should not appear too military." But of his own accord he began to appear at Militia gatherings and in some cases to address them, and he identified himself whenever occasion offered with the new Militia policy. He was not blind to the difficulties of the situation. The new policy should have originated with and been expounded by the Minister of Militia; instead, that oracle remained silent, and it was left for the general-officer-commanding to do not only the spade work but the exposition. Yet as both tasks lay within that officer's duties, and the principles had been publicly blessed by the Prime Minister and were accepted by the mass of the

Canadian people, he could only hope for the best. But he saw that in such a matter the acceptance of a plan was only the first step, and that the result depended on the spirit with which it was enforced; and between Hutton's vigour and ministerial apathy a great gulf was fixed. Moreover, there were the old difficulties of emphasis and interpretation, which are apt to mar any formal agreement.

The Governor-General was a profound believer in the future of the Militia, and inclined to attribute its defects, in part at least, to the British soldiers who had been sent out to command it. In a letter to Wolseley on April 21, 1899, he summarized his views:--

"These officers have been keen enough as regards soldiering on stereotyped lines, but they have not seemed to me capable of making sufficient allowance for colonial shortcomings, due very much to want of knowledge of military routine (not to any insubordinate spirit) and to the criticism and political influences which have pervaded military matters. . . . Hutton has attacked these difficulties with a very great deal of tact. He has spoken out very freely as to abuses . . . but at the same time he has indicated what ought to be done, and has put forward the view that it rests with the people of Canada to decide whether they will have an efficient force or allow the old evils to continue. The country itself is very military in feeling, and he has struck a right note, with the result that the people and the press generally are on his side. . . . He really has put life into everything, is all over the place organizing and inquiring, and entertains a great deal, feeding military, political, and civilian society with great judgment, and evidently excellent effect!"

Minto went on to say that he himself had made a point of magnifying the social position of officers and inviting them to entertainments "on account of their military rank." But he added that there was an enormous amount to be done. The Royal Regiment of Canada (the infantry portion of the permanent Militia) had not gone through a musketry course for three years, and many of the scattered battalions of the active Militia had not advanced beyond company drill and had never been brigaded. Above all, there was no departmental organization, and without such machinery it was impossible to progress. Yet, as he told Wolseley and other correspondents, he was confident that reform was on its way, and his one fear was the malignant effect of political interests.

Whenever he talked to Sir Wilfrid Laurier on the matter he found him broad-minded and sympathetic, but even from Sir Wilfrid he could not get the assurance he wanted about that vital question on which the discipline and efficiency of a national army must depend. There is a note of a conversation* four years later in which the Prime Minister frankly stated a view which was in the warp and woof of Canadian politics.

"As regards the existence of political influence Sir Wilfrid took up the line that in this country it was advisable to have a fair division of political influence in the force; that Sir Frederick Borden had done a great deal to eliminate political influence from the Militia; that when the Liberal party came into power they found the Militia a hotbed of Toryism, and that now, though he recognized the desirability of getting rid of politics as much as possible, yet as a matter of fact, if in the case of the raising of a new regiment the Conservative influence was predominant, Liberals would simply refuse to join the corps, and such regiment would become, as formerly, a Conservative machine. I told him that to me the recognition of politics in the Militia seemed entirely unnecessary, and that it simply rested with the Minister of Militia, when recommendations were placed before him, to uphold the selection of those men who were the most capable professionally. This view, however, I know it is impossible to persuade Sir Wilfrid to accept."

* June 14, 1904.

That a man of Laurier's quality should have explicitly stated a view so apparently indefensible pointed to certain intricacies in Canadian public life of which no newcomers could be wholly cognizant; but they were clearly difficulties which must stand most formidably in the way of that national army ideal which Minto and Hutton had set before them.

III

The campaign for Militia reform had already borne fruit in a new popular interest in defence questions when from South Africa came the first mutterings of the coming war. Minto shared to the full the new faith in the possibilities of an Empire, of which all the parts should be drawn into an organic union, but, as was his habit he envisaged that future soberly, practically, and without rhetoric. He profoundly admired the Colonial Secretary but he was no blind hero-worshipper; he had not been sent to Canada as was rumoured in some quarters, to carry out Mr. Chamberlain's policy, for he had^ever been closely in touch with Mr. Chamberlain, and had often criticized him. On South African questions he had found himself out of sympathy with Mr. Rhodes and his followers and he had vigorously condemned the whitewashing of the Jameson Raid; his inclination was rather toward the Boers and their wily President than towards the new-rich of Johannesburg. But in the years between 1895 and 1899 while Lord Milner was striving to clarify the issue, he had come-- reluctantly, if we may judge from his private letters*--to the decision that the Government of the Boer republics was pursuing a course which must be relinquished or end in war, and that if war came, Britain, in spite of many blunders of detail, would be justified. This was also the view of Sir Wilfrid Laurier and most of his Ministers. On July 31, 1899, a resolution, moved by the Prime Minister, was unanimously carried in Parliament, expressing the sympathy of Canada with the efforts of Britain to obtain justice for British subjects in the Transvaal. It was President Kruger's denial of the franchise which specially influenced Sir Wilfrid, and his hope was that "this mark of sympathy, of universal sympathy, extending from continent to continent and encircling the globe, might cause wiser and more humane counsels to prevail in the Transvaal, and possibly avert the awful arbitrament of war." On this point Canada was nearly unanimous, but Canada was neither well-informed nor greatly concerned. The trouble seemed small and remote to a people very much busied with its own affairs.

* He wrote to his brother Arthur on 28th September: "It will be a war, if we fight, which, in my opinion, will always be wrapped in remorse, however well our soldiers come out of it. . . . I would fight for the preservation of the paramount Power if it is in danger, but it is the policy which has led up to it which has been so fatal. We have never been courteous to the Boers. . . . In my opinion the last phase of South African history began at Majuba Hill, when we chose to let an ignorant people who had beaten us three times remain with that idea in their heads; but, having done so, we might have behaved with greater dignity. . . . We shall win and get all South Africa; but how shall we have got it? And what a mean heritage of bad feeling we shall have! . . . I don't yet believe in war, but I can't put half my heart in it if it does come."

In the spring of that year there had begun the intricate negotiations concerning Canada's share in a possible war which must be carefully traced. In March

1899 the War Office and the Admiralty raised the question of the powers of Britain under the Militia Act to require the Canadian Militia to serve outside Canada in time of war. Section 79 of that Act apparently gave the right to call out the Militia for service "within or without Canada," but Sir John Macdonald in 1885 had been of opinion that this referred only to crossing the frontier in the event of war with the United States, and that there was no power to move troops outside the North American continent. This was also Minto's interpretation; but when he consulted Laurier and his Cabinet he found that they took a different view. On the letter of the Act they held that in time of war the Imperial Government could move Canadian troops anywhere--a point in which they were probably right; but Sir Wilfrid added that the decisive question seemed to him to be, not whether the theatre of war was at home or abroad, but whether the troops were required for the defence of Canada. "They no doubt feel quite safe in this opinion," Minto wrote, "as there is not a single regiment of the active Militia capable of being sent out as a unit on foreign service." In putting the question before the Prime Minister Minto had added that he was inclined "to draw a distinct line between an official calling out by the Queen of Canadian troops for foreign service, and the offering of Canadian troops by the Dominion, which I feel certain would be enthusiastically made if the Empire were threatened." Canada had never shown a lack of fighting spirit. Her sons had fought in thousands for the North in the American Civil War; they had volunteered in the Crimean War and the Indian Mutiny;

they had offered themselves in the Sudan War of 1884, but as their Government, while ready to facilitate the raising of a contingent, had felt itself unable to pay for it, the offer had not been accepted. In any war of Britain's it might be assumed that some kind of Canadian force would be available; the questions were, whether the British Government could count, as of right, on any definite numbers, and whether the Canadian Government could or would offer, as of grace, to equip a contingent. The first question Sir Wilfrid Laurier answered in the affirmative, provided the war were for Canada's defence; as to the second he gave no sign.

In a letter of 3rd July Mr. Chamberlain forecast the ultimatum to President Kruger, and asked categorically whether, should this happen, there would be an offer of Canadian troops to serve with Her Majesty's forces. "Such a proof of the unity of the Empire would have a great moral effect and might go far to secure a pacific settlement. Is such an offer probable? If so, it should be made soon, but I do not desire that it should be the result of external pressure or suggestion." What at this stage was desired was an imperial demonstration to prevent war. Minto at once communicated with Laurier, to whom he wrote:--

"In this particular crisis the demonstration of such strength would be invaluable; but its effects would, I think, reach far beyond the difficulty of to-day. It would signify the acceptance of a principle which I believe would tend not only to strengthen enormously the

Empire generally, but which would also consolidate the individual strength, credit, and security of each of the offspring of the mother-country. Of course, I am quite aware that questions of imperial emergency may arise in which a colony, deeply interested in its own development, may very justly not see its way to assist; but a proof of a possible imperial unity, once exhibited before the eyes of the world, would, I believe, do much for the future history of the mothercountry and her colonies. It is a principle which appears to be fraught with great possibilities, and personally, as an old friend of Canada, nothing would please me better than seeing her first in the field in accepting it."

Minto honestly put all his cards on the table. Any Canadian offer must be spontaneous; but it was his duty, as a friend of the Prime Minister and a well-wisher of the country, to put before him the chances and hopes of the situation as he himself saw them.

The immediate result was the resolution of sympathy with British subjects in the Transvaal moved in Parliament on 31st July--a course which Sir Wilfrid had refused to follow three months earlier. "Personally," he had then written to Minto, "I feel very strongly with them, but it would be more than questionable wisdom to pretend to have a word to say in such a question. I told those who approached me very flatly that we might leave the matter in the hands of Lord Salisbury." Things had moved since then, a crisis was imminent, the Opposition was pressing the Government for a declaration, and individual members of the Opposition were urging an offer of troops, while the British press kept dropping hints to the same effect. A few days later Parliament was prorogued, but before it rose Sir Wilfrid had replied to Minto's letter. "I am sorry that my colleagues do not agree to that proposition, and I must add that I share their views. The present case does not seem to be one in which England, if there is war, ought to ask us, or even to expect us, to take a part; nor do I believe that it would add to the strength of the imperial sentiment to assert at this juncture that the colonies should assume the burden of military expenditure, except--which God forbid!--in the case of pressing danger." There was reason in these words, for the principle to which the Governor-General had referred was an intricate matter. He hoped for a beau geste, which would have a direct political importance and a great indirect sentimental value; but in the armed contribution of a self-governing colony there were many constitutional ramifications which the premier of such a colony was bound to consider. A war was in prospect which could not be regarded as imperilling the existence of the Empire, and which by no stretch of imagination could be considered as one of Canadian defence. If Canada volunteered to share in it officially, the step might involve a new doctrine of Canadian responsibility within the Empire. No Canadian statesman of any party--certainly not Sir John Macdonald--had definitely accepted the principle of Canada's duty to share in imperial defence; and this appeared to be scarcely even a question of imperial defence, for the coming campaign was looked on as a simple matter, likely to be soon finished, and involving only the interests of one locality. On the general question of the desirability of closer relationship between all parts of the Empire there was small difference of view; but this method of bringing about a closer relationship opened out at once a series of problems which went to the root of colonial autonomy. Canada might well find herself committed to the course of sharing in all British wars, however remote their interest for her and however little she was privy to the policy which had led to them; and, as a consequence, of greatly increasing her military estimates and losing something of her freedom.

It was a prospect which any responsible colonial statesman must view with serious anxiety. Moreover, the Liberal Government had their own special difficulties. They depended for their power largely on Quebec, and French Canada was apathetic or hostile in the face of the new imperialism. A rash step might not only involve the Dominion in an undesirable external policy, but lead to deep racial bitterness within its borders. Sir Wilfrid Laurier had every reason for moving circumspectly, and Minto, in acknowledging the resolution of 31st July, admitted the grave implications of any step. A month later the former, in a speech defending his policy, told his audience: "So long as I have the honour to occupy my present post you shall never see me carried away by passion, prejudice, or even enthusiasm. I have to think and consider." Beyond doubt his interpretation of his duty was just.

* He wrote to Arthur Elliot (28th September): "From the point of view of a Canadian statesman I don't see why they should commit their country to the expenditure of lives and money for a quarrel not threatening imperial safety and directly contrary to the opinion of a colonial government at the Cape. They are loyal here to a degree, and would fight for the old country if in a difficulty to the last man, but I confess I doubt the advisability of their taking part now, from the point of view of the Canadian Government. Sir Wilfrid told me the other day that if the question was reconsidered he should call a Cabinet Council and ask me to be present. I hope he Won't, for I should be in a nice muddle-my chief at home thirsting for blood, all my friends here ditto, and myself, while recognizing imperial possibilities, also seeing the iniquity of the war, and that the time for colonial support has hardly yet arrived." It needed the offers of the other colonies to change his view on this last point.

Minto had the enthusiasm which the Prime Minister lacked, but on him also it was incumbent to move warily. He desired that the conundrums which so perplexed Sir Wilfrid should be solved by Canada definitely accepting the policy of sharing in imperial defence; but he recognized that such a step was a momentous departure, and must be taken on Canada's own initiative. On one point he was early satisfied; Hutton's work had not been in vain, and the new military ardour which he had kindled would soon reveal itself in an overwhelming popular demand for Canada's participation in the war. Throughout August and September offers of service poured in from commanding officers of battalions of the active Militia, and these were duly submitted through the Militia Department and the Governor-General to the Imperial authorities. Other colonies offered contingents, but no such offer came from Canada. Meantime, Hutton, as he was bound to do, had worked out, in consultation with Minto, a detailed plan for a Canadian contribution, should the occasion arise. The first idea was a small brigade of all arms; but this seemed to be impossible, and an infantry battalion of eight companies was substituted. Every arrangement was made for raising, equipping, and transporting this battalion, and the plan was duly handed to the Minister of Militia, who was personally favourable to the policy of contributing troops. During these months opinion in the Cabinet, fluid in July, had, under the guidance of Scott and Tarte, hardened against it, but in Canada generally there was a growing party in its favour, and Ontario enthusiasts were laying plans to force the Government's hand. Hutton, having prepared a scheme in every detail for a contingent should it be decided to send one, thought it wiser to vanish for a little from the scene of action, lest he should appear to be implicated in such coercion, and started for a tour in the West. He was less happily inspired in a visit which he paid to Mr. Scott on his way through Ottawa, when he told him that if war came public opinion in Canada would force the Government to send troops, a view angrily denied by that Minister. The incident gave colour to the notion, now firmly implanted in the mind of the Cabinet, that Hutton had been offering a contingent to the War Office behind its back.

On 3rd October the Canadian Military Gazette, an unofficial publication, announced that if war broke out the Canadian Government would offer a force from the Militia for service in South Africa, and proceeded to give the details of Hutton's scheme. With the article Hutton had nothing to do; it was the work of some one who shared his views and was familiar with his work, but he would never have assented to an attempt at the coercion of his superiors, which would have been in a high degree insubordinate and in flat contradiction of the principle he had repeatedly announced--"The general-officer-commanding only carries out the policy indicated to him by the people speaking through their representatives." Sir Wilfrid Laurier, in an interview published in the Toronto Globe, denied the rumour. The Militia Act, he said, empowered the Canadian Government to send troops to fight abroad if Canada were menaced, but there was no such menace from the South African Republics. Even if the Government desired to do so, they could not send troops without permission of Parliament. There had been no offer of an official contingent to Britain; only individual offers had been transmitted home.

The announcement opened the flood-gates of the storm. Sir Wilfrid departed for Chicago to keep an engagement, and in his absence controversy raged throughout the land. It was very plain that a great majority of the people desired that Canada should do what every other British colony had already done and offer a contingent, and Sir Charles Tupper marshalled the forces of the Conservative Opposition to the aid of the popular clamour. On 10th October the Boers invaded British territory and war began. Sir Wilfrid returned on the 12th to find his Cabinet divided and the country in an uproar.

Meantime, on 3rd October an important cable had been received from Mr. Chamberlain:--

"Secretary of State for War and Commander-in-Chief desire to express high appreciation of signal exhibition of patriotic spirit of people of Canada shown by offers to serve in South Africa, and to furnish following information to assist organization of forces offered into units suitable for military requirements. Firstly, units should consist of about 125 men; secondly, may be infantry, mounted infantry, or cavalry--in view of numbers already available, infantry most, cavalry least, serviceable; thirdly, all should be armed with .303 rifles or carbines, which can be supplied by Imperial Government if necessary; fourthly, all must provide own equipment and mounted troops own horses; fifthly, not more than one captain and three subalterns each unit. Whole force may be commanded by officer not higher than major. In considering numbers which can be employed, Secretary for War, guided by nature of offers, by desire that each colony should be fairly represented, and by limits necessary if force is to be fully utilized by available staff as integral portion of Imperial forces, would gladly accept four units. Conditions as follows: Troops to be disembarked at port of landing South Africa, fully equipped at cost of Colonial Government or volunteers. From date of disembarkation Imperial Government will provide pay at Imperial rates, supplies and ammunition, and will defray expenses of transport back to Canada, and pay wound pensions and compassionate allowances at Imperial rates. Troops to embark not later than 31st October, proceeding direct to Cape Town for orders. Inform accordingly all who have offered to raise volunteers."

A needless mystery was made of this telegram, and it was assumed by some that it was a design on the part of Mr. Chamberlain to commit Canada by accepting an offer which had not been made. It was obviously a circular message sent to all colonies who had offered troops officially or unofficially, and it might be taken in Canada's case to refer to the individual offers of service already transmitted home. Nevertheless, it put _the Canadian Government in a quandary. If the various battalion commanders and regiments that had volunteered went abroad for service it must be with the Government's sanction and assistance. Having gone thus far, they must perforce go further, in view of the attitude of other colonies and the growing popular clamour in Canada. The alternatives were to equip an official contingent, or to tell Mr. Chamberlain that he had made a mistake and that the Government could not agree to the acceptance by Britain of the offers by individuals which had been transmitted; nay, the practical choice was narrowed to an official contingent or resignation.

Minto was in New York when Mr. Chamberlain's cable arrived and Hutton was in the North-West. The message was at once forwarded to Sir Wilfrid, and a copy sent to Minto, and it would have remained private had not the British press published the pith of it, so that its contents were almost at once accessible to the Canadian people, and added fuel to the fires of agitation. At first there was no sign of yielding on the part of the Cabinet, and on 4th October Mr. Chamberlain wrote to Minto, in deep disappointment, a letter which seems to contradict the obvious meaning of his telegram of the previous day. "We do not intend to accept any offer from volunteers. We do not want the men, and the whole point of the offer would be lost unless it was endorsed by the Government of the Colony." Till Sir Wilfrid's return on the 12th, Minto scrupulously refrained from any communication with the Imperial Government. After that day the Cabinet sat almost continuously. There were three parties--the intransigents from Quebec, who objected to any contribution; those who sought a half-way house on the terms of the telegram of 3rd October; and those who wanted a Canadian contingent, paid for by Canada and preserving its individuality. The struggle really lay between the first and third, between Mr. Tarte, who based his opposition on the ground that if Canada were to share in Britain's wars she must share in Britain's councils, and the Ontario leaders, who knew the drift of popular feeling in their province. On the 12th Minto cabled home that there was no hope of a contingent, but next day the pressure of public opinion convinced the doubters and carried the day. An order-in-council was passed, an ingenious document framed to preserve an air of consistency. After reciting Mr. Chamberlain's proposals of 3rd October, it went on:--

"The Prime Minister, in view of the well-known desire of a great many Canadians who are ready to take service on such conditions, is of opinion that the moderate expenditure which would thus be involved for the equipment and transportation of such volunteers may readily be undertaken by the Government of Canada without summoning Parliament, especially as such an expenditure, under such circumstances, cannot be regarded as a departure from the well-known principles of constitutional government and colonial practice, nor construed as a precedent for future action. Already, under similar conditions, New Zealand has sent two companies, Queensland is about to send 250 men, and West Australia and Tasmania are sending 125 men each. The Prime Minister therefore recommends that out of the stores now available in the Militia Department the Government undertake to equip a certain number of volunteers, not to exceed 1,000 men, and to provide for their transportation from this country to South Africa, and that the Minister of Militia make all necessary arrangements to the above effect."

In his letter to Mr. Chamberlain of 14th October, Minto describes the situation as he saw it:--

"I think it is clear that the troops would not have been offered unless the manifestation of public feeling had strengthened the hands of the Ontario member of the Cabinet, and this outburst of public dissatisfaction was no doubt brought about by the sense of the cable of 3rd October becoming known, and by the natural irritation caused here by seeing other colonies sending their contingents while Canada was left out in the cold. . . . Sir Wilfrid's position has been a peculiar one. I understood from him originally that, as I think I have told you, he personally was rather inclined to make the offer; but latterly he seems to have changed his ground. He says now that, though he thoroughly approves the action of the Imperial Government in South Africa, and admits the undoubted necessity of war, he has not been inclined to admit the policy of this colony accepting pecuniary liabilities for the old country. He says that it is contrary to the traditions of Canadian history, and that he thinks Canada would render imperial service in a better shape by contributing to such works as the Canadian Pacific Railway and the defences of Esquimalt, etc. He considers, however, that the acceptance of your offer to contribute to pay and transport of troops so minimizes the expense that the principle of non-acceptance of pecuniary liability is hardly departed from . . . He is thoroughly imperialistic, though he may have his doubts as to colonial action. I like him very much. He takes a broad view of things, and has an extremely difficult team to drive. But he is a Frenchman, and in saying that I think one covers almost the entire reason for the Quebec opposition. Quebec is perfectly loyal, but you cannot on such an occasion expect Frenchmen to possess British enthusiasm or thoroughly to understand it. . . . I have myself carefully avoided any appearance of pressing for troops, but I have put what I believe to be the imperial view of the question strongly before Sir Wilfrid, and I have pointed out to him the danger of a refusal being looked upon in the old country as want of sympathy here, particularly at a time when we must depend so much upon her good offices re Alaska, and no doubt in many other future questions."

The Government had capitulated to popular opinion. To preserve their existence they had done reluctantly what they had declared to be indefensible in principle and beyond their competence. Such a decision carried no honour with it, and incontestably they lost in prestige, for Canada had appeared last in the list of imperial contributaries. Their hand had been forced by the logic of events, and not by the Imperial Government, though Mr. Chamberlain's telegram had played a part for which it had probably not been designed. In March 1900 Sir Wilfrid told Mr. Bourassa in Parliament: "No, we were not forced by England; we were not forced by Mr. Chamberlain or by Downing Street to do what we did. . . . We acted in the full independence of our sovereign power. What we did we did of our own free will." In the Cabinet there was much bitter feeling-- against the home authorities who had landed them in the dilemma;* against the Governor-General, who was suspected of having been in league with these home authorities; above all, against Hutton, who was credited with every kind of Machiavellian plot. It is clear that such suspicions were wholly unjustified; Hutton was indeed largely responsible for the result, but it was because in carrying out the strict duties of his office he had educated and stimulated that Canadian public opinion which carried the day against the inertia of Ministers.

* The Canadian Government were entitled to complain of an apparent lack of candour in Mr. Chamberlain's attitude. His letter to Minto of 4th October expressly ruled out the kind of contribution accepted enthusiastically in his telegram of 3rd October, and the fact that the contents of that telegram were allowed to leak out to the British press naturally suggested an attempt on the part of an astute man of business to manoeuvre the Dominion into the decision he desired.

Minto had played a difficult part with complete correctness, and this was presently recognized by his critics. Mr. Scott confessed to him that the Government had made a blunder, and Mr. Tarte, that pedantic devotee of imperial federation, accepted the inevitable and promised the Governor-General to do his best for the success of the contingent. There was something about Mr. Tarte's fire and gusto which appealed to Minto. "It is pleasant," he wrote to Mr. Chamberlain, "to find one man with the courage of his opinions even though he is wrong." It is difficult for the forthright and simple man to sympathize greatly with the embarrassments of a party leader, or for one unversed in the niceties of constitutional law and practice to grasp the importance of what seems to him a trivial debating point. In addressing the first contingent as it was leaving Quebec, Minto declared that "the people of Canada had shown that they had no inclination to discuss the quibbles of colonial responsibility." It was his only unguarded word on the whole matter, and it was unjust to the genuine constitutional difficulty which Sir Wilfrid Laurier had to face, and which Minto himself had repeatedly acknowledged. It is true that Sir Wilfrid shirked that difficulty and decided on grounds of party expediency, but there is no reason to believe that it did not weigh heavily with him in determining his original policy of refusal.

The first contingent crossed the sea,* to be followed soon by a second contingent; the Government raised an infantry battalion to garrison Halifax and so released the Leinsters for active service; Lord Strathcona, as a private contribution, furnished three squadrons of mounted rifles who won fame as Strathcona's Horse. Canada played an honourable and distinguished part in the South African War, as Paardeberg testified, and Hutton, then commanding a mounted brigade in the field, saw with pride the prowess which he had helped to create. In everything that concerned the contingents Minto took the keenest interest, and it was largely due to him that they were kept intact as separate units, and not split up among British regiments, and that in the selection of the officers military competence and not politics prevailed.** The whole incident was an episode--a creditable and heartening episode, with a good moral effect--but no more. No constitutional precedent was created, no political conundrum was solved, no principle was established. Statesmen on both sides of the House agreed to treat it as an isolated and unrelated effort, marking no advance in imperial theory. The vital questions--the future provision of Canada for her own defence and her relation to the defences of the Empire--were by general consent never raised. When Mr. Bourassa in the spring of 1900 asked Parliament to put on record that the sending of the contingents did not create a precedent, he was heavily defeated, but his motion represented the facts. Indeed, looking back after the lapse of a quarter of a century, it may be argued that Canada's participation in the South African War was a movement retrograde in its results. It tended to increase her particularism and foster a baseless sense of security. The praise justly given to her troops was naturally unqualified by insistence upon their weak points, and the mistakes made by British generals and the defeats suffered by British regulars gave her a wrong idea of her own powers of self-defence, and--combined with the spectacle of Boer success--made her underestimate the value of regular training. She was more inclined than ever to trust to improvization and to cavil at any attempt to standardize the military system of the Empire. The South African War was destined to produce a harvest of false generalizations, and the vision of a Canadian national army lapsed into forgetfulness.

(* Footnote: Minto wrote to his wife describing the departure:-

"Everything was a magnificent success; the service in the Cathedral most impressive; the whole centre full of soldiers in uniform: the singing was splendid, every one joining in. About five hundred took the sacrament, the General and I going up first. The troops were drawn up on three sides of a square on the esplanade, just in front of the Garrison Club, with their backs to the ramparts, close to the St. Louis Gate. The Stand faced the Square. My procession--self in blue uniform, cocked hat, etc.-was formed at the Club. We walked on to the ground and I went straight to the saluting point, and the band played 'God save the Queen'; then I made my speech, then came Sir Wilfrid, then the Mayor's address; then Otter replied, and the General said a few words. At the close of my speech I told Otter to tell the men to take off their helmets, and to give three cheers for the Queen, taking the time from me. It was a very fine sight.")

** Footnote: Wolseley wrote to him: "I wish you were there in command of all our mounted troops, and, I have no doubt, so do you; but you are too much needed where you are. I know how much we have to thank you for the Canadian contingent. It is not because it adds to our strength so much as because it serves to draw the Dominions and the mother country together, that I value this move."

IV

The Laurier Government, angry at their damaged prestige, and irritated at being compelled to carry out a policy which had not been theirs, found a scapegoat in Hutton. The conduct of the Governor-General had been too correct for criticism, but that of the General commanding the Militia gave many chances to his ill-wishers.

Lord Minto as Governor-General of Canada, 1899

Hutton, instant in season and out of season, was too single-hearted in his purpose to walk warily. His ardour had made him many friends, but not a few implacable enemies. He had carefully refrained from flirting with the Opposition, but his constant speeches, tuned to a high pitch of imperial sentiment, and his frequent direct and indirect communications to the press were bound to be interpreted as a criticism of Ministers. Ill-advised utterances in private conversation, much magnified by gossip, reached their ears and increased their annoyance. It is fair to recognize that he was for the Government a most uncomfortable subordinate, though he cannot be said to have exceeded the formal limits of his duties; it is not less fair to grant that in the pursuit of these duties he met with no encouragement from the Government and every kind of vexatious obstacle. The Minister of Militia had, as Lord Rosebery said of Addington, the indescribable air of a village apothecary inspecting the tongue of the State. He had fitful moments of vigour and reforming zeal, but au fond he was a politician, studying earnestly the political barometer. Suspicion of Hutton was soon changed to direct antagonism. Various disciplinary questions were settled in the General's favour owing to Sir Wilfrid's wise habit of consulting Minto; but presently the air became electric, the General was kept in the dark about vital matters concerning his command, and had to suffer much incivility. He kept his temper surprisingly well, but daily the position became more uneasy. He longed to be in the field, but when he asked for leave of absence for that purpose he was told curtly that he must first resign his post. The Cabinet would gladly have seen him in South Africa, because they wished him out of Canada, and they waited anxiously for the chance to dispense with his services.

That chance came in January 1900 on the question of buying horses for the second contingent. Hutton had appointed, with his Minister's approval, a committee under Colonel Kitson, the commandant of the Royal Military College at Kingston, to supervise purchases in the open market. It seems to have been suspected that the arrangement would be favourable to horse-dealers of the Conservative persuasion, so, without consulting the General, Dr. Borden appointed a Liberal member of Parliament, connected with the horse trade, to report upon all purchases. Hutton took the slight well, but the subsequent letters from the Minister were so elaborately rude that it seemed as if they were intended to force his resignation. He had an interview with the Prime Minister, who could not be other than courteous, but it was made plain to him that his whole work and attitude met with the disapproval of the Government. "I plead guilty," said Hutton, "only to having roused the latent military enthusiasm through all ranks of the Militia, and having strengthened the innate feeling of patriotism towards the old country and the Empire, which already existed in all parts of the Dominion." To this Sir Wilfrid made the significant answer that "he could see little difference between inculcating patriotism and arousing military enthusiasm, and party politics."

The next step was an interview between the Prime Minister and the Governor-General. Sir Wilfrid did not accuse Hutton of more than want of tact in dealing with Ministers and injudicious expressions in public speeches, and admitted that the horse-coping episode might easily have been smoothed over; but he declared that matters had come to a deadlock, and that there was no other course left to him but to ask for Hutton's recall. Minto replied vigorously that in his view Hutton was in the right, that the latter had fought against political influence in Militia administration, and that in this lay the secret of the whole trouble. If the Cabinet asked for his recall he would, of course, transmit the request to the Imperial Government, but he would feel bound in a covering dispatch to state strongly his own opinion; a course which Sir Wilfrid said might compel the resignation of his Government. The Prime Minister suggested that Hutton might be allowed to go to South Africa in command, say, of Strathcona's Horse, but Minto declared that that would be a "palpable makeshift" which he could not accept. As he wrote to Mr. Chamberlain, he considered that the question of the G.O.C. in Canada should be put once for all on a proper basis, and that he ought, if necessary, to accept the Government's resignation, "I do not admit any right on the part of any Government to expect me to refrain from commenting to you adversely on their action."

On 20th January Minto submitted a memorandum setting forth his views; it was meant to be for the confidential information of the Prime Minister, but by some mistake it was submitted to the Cabinet. In it he pointed out the mischief of political interference with the Militia, the ineptitude of Dr. Borden's behaviour in the horsedealing case and the discourtesy of his whole attitude, and the difficulty of finding a successor to Hutton, unless the position of the G.O.C. was properly maintained. He added the incontrovertible truth that, while by statute the Minister of Militia was supreme, yet, by accepting the G.O.C. as his military adviser, he placed matters of military routine and detail in his hands, and that interference in matters thus delegated would make the post of G.O.C. untenable by any self-respecting man. The Cabinet replied with an immensely long discourse on constitutional law, drawn up by the Minister of Justice, which Sir Wilfrid handed to Minto with some amusement. The reasoning of the discourse was impeccable, but it was wholly irrelevant to the question at issue. Minto drily rejoined that he accepted every word of the document; but that the dispute was not as to constitutional principles but as to the "best practical adaptation of them and as to the proper line of demarcation between civil and military authority in regard to the smooth working of the mechanism of an army;" and expressed his "surprise at the suggestion that he could possibly advocate for any military officer a position independent of responsibility to a Minister of the Crown."

Further discussion with Sir Wilfrid did not alter the position. Minto laboured hard to bring about a settlement, for, apart from other reasons, he saw that Hutton would be hard to replace during the war, and that, with his military secretary, Laurence Drummond, serving in South Africa, he would be left alone to grapple with the Militia Department. But the Cabinet was adamant, and on 7th February an order-in-council was passed asking for Muttons recall. Minto had hesitated for a little as to whether he should sign this order, but on reflection, as he wrote to Mr. Chamberlain, the wiser course seemed to be to sign it, to make his protest to the Council, and to forward the whole correspondence to the Imperial authorities. "'It would be a great mistake to push an advocacy of the General's position to extremes. Though he has many supporters, anything like an attempt to over-press the Government to retain him would in all probability be taken as unjustifiable imperial pressure and be resented accordingly, so that there seemed to be no doubt as to my signing the request to H.M.'s Government for the General's recall. But it also appeared to me that, considering the manner in which other generals have disappeared from Canada with no apparent reason placed before the public, it was right that my Government should accept the official responsibility for their General's removal."

On 3rd February Minto had submitted to the Council a formal statement of his views; on 8th February he put them before Mr. Chamberlain in a dispatch covering the order-in-council and copies of the correspondence; on 9th February Hutton was informed by Lord Lansdowne of his selection for active service in South Africa and ordered home. Next day he sent in his resignation, which was at once accepted, and on the 13th took a friendly farewell of Sir Wilfrid Laurier. He left Canada amid many demonstrations of popular regret, which did much to salve his wounded pride. From New York he wrote to Minto: "Personally I can never forget all your Excellency's kindness and thought. It has been your sympathy and constant encouragement which have alone enabled me to stand the discourtesies and annoyances extending over so many months." To complete the tale: Mr. Chamberlain's dispatch of 17th April recorded his deep disappointment "that Ministers should have found themselves unable to allow General Hutton to complete the work he had begun," and expressed the view that "although the responsibility to Parliament must be maintained, it is desirable that the officer in command of the defensive forces in Canada should have a freer hand in matters essential to the discipline and efficiency of the Militia than would be proper in the case of an ordinary civil servant even of the highest position."

Minto's action was much criticized, but it is impossible to doubt that he was right--both in signing the order-in-council and in making his protest. The "stiffness" which Sir Wilfrid attributed to him was in this case clear-sightedness and courage. He stated the case to Mr. Chamberlain with complete fairness. Hutton was undoubtedly difficult; he might strive to be decorous, but cumulatively by endless little indiscretions he exceeded decorum. His fortitude in re was not combined with suavity in modo; he was a gadfly whose business it was to sting lethargy into action, and there were naturally protests from those who smarted under the sting. He was not the best man to work with the Government of a jealous young democracy. But the fact remained that the policy he represented was vital to Canada as a nation, that it was not questioned by Ministers that he had substantially kept inside the constitutional limits of his office, that he had done and was doing much valuable work, and that he fell a victim less to his defects than to his merits. He had suffered an unwarrantable interference in matters which were strictly within his province, and that interference had been due to the inclination to "graft" and patronage engrained in Canadian political life. Unless this root of evil was extirpated there could be no health in the Militia, and with Hutton's failure vanished the hope of a national militia army.

It was for this reason that Minto was compelled to take a stand in opposition to his Ministers. Hutton was sacrificed to their pettiness--not so much Sir Wilfrid's, for he admitted that he could have worked with him, but that of lesser folk; and in the interests of his party the Prime Minister not very willingly and rather shamefacedly took up the quarrel. In these lesser people two other motives were no doubt at work. It was the dark season of the South African War, and the repute of imperial officers was a little tarnished, and the ardour of the more recent converts to imperialism notably abated. "I ask myself," Dr. Borden had told Hutton after Colenso, "in face of the reverses which the British army has received, if it is worth the while of Canada to remain part of the Empire." Also, Hutton was too popular. He had behind him a large following of which he was sometimes injudicious enough to remind Ministers--an unpalatable thought to those who had come to believe that they were the sole rightful interpreters of the people's will.

During his term of office Minto had to face a second dispute over the personality of the Militia commander, but happily one which raised a less difficult question. A temporary successor to Hutton was appointed, and Mr. Brodrick, when he became Secretary for War, exerted himself to find a man who would be at once acceptable to the Canadian Government and would carry out the reforms in the Militia, as to which he and Minto were in complete accord. After many failures he persuaded Lord Dundonald to accept the post. Lord Dundonald at the time was a conspicuous figure in the public eye. He had done good work with the cavalry in South Africa, and had led the first troops that relieved Ladysmith; he was a keen professional soldier; he belonged to an ancient and famous Scottish house, which was in itself a recommendation to a country so largely peopled from Scotland. But he had certain personal characteristics which made friction inevitable. His candour had little geniality; he was extremely sensitive, like many shy men, and had developed a protective armour of stiffness and reserve, which was not far removed from egotism. A touch of the theatrical in his conduct was a further danger; he was very willing to appear to the world as riding the storm and holding the gate. At first he was not unsuccessful. Much excellent work was done in Militia reorganization in the light of South African lessons, and the Militia budget was substantially increased. But rifts soon opened between him and the Government. His pleas for larger estimates and for extensive fortifications on the United States border were rejected, and in the discussions on the revision of the Militia Act he was profoundly irritated by the ignoring of his views on certain clauses. A multitude of petty differences of opinion with Sir Frederick Borden exacerbated his temper, and he gradually slipped in his public utterances into a tone of sharp criticism of the Government of which he was the servant.

The crisis came in the summer of 1904. A new regiment, the 13th Scottish Dragoons, was being raised in the Eastern Townships, the constituency of a member of the Cabinet, Mr. Sydney Fisher, who was temporarily acting as Minister of Militia. Among the names of officers submitted to the Governor-General for approval, one, that of a prominent Tory politician, was scratched out by Mr. Fisher on his own responsibility. Minto signed the list, and returned it to Dundonald, who made no comment. But on 4th July the latter at Montreal made a public speech in which he violently attacked the Government for introducing party politics into the Militia administration. Such action was a grave breach of discipline, and Minto saw at once that it made Dundonald's position impossible, and frankly told him so. The General commanding the Militia had been sedulously cultivating the Opposition and the Opposition press, and he was not displeased to find himself in the role of a popular saviour defying the machinations of the politicians. Mr. Fisher's action had been no doubt irregular, but Dundonald's correct views on the evils of political wire-pulling could not atone for a flagrant breach of discipline and an utter disregard of the constitutional position of his command. In a private memorandum Minto wrote: "I entirely agree with my Government as to the immediate necessity of Dundonald's dismissal. As to their support of Fisher I entirely disagree with them; but surely the question as to whether public departments are to be run on political lines is not one to be settled by the Governor-General, but by the Dominion Parliament and the people of Canada. . . . I don't care a damn what any one says, and have not a shadow of doubt this is right."

He was strongly pressed to refuse to sign the order-incouncil for Dundonald's dismissal, and much criticized when he signed it. But he had no doubts as to his course. Dundonald's case was wholly different from Hutton's; the latter had laboured earnestly to carry Ministers with him and had never been willingly guilty of insubordination; the former had chosen the path of flat defiance. Dundonald's attitude was revealed by his conduct when the order was passed. He wanted Minto to delay it that he might have a chance of starting a political campaign, and was surprised when Minto told him that he would never be a party to such a course. At the same time Minto wished to use the occasion as a warning against political jobbery in the Militia, and pressed Sir Wilfrid to ask also for Mr. Fisher's resignation--a course which the Prime Minister declined to take. Minto signed the order, and contented himself with repeating his views on political interference in a private memorandum to Council, and in endeavouring unsuccessfully to get from Ministers some recognition of the good work accomplished by Dundonald in spite of his indiscretions. A hot controversy followed the incident, for the Opposition were on the General's side, and Dundonald, like his famous ancestor, was not without some of the gifts of the demagogue. Moreover, he was a Scot, and Canadian Scots were prompt to resent Sir Wilfrid's description of him as a "foreigner," at once modified to "stranger"--the consequence, perhaps, of the Prime Minister's habit of thinking in French. The mass meetings held in Toronto, Ottawa, and Montreal were nearly as critical of the Governor-General as of the Government. Minto's action was a proof of his full understanding of his constitutional duties, and his appreciation of those small differences in the facts which may involve a momentous divergence in principle; the policy which he had vigorously resisted in the case of Hutton he accepted promptly in the case of Dundonald.*

* Footnote: His action has been curiously misunderstood by certain Canadian writers. Professor Skelton in his Life of Sir Wilfrid Laurier says that "he endeavoured to induce Sir Wilfrid to abandon or postpone the dismissal" (II., page 201), and Mr. J. W. Dafoe in his brilliant little sketch of Laurier says that "he resisted signing the order-in-council until it was made clear to him that the alternative would be a general election in which the issue would be his refusal" (page 80). The writers seem to be confusing the Hutton and Dundonald affairs, for I can find no evidence from the correspondence and notes of conversations of any delay in the latter case. Minto accepted at once the view of the Cabinet on the necessity of Dundonald's dismissal.

In a conversation with Laurier in June 1904, Minto secured from the Prime Minister a remarkable condemnation of political influence in spheres which should be free from politics. It was, said Sir Wilfrid, the great evil of democracies, and he deplored the case of Quebec, "which was full of small political organizations who entirely controlled numerous public appointments." His view seems to have been that the whole business was indefensible, but that while life was lived in faece Romuli and not in the Platonic state, the evil must be accepted and the abuses of one party balanced by the abuses of the other. It was the view of a practical party leader, not very heroic, perhaps, but with a certain crude justification. So long as the people accepted the system, the system would continue. Canada suffered from the misfortunes incident to all young countries, where the ablest and strongest men are content, as a rule, with private life, and are too busy in developing the land's resources to have time to take a share in the land's government. Such a situation leaves a free field for the wire-puller. Moreover, in Canada parties had come to have a hereditary and sentimental sanction, so that the people were sharply brigaded between them without much regard to doctrine. A man was born a "Grit" or a Conservative, traditions and environment determined his political allegiance, and party loyalty had come to be reckoned a moral virtue. In Lord Bryce's words:* "Party seems to exist for its own sake. In Canada ideas are not needed to make parties, for these can live by heredity, and, like the Guelfs and Ghibellines of mediaeval Italy, by memories of past combats." In such conditions the statesmen who tried to exclude party influence and "graft" from any domain of public life had the hopeless task of Sisyphus.

* Quoted in Dafoe's Laurier, page 176.

But this maleficent growth was bound to strangle at birth any true system of national defence. There was another and a not less grave obstacle to be faced by the military reformer. The Canadian people could not be apprehensive of danger except from the direction of the south. The Venezuela crisis and the vapourings of American politicians alarmed the country from Halifax to Vancouver, and on the basis of this alarm Hutton began his reforms. But the fear soon passed, and the enthusiasm at the start of the South African War was not less short-lived. Canada, desperately busy in developing her rich heritage, lost interest in schemes for her defence, for the imagination of most people has but a short range, and dangers which are not visible to the eye are soon dismissed as academic.

Before the end of Minto's term of office certain vital changes were made in the Militia Department. In 1904 the Militia Act was revised, and the Government were permitted to appoint to the command of the force, if they so desired, a Canadian Militia officer. A Militia Council was also created, on the lines of the new Army Council in Britain, with the Minister as president, and with as its first member a Chief of Staff, who was destined to take the place of the old G.O.C. Moreover, the doubt as to the powers of the Imperial authorities to call out the Militia for service abroad was settled by an explicit statement that the force in time of war could only be called out by the Dominion Government, and that its service, whether within or without Canada, was restricted to the defence of Canada. In the following year the fortified harbours of Halifax and Esquimalt, hitherto maintained and garrisoned by Britain, were taken over by Canada, and the numbers of the permanent Militia were consequently increased. The result was that the defence of the country and the control of the armed forces of the Dominion were wholly vested in the Canadian Government.

Minto, as was to be expected, took an eager interest in the changes, and in many letters to Mr. Chamberlain, Mr. Brodrick, Lord Lansdowne, and Mr. Alfred Lyttelton, and in conversations with Sir Wilfrid Laurier and Sir Frederick Borden he pressed his views. He was the first to suggest that Halifax and Esquimalt should be handed over to Canada and their command amalgamated with that of the Militia, for he thought that the increased importance of the post would attract the best type of soldier--"capable," as he told Mr. Chamberlain, "of looking beyond purely military needs, and of dealing tenderly with political necessities and the many disagreeable surroundings of official life in a new country, and at the same time possessing strength of character enough to wear down abuses by tact and deliberation." To the Militia Council he was favourable, but he was resolutely opposed to the throwing open of the chief command to Canadian officers. He was most anxious to open up to keen Militia officers a real career, and laboured to devise a system by which a certain number of imperial appointments would be available for them. But he did not believe that the time was ripe to hand over the defence of Canada to a Canadian soldier, and his reasons were threefold. The first and most important was the matter of technical competence. Canada simply did not possess men of the professional knowledge capable of bringing the Militia to the standard of training required by modern military standards. It was no discredit to Canada, but it was a fact which could not be blinked. In the second place, it was unfair to expect a Canadian commander to fight against the traditions of political interference which were ingrained in public life, and which at the same time must disappear if true discipline was to be maintained. Finally, he dreamed of a Canadian force trained on the same lines as other forces in the Empire, and so linked with these forces that in a great war co-operation--should Canada decree it--would be swift and smooth and irresistible. For this there must be a trait d'union, and that for the present could only be found in the link provided by an imperial commanding officer, familiar with imperial staff work. Minto laboured in argument, but the home authorities were apathetic and the Canadian Government resolved. Slowly the vision of a Canadian national army, on a plane with other national armies within the Empire and part of one great system of imperial defence, faded out of the air.

There are many views on the doctrine of Empire, and a dozen types of constitution have been canvassed, from the close mechanism of federation to the loose tie of allied nations. But, whatever the doctrine, the one insistent interest which can never be questioned is that of common defence. Canada relapsed into a provincial system of a small permanent Militia, an imperfectly trained active Militia, and a water-tight staff. She did not even, like Australia, have any custom of universal training. Her statesmen of all parties, however restive they might normally be under imperial demands, had eloquently proclaimed that should Britain and the Empire ever be in danger the country would rise as one man in their defence. They were justified in their faith. When in August 1914 Germany flung down the challenge, Canada did not waver. Her response was instant and universal; she put armies into the field larger than any army of Britain in the old wars, and at Second Ypres, at Vimy, at Passchendaele, at the Drocourt-Queant Line won victories which were vital to the Allied triumph. But everything had to be improvised, and improvisation takes time. It was eight months before the first Canadian division could take its place in the field, and meantime the whole burden of the defence, not of Britain alone but of Canada, fell on the worn ranks of the British regulars. They did not fail in that desperate duty, but most of them died of it.

CHAPTER SEVEN

GOVERNOR-GENERAL OF CANADA, 1898-1904 (continued)

Imperial and Domestic Problems

WHEN in the mid 'nineties the doctrine of a united Empire, preached by Sir John Seeley and made romantic by Cecil Rhodes, became in Mr. Chamberlain's hands an explicit policy, it took for its text Disraeli's famous declaration in 1872: "Self-government, in my opinion, when it was conceded, ought to have been conceded as part of a great policy of imperial consolidation. It ought to have been accompanied by an imperial tariff . . . and by a military code, which should have precisely defined the means and the responsibilities by which the colonies should be defended, and by which, if necessary, this country should call for aid from the colonies themselves. It ought, further, to have been accompanied by the institution of some representative council in the metropolis, which would have brought the colonies into constant and continuous relations with the home Government." Each detail of this creed--constitutional, military, economic--was emphasized in turn by the new imperialist school; but naturally the constitutional took precedence, and its first and obvious form was the scheme of imperial federation.

Sir Wilfrid Laurier was in 1897 the hope of the federationists. In his own words, they looked to him to act as the bell-wether. The measure of imperial preference which he had carried in that year as a shrewd stroke in domestic politics seemed to outsiders a step in a bold imperial statesmanship. He told a Liverpool audience in his eloquent way that the time might come when Macaulay's New Zealander would "stand at the gate of Westminster Palace asking for admission into that historic hall which, having been the cradle of Liberty"--the rest of the sentence was drowned in the plaudits of his hearers. His views beyond doubt at this time leaned to a scheme of federation, and the Conservative Opposition, while in Ontario accusing him of lukewarmness in the cause of Empire, in Quebec tried to win favour by attacking his imperialist proclivities. When in the spring of 1900 he replied to Mr. Bourassa's criticisms in Parliament, he declared that Canada's assistance in future wars must be dependent on a new constitutional arrangement. "If you want us to help you," he told the people of Britain, "you must call us to your councils." It was natural that Mr. Chamberlain should look on the Canadian Premier as his first lieutenant.

But Sir Wilfrid was not the type of statesman who is deeply concerned with constitutional theories. A man who is leader of a party for thirty-two years and Prime Minister for more than fifteen must be something of an opportunist, and his theory must be elastic enough to take its shape from changing facts. If the principle of federation seemed to him attractive, he was not prepared to take any step towards its realization till compelled by an overwhelming pressure of circumstance, for he was aware how delicate was the imperial organism, and knew that the imposition of a new and rigid pattern might kill its growth. So accomplished a rhetorician could not avoid making play with the picturesque dream of a united Empire, but it did not lie close to his heart. The development of Canadian nationalism appealed more deeply both to his sentiment and his practical judgment.

Minto also was no lover of theories, and was chary of bold expansive constitutional novelties. He felt that the easiest path to Empire union was through executive co-operation, and that was why he flung himself into the question of defence. This identity of instinct made him read Sir Wilfrid's mind with remarkable acumen, and incidentally the mind of Canada. "People at home," he wrote to his brother Arthur, "do not appreciate the growing aspirations of the young nationalities we call colonies. . . . The more I see the more convinced I am that, whatever they may say, the strongest feeling of Canadians is a feeling of Canada's national independence. On the slightest pretext they resent instantly anything they can twist into meaning imperial interference." Of Laurier he was warmly appreciative. To the same correspondent he wrote: "Far the biggest man in Canada is Laurier. He is quite charming, and if there is a change I shall miss him more than I can say--and he is honest." But he had no illusions about the ultimate policy of the Prime Minister or about the inner core of Canadian feeling, which the Prime Minister was bound to interpret. Men like George Parkin, the Principal of

Upper Canada College, Toronto, with whom he maintained an affectionate intimacy, were imperial enthusiasts after the British type, and others, like Sir William Mulock and Mr. Israel Tarte, seemed to be convinced federationists; but Sir Wilfrid's wary, non-committal opportunism was, he knew, in the last resort Canada's attitude.

When Mr. Chamberlain in March 1900 mooted the idea of an Imperial Advisory Council Minto discussed the matter with Laurier and found him shy and unsympathetic. In a private letter to the Colonial Secretary in April 1900 he set out the facts as he saw them:--

"Sir Wilfrid's own inclination towards an imperial federation of any sort is, in my opinion, extremely doubtful--in fact, though his recent speeches appear to have been taken in England as enthusiastically imperialist, I am convinced they guarantee no such opinion. His speech in the House was very eloquent, and the 'call us to your councils' phrase appears to have been accepted as indicating a wish to be called--the very last thing Sir Wilfrid would want, and the speech itself did not justify that interpretation of it. He recognized the strong British devotion to the motherland existent here, and the imperial feeling at home stronger perhaps than here, and got a chance for his great eloquence. But I should say that seriously he is devoid of the British feeling for a united Empire, that it has no sentimental attraction for him, and that a closer connection with the old country he would consider from a utility point of view and nothing more. He recognizes the fact that his Canadian fellow-countrymen must follow the Anglo-Saxon lead, and will do his best to educate them up to it; but I believe it to be much more with the idea of the welding together of a Canadian nation than of forming part of a great Empire . . . and though he has never actually said so to me, I suspect that he dreams of Canadian independence in some future age. He thinks the arrangement of tariff questions far more likely to bring about imperial unity than any joint system of imperial defence; the former may be made to appear magnanimous in an imperial sense, but it would hardly be advocated by a colonial Government except in a belief in some practical gain to the colony from it, whilst the latter, upon which the safety of trade must depend, probably appears before the public merely as a direct increase in military expenditure to meet an obscure danger not generally realized."

Minto's reading of Laurier's mind found remarkable vindication at the post-war Imperial Conference of 1902. The Dominion representatives one and all--even the ardent Mr. Seddon--fought shy of Mr. Chamberlain's Imperial Council, fearing lest it might conflict with their own parliaments. The Conference decided that the "present political relation was generally satisfactory under existing conditions." The "bell-wether" declined to lead the way; he had lost his old federationism and was moving slowly to another view of imperial relationship. He wanted to let well alone, for of the two factors in

Empire development, colonial nationalism and the imperial tie, he believed that the former must for long require the chief emphasis. His conception now was of Canada as a "nation within the Empire," and he left the best machinery of co-operation to reveal itself. It is probable that at the back of his head he conceived of an ultimately independent Canada; Minto always thought so, and Sir Wilfrid's biographer assents.* But independence at the moment was as futile as federation, for it did not fit the facts; and we may take his words in 1909 as the confession of faith of a man who was above all things a realist, and was determined to make dream wait upon fact. "We are reaching the day when our Canadian Parliament will claim co-equal rights with the British Parliament, and when the only ties binding us together will be a common flag and a common Crown." This was likewise Minto's conclusion--also based on observed facts--though he might have wished it otherwise. It is no disparagement of the idealists who from the 'nineties on have preached organic imperial union to say that they misjudged the course of events, for their ideals, even if unrealized and unrealizable, have had a potent influence on political thought; but it was those who, like Minto, looked forward to alliance instead of federation, to executive co-operation rather than a legislative partnership, who judged most shrewdly the trend of Empire development.

* Skelton, II.

A statesman, it has been said, should be subtle enough to deal with things, and simple enough to deal with men.* Minto had that large secure judgment of his fellow-creatures, at once shrewd and charitable, which comes from mixing with every type of humanity. While imperialists in Britain and Canada tended to picture the French-Canadians as a race brooding darkly over ancestral hatreds and dreaming of separation, he laughed the bogey to scorn. There were elements, indeed, of danger, as he saw, in French Canada--the dregs of an ancient jacobinism and recurrent waves of clericalism-- but the attitude of the vast majority was acquiescent and decorous. As a mere matter of self-interest the British Crown was their best protection. America had nothing to offer; an independent Canada would raise awkward questions for them; the Crown was the guardian of their Church, their language, and their peculiar traditions. They were a social enclave which could only maintain its particularism under the aegis of a tolerant Empire. Minto had no patience with the nonsense commonly talked on the subject. In November 1900 he wrote to Arthur Elliot: "The writing of the leading Opposition papers in Ontario has been positively willed, simply aiming at stirring up hatred of French Canada. It is perfectly monstrous . . . I believe myself that the French-Canadians are very much maligned as to their disloyalty. French Canada does not wish to be mixed up in imperial wars, and is lukewarm, but at home you do not call a man disloyal if he disapproves of the War. Here, if he is only lukewarm, and is a French-Canadian, he must be a rebel! That is the British bulldog argument." And six months later he wrote: "I think pig-headed British assertiveness is much more to be feared than French sympathies." The fault of the French-Canadian, as he saw it, was not disloyalty but parochialism, and this parochialism, in view of his past history, was intelligible and inevitable. How could men of another blood kindle to the racial mysticism of the imperial creed. For, be it remembered, the imperialism preached by Mr. Chamberlain had a strong racial tinge. As early as his visit to Canada in 1887 he had eulogized "that proud, persistent, self-asserting and resolute stock that no change of climate or condition can alter, and which is infallibly destined to be the predominating force in the future history and civilization of the world"; and he had added, "I am an Englishman. I refuse to make any distinction between the interests of Englishmen in England, in Canada, and in the United States." The habitant could understand his own ancient loyalties, he might even be fired by Canadian nationalism, but it would have been a miracle if he had discovered enthusiasm for a creed which claimed the earth as an inheritance for men of another blood.

* The phrase is the late Sir Walter Raleigh's.

Mr. Chamberlain, having failed in his plans of union on the constitutional and defence sides, turned in the summer of 1903 to the economic. Minto had never given much attention to fiscal and tariff questions, but Mr. Chamberlain's arguments seemed to him to be on the face of them incontrovertible. In protection per se he had little interest, but retaliation appeared to him to be axiomatic, and imperial preferences looked like the method of executive co-operation, which he judged to be the right development of imperial relations. With Arthur Elliot, who as a free-trade Unionist felt himself obliged to resign his post in Mr. Balfour's Government, he had lengthy arguments, and his letters reveal his difficulty in understanding any detail of his brother's attitude. Minto hoped for an instant response from Canada, for Canada was a protectionist land and had already taken a first step in imperial preference, and Sir Wilfrid Laurier at the Conference of 1902 had encouraged Mr. Chamberlain to turn to the economic side of imperial union. But he realized, too, certain difficulties in the situation, which he expounded to the Colonial Secretary in a letter of July 17, 1903:--

"Canada is in a state of evolution. At present I see no one in the Dominion capable of directing her future. Everything is in a state of drift. The chief attraction in public life is the so-called development of the country, meaning, I am afraid, to a great extent financial transactions not creditable to her public men; and influences and inclinations are, so to speak, aimlessly floating about, waiting for some power which will eventually control them. British sentiment is one such influence; it simmers quite honestly in the hearts of the English-speaking population, but there is no strong man here to put life into it. It has plenty of enemies, and, admitting its genuine existence, one has still to consider the mixed social characteristics which surround it, and the effect they may eventually have upon it. I do not doubt the loyalty of Canada, but I believe the strongest feeling of her people is that of Canadian nationality. There is no reason why, if Canada and the motherland share mutual interests, her national ambitions should be anti-imperial; if they do not, the tendency will be towards eventual separation. There is, too, even among the most British society of the Dominion, that disagreeable cavilling feeling towards the old country . . . and the exaggerated suspicion of anything that can be twisted into meaning imperial interference."

Minto believed that Mr. Chamberlain's proposals were the turning of the ways in British history. He thought that if Britain refused to develop a line of policy which Canada had herself inaugurated, the tendency would be for the Dominion to turn her mind to reciprocity with the United States. Here, as in the question of defence, he longed for qualities in the Prime Minister--qualities of dash and daring--which the Prime Minister did not possess. The response from the Laurier Government was polite, but tepid. On 27th July Mr. Chamberlain wrote to Minto a letter which frankly set out his policy so far as it concerned Canada:--

"I am not by any means entirely satisfied with the action of the Canadian Ministers. Seeing that in all these conversations they pressed for the adoption of the policy I am now advocating, I certainly hoped for a warmer and more indisputable welcome. I have been ready to sacrifice anything to secure what I believe to be a great imperial object. If I fail, of course my political career will be closed, but with proper co-operation I do not think I shall fail in the long run, although I may not win uno saltu. Colonial politicians, however, are more timid, and they do not seem to me to venture to put great questions on the highest level. They attach more importance to a few votes than to great principles, and the prospect of an imperial union, which they perhaps do not appreciate at its true value, is not sufficiently attractive to them to justify any risk of losing political support. . . . What I have to do is to convince my own people first. . . .

"The change will be carried, if at all, by mixed considerations of sentiment and interest. As to the former, I hope it is strong in Canada, and that there is some appreciation of what an Empire really means as contrasted with the parochial life and small ambitions of little states. If the Empire breaks up into atoms, each one will be comparatively insignificant, powerless, and uninteresting. If it holds together it will be the greatest civilizing influence in the world.

"As regards interest, the colonies will no doubt take steps to guard their growing manufactures from extinction. On the other hand, our people will not assent to a tax on corn and meat or other articles of primary necessity, unless they are satisfied that they will have something substantial in return in the shape of increased exports of manufactures. This cannot be secured entirely by the mere increase of differential rates against foreign nations. The business of foreign countries with Canada is either comparatively small, or it is in articles which we do not make or produce. We must, therefore, look to an expansion due to other causes than a mere reduction in the imports of other countries.

"It seems to me that what we both want is possible. Canada may preserve her present industries, but give us a full share in her future expansion. If she has, for instance, decided to establish, or has already established, the great primary industries such as iron-making and cotton-spinning, and requires a small protection against us to prevent them from being overwhelmed, such a course might be taken; while, at the same time, she might leave to us the smaller industries not yet established in Canada, in regard to which there is no vested interest, and which together will make up large sums. In other words, let Canada continue to protect what she has got, and adopt free trade, or nearly free trade, so far as we are concerned, in regard to all the industries that up to the present time have not been established.

"I feel strongly with you that we are at a parting of the ways, and, although I am not disposed to prophesy anything with confidence, I think that unless we succeed in doing something to unite our business interests more closely, sentiment alone will not keep the Empire together."

Mr. Chamberlain resigned the Colonial Secretaryship and devoted himself to his crusade, but there was no such missionary zeal in the protectionist

Government of Canada. Sir Wilfrid accepted the scheme in principle, but would take no overt step to show his approval. Minto summed up his attitude thus to Mr. Chamberlain: "Canada does not want to appear as a beggar, asking a favour of the motherland; she does not want to interfere in what is becoming a party fight at home; the matter is one which the old country must first settle for herself, and then Canada will know what to do. Canada believes that preferential trade between the motherland and herself would be advantageous to both parties, but the former, with whom the decision rests, must not put herself in the position of making, or appearing to make, sacrifices for Canada."

It was a discreet and impregnable attitude, but it was not heroic, and to Mr. Chamberlain, prepared to hazard everything for what he believed to be a shining ideal, it seemed shabby and faint-hearted. Minto could not understand how those who accepted the end could be unwilling to urge the means, and Mr. Chamberlain wrote to him, in sadness rather than in bitterness, that Sir Wilfrid was clearly "not a man with whom to go out tiger-hunting." Sir Wilfrid was not; he was little inclined to court danger, and his courage was reserved for the time when danger was present and inevitable. But there was more in the Government's lukewarmness than the temperament of its leader. Canadian Liberals were influenced by the not very honest "dear loaf" campaign of their British namesakes. Canadian Conservatives were not enthusiastic about the free field claimed for British manufactures in Canada, and Canadian manufacturers were disinclined to admit that there were any articles which sooner or later somewhere in the country they could not produce. The British proposals seemed too much like a stereotyping of Canada's present industrial position, and Canada, intoxicated with dreams of a vast future, was averse to any economic delimitation. Moreover, the imperial preference side began soon to fall into the shade, and Mr. Chamberlain's campaign, as it developed, became more and more a plan for the protection of British industries. Sir Wilfrid judged truly the feeling of his countrymen. They were not greatly interested; there was no force of popular sentiment which would force the Government's hand, and the Government was without inclination for imperial adventures. Minto, sharing to the full in Mr. Chamberlain's views, set down Canadian apathy to Sir Wilfrid's weakness; but it is not weak to refuse to be drawn into a course for which you have little zest. The man who is seeking new worlds to conquer will never see eye to eye with the man who is engrossed in the development of his township.

II

A Governor-General must play a large part in the foreign relations of the dominion where he represents the British Crown, since he is the exponent of the British point of view, which has of necessity to embrace a wider orbit than that of the local government. Canadian foreign policy was at the time confined to her relations with America, as to which there were many long-standing problems that at any moment might become acute controversies. Minto shared the view which Queen Victoria had expressed to him at Balmoral, that there was a great deal of cant in the current talk of kinship between the United States and Britain. He was of the opinion that Sir Wilfrid Laurier set down in a letter to him in 1899-- "Our American friends have very many qualities, but what they have they keep, and what they have not they want. Perhaps," Sir Wilfrid added, "we, too, are built up the same way." The influence of the "big interests," which everywhere he detested, seemed to Minto to have reached in America the dimensions of a scandal, and he found in her people a lack of that sporting equity which he valued above all other human qualities. In any controversy with the United States he was therefore likely to have a strong a "priori" leaning to Canada's side.

The Washington Treaty of 1871, which dealt largely with fisheries and trade, was abrogated in 1885, and the fishing question was governed by the old treaty of 1818. This was manifestly an out-of-date machine, so a special commission, of which Mr. Chamberlain was a member, was appointed in 1887, and the Chamberlain-Bryan Treaty was produced, which, however, the United States Senate declined to ratify. The consequence was an annual modus vivendi, till in 1897 the Governments of Britain and America agreed to a joint High Commission, which should settle all outstanding differences, such as the matter of trade reciprocity, the Alaskan boundary, the Atlantic fisheries, and the seal fishing in the Behring

Sea. Lord Herschell, the chairman, died during the sittings, and the deliberations came to an untimely end, principally because, though agreement seemed to be in sight on the other points, a violent divergence of views was apparent on the Alaskan frontier question. On this the difference of attitude and interests between Canada and her neighbour came to a head, and it formed in many ways the most delicate and troublesome problem of Minto's term of office.

Alaska had been first explored by the Russians Behring and Cherikov, and its coast had been first charted by Captain Cook in 1778 and Vancouver in 1793-94. The land originally was Russian territory, and its relations with America were fixed by treaty in 1824, and its boundary with the British possessions by the treaty of 1825. In 1867 Russian Alaska was sold to the United States, but the frontier question with Canada was not scientifically determined. Towards the close of the century the matter was made urgent by the discovery of gold in the Klondyke and the rapid development of the Yukon district. Canada needed ports for her hinterland, and the question of police regulations was insoluble so long as the boundary line was vague. There were many suggestions made for a compromise, but America stood on what she believed to be her legal rights given by the treaty of 1825. Arbitration was proposed under an impartial tribunal and an umpire, but this America rejected. The feeling in Canada may be judged from a letter of Minto's to Arthur Elliot in August 1899:--

"The States are impossible to deal with. Their leading men, however high-minded personally, are entirely under the influence of local organizations which they can't ignore. No one for an instant expects fair play from the States either in business or in sport. The feeling here is very strong against them, and it is only human nature that it should be so. On the other hand, thinking people of course see the vital necessity of being on friendly terms with them. Canadian statesmen fully recognize the overwhelming importance of this; but one can't forget that you have an unruly mining population on the debatable frontier of Alaska, rubbing up against Canadian posts, and a good hearty hatred between a large part of both nations."

The ordinary reader, when he first approaches the subject, is inclined to be amazed at the unreason and truculence of the American attitude, and to set it down to that highhandedness in international questions which has occasionally distinguished a nation accustomed more than others to proclaim the majesty of international law. Here was a long strip of coast, running far to the south and overlapping British Columbia, which had been given by an old treaty to Russia because of the rights created at that date by occupation, when America had no interest in the region. It was fair to argue that the whole position as between two friendly neighbours should be revised by arbitration in the light of the facts of Canadian western development. Arbitration seemed to be a pet American procedure. In 1895-96 President Cleveland had compelled Lord Salisbury to accept it in a boundary dispute with Venezuela--had insisted on it, indeed, with notable discourtesy. But now, when a neighbour asked for arbitration in a case far more difficult than that of the Venezuela frontier, America would have none of it. She was indignant when it was suggested that Alaska should be included in the reference of the Herschell Commission, and on that very score the Commission failed. She was in effective occupation of the coast strip; "what I have I hold," seemed to be her answer, irrespective of law or decency.

Then Britain proposed arbitration anew, and there is reason to believe that President M'Kinley would have accepted it. Even John Hay, his Secretary of State, though he did not like it, felt some difficulty in refusing what America had demanded in the case of Venezuela. But in September 1901 M'Kinley was assassinated, and Theodore Roosevelt succeeded him as President; and one of Roosevelt's first acts was to refuse categorically any suggestion for arbitration. What were his reasons? He was a wise and a strong man, a lover of his country, but a lover also of fair play and international righteousness. Had he been convinced that America was behaving dishonourably, we may be certain that he would have done what he held to be right and consigned all intriguing interests and threatening electorates to the devil. On what did he base his unhesitating refusal?

In the first place--if we may guess at his thoughts--he regarded the treaty of 1825 as a legal document to be interpreted judicially. It was the title-deeds of America's property on the southern Alaskan coast. For seventy years a certain obvious interpretation of it had held the field, which showed the boundary running round the heads of many inlets. It was clear to him that it had been the intention of the treaty to give Russia not merely a string of isolated headlands, but the unbroken lisiere. Now Canada had made the mistake of overstating her case. She claimed that the line should run across the mouths of the fjords, leaving her the deep inlets behind. To Roosevelt and to the American people the claim seemed preposterous, both on the wording of the treaty and on the prescriptive right given by the assumption of seventy years. Had there been an arbitration, this extreme case of Canada's would have been put forward as a bargaining counter, and, since arbitrators invariably compromise, Canada would have received more than her due. He felt that he had no right to play fast and loose with the property of his country; it was not only Seattle and the West that would object, it was the whole American nation. He strongly desired a settlement, but he did not believe that any settlement would endure which violated plain legal rights. All he was concerned with was to have these rights explicitly ascertained, and for that the proper instrument was a judicial commission.

It was believed at the time in Canada that the negotiations with America over the revision of the Bulwer-Clayton Treaty, in order to assure her control of the Panama Canal, gave Britain an opportunity for bartering concessions in Central America for concessions in Alaska. The opportunity, if it ever really existed, was missed, and the Alaska question was referred to a commission of "six impartial jurists of repute," three British and three American. This was not satisfactory to Canada, for it seemed likely to lead to a deadlock, but Laurier accepted the proposal, it being understood that the British three would be an English and a Canadian judge and the English Chief-Justice. To the amazement of the world the American trio consisted of the Secretary for War, Mr. Elihu Root; Mr. Henry Cabot Lodge, the Senator for Massachusetts; and Senator Turner of Washington. Mr. Root was a great lawyer, but he was also a member of the American Executive; Senator Lodge had publicly described the Canadian case as "a baseless and manufactured claim," and Senator Turner represented those Western interests which were hostile to Canadian trade. Where were the "impartial jurists"? Roosevelt's motive in the appointments seems to have been that he was determined on a speedy settlement which would remove "the last obstacle to absolute agreement between the two peoples," and that he was convinced that his case was so unanswerable that he did not need to seek an appearance of impartiality.

Canada, who had argued herself into a belief in the justice of her full claim, could scarcely be expected to approve this conduct or appreciate the motives behind it. On March 1, 1903, Minto wrote to Arthur Elliot:--

"The U.S. have behaved quite disgracefully. Briefly, we accepted their proposal, or rather Herbert and Hay's arrangement for the judicial discussion of the frontier dispute--three 'impartial jurists of repute' on each side. This was entirely contrary to what Canada has always sought for, viz., arbitration with a court selected under unprejudiced conditions and an umpire; but, being honestly anxious to have the arguments on both sides fully considered, we agreed to the Hay-Herbert treaty, pointing out that it was not what we hoped for, but that the immense importance of a friendly international consideration of the subject had decided us to accept the terms proposed. The pourparlers were perfectly distinct that on one side we should have the Chief-Justice of England and two judges of the High Courts of England and Canada respectively--assuming, of course, that the U.S. commissioners would be jurists of distinction not at present mixed up in politics. Imagine our surprise when Roosevelt appoints Root, his Sec. of S. for War; Lodge, who has given vent to the most anti-British views on Alaska; and Turner, the Senator for Washington State and the representative of the Pacific ports interest, in opposition, of course, to our Alaskan coast trade. It's the most monstrous thing. . . . The first inclination was to retire altogether as far as Canada was concerned from the bargain. On second thoughts, however, it seems better, while protesting against the U.S. action, to accept the President's nominations; but I have impressed upon Sir Wilfrid and upon H.M.'s Gov. that in my opinion we ought to insist on sticking to our side of the bargain, and appointing the Chief-Justice and other judges on our side as originally intended. For some reason or other H.M.'s Gov. seem to have got it into their heads that because the U.S. are appointing partisans, therefore we must give up the judicial character of our representatives. I think exactly the opposite. If both sides appoint partisans the tribunal must lose all dignity and weight, whereas if we stick to the bargain like gentlemen, we shall not only gain by better professional arguments, but will place the U.S. before the world as not having played up to the terms of the treaty which they had agreed to."

Minto's good sense--with which Sir Wilfrid Laurier was in full accord-prevailed. It was considered wise to appoint, in addition to Lord Alverstone, two Canadian judges, Sir Louis Jette and Mr. Justice Armour, the latter of whom died in London and was succeeded by Mr. A. B. Aylesworth, a leader of the Ontario bar. In October 1903 the tribunal reported. By a majority of four to two, Lord Alverstone voting with the American representatives, it was held that the boundary should run, not across the mouths, but round the heads of the fjords, and that the Portland Channel, the southern limit, should be taken as running in such a way as to give Canada only two of the four islands claimed. In effect the verdict accepted the case of the United States.

There was an instant uproar in Canada, and the bitter part of the the pill was the Portland Channel. It appeared that Lord Alverstone had admitted the strength of the British case on 12th October, and had delivered on 17th October a judgment contradicting his expressed opinion, and the natural deduction was that, in his anxiety to settle the matter, he had compromised, and acted as a diplomatist and not as a judge. The two Canadian commissioners protested publicly, and Minto lamented the awakening of all kinds of old separatist and anti-British ghosts which he hoped had long been laid in their graves. It may be safely said that for the allegations against Lord Alverstone there was no foundation. The English Chief-Justice was not a great lawyer or a conspicuously strong man, but he was a very honest one, and he was incapable on such a tribunal of forgetting the primary duties of a judge. The best legal view at the time was that the question of the Portland Channel was one of extreme difficulty in which the merits were evenly balanced, and that the American contention was at least as justifiable as the Canadian.

Now that the irritation has long been forgotten, the considered opinion of Canada accepts the finding as a reasonable settlement. Undoubtedly President Roosevelt, however excellent his intentions, and however cogent his grounds for refusing an arbitration, played a blundering part, for his choice of the American commissioners was one of those pieces of folly and bluster which sometimes marred his great career. If his case was as strong as he believed it to be, and as it no doubt was, to pack the court with partisans was to make certain that any decision would be suspect in the eyes of Canada and the world; and he did not help matters when, after the decision was announced, he proclaimed it to the housetops as "the greatest diplomatic victory of our time." Minto, on the contrary, showed a restraint and wisdom which had a soothing effect on the exacerbated temper of his Government. He had been as angry as any Canadian at the American appointments, but he did not question the justice of the verdict. He calmed down those who demanded that in future Canada should have the "treaty-making power" by suggesting that in that event Canada must shoulder the whole burden of her defence. He made himself a complete master of the facts of the case, and defended Lord Alverstone much better than that honest gentleman defended himself. He went over every argument with his Ministers in long conversations, the notes of which show not only his trenchant good sense but an unexpected legal acumen; while his letters to Sir Wilfrid contain an argument on the Portland Channel which was certainly not bettered by counsel during the hearing of the case.

III

Canadian internal politics were no part of Minto's province, but there was a margin of domestic questions where the Governor-General had a certain status, and was free to inquire and advise. Notable among these was the administration of the new Yukon province, the position of the Indian remnants, and matters of historical and antiquarian interest, which are apt to be ignored in a country borne on the high tide of commercial triumph. In July 1900, while Sir Wilfrid Laurier was in the thick of preparations for a general election, Minto left Ottawa for a prolonged tour in the North-West. It was a land he had not visited since he went to Vancouver with Lord Lansdowne fifteen years before, and every mile was a revelation, for the old villages had swelled into towns, and towns had been transformed into cities. He left Vancouver on 8th August with Lady Minto, and, travelling by way of Skagway and the White Horse Pass, reached Dawson City on the 14th. For four days he led a strenuous life, of which the burden was not lightened by excessive proffers of champagne. "It has been a wonderful experience," his diary records. "There seems to have been an idea that we would hold ourselves aloof, and refuse generally to meet all classes or interchange ideas. We have done our best to see every one and do everything that time allowed. I have received petitions from the citizens and the Board of Trade, and discussed matters with the politicians, and have had many conversations with miners and others interested in the country. I have no doubt that my search for information will be bitterly resented by those in power, but to have refused to listen would have been, in my opinion, miserable." Among those who resented his conduct was certainly not Sir Wilfrid, to whom the Yukon was a perpetual source of disquiet, and who gladly welcomed an honest and first-hand opinion. The enthusiasm attending the Governor-General's departure from Dawson was in marked contrast to the apathy shown on his arrival. The miners felt they had found a friend who understood them. They presented Lady Minto with a gold basket, made in Dawson, filled with nuggets, and with hearty hand-shakes and amid ringing cheers the party embarked on the paddle-boat, Sybil, on their return journey down the Yukon River.

In Minto's view the direction of the Yukon at that time was a disgrace. It was too far away to be effectively governed from Ottawa, and corruption, which was always an ugly background force in Canadian politics, walked there open and unashamed. The place was a Territory, administered by a commissioner and five others appointed by the Governor-General-in-Council, to which body two elected members had just been added. The problem, it is true, was far from easy. The population was rough, mixed, and nomadic, and of the 17,000 in Dawson City 75 per cent, were American subjects. The system of getting gold was entirely "placer" mining, which is not easily developed into a systematic industry. Distance and the difficulties of transport made supplies costly, and administrative blunders added to the expense of living and intensified the gambling atmosphere. "Prices are enormous," Minto wrote to Arthur Elliot; "an egg 75 cents, a bottle of champagne cheap at 20 dollars, but every one drinks it on every possible occasion; hay very cheap when I was there at 300 dollars a ton (I believe it has been up to 600 dollars). The high prices are to a great extent of course due to expense of freight, but also to the misgovernment which has so taxed the gold output that there is a feeling that only gambling prices are worth going in for. Liquor is only allowed in by a system of permits, the Minister of the Interior disposing of these permits to his friends at a royalty of two dollars a gallon, and they selling it in Dawson for four and five dollars a gallon to speculators there."

It is the tale of all new mining camps. A remote government treats them as a milch-cow for revenue and a field for patronage, and forgets its duties. In a long private letter to Mr. Chamberlain, Minto set out the reforms which seemed to him essential. The excessive royalty on the gold output--10 per cent, on the gross--should be reduced; the liquor permits system should be abolished, since it put the trade into a few corrupt hands; there should be a change in the system of the reservation of claims for the Dominion Government, which was no less than an invitation to official dishonesty; above all, a reasonable proportion of the revenue should be spent on the improvement of the country. There was nothing new either in the complaints or the proposed reforms, for Canada had been humming for the past year with talk of Yukon scandals. Sir Wilfrid was far from easy in his own mind about the matter, and he could not disregard the emphatic comments of the Governor-General. The gold royalty was reduced, and other reforms were in process, when the Yukon question was suddenly transformed into the Alaskan boundary controversy. In a few years the decline of the placer mining stripped the problem of its urgency, for the wilds closed in upon many mushroom settlements, and the torrential growth checked and ebbed.

For the Indians, the ancient owners of the land, Minto had at all times a peculiar tenderness. In his early wanderings he had been brought much into contact with savage tribes, and in particular had seen how the frontier officers in India kept the peace by a wise tolerance, when the harsh hand would have led to strife. In the Batoche expedition he had had experience of the red man, and was eager to preserve something of his traditional life from the steam-roller of civilization. We find him, on his way back from his Yukon journey, visiting the Sarcee and Blackfoot Reserves, of which he wrote to Queen Victoria:--"The Indians, too, have made great advances, and though they met me with all their old barbaric pomp, bead-work, feathers, and tomahawks, I am told I am probably the last Governor-General who will receive such a welcome, and that my successors will have to be content with chiefs in tall hats and black coats. I suppose one must not regret the coming change, but I confess the wild red man has charms for me."

Two years later he was at Fort Qu'appelle and held a pow-wow with the chiefs of a neighbouring reserve and heard their grievances. One of them was the Sioux, Standing Buffalo, with whose intelligence he was much impressed, and he listened patiently to the tale of their woes. The foremost was the suppression of their traditional dancing. "The Commissioner for Native Affairs," says the journal, "is evidently opposed to dancing. He is a tall cadaverous Scotsman, more like an elder of the Kirk than anything else, and had the most depressing effect on me. . . . I cannot conceive his ever approving of dancing! But why should not these poor people dance? It is their only amusement, and sober beyond words in comparison to a Scottish reel.

Lord Minto and "Dandy," 1900. (Photo by Topley, Ottawa)

Of course the Sun Dance and its cruelties it was right to stop, but surely not all dancing. . . . The ridiculous wish to cut it down, root and branch, on the part of narrow-minded authorities ^makes me sick, and I said plainly that I saw no harm in it, and was in no way opposed to it. I suppose I shall be reported, as usual, as in violent opposition to my Ministers. I don't care a damn, as I am convinced all reasonable people who know the Indians agree with me, and I believe my speaking out occasionally does much good." So we find him to the end of his tenure of office pleading the cause of the Indians, especially of his friend Standing Buffalo, to Indian commissioners and Lieutenant-Governors, without much assistance from the Prime Minister. Sir Wilfrid, who might have been expected to have a tender side towards the ancient ways, had no wish to rouse the Canadian equivalent of the Nonconformist conscience.

Some months after Minto's return from the Yukon a Dawson paper thus described his visit and its results:--

"For a Governor-General in an aggressive young colony like Canada to be actively interested in affairs necessitates the constant exercise of the greatest common sense. An illustration was afforded in Dawson. The complaints from the territory percolating through to the outside were loud and deep. The Government had considered it necessary on the floor of the House to protest that there was really nothing wrong here excepting the people. Lord Minto was not content to come here and be blind and deaf. The Administration desired it. There were many staunch supporters of the party in power who stood prepared to take mortal offence did the Governor-General make any capital for the Opposition.

"A weak man would have taken the hint and remained silent, leaving abuses unredressed and the people oppressed. A cowardly man would have avoided the dangerous shoals by retiring from the public behind official dignity and red tape. A stupid man would have had the party and Government about his ears in a week. But Lord Minto avoided every pitfall. He first insisted upon receiving the people here and hearing their complaints: the Administration stood off in affright! The Governor-General even invited bills of rights and memorials recapitulating abuses; and the stauncher members of the party almost collapsed! He cross-examined his callers closely, showing the most intelligent and sympathetic understanding of the questions brought before him. The wise ones winked knowingly, and intimated that the Governor-General would avoid the rocks by shelving the complaints; that the memorials would be pigeon-holed and never resurrected; that, in short, it was all a 'stall.'

"He left Dawson, and it is a matter of Yukon history that after his departure he was silent as the grave. Not a word came back to Dawson; not a word reached the outside papers. Ottawa gossip never even discovered he was having anything to say to the Ministers, or reporting to them his discoveries while here. And the only way in which we know we were not forgotten was that, commencing some twenty days after his departure, the very reforms were begun for which he had been petitioned. Day by day the abuses were removed, until presently everything complained of to Lord Minto had been remedied without a word of explanation. Moreover, it was to be observed that so cleverly had his recommendations been made that his standing with the Canadian Government and in official circles was higher than ever. He had dared to be more than an official puppet; had put his spoke in the Canadian wheel; had not feared to essay the amendment of palpable abuses; and yet had interfered so cleverly that there was not the slightest soreness discoverable anywhere."

That was the kind of recognition which Minto desired. He was a man of action, and, though his position forbade him to act himself, he could get things done by others. He adhered scrupulously to constitutional form, and he did not seek personal repute or advertisement, but he secured results without friction, where the gushing popularity-hunting type of Governor would have utterly failed. Dr. Doughty has written of him: "Sir Wilfrid Laurier said once: "Lord Minto is the most constitutional Governor we have had.' And yet perhaps no other Governor succeeded so completely in imposing his own policy upon the Government. He would suggest, persuade, insist; but when once his point was gained, there was complete self-effacement, and the measure became that of his advisers, even in its inception. He might be the discoverer of the evil and the author of the remedy, but the action must be taken by, and the credit belong to, the Government of Canada."

He would have asked for no finer tribute. It is a definition of the essential function of a wise viceroy in a free Dominion.

CHAPTER EIGHT

GOVERNOR-GENERAL OF CANADA, 1898-1904 (continued)

Social and Personal Relations

A GOVERNOR-GENERAL lives an intricate and crowded life in the public eye, and he is fortunate if from the whirl of minor duties he can snatch time for study and reflection. His mind may be absorbed in some grave discussion with his Ministers or the home Government, but he must present himself smiling at a dozen functions, and let no one guess his preoccupation. He must perpetually entertain and be entertained: he must show interest in every form of public activity, from a charity bazaar to a university celebration; he must be accessible to all men that he may learn of them and they of him; he must visit every corner of his domain, and become, for the time being, not only one of its citizens, but by adoption a perfervid son of each town and province. These things are the imponderabilia of governorship, not less important than a cool head and a sound judgment in the greater matters of policy, and many a man who is well fitted for the latter duties fails signally in the other. We have seen Minto's work on the political side; in its social and personal aspects its merits were no less conspicuous. To the task indeed he brought splendid endowments. He had remarkable physical strength, and could go through a long ceremonial day without loss of vigour or temper. He mentions in his journal that at the age of fifty-six he wore glasses for the first time in reading, which shows how little he had to complain of in bodily powers. He was also endowed with the liveliest curiosity about all sorts and conditions of men, their business, their sports, the whims and humours of their lives. Being the extreme contrary of an egoist, it was easy for him to enter into other people's interests, and his sympathy was no painfully adopted pose, but sincere and spontaneous. Lastly, he had a wife who shared his happy temperament, and relieved him of more than half his burden. Lady Minto's energy was unflagging, and her tact infallible. She busied herself with every form of social work, interesting herself in the charities already established, and raising a fund in memory of Queen Victoria which was devoted to establishing cottage hospitals in outlying districts. She accompanied him everywhere, and everywhere made friends. Few Governor-Generals have made a greater success of that delicate and arduous duty, official entertainments. There was a cordiality about the reception of each guest which gave the impression of an individual welcome, and the happy atmosphere could not fail to leave its impression on the stream of visitors who crossed the threshold, for the hospitable doors of Government House were always open. The secret of this success was apparent: the whole establishment worked for the common end with a spirit of co-operation which produced a harmonious household, for there was a magnetism about Minto which called forth the best in others. He had the good fortune to be assisted by the most competent staff; his first military secretary was Laurence Drummond, to be followed two years later by that officer of the Coldstream Guards who, as Sir Stanley Maude, in the Great War saved our fortunes in Mesopotamia. Minto was no lover of functions, but he accepted them cheerfully, wearing on every possible occasion his military uniform in preference to the diplomatic gold coat. "You are so absurdly fond of my bare legs and dancing pumps," he wrote to his wife. "What I feel is that all my service till I came here has been military service, every little honour I have won is for that, and on retirement I was given the right to wear a General's uniform, and I shall always do so. I hate these bare-legged people." He could find a source of humour even in boredom.

"An awful dinner last night," he told his wife; "timed for 7 and we did not get home till 2 a.m. The toast list was sent to me beforehand, and, to my horror, five toasts and seventeen people to speak. I violently remonstrated, but was assured the speeches would be very short. They were yards long! At last, when I was getting desperate, and was just going to propose Sir . . . 's health to close the proceedings, to my dismay he jumped up and proposed mine for the second time. We were by that time so overcome with emotion at each other's eloquence that we simultaneously broke up. X made a tremendous speech, and, trembling with emotion, proclaimed a Monroe doctrine for Canada, and that she must absorb the States and rule the world. As he had a U.S. professor next door to him, who had just made an excellent speech, I quite expected war would be declared this morning."

The group of high-spirited and extraordinarily handsome children became something of a legend, and their doings and sayings did much to add to the lively interest which Canada took in Government House. A happy home life is not only an indispensable background for a busy man, but, if that man be Governor-General, it is an element in his influence and a direct aid to the popularity of his regime. The atmosphere of Government House, with its warm family affection, its gaiety and its simplicity, was a rest and a refreshment to all who entered it. Minto's journals and letters are full of his children and his pride in their achievements, and the humours and surprises of the young; the remarkable talent that Eileen showed for acting; Ruby's success in taking a first-class at the Toronto College of Music; Esmond's wit and charm; Larry's and Violet's horsemanship. He tells this story of his youngest daughter, who accompanied him on a journey to Lake Tamiscaming. "As we arrived at the station a poor man was brought in horribly mutilated by a blast on the new railway near here. He was quite insensible and practically dead, and they put him in the booking office. I hoped Vi had not seen him, but she had, and assumed he was in frightful agony and asked me angrily why they did not kill him now, at once: 'Do have him killed, Father.' So thoroughly practical and so like old Vi--it would so often be much the best plan."

There were other entertainments at Government House than formal parties, one of the most successful being a children's fancy dress ball at the Christmas of 1903, when the chief characters were taken from Alice in Wonderland and Through the Looking-Glass, his youngest daughter Violet filling the part of Alice, and Esmond, then seven years old, that of the White Rabbit. There were also many dramatic performances, brilliantly stage-managed by Captain Harry Graham. There were unrehearsed performances too, such as the fire that broke out in the new wing of the house on the early morning of Easter Sunday 1904, when Lady Minto was lying helpless with a broken leg. "My own bedroom," Minto writes in his journal, "was so full of smoke I could hardly breathe in it. We made a stretcher out of a screen and carried Mary down to the oval room. She really behaved magnificently; my fear was that she was too cool and would not allow us to hurry her enough. The children's wing was almost totally destroyed, and much damage was done by water before the fire was extinguished. The younger children had been taken for safety to the stables, and were found there later, kneeling by the corn bin, earnestly praying for their mother's safety."*

* This was not the only experience the Mintos had of fires, for in the same month four years earlier four miles of the town of Ottawa had been burnt, and the Governor-General had himself assisted the fire brigade in fighting the flames.

There were certain incidents which belonged to the social and ceremonial side of Minto's duties which gave him as much thought and trouble as the major problems of politics. Two of them are worth noting, as an example of the kind of difficulty which beset the Governor-General's path. When in January 1901 Queen Victoria died, it seemed to Minto only fitting that there should be an official memorial service in Ottawa. He consulted Sir Wilfrid Laurier, who approved, and it was decided that a service should be held in the Church of England Cathedral, at which the Governor-General and Ministers should attend in state. It was arranged that Minto should issue the invitations, that the Primate should officiate, and that the Government should contribute to the Cathedral decorations. Suddenly there arrived a note from Sir Wilfrid saying that there could be no state service, as there was no state church in Canada, and that Ministers could only attend the services of their own communions. Minto was naturally surprised, not at the information about the state church, but at Sir Wilfrid's conclusion. It seemed to him reasonable to hold the memorial service for the dead Queen in the church to which she had belonged, though the Prime Minister was a Catholic. Moreover, there was an exact precedent. The body of Sir John Thompson had been brought from England in a man-of-war, there had been a state funeral at Halifax, and a state memorial service in the Roman Catholic Basilica at Ottawa, for all of which the Government had paid. Sir Wilfrid, much embarrassed, explained that Sir John's had been a "burial" service with the body present; but Minto replied that the body had remained at Halifax, while the memorial service was held at Ottawa. There was indeed no argument possible on the Prime Minister's side; he had been willing enough, but had changed his mind because of the objections of certain of the Ministers, notably Mr. Scott, who was a narrow type of Catholic. Meantime the Ministerial press accused the Governor-General of having taken a highhanded line on his own authority and of attempting to force a state church upon Canada. Minto very properly issued a contradiction, pointing out that every step he had taken had been with Sir Wilfrid's assent, and the consequence was that Ministers looked extremely foolish. The whole affair was scarcely to the Prime Minister's credit; he had agreed without consulting his Cabinet, and at a hint of opposition had chosen to leave the Governor-General in the lurch. The result was that the solemnity of the occasion was somewhat marred: the Catholic Mayor of Quebec, who was also Prime Minister of the Province, attended in state a service in the English Cathedral in that city; at Ottawa Sir Wilfrid went to the Roman Catholic Basilica, while Minto with some of the Ministers went to the English service--accompanied, to the amazement of the citizens, by that stout Catholic, Mr. Israel Tarte.

A second incident was the visit of the Duke and Duchess of Cornwall and York in the autumn of 1901. The Government at first showed complete apathy in the business; Mr. Scott was doubtful about Canada's welcome, but waived his objection in haste when Minto proposed to cable his views home and suggest that the visit be countermanded. Then Ministers desired to make arrangements themselves, which was manifestly an impossible plan, but Minto pointed out that he would be held personally responsible for the details, and they willingly relinquished the task. The organization from beginning to end was the work of the Governor-General and his staff, and it was no small undertaking. The time was limited, the Royal visitors wished to travel Canada from East to West, local susceptibilities had to be considered in order that no area might be neglected, and it was equally important that the Duke and Duchess should not be overweighted with duties but should have a reasonable share of leisure and amusement. There were anxious hearts at the Citadel before the Ophir arrived at Quebec, but the success of the visit was complete and unequivocal. Minto's letter of October 25, 1901, to King Edward is the best summary:--

"It is a great pleasure to me to be able to tell your Majesty of the immense success of their Royal Highnesses' visit. From the day they arrived at Quebec till their departure last Monday their stay here has been a series of ovations, and I hear nothing on all sides but expressions of pleasure, not only as to the success of the tour, but as to the affectionate impressions they have left behind them. . . . Their Royal Highnesses held receptions at all the chief towns, which were very largely attended. They were arranged on the lines of the state receptions held at Ottawa, though there was at first considerable divergence of opinion as to the best manner of conducting them--whether they should simply be receptions in the ordinary sense of the word, a few selected people being brought up and introduced, or whether people should 'pass' and bow without shaking hands, or whether every one should shake hands. Their Royal Highnesses adopted the last course, and it has been deeply appreciated as a personal intercourse between themselves and the Canadian people, which will always be remembered.

"Your Majesty will have seen from the newspapers that I did not accompany their Royal Highnesses across the continent. . . . I confess I was at first much in doubt as to what to do. I was very anxious to give all the help I could, and felt that I might be able to give a good deal of help from my acquaintance with leading people in the North-West and in British Columbia. But at the same time I felt that it was only natural that Lieutenant-Governors should wish personally to take the lead in doing honour to the Duke and Duchess, and that I should perhaps be rather in the way at small Government Houses, where two staffs would multiply difficulties. So I hope your Majesty may think I decided rightly in not going across the continent. Lady Minto went everywhere with the Duke and Duchess, and was, I hope, an assistance to them. I met them on their return from the West at a place called Poplar Point, in Manitoba, where we had two days' duck shooting, which I believe the Duke enjoyed. I think that eleven guns got about 700 duck in a day and a half's shooting, and a detached party of four guns got about 200 more. I had great difficulty in arranging this shoot: my Ministers were opposed to any shooting at all, and I finally had to insist on it on the ground that it really was absurd to say that H.R.H. should not be allowed a day and a half's relaxation. . . . I am sure your Majesty will understand that the organization of the tour was not without its difficulties. There was at first an inclination to do nothing to prepare for the reception and to leave everything to chance. It was hopeless, too, to endeavour to explain that their Royal Highnesses' time was limited, or that it was fair to consider their powers of endurance. Consequently it rested with me to undertake many refusals and curtailments of ceremonies, the necessity for which people here are unwilling to admit. But it is an immense satisfaction to realize that Canada's reception has been a triumphant demonstration of loyal sentiment. The letter of hearty thanks which the Duke has addressed to me, expressing his sincere appreciation of the reception he had received throughout Canada, has given great pleasure everywhere."

The weeks passed at the Citadel during the autumn of each year were of special interest to Minto. Quebec had a peculiar attraction for him, and he spent many an afternoon wandering through the Old Town searching out its historical treasures and examining the details of its battlefields. His interest led him to desire a deeper and more accurate knowledge, and on making inquiries for the historical manuscripts Minto found that these valuable records were not available, and that the whole of the Canadian archives were in a state of dire disorder. They were rotting uncatalogued and uncared for in cellars and basements: no one department was responsible for their custody, and no attempt was made to fill up the gaps in them, with the result that they were virtually useless for the purposes of the scholar. In a long letter to Sir Wilfrid, Minto pointed out what appeared to him the iniquity of the neglect: "My researches have aroused in me such interest and concern that I cannot refrain from speaking strongly. Prior to 1882 many papers were committed to the flames; I have heard of large consignments of unsorted documents, some of which were known to be valuable, being removed from the Privy Council Office for the benefit of the paper factories. It is not only in the Government offices that these records exist, but many are scattered throughout the country in the old Hudson's Bay posts, utterly neglected, which are of the greatest historical value. It appears to me that the appointment of a Deputy Keeper of the Records would be of the greatest value to the history of the Dominion, and would effect a substantial saving on the extravagant system which at present exists. For this appointment, both on account of his ability and literary taste, I should like to mention Mr. Doughty, the Parliamentary Librarian, with whom I have been in close touch in connection with the old plans of the defences of Quebec."

Minto pressed the question, with the result that the present Archives building was erected, and the Government laid the foundation of a new system of safeguarding and completing the public records which has grown to-day to be one of the best in the world. He secured for Canada the originals of the despatches to the Governor-Generals, as well as many valuable documents from private muniment rooms. He also took up the matter of the teaching of Canadian history in schools, and, being dissatisfied with the existing text-books, induced the Government to undertake the preparation and issue of documents for Canadian history, of which the Board of Historical Publications of Canada and the brilliant work of Dr. A. S. Doughty were the ultimate fruit.

Minto also interceded with the Prime Minister for the preservation of the Plains of Abraham, having discovered to his horror that it was proposed to desecrate that historic ground by building and road-making, and that Sir Wilfrid had actually signed, without reading it, an order-in-council for the purpose. He at once took the matter up and converted the Prime Minister to his views, so that legislation was passed preserving the Plains for all time as a national memorial.

The Governor-General had an unusual experience one winter in reaching Quebec:--

"Left Government House in the worst blizzard I ever saw. Telegrams from Quebec told us of a terrible storm raging there, but I thought it was best to push through if possible. We arrived at Levis about midnight. The ice-bridge jam gave way last night, and the river was passable only in canoes; the banks were piled with rough ice and fields of icebergs were floating down the river. It is very rare that the ferryboats fail to keep the river open, and canoes are now seldom used. It was a most thrilling experience. We got into our canoe on dry land and were pushed and towed partly over the floes of ice and partly in the open river. We had eight men to each canoe, who paddled in the open water and were wonderfully quick in jumping out and pushing the canoe over the ice, singing French-Canadian songs as they paddled. I would not have missed the passage for anything. In these days of ice-breakers such a crossing is almost unique. At the landing sleighs had been provided for us, and the Snow Shoe Clubs in their costumes escorted us to the Citadel, which we found warm and comfortable."

II

The Governor-General travelled throughout the length and breadth of Canada, covering 113,000 miles during his term of office. Generations of Whig decorum had not killed in him the moss-trooping instincts of Liddesdale; his love of adventure, often of the roughest kind, and of every description of sport, brought him very near to the heart of the country. His bodily fitness and the hard training in which he always kept himself made expeditions possible for him which would have broken up younger men. His old family connections, too, and his share in the little war of 1885 stood him in good stead, and wherever he went he found friends--Border Scots who remembered the Elliots, and men who had been with him at Batoche.

"Arrived at Winnipeg, where we met with a most extraordinary reception. A huge crowd packed the streets, and we passed through a narrow line of people all carrying torches. It is said that Canadians can't cheer, but there was no doubt about it at Winnipeg, and people kept running out of the crowd to shake my hand, Hawick men shouting 'Terribus.'* The enthusiasm continued the whole way to Government House. Winnipeg is intensely Scots: the Mayor in one of his speeches said that though they were very proud to welcome the representative of the Queen, their demonstration was for Lord Melgund, who had fought for them in 1885. . .

* The rallying cry of the men of Hawick.

"Attended church parade in uniform. I marched at the head of the 90th, very full of old recollections of 1885, and with rather a lump in my throat. I was with them so much; they and the Scouts bore all the brunt of the early days of the campaign. It was with a strong party of the 90th that I went, two days after the fight at Fish Creek, to recover the bodies of the men left there. And as we passed the gate of old Fort Garry one could not but think of Wolseley, and Buller, and the Red River Expedition, and all the history they have shared in since then, when there was scarcely anything but the Hudson's Bay Fort and a few nouses with about 200 inhabitants where the great city now stands. In 1885, when I first knew it, the main street was a quagmire, and the population about 25,000. At the last census it was returned at 95,000. Huge buildings, banks, and warehouses rivalling London and New York are springing up everywhere alongside the old wooden shacks of days gone by. It has become a vast railway centre with a hundred miles of sidings. It seems a fairy tale."*

* It was from Winnipeg four years later that Minto received his most touching farewell. The Town Hall was illuminated with "Au revoir, Minto": the Governor-General's train stood for some time in the station, and the crowd made the most remarkable demonstration. Thousands surrounded the car; they climbed on the wheels, on the footboard, and clung to the door. Again and again Minto had to appear; he thanked them and tried to bid them good-bye, but they refused to disperse until the train slowly moved out of the station amid ringing cheers.

The Mintos paid two visits to the United States. The first was in October 1899:--

"We left Ottawa and arrived at New York on 1st October, to be the guests of Colonel Roosevelt, Governor of New York State, in order to attend the International Yacht Race between Sir Thomas Lipton's Shamrock and the United States yacht Columbia. Roosevelt's home is Sagamore Hill, Long Island, a small and unpretentious house. . . . In the afternoon I took a walk with Colonel Roosevelt, who is quite one of the most remarkable men I ever met, bubbling over with energy of mind and body; hardly ever stops talking, a great sense of humour, and an excellent raconteur; I should think afraid of nothing physically or morally, and absolutely straightforward. Though a great sportsman--the house is full of magnificent heads--he has much literary talent, and has written many books, sporting and historical, and is considered to be in the running for the Presidency. He is rather fat and short, with a bull-dog expression, and a way of gnashing his teeth when eager in conversation. I delighted in him."

During one walk Roosevelt led Minto to a precipitous cliff and pointed out a zigzag path by which he advised him to descend, saying that he himself preferred climbing down the face of the rock. To his surprise Minto at once volunteered to accompany him, and the Governor of New York State and the Governor-General of Canada raced together to the bottom. At the close of the visit their host, on wishing Lady Minto good-bye, confided to her that he had dreaded their arrival, his idea of an English peer being somebody "wedded to a frock coat and a tall hat, who had rarely left the London pavements."

The second crossing of the border took place in May 1903. During one of his arduous official tours in Western Ontario--when it was no exception to visit from five to six towns in one day, inspecting every charitable institution of importance, replying to a dozen or more addresses, and holding receptions of nearer thousands than hundreds--Minto was invited to visit Detroit. The journal contains this account:--

"Our reception at Detroit took us entirely by surprise. We found Colonel Hecker's yacht full of lovely ladies in the latest Paris fashions, and on landing we found a carriage, and the Mayor, waiting to escort us. The streets were cleared of all traffic, and the Mayor said there were some 150,000 people along the line of our route. Every window was crowded, and our reception was enthusiastic. 'The Fighting First,' a regular regiment home the day before from the Philippines, headed the procession in khaki, then the National Guard, then the Naval Reserve, all in open columns of companies. A small boy marched alongside of our carriage yelling: 'What's the matter with Lady Minto--she's all right,' after the custom of the New World. After marching through the chief parts of the town, the troops formed line along the magnificent principal street, and the bands played 'God save the King ' as we passed. We were then taken to the hotel, where a deputation from both Houses of the Legislature of Michigan State presented me with an address of welcome, unanimously voted by both Houses, for which I expressed my thanks. The Mayor made a very nice speech, to which I replied, saying that I could only suppose the enthusiasm of my reception was intended as a testimony of friendship for the King whom I was so proud to represent. Then followed a supper and a reception of the leading citizens, when we were presented to the officers of the 'Fighting First.' The City Hall was illuminated with a 'Welcome' to us, and then we returned in our yacht to our own side. It was a most remarkable ceremony from first to last. Everything perfectly organized, and I am at a loss to account for the enthusiasm. Whether it was all the American wish to lead the world, even as to receptions, or whether there was any inspiration from Washington, or whether the large Canadian population of Detroit had anything to do with it, I don't know; but it is impossible to think that there was not some friendly feeling underlying it all."

The journal throughout his term of office is full of notes of camping expeditions, sometimes part of an official tour, sometimes snatched in the intervals of business. Twice with his family Minto camped on the shores of Qu'appelle Lake, celebrated for its duck shooting; but what he enjoyed most was revisiting the scenes of the Riel Rebellion and living over again his old campaigning days.

"Moved to Edmonton during the night. Received an address on the hill above the Saskatchewan on which the town stands. The beech woods a mass of yellow. The escort must have been a pretty sight as they crossed the bridge and rose the hill. Just as I got off my horse a man in the crowd shouted out, 'We'll give the Indian war whoop for our fighting Governor-General;' they gave three cheers and then yelled the war whoop. I suppose I, and those in the Riel Rebellion in 1885, will be the last to hear the Indian war whoop in battle.

"We lunched with Bishop Grandin, a delightful old man, at the Mission at Fort Albert, where I met an old soldier who told me that he had served with me in the Mounted Infantry in Egypt in 1882. Just as I was leaving a priest came up and spoke to me: 'Had I ever seen him before?' I said, 'Yes, I think in a cottage at Batoche fifteen years ago.' He then told me that he was the priest to whom I gave a safe-conduct and a message to the rebels. I remembered it all perfectly, and had always a hope that the rebels might surrender without further loss of life.

"Three curious things have happened to me today. The war whoop, the old soldier, and the priest.

"(Batoche) Strolled with Mary and the girls to the church. The last time I saw it it was full of our wounded, and I had given orders for them to be ready to move at once if we had to fall back. Places and scenes came vividly before me. . . .

"We had a most interesting day too at Fish Creek. We lunched in the hollow leading to the ravine where I was twice fired at and where Middleton had his cap shot through. I was told long afterwards that it was Gabriel Dumont who fired at us. I walked over to Père Moulin's house in the moonlight, and had a last look at the church and the open ground in front of it, so full of memories. When I last saw it the bush to the right was on fire, and things were not going well. I went into Batoche's house and saw the room in which poor Jack French was killed, shot through the window. He was a fine gallant fellow and much liked. . . . A day full of interest, but rather sad; recollections of hard but very happy times and many old friends. Our camp here has been luxurious, very different from the old campaigning days. Mary is sitting here beside me. Our tent opens towards the beautiful Saskatchewan."

In September 1904 Minto introduced a new feature into the usual autumn programme, starting with Maude, and an escort of North-West Mounted Police commanded by Gilpin Brown, on a 400-mile ride from Edmonton to Saskatoon, in order to acquaint himself with the conditions of the country:--

"The prairie looking lovely in all the glory of autumn tints, golden beech, and crimson-leaf dwarf rose, and the magnificent outline of the Rockies always in the background. My staff laugh at me because I say that if I began life over again I would choose the Bow River country for a home. To me, too, even the flatter prairie has a charm.

"September 21st.--Struck our camp for the last time. In all probability my last camp on the prairie. Such a pretty place on the banks of the North Saskatchewan. Last night brilliant moonlight--a couple of coyotes speaking to each other not far off, and the rush of a flight of ducks over my tent about midnight. It is a dreadful pang leaving it all. The population of these parts is entirely old country. It is curious to find refined ladies and gentlemen in this rough Western life, but they are splendid, full of ideas and energy, and the more I see the more I admire the vanguard of the best of our people, and the more I dislike the self-satisfied luxury of home.

The people of the Far West, the Indians, the Mounted Police, are generally far better fellows."

III

To the wonderful Canadian rivers Minto and his family owed their chief enjoyment. Those mighty waterways, with their relentless currents and snowy rapids, cast a spell over them. River expeditions were made almost every day during the summer, sailing, canoeing, or rowing, and on more than one occasion at considerable personal risk. Unexpected squalls would arise, when the waves would well-nigh swamp the frail canoe, or the sail would hardly be lowered in time. The calm cool evenings on the Ottawa, after the great heat of the day, with the sun setting in a pageant of crimson, brought rest and contentment. Minto could handle a canoe as well as any half-breed, and he never forgot his "wet-bob" exploits at Eton. "I have just returned from dining at the Shack on the Gatineau," he wrote to his wife, "Lawless, Hanlon and some rowing men, Bill Lascelles and self. Hanlon, as I dare say you know, was champion sculler of the world for years, probably the best that ever rowed. You would have been amused this afternoon: of course they did not know I knew anything about sculling. Well, Hanlon came up in a light racing boat, and after dinner Bill, goodness knows why, said he must go out in it. I thought it odd if he knew nothing about it to venture in an outrigger with a sliding seat. However, out he went, and sort of floated into the middle of the river, where he became powerless to move either way, and Lawless had to go out in a canoe and somehow bring him in. So I thought I would give them a show. I believe they thought me mad, and that I was bound to capsize, so I handed my watch to Hanlon, who evidently considered it all up with me, and quietly seated myself, being certain I should feel just as I did thirty years ago. I made them push me out, and I fancy they were utterly overcome by surprise at the first few strokes I took, when they all burst into wild applause. In a few minutes I felt I was quite in good form, and left them all gaping with wonder!"

One of the recognized Ottawa expeditions was to shoot the lumber slides on the Chaudiere Falls, a comparatively tame performance; but to add zest to the exploit the Governor-General was advised to use a lumberman's boat instead of a prosaic raft. Arrangements were accordingly made, and the Mintos, accompanied by the Drummonds and the Grenfells,* embarked above the Falls, quite unaware of the extreme danger of the adventure. Once in the boat it was too late to draw back. The lock gates were open, the river was exceptionally high, the current carried them off, and soon they were plunging down a drop of twenty feet into the surging rapids of the Falls. The nose of the boat was completely submerged, and the two men who were attempting to guide her were powerless. The torrent took command and flung the boat like a cork first one way then the other, till, with its drenched occupants, it was providentially carried into calmer waters.

* Lord and Lady Desborough.

In the early spring of 1902 Minto had another narrow escape from drowning. When walking one day on the frozen Ottawa River the ice suddenly gave way with him and he found himself in the water:--

"At first I thought it was only the snow crust, but soon realized it was more than that. I could see the solid ice about three feet below the surface, and close to it was the unmistakable black-looking deep water, just under my head. I fell full length, and luckily the crust supported my arm, but on the right side I was wet up to the neck. I cautiously raised myself on to the crust on my hands and knees and was then all right. I must have struck an air hole connected with the deep water, and only thinly covered. It does not do to take liberties with the Ottawa River!"

It was a great grief to Minto that the fishing on the Cascapedia was no longer the perquisite of the Governor-General; for the enjoyment of this sport he had to be beholden to private owners, or to accept the hospitality of the American clubs who had purchased the fishing of many Canadian rivers. The luxury of the newcomers seemed to him to suburbanize the sport. "Very hospitable, certainly," the journal notes, "but an unworkmanlike look about them; very smart sporting clothes, looking as if they never had been and never would be rained on. X himself in a grey hat and white puggaree, variegated waistcoat, new putties under white low gaiters, and brand new leather boots. He would have startled them on the Tweed." Minto loved the river, frozen or running free; the whole family skated, Lady Minto brilliantly, and during their term of office the Minto Skating Club was inaugurated, which has since produced competitors for the world's championship. Throughout the winter there were weekly skating parties, but the favourite entertainments were by moonlight, when the bonfires blazed and the rinks were brilliant with fairy lights. There would be an occasional tramp with the Snow-shoers in their picturesque costumes to the rhythm of French-Canadian songs. Minto also took up ski-ing with enthusiasm, and with Lady Minto and the children was often seen careering over the snow-clad hills at Fairy Lake.*

* As a Scotsman Minto was also a curler, and had the pleasure of entertaining the Scottish team that came over to play Canada. In the dry and electric air of the Canadian winter it is possible to light the gas by placing a finger on the jet. This was pointed out to one of the visitors, who duly performed the feat, and observed that "it cowed a'." "When I get hame," he said, "I'll hae some queer things to tell the wife, but I'll no tell her that. She would say I had been drinkiin'."

No sport came amiss to the Governor-General, and an adventure while on a moose-hunt in the Matawa district of Ontario is described in a letter to his wife:--

"We started at 8:30 a.m. through nice open bush. I got a shot at a moose in the afternoon, and thought I had killed him, but he went on. He was close in front of us, but we could not quite manage to get up to him. As it was getting late we thought we had better make for camp; the guide assured me we should get the moose the next day, so we started for home. We tramped along for some time, but before long I was convinced that neither of the guides knew in the least where we were; however, we struggled on due north, steering by the compass. At last we came down to a little lake; it was getting dark, and the guide, Frank Le Claire, pulled up, looked at me and said, 'We must make fire.'"

It is a pretty dismal feeling to be utterly lost in these huge forests. We had practically nothing to eat, and very thin coats on, though we luckily had our sweaters. We had eight small biscuits left from our lunch, some tea, and a spoonful of whisky in my flask. There was nothing for it but 'to make fire,' and the guide at once tackled a huge dead pine with his small axe, an enormous tree which came down with a tremendous crash. It was rotten all through, and the hollow tree formed a sort of draught chimney, at the end of which we lighted our fire, and kept it burning all night. It was certainly an unpleasant experience, bitterly cold, but fine, the new moon just showing itself. The guides cut us some spruce boughs, and we lay down on these, getting roasted on one side so that our things scorched, and frozen on the other, so that one had to keep revolving like a kitchen spit.

"The morning came at last; we started again at 7:30 a.m., still steering north. A very rough walk till we hit a lumber trail. Soon we got down to the lake, doubtfully frozen over, and nervously crossed till within a few yards of the other side; but seeing no signs of the trail in the bush, and not knowing where in the world we might get to if we still went on our course, we decided to turn back to our bivouac and take up our old trail of the day before and hunt it out if we could stick the distance, as we knew it must eventually get us home unless snow came and obliterated our marks. About 4 o'clock, after tramping all day through the snow, we heard a shout, and to our intense delight found that one of the guides had come out from the camp to meet us, bringing whisky and sandwiches. We had practically eaten nothing since 12 o'clock the day before, and had had tremendously hard walking, up to our knees in snow. Another hour brought us into the camp. I do not think I have ever had such a hard time, and have never been so played out; we had been on the go for about 34 hours. I wondered how much further it was possible for us to keep on. To-day we felt we must have a rest, but the guides went out, and the Indians have just brought in my moose, a splendid head measuring 49, and the whole establishment is wild with excitement."

Canada is not famous as a hunting country, and Minto had few chances of indulging in his favourite pursuit. On one occasion, however, shortly after his arrival in the country, he was out riding with his children--

"When, to our intense surprise, we heard hounds running in the cemetery, and five and a half couple crossed the road, running hard, with a tremendous cry, and not a soul with them." The promise of this ghostly hunt was not fulfilled, but the journal records one day with the hounds at St. Anne's, near Montreal: "What recollections of old days! Red coats and all the panoply of the chase! We found in a large wood and went away very fast for twenty minutes quite straight and lost him. Found again late in the afternoon, over very difficult country, stone walls, and stiff timber with no end of ditches. My horse was the cleverest I ever rode. A very good day's sport!" The gusto with which he recounts the details of the run showed that the passion of the old Limber days had not abated.

IV

In June 1902 Minto returned to England on a flying visit to attend the Coronation, where he was just in time to prevent the announcement of a peerage for Sir Wilfrid Laurier which Sir Wilfrid had refused. He found it difficult to get any serious talk with the Ministers.

"They are generally head over ears in work and interested only in their own departments. Mr. Chamberlain's accident too has prevented my having much conversation with him. He himself has done a great work in developing the colonial and imperial connection, but I doubt if he is in touch with colonial sentiment--I mean, if he entirely realizes the sentimental affection for the motherland, or judges fairly of the unwillingness of colonial statesmen to commit themselves hastily to an imperial policy. He appears to be a hard-headed man of business, bent on the idea of utilizing our colonial possessions for imperial benefit. . . . He is a very strong man but not a sympathetic one, and therefore his colonial administration is not without risk. I suppose my eyes have been opened by my life on the other side of the Atlantic, for I confess I feel that there is much that is very insular at home in ideas and knowledge of mankind."

About military affairs Minto was pessimistic. He thought Lord Roberts incapable of carrying through any real army reforms, and the conditions of the War Office seemed to him primeval chaos. "Kitchener said at luncheon the other day at the Duke of Connaught's, 'One could run a War Office elsewhere for a year without the War Office finding one out.' There have only been telephones at the War Office for the last few months, for fear, it is said, that some one should say something down them of which there was no record!" *

* The journal for 1902 closes with this entry: "This year has been full of events; the Peace, the Coronation, and all its sensational interest, and latterly the completion of the Pacific Cable and the 'All-round-the-World' message to me, and still more Marconi's wonderful success, and my wireless message to the King. For the future Sir Wilfrid's delicate health makes me

anxious both in a public and a private sense, for he is a great friend, and a stormy session is approaching. . . . And now we shall advance at midnight for the next campaign. The bells are ringing in the New Year, and Mary wishes me a happy one."

In April 1903 Mr. Chamberlain, in terms of high compliment, begged Minto to remain another year in Canada, since the office was in reality a six-year appointment, though custom had curtailed it to five. Minto consented, as he was bound to do, especially as Sir Wilfrid Laurier added his entreaties. That same month we find the first mention of the possibility of his going to India as Lord Curzon's successor. Mr. Chamberlain referred to it in his letter, and Sir Wilfrid spoke privately to the Governor-General, saying that he would do all in his power to urge the appointment, adding that Minto had "his foot in the stirrup, if he was not yet in the saddle," and that he would be glad to see Lord Palmerston's advice followed--"When in difficulty send an Elliot." There had been other suggestions as to his future, one of which, the Embassy at Washington, he had unhesitatingly rejected. India appealed to him on every ground of past connection and present-day opportunity; but it was never his habit to ask for things, and for the next eighteen months the subject dropped. Lady Minto, who was in England in the summer of 1904, reported that the inclination seemed to be to send a Cabinet Minister, somebody like Lord Selborne, and that Lord Curzon had told her that no man over fifty should be appointed, as the post was the most arduous in the Empire. The letters Minto wrote to his wife during these brief absences are perhaps the most full and characteristic of all his correspondence, for from her he had no reservations, and to her he could reveal much which his natural reticence withheld from others.

The extra year of office passed, and in August 1904 came the last state function, the prorogation of Parliament, when the retiring Governor-General received an address of thanks from both Houses, Lady Minto taking her place on the dais beside him, and the speeches of Sir Wilfrid Laurier and Sir Robert Borden constituted such a tribute as no man could listen to unmoved. Minto had before this been privately informed that his successor would be his brother-in-law, Lord Grey. He paid a farewell visit to Quebec--"Our last night at the Citadel; very sad; everything full of old recollections"--and then started with his wife and eldest daughter for a final trip to the North-West and British Columbia. The tour was saddened by a horrible railway accident near Sintaluta, in which five lives were lost and the Governor-General's party had a narrow escape. The journal, amidst its lists of addresses and receptions, falls often into a mood of wistful regret, for Minto was too deeply in love with the country to leave it easily. When he records "Struck our camp for the last time--my last camp in all human probability"--it is the reflection of a man who, in the great spaces of the prairie and amongst the pioneers of a new land, had found a life after his own heart.

On Friday, 18th November, the party sailed in the Tunisian from Quebec, after a trying time of presentations and farewells. There had been far more in the leavetaking than a formal ceremony, for there was affection on both sides, and if Minto was loth to go, Canada was loth to lose him. Says the journal:--

"At sea. So our life in Canada is over at last, and it has been a great wrench parting from so many friends and leaving a country which I love and which has been very full of interest to me. We have had nothing but 'good-byes' for weeks. . . . We left Government House, Ottawa, for the last time in brilliant sunshine, and drove to the Armoury, where I received a farewell address, Mary afterwards being presented with a beautiful diamond maple leaf by Belcourt on behalf of the city. Her speech in expressing her thanks was perfect. The station was crowded with our friends; the inside of the car was decorated with flowers, and the band played 'Auld Lang Syne' as we moved off. We arrived at Quebec and drove to the Frontenac as guests of the city. The last evening we gave a banquet, and our guests accompanied us to the wharf through an avenue of lighted torches, and amidst cheering and waving of handkerchiefs we put off at 10 p.m., the old Citadel blazing away her nineteen guns.

"So ends our career in Canada. Innumerable addresses and speeches, but it has been a very affectionate farewell, and one cannot but feel very pleased at what has been said on every side. I cannot write a memoir now, but the six years have been far from ordinary ones, very full of history, imperial and Canadian, with much that is fraught with meaning for the future. And now the task is over, and I am grateful for the appreciation of the country I have worked for; and through it all Mary has been more than splendid."

Minto arrived at Liverpool and found a host of friends to greet him. Mr. Alfred Lyttelton had succeeded Mr. Chamberlain at the Colonial Office, and his official dispatch was cordial in its tribute:--

"The six years during which you have represented the Sovereign in Canada have been marked by events of great importance to the Dominion and the Empire at large, including a war in which the military forces of the United Kingdom and Canada acted together in an imperial cause. These years have also been marked by a splendid development in the prosperity and greatness of Canada, and His Majesty's Government has been glad to recognize that during this period the highest office in the Dominion has been held by one upon whose discretion, ability, and courageous sense of duty they could confidently rely on all occasions. . . . I also note with pleasure the appreciation of the admirable qualities and services of the Countess of Minto, shown by the Canadian Parliament and people."

It had been a happy time, and Minto brought away from it that legacy of delectable memories which is the reward of the traveller. Lady Minto, in a paper in the

National Review in March 1905, tried to tell something of the wonders of the great Dominion. "With vivid distinctness scenes too numerous to recount come back to me. I see again the foaming waters of the St. John River racing in wild career through turbulent rapids for 45 miles to the Saguenay, my frail canoe tossing like a leaf on the mighty stream, gliding swiftly past the treacherous whirlpools and the sharp rocks, safe in the skilful hands of the half-breeds. And now I am galloping once more on the boundless prairie, over that fragrant carpet woven of wild spring flowers, elated by the pure air and transparent atmosphere, exulting in the freedom of my life. And now the silence of the night has fallen, and in the awe-inspiring forests or in the sweet stillness of the prairie the camp sleeps, watched over by a myriad stars." Minto, no less than his wife, was intoxicated by the beauty of Canada's deep winters and riotous summers and flaming autumns. To a Border Scot the land provided on a magnificent scale the fir woods, the clear waters, and the wide spaces of his own countryside. With all classes of the people he felt an immediate kinship, and he could appraise the quality alike of an Indian chief and a Montreal lawyer, a Scots settler in Manitoba and a Quebec habitant. He shared in their hopes, rejoiced in their triumphs, and mourned with them in their sorrows. When the skating tragedy took place at Ottawa in December 1901, of which Mr. Mackenzie King has written in his Secret of Heroism, it was the Governor-General who was out at dawn next day helping to recover the bodies. The humanity learned hi the democratic Borders, and ripened by years of racing and soldiering, enabled him to meet men of every rank and breed with friendliness and understanding.

Minto gave much to Canada, but he received much in return. He was enabled to look within the mechanism of the constitutional State. His party politics, never cherished with much conviction, were mellowed and liberalized by an insight into the eternal difficulties of all parties and their curious alikeness in fundamentals. He acquired perspective, and learned to separate the accidental from the essential. His imperialism, which had been a dream, became a reasoned faith. More and more he came to value the moral qualities in statesmanship above the intellectual; for, since democracy among men of British blood is practically the same whatever party governs, excellence is found rather in character than in creed. His flair for the true constitutional path, an inheritance from his Whig forbears, developed into a sure instinct, which was often in advance of that of Ministers both in Canada and at home. Earlier in his life he had disliked the game of politics, now he came to see the gravity of it, and he exerted himself to ensure that it was played wisely and honestly. There was much in the Canadian parties that he disliked, but he saw that reform could not come merely by reprobation, and he did his best to set before the youth with which he came in contact a high, if undogmatic and unpharisaic, ideal of public service. To Mr. Mackenzie King, then a young man on the threshold of his career, Minto wrote:--

"Though I thanked you for your speech a few days ago, I have always meant to write and tell you how glad I am to have a copy of it. If you will allow me to say so, the speech was a most eloquent one, and not only that, but it gave expression to opinions which, in my estimation, it is impossible to over-value. To me it seems all-important that the young men who are coming on, and who will make the history of Canada, should speak out clearly and decidedly in their insistence on the manliness and purity of public life. Nothing, in my opinion, can be more unfortunate to a country than that its people should be ready to accept as a matter of course a low standard of public and political morality.

"I know how difficult it is from the nature of things for people to speak out as they would often like to do. At the same time I sometimes think that public opinion in Canada is too apathetic, and not prone enough to be outspoken on public affairs. Many of the best brains in the country are no doubt engaged in business and professions and are not available for political careers--but even they can make their voices heard; and I venture to think that more of them might be inclined to enter the political lists than do at present. Anyhow I am thoroughly with you in the all-importance of the pure public spirit of rising Canada."

Minto's main task had been the harmonizing of forces which might well have clashed--the nationalism of Canada and the new self-conscious imperialism of Britain. Largely owing to his patience and tact any shadow of conflict was avoided. In the matter which he had most at heart, imperial defence, his prescient warnings were indeed neglected, but Canada was enabled to advance towards her national destiny unhampered by a too strait imperial bond, while at the same time the more potent and delicate ties with the mother-country were notably strengthened. In his term of office he had to deal especially with two distinguished figures who had a real formative effect on his mind. Of the two Mr. Chamberlain's influence was perhaps the lesser. Minto respected him extremely, and shared most of his views; to him the Colonial Office without Mr. Chamberlain was like the War Office without Lord Wolseley; but in temperament the two had little in common except courage. Their relationship was one of mutual loyalty and respect, but scarcely of intimacy. With Sir Wilfrid Laurier, on the other hand, Minto frequently disagreed, and was often exasperated. He believed that excessive temporizing for the sake of party unity was bad tactics even for that purpose, and he had little patience with the type of mind which seemed to be content to govern adroitly from day to day without any policy worthy of the name. But it is impossible to read his letters and journals without realizing that there was growing up in him a feeling that after all Sir Wilfrid might be right-- that in a new land, with so many incompatible elements inside her borders, the slow game might be the wise game, that the time was not ripe for a clenched and riveted formula of Empire, and that the true solution must be left to the processes of time. At any rate, lover of decided action as he was, in his public conduct the Whig element in Minto dominated the Liddesdale impetuosity, and it would appear that history has vindicated both him and his Prime Minister. Of the affection between the two men there was no question. Sir Wilfrid's graciousness and charm won the heart of one who was always a lover of gentleness. Once Lady Minto, speaking of him to Mr. Chamberlain, said that, whatever his foibles, he was a great gentleman. "I would rather," ran the reply, "do business with a cad who knows his own mind." Minto would not have assented. Under no circumstances did he believe in the cad.

BOOK THREE

CHAPTER NINE

VICEROY OF INDIA, 1905-6

AFTER his six strenuous Canadian years Minto hoped for a rest at home, and longed especially for that Border country life which lay always nearest to his heart. But a retiring Governor-General is not readily permitted to sink into the ease of a private citizen; he became the quarry of a thousand organizations in quest of a president or an apologist; and even when he escaped to Minto he found leisure hard to come by. He was busy with improvements on his estate, including the installation of electric light and the building of a new wing, and these, with a little hunting and a number of visits, filled his time in the winter and spring of 1904-5. In May he went to Rome, at the request of the Board of Agriculture, as one of the British delegates to the International Agricultural Congress, and after a brief stay returned in July to politics and dinners in London, including a banquet to his old tutor, Dr. Warre, on his retirement from the headmastership of Eton. By the 12th of August he was back at Minto, filling his days, like Sir Walter Scott, with the overseeing of his improvements. The place was in the hands of workmen, and he and his wife were installed in the factor's little house at Cleughhead.

Absorbed in domestic plans, and already half drawn into the machine of British affairs, Minto had almost forgotten the possibility of the Indian viceroyalty which had been mooted a year ago before he left Canada. There seemed to be many candidates, and it had been his fashion to wait in these matters upon the hand of Providence. Therefore it was with a real surprise that, on the morning of 18th August, as he was walking down to Minto before breakfast, he opened a letter from Mr. St. John Brodrick, which told him that Lord Curzon had resigned and that he was nominated as his successor. In the garden afterwards, when the hot August sun was beginning to drive the mist from the hills, he told his wife. "The greatest appointment I have ever hoped for," he wrote in his journal, "and still what a pang to leave the dear old place again--and all the difficulties about the children. Mary took it so well. I know she feels the same as I do, and it is a recognition of all her good work quite as much as of anything I have ever done. But it is a very high trial."

The appointment was to be curiously informal in every detail. Minto never heard a word directly from the Prime Minister. The Prince and Princess of Wales were on the eve of departing for India, and it was arranged that Lord Curzon should meet them at Bombay, and that he should receive the incoming Viceroy in the same place instead of in Calcutta--a departure from precedent fraught with possibilities of contretemps. Minto paid a visit to the King at Balmoral, and then set himself to the exhausting business of farewells. He found it hard to tear himself from his home, which he had just recovered and beautified, for the spell of the Border grows the stronger for absence, and many of the old folk about the place he could not expect in the course of nature to see again. He had the regulation talks with Mr. Balfour, and with Mr. Brodrick, the Secretary of State for India, but as the Conservative administration was tottering to its fall these were naturally of a slighter character than usual. It was tacitly recognized that in a month or two he would be the servant of a very different government. He took counsel of the Nestor of imperial administration, Lord Cromer, "the only one among all the public men I know who has impressed me as a really big man." There were the usual dinners--one, especially, composed entirely of old Eton, Cambridge, Army, and hunting friends, when Minto very modestly set out his hopes. "I am succeeding," he said, "a brilliant ruler who, in perfecting the machinery of state, has given evidence of abilities and talents which no successor can hope to emulate. And yet my racing days have taught me that many a race has been won by giving the horse a rest in his gallops." On 2nd November the Mintos left London, almost on the same day as seven years before they had sailed from Liverpool for Canada, and on the afternoon of 17th November arrived at Bombay.

II

When in 1806 the first Earl of Minto went to India as Governor-General, it was in succession--save for the brief interludes of Cornwallis and Sir George Barlow--to the great era of expansion under the Marquis Wellesley which had made the British Government paramount throughout the peninsula. His task was to consolidate what had been won, to join the raw edges which are left by change, and to make of the new order of things a harmonious and organic polity. The duty which fell to his descendant a century later was not dissimilar. The history of India does not permit itself to be summarized in a paragraph, but it is necessary to glance briefly at the decade which preceded Minto's arrival.

The age of the conquering Viceroys ended with Dalhousie, and with him, too, began the succession of rulers who have given their minds to the development of the wealth of the land and the prosperity of the Indian people, for even the great reforming regime of Lord William Bentinck had been devoted rather to the elimination of old abuses than to positive advances in what the modern world calls civilization. The Mutiny obscured for a moment the work of the greatest figure among the Viceroys, who completed the task of Wellesley and continued the policy of Bentinck, but the foundations remained, and the India of to-day is in the main Dalhousie's creation. The post-Mutiny governors, after the transference in 1858 of all India to the British Crown, had the same types of problem to face, which they dealt with after their individual fashions. They had the permanent question of frontier defence--the belt of wild tribes in the mountains of the North-West, the uncertain Power of Afghanistan, and the potential menace of Russia from beyond the trans-Himalayan deserts. They had the difficult business of finance, complicated by the falling rupee, and an intricate group of economic problems, dating from Dalhousie's reconstruction. They had the more purely administrative questions, the efficiency of the civil service, the degree to which decentralization was possible, the nature and strength of the armed forces of the Crown, both British and native, and their relations to the civil government. And behind all, they had the problem of the Indian people, their education, the effect upon them of Western ideas, the question of how far and to what end they should be trained in political responsibility. Different Viceroys concentrated on different aspects of their task; Lytton was preoccupied with the frontier, Northbrook with finance, Ripon with the application to India of Gladstonian Liberalism, Dufferin with administrative reforms; and to the idiosyncrasies of each must be added the idiosyncrasies of the various British Governments which they served. But behind all the transitory viceregal race there was the continuity of the greatest civil service since the days of the Roman Empire, a body of highly-trained and devoted men, working with a vast accumulated body of knowledge to aid them and in the spirit of a high and unselfish tradition. India was virtually a bureaucracy of the most efficient type, for the machine was stronger than any Viceroy, great as were the Viceroy's powers, and far stronger than even the most vigilant Secretary of State. For, since the passing away of the East India Company, Britain had infinitely less knowledge of her Indian dependency. In the old days at each renewal of the company's charter there had been a more or less thorough inquisition into the state of Indian affairs, but now the home country was content to trust to the India Office and the Viceroy, and an Indian discussion in the House of Commons became a byword for apathy and dullness. The mood of the Indian people could only be guessed at even by the well-informed at home, and its aspirations became little more than rhetorical speculations in party debate.

In 1899 Lord Curzon, then scarcely forty years of age, succeeded Lord Elgin. He had imagination and enthusiasm, complete self-confidence, a high courage, and an industry and a speed which left his colleagues panting behind him. This is not the place to enlarge on that remarkable term of office. To each of the standing problems of Indian rule he brought his own weighty contribution. He continued the policy begun by Lord Elgin on the North-West frontier, withdrew British garrisons from the tribal zone, putting tribal levies in their place, and created a new North-West frontier province. By comprehensive schemes of irrigation, by reforms in the collection of land revenue, and by the institution of co-operative credit societies, he laboured to put agriculture on a securer basis. He overhauled the whole administrative machine, reformed the police, lopped off dead wood from the civil service, and checked that addiction to paperasserie which is the foible of even the best bureaucracy. Inspired with the romance of India's history, he showed a reverent concern for her great public memorials. He was aware of the growth of the selfgovernment movement, which, from the small beginnings of the first Indian National Congress of 1885, had now become a power, and, believing that the ills caused by a smattering of Western education could only be cured by a better and fuller knowledge, he strove to broaden the whole educational system, and in spite of much opposition carried his Universities Act of 1904. To a casual observer the spectacular and controversial character of some of his reforms was apt to obscure the enormous mass of sound and painstaking work, the beneficial effect of which was beyond question.

But the wisest changes, if they are many and sudden, will produce a revulsion. On the long view, it may fairly be said that Lord Curzon had provided for India a diet which, though wholesome in quality, was too large in quantity for a normal digestion. No Viceroy had ever sought more earnestly the welfare of the Indian people, but there comes a time in the development of a race when they are less grateful for wise ruling than for permission to blunder on their own account. He had underrated the dissatisfaction which a cyclone of reform from above would produce not only among the cruder vested interests of the Indian bar and Indian journalism, but among even honest and public-spirited citizens. The event which caused his resignation was, indeed, a comparatively trivial matter as far as Indian policy was concerned, being no more than a difference of opinion with Lord Kitchener as to the method by which military proposals should be presented to the Viceroy's Executive Council--Lord Kitchener demanding a single department presided over by the Commander-in-Chief as an ordinary member of Council, and Lord Curzon objecting that the civil power would thereby be deprived of independent military advice, and all military authority would be concentrated in the hands of the Commander-in-Chief. It may be fantastic to argue, as some have done, that Lord Kitchener's victory was responsible for the breakdown of the Indian army system ten years later in Mesopotamia, but it is doubtful whether much was gained by the change either in administrative efficiency or economy. Lord Curzon was tired and out of health, and a difference which might easily have been settled was allowed to become a clash of adamantine principles. More serious was the other step which the Viceroy took in his last year of office. The Presidency of Bengal was proving unwieldy for a single provincial government, and Lord Curzon decided to separate the flat wet plains and jungles of the eastern section and combine them with the province of Assam. This gave the Mohammedans a majority in the new province, and thereby inflamed the Hindus of Bengal, who saw in it a menace to their religious preponderance, and to the importance of Calcutta. The cry arose that the Bengali nation had been insulted and split in twain, and, the sensational triumph of Japan over Russia having kindled the race-consciousness of the East, in the autumn of 1905 a very pretty campaign began of boycott and agitation.

The first Minto had followed on the stirring times of Wellesley, and had rightly hoped for a period of peace and internal development, which he did not obtain. His great-grandson entered upon office with the same hopes, and was to be doomed to the same disappointment. In India it is unsafe at the best to forecast the future. "No prudent man," said Dalhousie, as he left with the seal of death on him, "would venture to predict a long continuance of peace in India. . . . Insurrection may arise like an exhalation from the earth;" and his successor, Canning, speaking at a farewell banquet in England, declared in prophetic words: "I wish for a peaceful time of office. But I cannot forget that in the sky of India, serene as it is, a small cloud may arise, no larger than a man's hand, but which, growing larger and larger, may at last threaten to burst and overwhelm us with ruin." Already the cloud was larger than a man's hand. There were the smouldering embers in Bengal, rapidly being fanned into flame; there was a general unsettlement of men's minds owing to a plethora of sudden changes, the vigour of which had not perhaps been softened by tactfulness in method. Peace and quiet might be what India needed, but it was far from certain that they were what she would choose. From the beginning of his term of office it was clear that the land stood at the parting of the ways, and that it lay with the new Viceroy to make decisions as momentous as any taken by his predecessors.

In Canada Minto had learned the duty of a self-effacing governor, quick to understand the nuances of constitutionalism, and exercising his power by suggestion and counsel. His new position was very different, for he was in a land remote from the forms and spirit of Western democracy, wielding through his Council an executive authority far greater than that of an ordinary monarch. His business was to govern as well as to reign. His position was not only the most responsible in the overseas British Empire, but by far the most onerous, and its laboriousness had been increased by Lord Curzon's passion for drawing into his hands the minutest details. In addition to the normal routine which filled most of the hours of a working day, he must exercise a personal influence, for in the East the personal factor is omnipotent, journeying throughout the length of the land, to meet and learn from every class and condition. He must be patient and tactful and urbane, for in recent years many nerves had been frayed and tempers ruffled. He must not become so immersed in detail as to miss seeing the wood for the trees, for his first duty was the long view. As Minto reflected upon his burden it must have occurred to him that at last his ambition had been gratified, and that he had found a form of soldiering. The position of a Viceroy is like that of a general; he has to forecast the campaign, to take in the last resort great decisions alone, to foster the moral of his army, which is the three hundred millions of India, and to check ruthlessly in the common interest any impulse to anarchy. The words which his great-grandfather used a century earlier must have often recurred to his memory, as a reminder of the solemnity of his charge: "I entreat them to be persuaded that no man of honour at the head of a government will ever compromise with revolt; he has no option but to maintain the contest or abandon his trust and fly from his duty." And he may well have reflected that the giving effect to this maxim might be for a far-sighted and liberal mind one of the most difficult of human tasks.

III

The arrival at Bombay was an embarrassing affair, with Lord Curzon waiting on the eve of departure and the officials of the Bombay Government unable to cope with a situation which had no precedent. Minto landed late in the afternoon, too late, it was judged, for a public reception. He had a long talk that evening with Lord Curzon, who left early next morning, when the deferred public reception of the new Viceroy at last took place. Minto was conducted to the Secretariat, where the warrant of appointment was read, and he took his seat as Viceroy, but the whole ceremony was something of a muddle. The subject may be dismissed with the dry note which is to be found in the official report on his administration: "These proceedings were not entirely in accordance with precedent, and Lord Minto has decided that they shall not be taken as a guide for the future."

On 22nd November the Mintos arrived in Calcutta, where their reception made amends for the informalities of Bombay. The first impression of a Viceroy must be of a ceremonial state almost too heavy to be endured, of a cloth-of-gold ritual which stiffens all the movements of life. A household of seven hundred native servants, whose tasks are infinitely and rigidly differentiated, leaves upon the newcomer a sense of living alone in the heart of vast solitudes, from which it is possible to get only a distant prospect of the normal world. The Viceroy has immediate duties to turn his mind from this weighty magnificence, but his wife must grapple with it and domesticate it. Lady Minto's first feeling was one of an immense loneliness. "Letters are brought in from A.D.C.'s saying that they await my commands-at present I have none to give them. Apparently in future I shall have to send for any one I may wish to see, as no one intrudes upon the sacred presence uninvited. I am bound to say a deep depression has taken possession of my soul!" Nothing cheered them both so much as to come across traces of the family traditions which linked the quiet home by Teviot with this gorgeous East. The portrait of the first Earl hung conspicuously in the Council Chamber of Government House. Almost the first deputations which Minto received were from the four Maharajas of Patiala, Jind, Nabha, and Behawalpur, states which the first Lord Minto had protected against the encroachments of Ranjit Singh, who was seeking to extend his territory across the Sutlej. It was pleasant to find that India had a long memory.

Christmas was a season of functions--the state visit of the Tashi Lama of Tibet, a young man in a yellow bishop's mitre, with a tom-tom-beating escort on shaggy ponies, and the Tongsa Penlop of Bhutan, a famous figure in the Lhasa expedition. On 29th December the Royal party arrived in Calcutta, and till their departure on January 9, 1906, the Prince and Princess of Wales and their hosts led crowded lives. At first there had been a threat that the native population would boycott the visit, but Minto took the bold step of sending for Mr. Gokhale, the leader of the Indian progressives, and talking to him with so much effect that all danger from that source was removed. It was a visit in which the future monarchs of Britain won golden opinions from every class, European and native alike, for their graciousness and friendly simplicity, and it was of the first importance, too, in the development of Indian policy. The Prince, in his speech at the Guildhall on his return, declared as the moral he had read from his tour the need of a closer and wider sympathy between government and governed in India, and it fell to Minto to provide means for the realization of this ideal.

By the early months of 1906 the new Viceroy was in the toils of the laborious routine of his office, and attempting in his scanty leisure to bring into focus the multitude of new problems which each day presented. His indefatigable predecessor had drawn all the details of administration to himself, and this centralization, beneficial as were many of its results, involved the emasculation of the local governments, and a dead-weight of detail for the Viceroy. The Members of Council had been stripped of all real responsibility, and from coadjutors had become clerks. In Colonel Dunlop Smith, Minto had a most capable private secretary who laboured to spare him, but the system of bringing the most trivial of matters to the Viceroy for decision, of using, in Burke's phrase, the "extreme medicine of the constitution as its daily bread," could not be altered in a day. "Every morning about eight," Lady Minto writes, "heavily laden servants stagger upstairs with innumerable papers. These colossal files, with their distinctive labels and huge red tickets with 'Urgent' printed in aggressive letters, are built in a zareba on the floor round his writing table and almost hide him from view." It was not easy to wade through morasses of the inessential--to sanction the spending of a thousand rupees on building a bathroom for a remote official or decide whether a man should have leave to visit his dentist--and at the same time to keep the mind clear and fresh for the consideration of the greater matters of policy. From that folie de doute which prevents a man from delegating work and makes him nervous about the most microscopic detail to which he has not given personal attention, Minto was conspicuously free. He thought of government as an exercise in co-operation and not as an anxious dictatorship, and he steadily refused to be buried under a drift of files. From the first he strove to restore the responsibility and initiative of the Executive Council, and he insisted on making leisure for himself to study and meditate upon the larger questions of Indian rule. He was not sent to India to be an under-secretary but a Viceroy.

IV

Before the close of 1905 Mr. Balfour's Government had fallen, and the election of January 1906 brought the Liberals into power with a majority almost too big to be comfortable. The new Government entered upon office with a large programme of reform, and, since they had defeated decisively the imperialist policy of Mr. Chamberlain, it was assumed by many that their accession would involve some radical changes in the administration of the Empire. Mr. John Morley, who had his choice of many posts, selected the Secretaryship for India, and, whatever doubts may have been in Minto's mind as to future unanimity, he welcomed the appointment to the India Office of a man so able, so generally esteemed, and so powerful in the councils of his party, as a proof that India would not be relegated to the position of a forgotten side-show in British policy. He had met Mr. Morley in Canada and had greatly liked him, and the first letter from the new Secretary of State recalled the meeting. "The conversation we had when you so kindly sheltered me at Ottawa last year convinces me that we speak the same political language, even though we may not always say precisely the same things." Their relations thus began on a note of friendship, a friendship which through frequent differences of opinion was never impaired. The many private letters which passed during this period between Whitehall and Calcutta form a body of correspondence as fascinating in its revelation of temperament and mind, and as politically informative, as any in the archives of the British Empire. Lord Morley has happily given to the world many of his letters, and it is our privilege in these pages to supplement them by certain quotations from Minto's side. He has also published in his Recollections* a tribute to his correspondent, based upon five years of intimate colleagueship:--

"Lord Minto, the new Viceroy, had all the manly traditions and honourable associations that gather round the best of youth at Eton and Trinity. In stock he was descended from patrician Whigs, and he had his share of the intuitive political perception that belonged to that sect since its rise at the revolutionary settlement. His temperament was theirs. He had seen active service under Roberts in India; he had fought on the side of the Turks against Russia: nor, in truth, did friendly feeling for the Ottoman ever leave him. As Governor-General of Canada he had acquired insight into the working technicalities of public administration in a free parliamentary system. Such habits of mind he joined to the spirit of the soldier. The Indian Viceroy is not bound to know political philosophy or juristic theory or constitutional history; he is first and foremost an administrator, and the working head of a complicated civil and military service. Nature had endowed Lord Minto with an ample supply of constancy and goodhumour. His loyalty, courage, friendliness, straightforwardness, and pressing sense of public duty were all splendid; so was his rooted contempt for those in whom he found such excellences languid. A Viceroy needs to be a judge of men, whether with dark skins or white, and Lord Minto mixed tact and good cornmon sense and the milk of human kindness in the right proportion for discovering with what sort of man he had to deal. He liked people, though he did not always believe them, and he began by a disposition to get on with people as well as they would let him. If he found on trial what he thought good reason for distrusting a man, he did not change. His vision was not subtle, but, what is far better, it was remarkably shrewd. A bare catalogue of qualities, however, is not all; such lists never are, nor can be. It is the summary of them, the man himself, that matters. His ancestor, an idolater of Burke, and Indian Viceroy a hundred years before, once dropped the ingenuous but profound remark, 'How curious it is to see how exactly people follow their own characters all through life.' Our Lord Minto was a first-rate case. You were always sure where you would find him; there was no fear of selfishness or pettiness drawing him for a single passing moment from the straight path; his standard of political weights and measures was simple--it was true to the right facts, and it was steadfast.

"In early days at the India Office it was refreshing to hear from him how grateful he was for my proposal that he should pardon three hundred students who had been injudiciously dismissed from their school. 'For,' said he, 'I do believe that in this country one can do any amount of good, and accumulate a very growing influence, if one only gives evidence of some feelings of sympathy.' This was the result of a sure instinct. It went with a strong and active conscience, not a weak one; with a manful sense both of public responsibility and of practical proportion. The sympathy of which he spoke was much more than humane sentiment; it was a key to sound politics, and I very soon made no doubt that, though he did not belong to my own political party on the Thames at Westminster, we should find all that was wanted of common ground on the banks of the Ganges. Good mutual understanding between Secretary of State and Viceroy makes all the difference, and between us two it never failed. We were most happily alike, if I may use again some old words of my own, in aversion to all quackery and cant, whether it be the quackery of hurried violence dissembling as love of order or the cant of unsound and misapplied sentiment, divorced from knowledge and untouched by cool comprehension of realities."

* Vol II, pages 121-123. In a presentation copy to Lady Minto the author has written the following tribute:--

"To Lady Minto, with warm respect, in grateful memory of an able, straightforward, steadfast, unselfish, and most considerate comrade in tasks of arduous public duty. MORLEY OF B. April 25, 1919."

Every item in this wise and generous tribute was, we may be assured, deeply felt by the writer, and every phrase is true. Minto had not the literary skill of his colleague, and he has left us no such exercise in the art of Theophrastus; his estimate of Mr. Morley is to be gathered only from fragments of his letters and conversations. But it is clear that from the very outset he had arrived at an accurate judgment of the Secretary of State. A warm regard soon ripened into affection; he admired the brilliance and diversity of his talents, and was grateful for the treasures of wisdom, drawn from a rich memory of the world's thought and literature, with which he brightened his correspondence. This, he felt, was a compliment of which any man might well be proud. But he had to meet Mr. Morley not as a private friend, but as a Secretary of State, and as a Secretary of State he had his drawbacks. His clear-cut personality, free from ragged edges and indeterminate colours, was not the one best suited to the task of administration. His life had been that of the scholar and the teacher, and even in Parliament his power lay rather in debate than in the arts of leadership. He was not, like Sir Wilfrid Laurier, a skilled party tactician, but an exponent of principles, and an inspirer, rather than a framer, of policies. His intellectual allegiance was owed to a school of thought which tended always towards rigidity in theory, and rigidity in theory is apt, if the thinker becomes a statesman, to develop into absolutism in practice. He had had no training in affairs such as falls to the lot of the humblest country gentleman, and had never had his corners rubbed off by mingling with the ruck of humanity. The scholar, especially a scholar of Mr. Morley's type, transferred to the seat of power, is always apt to order things with a high hand, because he has little knowledge of the daily compromises by means of which the business of the world is conducted.

The innocent vanity of the scholar, too, may easily acquire that touch of arrogance which brings it near to folie des grandeurs, and is indeed the almost inevitable concomitant of a quick imagination. Mr. Morley was attracted to the India Office by his susceptibility to historic state; he loved to sit in a large room and issue decrees to high officials; it delighted him to feel that he had the control of the fortunes of some hundreds of millions of human souls; there was even satisfaction in the thought that troops might move at his command in just and beneficent wars. It is a curious trait to record in a follower of Comte, but he had no general humanitarian sympathies. Indeed, he had a strong distaste for all coloured races, and little imaginative insight into their moods and views. "The real truth," he told Lady Minto in a delightful letter, "is that I am an Occidental, not an Oriental; don't betray this fatal secret or I shall be ruined! I think I like Mohammedans, but I cannot go much further than that in an easterly direction." He had a prejudice against bureaucracy, but had himself the temperament of the austerest bureaucrat; he professed a distaste for militarism, but he had an odd liking for soldiers, and his affection was vowed in history to figures like Cromwell and Strafford. He called it a "wicked thought," but it was a self-revealing suggestion of his that "Strafford was an ideal type, both for governor of Ireland in the seventeenth century and governor of India in the twentieth century." Indeed, if an irreverence may be permitted which its subject would assuredly have forgiven, there was about Mr. Morley at the India Office the air of a colleger who is admitted in his last year at school to the companionship of the captains of the boats and the cricket eleven, and who is intoxicated with his new society and inclined to forget the scholar in the sportsman. He was like Dr. Johnson in his capacity as Mr. Thrale's executor, striding about the brewery with a great inkhorn and rejoicing in the playing of a novel part.* There are many passages which express his distaste for the doctrinaire, but no man so ready as he was to put his philosophy of life into maxims and aphorisms could escape a touch of doctrinairedom. His school of thought had taught him high-flying doctrines of parliamentary supremacy, and there was a risk that he might incline to views about the government of India which were not the less despotic because the despotism was parliamentary. His rule was in danger of becoming autocratic and inelastic; he would certainly override his own Council, he would probably pay small respect to the Viceroy's Council, and he might end by ignoring the Viceroy himself.

* Once, when lunching at 10 Downing Street after he had become Lord President of the Council, he was asked by his old friend, Mr. Thomas Hardy, what books he had been reading lately, and replied loftily, "I never read anything"--seeming, said Mr. Hardy gently in telling the tale, "to draw an invisible ermine about him, as though he were a sporting peer who never read anything but the Pink 'Un."-Quarterly Review, January 1924.

Minto shrewdly assessed the temperament of the Secretary of State and set himself to counteract its dangers. His aim was by patient argument and adroit suggestion to get Mr. Morley to believe that the policy of the Government of India was initiated by Whitehall; it mattered little who got the credit so long as the work was done. He avoided scrupulously any conflict except on the gravest issues; in lesser matters he was only too willing to humour his colleague. Having no vanity himself, he was not offended by an innocent manifestation of it in another, especially when he had for that other a sincere respect and affection. He recognized, too, that the fates had been kind in giving him, in a new Government of unpredictable tendencies, just such a Secretary of State. To Mr. Morley he could look with certainty for support in all liberal and sympathetic policies, and, should it become necessary to take strong measures of repression, if he could convince Mr. Morley, he could count with confidence on the support of the Cabinet. A statesman of such an impeccable democratic record would soon silence the ill-informed critics of his own side, for he had about him an aura of earnest morality which would enable him to steal a horse with safety when another man dare not look over the hedge.

The first of Minto's tasks was to settle the quarrel on military administration which had led to the break between Lord Curzon and Lord Kitchener. With the latter he had only a slight previous acquaintance, and looked forward with some trepidation to their first official meeting. To his delight he found a man whom he could work with in perfect confidence and ease, a fellow-soldier who spoke the same tongue as himself, a friend whose humour and loyalty made him an admirable colleague. The new arrangement, which had been sanctioned in principle by Mr. Brodrick in the previous year, was worked out in detail, and, with some modifications, received the assent of His Majesty's

Government, and came into force as from March 19, 1906. The Military Department of the Government of India, which had existed for over one hundred and twenty years, was abolished; the administrative control of the Army of India was distributed between two new departments--the Army Department and the Department of Military Supply; the former was placed under the Commanderin-Chief, who was now directly responsible to the Governor-General in Council for the administration of the Indian forces. The scheme was accepted as a reasonable settlement both in Britain and India; the Cabinet contented itself with altering certain small provisions which the Government of India intentionally inserted that they might be altered. Mr. Morley told Minto that he did not consider the solution particularly brilliant, but that everything depended "upon the C.-in-C. being held by you strictly within the limits we are assigning to him;" the Viceroy, thankful to be quit of the business, told the Secretary of State that "it was refreshing to see ideas conveyed in a kind of English unknown to official language here." So in an atmosphere of mutual compliments an acrimonious controversy was laid to rest.

Following close upon it, came Mr. Morley's first suggestion of the new policy of the Foreign Office towards Russia, whose position in the world had been materially altered by her defeat at the hands of Japan. "Supposing," Mr. Morley wrote to the Viceroy, "you were coming to some sort of understanding with Russia-- a hypothesis which may be many hundred miles off realization--and suppose even that we held the upper hand in the negotiation, what would be the terms that you would exact from Russia as essential to a bargain? I mean what, from military, strategic, and political points of view, are the things that she is to undertake to do or not to do?" Minto took time to consider the question in consultation with Lord Kitchener, and the view of the two was set forth in a letter of 2nd May. Kitchener's conditions were that Russia should publicly recognize that Afghanistan was outside her sphere of influence and that its external relations must be conducted through Britain; that she should make no strategic extension of her present railway system towards the Indian frontier; that she should recognize the preponderating interests of Britain in Seistan and southern Persia, and that she should scrupulously respect the integrity of China in Kashgar and elsewhere, and refrain from all interference in Tibet. On 25th May Mr. Morley sent to India a draft of Sir Edward Grey's instructions to Sir Arthur Nicolson in Petrograd on the treaty so far as it related to Afghanistan, Persia, and Tibet, and Minto replied on 12th June, criticizing strongly the provisions as to Afghanistan. He was prepared for the most generous concessions to Russia in Persia, but he was nervous about the Indian North-West frontier. He doubted the wisdom of permitting communications between Russian and Afghan officials even on purely local matters; he questioned the advisability of a Russo-Afghan frontier commission, and he took the gravest exception to the proposed agreement of Britain not to extend her railways in the direction of the Afghan border during a period of ten years. He believed that railways were the true frontier defence of India, a necessary consequence of the frontier military policy.

"We must be masters in our own house. We surely cannot agree to sacrifice the security and internal improvement of a portion of our dominions for the sake of our relations with a foreign Power. . . We should have to stand still for ten years, to give up hopes of closer relations with our tribes, and, for the sake of our own safety, to go on fighting them as we have done for generations. . . . I cannot but feel strongly opposed to any agreement with Russia in respect to railways. I should be inclined to let her do what she wants. She has practically in respect to her propinquity to the Afghan frontier got all she wants now, or can get it at very short notice. I earnestly hope it may be realized how such an agreement would tie our hands. . . . I cannot but think that primarily the Amir is a more dangerous neighbour to us than Russia, and therefore in respect to India a more necessary friend. . . . To me it seems infinitely more important to keep on friendly and controlling terms with him than to enter into any bargain with Russia which might lessen our influence with him, or alienate him from us. I believe him to be sensitive, suspicious, and over-confident in his own strength, but in my opinion it is vitally important to keep on good terms with him. . . . If we are to enter upon an entente with Russia, let us bargain with her elsewhere than in Central Asia. . . . I have only given you my own views in answer to your letter, but I certainly think that, for reasons affecting the internal administration of India independently of imperial foreign policy, the Government of India should be fully consulted before any agreement is entered into with Russia."

This letter embodies Minto's main articles of frontier defence--that, having accepted the dubious plan of holding the marches with tribal levies, a road and railway policy was necessary to bring these tribes more closely under our influence, and to provide the strategical means for rapid military concentration; and that the Amir's friendship was the foundation of frontier peace. In a matter so vitally affecting the internal interests of India it seems a modest request that the Government of India should be consulted. In replying on 6th July to a letter of which he praised the "great clearness, ability, and force," Mr. Morley delivered a lecture on the principles and practice of statesmanship, a vigorous homily which is worth quoting as an example of the aptitude of the Secretary of State for discovering suddenly in the most prosaic connection that fundamentals were endangered:--

"You argue . . . as if the policy of entente with Russia were an open question. That is just what it is not. His Majesty's Government, with almost universal support in public opinion, have decided to make such attempt as Russian circumstances may permit to arrange an entente. The grounds for this I have often referred to when writing to you. Be they good or bad, be we right or wrong, that is our policy. . . .

"You say, 'If we are to enter on an entente with Russia, let us bargain with her elsewhere than in Central Asia.' But then this was not the question laid before you. The question was, in view of the policy resolved upon deliberately by us, what you thought of the line on which in respect of Afghanistan we intended to pursue our policy. An entente with Russia that should leave out Central Asia would be a sorry trophy of our diplomacy indeed. Anyhow, H.M.'s Government has determined on this course, and it is for their agents and officers all over the world to accept it. If there is one among them to whom it would be more idle to repeat the a b c of the constitution than to another you are that man.

"I am, however, a little frightened when you say at the end of your letter that 'the Government of India should be fully consulted before the agreement suggested is entered into with Russia.' If you mean the Government of India in a technical sense--as the G.-G. in C.--I must with all respect demur. For one thing the G.-G. is his own foreign minister, and the Foreign department is under his own immediate superintendence. Second, with sincere regard for the capacity of your Council, I fail to see what particular contribution they could make to questions of public policy. . . . Third, have you considered how in practice this 'full consultation' could be worked? Diplomacy, as you will agree, is necessarily delicate, flexible, elastic. Is Nicolson in his talks with Isvolsky to pull himself up by thinking how this or that proposal would be taken not only at Whitehall, but also at Simla? You know better than anybody how the pretensions of Canada (I don't use pretensions in any bad sense) fetter and shackle negotiations with the United States. The plain truth is--and you won't mind my saying it frankly because you will agree--that this country cannot have two foreign policies. The Government of India in Curzon's day, and in days before Curzon, tried to have its own foreign policy. I seem to see the same spectre lurking behind the phrase about 'full consultation.'"

In these sentences there is obviously much dubious doctrine, and what is sound is a little beside the point. Minto contented himself with replying that no one could be more opposed than himself to any attempt of the Government of India to have a policy apart from the policy of Britain. "But opinions are a different thing, and it is quite possible and often probable that the opinions of a subsidiary Government may be different from those of His Majesty's Government. In that case it seems to me all-important that the Secretary of State should have the opportunity of hearing these opinions and deciding upon their value."

In one detail of his frontier policy he had the Secretary of State's full concurrence--the fostering of friendly relations with the Amir of Afghanistan. Lord Curzon had tried to persuade Habibullah to visit India to attend the Coronation Durbar at Delhi; but the invitation had been perhaps too much in the nature of a command, and Habibullah took umbrage. Since then Sir

Louis Dane's mission had smoothed away the irritation, and early in 1906 Minto heard that the Amir was anxious to make a pleasure trip to the chief Indian cities. He sent him a cordial invitation to be his guest, and a ready acceptance followed. "I was determined," Habibullah told his durbar, "never to go to India in the manner desired by Lord Curzon. The attitude adopted by Lord Minto, however, is so friendly and free from motives that I cannot possibly hesitate to accept the invitation of His Excellency, which is couched in such terms of kindness expressing a desire for an interview between friends." It was the first time since the days of Lord Dufferin that the ruler of Afghanistan had consented to visit India.

The chief internal problem of the first half of 1906 was the agitation against the partition of Bengal, that vexed inheritance to which Minto had fallen heir. We shall presently see this volcano in irruption. But in the early months of the year Minto had begun to turn his attention to the matter which the Prince of Wales had made the keynote of his speech on his return, and which he and Mr. Morley had canvassed from the beginning of their colleagueship-the possibility of establishing a truer sympathy between rulers and ruled by admitting Indians to some share in the government of their country. It would be an idle task to determine whether the first suggestion came from the side of the Viceroy or of the Secretary of State, for both men were from the start at one on the desirability of the reform, if it were practically feasible. In Minto's mind the ruling motive was a sense of honour, the wish to fulfil the promise held out as long ago as the Act of 1833 and the Royal proclamation of 1858. Lord Curzon, labouring singleheartedly in what he believed to be the cause of the Indian people, had shown himself somewhat intolerant of the claims of the new educated public which Britain had created. On the ground of efficiency he had declared, with perhaps needless sharpness, that the higher ranks of civil employment must be reserved for Englishmen, "for the reason that they possess, partly by heredity, partly by upbringing, and partly by education, the knowledge of the principles of government, the habits of mind, and the vigour of character which are essential for the task." He had declared, too, that the West had a higher standard of truthfulness than the East, "where craftiness and diplomatic wile have always been held in much repute." These dicta, whatever their justification, were deeply wounding to Indian self-esteem, and they seemed to postpone the realization of Britain's solemn pledge till the Greek Kalends. Minto, with his lively sense of public honour, could not be comfortable in this blank refusal.

Moreover, as a practical man, he did not see the common sense of the attitude. He had to the full Lord Curzon's admiration for the qualities of his own countrymen, but his very pride in these qualities made him incline to the belief that they could maintain good government even when the problem was complicated by admitting Indians to a share in it. It was the boast of the British in India that they had been willing to face the facts of a new world and alter their administration accordingly; one of the greatest of them, Warren Hastings, had foreseen that the true task of his race was not in conquest but in what came after, when he said, "To obtain empire is common; to govern it well has been rare indeed." To Minto it seemed that to govern with the assent of the governed was less a moral than a physical necessity; the opposite was not so much wrong as impossible. As he looked around him he saw two currents of unrest--one the inevitable desire of men whom we had educated on Western lines to share in the government, the other the dark stream of anarchy and revolution, which had its springs as much in Europe as in India. If both were suffered to overflow there might be cataclysmic disaster; but the two were different in kind, and if the second was to be restrained, there was the more need for canalizing and regulating the first; otherwise the currents might join in a tragic inundation. He was incapable of taking a melodramatic view, and reading anarchy into what was natural and reasonable. There was a type of unrest which might fairly be called "loyal." In his own words, he saw that "beneath a seemingly calm surface there existed a mass of smothered political discontent, much of which was thoroughly justifiable and due to causes which we were bound to examine." He desired to check the revolutionary by preventing his alliance with the moderate reformer. The words which Mr. Gokhale used in the Budget debate in March 1906 seemed to him the bare truth. "The question of the conciliation of the educated classes . . . raises issues which will tax all the resources of British statesmanship. There is but one way in which this conciliation can be secured, and that is by associating these classes more and more with the government of their own country. This is the policy to which England stands committed by solemn pledges given in the past. . . . What the country needs at the moment above everything else is a government national in spirit, even though it may be foreign in personnel."

The first step was taken by the Viceroy. In March 1906, before leaving Calcutta, he raised boldly in private with certain members of his Executive Council the question of the desirability of appointing an Indian to its membership, since to him the path of executive partnership between the races seemed the simplest and most hopeful. He found the majority of his advisers strongly against the proposal, and he did not report the discussion to the Secretary of State, since he intended to open the whole question later. On 16th May, in connection with the position of Mr. Gokhale, he wrote to Mr. Morley deprecating the importation of British institutions into India en bloc, and Mr. Morley replied, agreeing, but arguing that British institutions were one thing and the spirit of British institutions another--"a thing we cannot escape, even if we wished, which I hope we don't. . . . I have no sort of ambition for us to take a part in any grand revolution during my time of responsibility, whether it be long or short. Just the very opposite. You need have no apprehension whatever of a private telegram reaching you from me some fine morning requesting you at once to summon an Indian Duma. On the other hand, I don't want to walk blindfold in the ways of bureaucracy." A week or two earlier Mr. Morley had quoted a frequent saying of Lord Cromer, which he had heard from Mr. Brodrick, to the effect that it had always been his habit in Egypt to employ a native whenever it was at all possible, even though a European might be more efficient. "That," said Lord Cromer, "is where the Government of India go wrong, and have always gone wrong; they find the native less competent, or not competent at all, and then they employ an Englishman instead. You lose more by the effect on popular content than you gain by having your work better done."

This was very much Minto's own way of looking at things, and in his letter of 28th May he emphasized this view and liberated his soul on the foolish exclusiveness of British society in India, instancing the case of Sir Pertab Singh:--

"I will tell you a story of Sir Pertab. Not long ago a young British officer of whom he was very fond died of cholera in his house. He was to be buried the same afternoon, and had just been put in his coffin in a room in which were Sir Pertab and an English officer, who, seeing that there would be some difficulty in carrying the coffin down to the gun-carriage at the door, asked Sir Pertab to send for a 'sweeper.' 'Sweeper!' said Sir Pertab, 'what do you want a sweeper for? I shall carry the boy down myself.' The English officer, knowing that this meant that he would lose his caste, implored him not to do so, but he insisted, carried the coffin on his shoulder to the door, walked by the gun-carriage, and again carried the coffin from it to the grave. Next morning a deputation of Brahmins came to Sir Pertab's house and told him that a terrible thing had happened the day before. 'Yes!' he answered, 'a young officer died here.' 'More terrible than that,' they said. 'You, a Rahtor Rajput, have lost your caste.' He flared up like a shot. 'Look here, you pigs! There is one caste higher than all other castes throughout the world, and that is the caste of a soldier! That is my caste!' Turning to one of his staff he angrily asked for his hunting whip, the Brahmins fled, and he remains as great as ever. And that is the man that we can't allow inside an English club at Calcutta!"

On 15th June, in a letter of Mr. Morley's occurred a passage of the first importance:--

"I wonder whether we could not now make a good start in the way of reform in the popular direction. If we don't, is it not certain that the demands will widen and extend into 'national' reasons, which I at least look upon with a very doubtful and suspicious eye. Why should you not now consider as practical and immediate things--the extension of the native element in your Legislative Council; ditto in local councils; full time for discussing Budget in your L.C., instead of four or five skimpy hours; right of moving amendments? (Of course, officials would remain a majority.) If I read your letters correctly you have no disposition whatsoever to look on such changes in a hostile spirit; quite the contrary. Why not, then, be getting ready to announce reforms of this sort?

Either you write me a dispatch, or I write you one--by way of opening the ball. It need be no long or highflown affair. I suppose the notion of a native in your Executive Council would not do at all. Is that certain? I daresay it is--and it would frighten that nervous personage (naturally nervous), the Anglo-Indian."

These suggestions were the "common form" of Indian liberalism, and Mr. Morley had adopted them partly from Minto's letters, partly from talks with Mr. Gokhale, and partly from Indian sympathizers at home. Minto replied on 5th July, agreeing heartily with the Secretary of State, and mentioning that the possibility of a native on his Executive Council had been simmering for months in his mind. On 11th July he wrote at greater length:--

"I need not tell you how heartily I am in accord with all you say as to the necessity of dealing with our Indian political future. Moreover, it appears to me that our opportunity has come. . . . I would for the present put aside the-question of the Council of Princes and the possibility of a native Member of Council. . . . What I think we have distinctly before us is the prolongation of the Budget debate, the encouragement of greater discussion at that debate not only on questions of finance, but on other matters of public moment, and also a larger representation on the Legislative Council of the Viceroy. . . . I believe, as a matter of sound improvement, we should do very right in commencing our reforms from the bottom of the tree. The Congress leaders would begin at the top. They want ready-made power for themselves. We must remember that our own people at home have been educated for centuries in the idea of constitutional government, and have only advanced by slow steps to the popular representation of to-day. Here everything is different. From time immemorial it has been a rule of dictators, and we must be very careful not to thrust modern political machinery upon a people who are generally totally unprepared for it. . . . What I should venture to propose to you is that you should let me know what you think of my crude suggestions, that we should put our ideas as far as possible into shape by private correspondence, and that I should then place the position before my Council for discussion, with the intention of our sending you our proposals in the shape of an official dispatch. I attach great importance to the official initiative being taken by the Government of India. It is better in every respect, both for the present and for the future, that the Government of India should appear to recognize all that is in the air here, and the necessity of meeting new conditions, and that they should not run the risk of being assumed to have at last taken tardy action out of respect to instructions from home."

VI

At the close of March the Mintos left Calcutta for a tour in the North-West, visiting Delhi on the way, where the Viceroy unveiled a statue of John Nicholson. It was his first breathing-space, and he exulted in the keen air of the frontier hills, and the revisiting of places where he had campaigned twenty-seven years before. At Mardan they saw the memorial to Cavagnari, and Lady Minto remembered with a shudder how narrowly her husband had escaped Cavagnari's fate.

"I saw the headmen at Dargai," Minto wrote to Mr. Morley on 18th April, "who presented me with an address in verse in Pushtu, the main point of which was a desire for improved railway communication. On the other side of the pass I again met all the leading men--a strong, manly, cheerful people, eminently respectable-looking in their long white dresses, who were fighting hard against us in 1895-97 and 1898. I am afraid my Border blood conduced to a certain amount of sympathy between us. I talked to all the leaders among them, and somehow could not help feeling that we liked each other, and they presented me with two of their standards, which, I believe, is an honour never paid to any one before, as no standard has ever been parted with unless it was lost in war. It is a peculiar society, perpetual bloodfeuds and little wars among themselves. Younghusband, commanding the Guides, Sir Francis's brother, told me the other day that only a few months ago he was coming back from playing polo in the Swat valley close to a village through which I passed, when to his astonishment he realized that a heavy musketry fire was going on, and he rode up to a line of warriors who were firing away merrily, and asked what on earth they were doing. They said they were only fighting about a piece of land, and that, though there 'were yet but five corpses, by God's grace there would soon be more.' Our frontier officers, like Roos-Keppel in the Khyber, and Deane, love these people. There is a curious feeling of fun and devilry in it all which is fascinating."

The last week of April found the Vice-regal household settled in Simla, the place which Minto had found odious on his first visit, but which he was soon to appreciate. It was a change of residence, but no change of life, for the inexorable files flowed in ceaselessly, and the Viceroy was fortunate if he snatched an hour's ride in the day. In June they had an alarming earthquake, and in July the community was saddened by the tragic news of Lady Curzon's death. Lady Minto was hard at work at her organization of the Indian Nursing Association, and preparing for the huge Fancy Fete in Calcutta which was to provide it with endowments. In this scheme she had Mr. Morley's warm support. "Do you know," he wrote, "that I have often wondered whether I would not rather be in Lord Shaftesbury's place on the Day of Judgment than in the place of all the glittering statesmen. I mean that I would rather have done something pretty certain-- nothing is quite certain--to mitigate miseries such as your Nursing Scheme aims at, than have done all the grand things about which high speeches are made and great articles written in the newspapers." There were expeditions in which the hard-worked Viceroy sometimes managed to join, and the marvellous ritual of the household never ceased to inspire awe. After a very wet ride they arrive at Fagu in the hills, and Lady Minto's journal notes: "The scarlet servants with immovable faces stood round the table as usual, looking as if they had never left Government House. Francis Grenfell told me he expected a picnic luncheon, but I informed him that the Viceroy must have his silver plate, his Star of India china, and every variety of wine, even if he happens to be on the highest pinnacle of the Himalaya mountains, and somehow they always appear as if by magic!"

Simla was scarcely less elaborate than Calcutta. "We counted the other day, when Rolly and I were absolutely alone, nineteen servants waiting about in the passages, and thirty-two men who compose the band playing in the hall below--fifty-one in all." It was a gay and intimate world, full of polo and tennis, gymkhanas, amateur theatricals, and endless dances, in which the three daughters, soon to be respectfully known throughout India as the "Destroying Angels," played a notable part. But it was a world in which perforce the Viceroy could have little share. The Secretary of State was courteous and kindly, but he was exacting, and cables demanding information arrived at all hours. Mr. Morley praised the "cool, equitable, and penetrating reflection" which Minto was giving to his problems, and wrote to Lady Minto:

"We have had widely different training and experience, but I do believe that, in the way we approach public business, Lord Minto and I are just the same. It is inevitable that in detail and carrying things out we should sometimes vary, and controversies cannot be avoided in all these complex and difficult affairs. But, at any rate, after our six months' experience, I am confident that neither on his side nor mine will a difficulty ever be made worse by any element of huffy personality." It was a fortunate state of things, for the problems themselves were of a magnitude to demand the undivided attention of both.

In July the difficulties in Eastern Bengal came to a head. The inevitable troubles connected with partition were not soothed by the personality of the first lieutenant-governor of the new province. Sir Bampfylde Fuller was a man of ability and energy, and single-hearted in his devotion to duty. But he had not the qualities of tact and judgment necessary for the delicate situation in which he was placed; he was impetuous and hot-headed, apt to use the strong hand, and not inclined to be too deferent to the views of his official superiors, who had to envisage the problems of all India. Already in the first six months of his tenure of office he had made many blunders, and greatly increased the Viceroy's burden. Mr. Morley was eager that he should be removed; Minto shrank, not unnaturally, from a step which would be certainly misconstrued by the critics of the Government; but he was convinced that Sir Bampfylde's administration was a serious danger, since he lacked the qualities of patience and discretion which could alone in time abate the partition ferment. Perpetual pin-pricks, on the contrary, kept the irritation alive. "What ails Fuller Sahib," Sir Pertab Singh once asked, "that he wants to blow flies from cannon?" Then in July an incident happened which was not quite unwelcome to either Viceroy or Secretary of State. Before the partition came into force the Government of Bengal had prohibited the participation of students in the boycott movement, and warned the heads of schools and colleges that, if this prohibition were disregarded, state aid-would be withdrawn, and Calcutta University would be asked to disaffiliate such institutions. In February 1906 the Government of Eastern Bengal asked that Calcutta University should withdraw recognition from two schools which had ignored the prohibition. Now, at that moment such action would have been dangerous, for Lord Curzon's University Act was not yet in full working order, Calcutta University was in process of reorganization, and if the disaffiliation request had been pressed forthwith it might have been refused, with the most awkward consequences. Accordingly, the Home department of the Government of India suggested semi-officially to the Lieutenant-Governor the advisability of withdrawing the request on the ground that "the political objections to pressing the application to the Syndicate outweigh whatever educational advantages might be supposed to attach to a withdrawal of recognition from the schools." To this Sir Bampfylde replied with an autograph letter to the Viceroy, in which he announced that he was unable to acquiesce in this view, and that if it were persisted in he must tender his resignation.

To his amazement Minto, after consulting the Secretary of State, accepted the resignation.* "I feel," he wrote, "that, as you had expressed your willingness to resign, it would not be right to ask you to undertake proceedings of which you did not approve." The incident produced a profound sensation, and there was much foolish talk of "throwing officers to the wolves." But there can be no doubt that Minto was right. Sir Bampfylde Fuller had not proved a success, and that he should have been unable to perceive the cogent reasons of the Government of India for refusing his request was sufficient proof that he had not the qualifications needed for a most difficult post. In substance his policy was sound, and a year later, when the Senate of Calcutta University had been reconstituted, it was put into effect by the Viceroy. But in the summer of 1906 it was premature, for it is a truism of statesmanship that what is wise at one moment may be foolish at another. As for the charge of disloyalty to a subordinate, it was more correct to say that the subordinate had been disloyal to his superior. To reply with a threat of resignation to a letter pointing out difficulties and suggesting a reconsideration of a demand was to fail in the first duty of a public servant. No Government could survive for long if, when an official differed from it and offered to resign, it felt bound to capitulate to the pistol held at its head.

* Footnote: Mr. Morley wrote to the Viceroy, November 2, 1906: " . . . The Fuller papers will be laid before Parliament in a day or two. One matter in connection with them lies rather heavy on my conscience, and it is this. There is not a word to show that the acceptance of Fuller's resignation had my entire concurrence; and I have a feeling that you may think it rather shabby in me, who clamoured every week for his removal, to remain in the innocence of a lamb before Parliament. The Office were obdurate against the production of my telegram on the ground that the Governor-General is technically and constitutionally the sole authority over Lieutenant-Governors, and on the further ground that both Governor-General and Secretary of State should communicate with one another in absolute freedom, and this freedom would be much impaired if either felt that his letter or telegram might be planted in a blue book. I will try to get it known in Parliament that I warmly concurred in your acceptance of the resignation. I only hope that you will believe I am not thinking of saving my own skin, which, after all this time, has become dreadfully indurated."

The sensation was short-lived. Sir Bampfylde Fuller behaved at first with discretion, but when in June 1908 he published in the Times his letter headed "J'accuse" he convinced reasonable men that, whatever his talents, he was unfitted for the more delicate tasks of administration. Mr. Morley's account of his interview with him in the following October is the best comment on a painful but unavoidable affair:--

"I had a talk with him yesterday which lasted two solid hours and a half. I did not grudge the time, though it was a pretty stiff dose. . . . His extraordinary vivacity attracted me; so did his evident candour and good faith; he soon became free and colloquial in his speech, playing with cards on the table, in which tactics I followed him, both of us being perfectly frank and entirely good-natured. He is certainly a shrewdish, eager, impulsive, overflowing sort of man, quite well fitted for government work of ordinary scope, but I fear no more fitted to manage the state of things in E. Bengal than am I to drive an engine. . . . 'Well,' said I, 'you have a right to present your case in your own way, My reply will be a very simple one, and it will be that; "You resigned not because you had been ill-supported by the G. of I., but because you could not have your own way in a particular matter where you took one view and the G. of I. took another. That is the only question that arises on this set of facts. My firm principle is that if any official resigns because he cannot have his way, I (if it be my business) will promptly and definitely accept his resignation, and I cannot see that Lord Minto had any other alternative. Your policy was not recommended by success. You talk of the injury to prestige caused by the acceptance of your resignation. You should have thought of that before you resigned. The responsibility is yours. I don't believe it is for the good of prestige to back up every official whatever he does, right or wrong."' The effect of this eloquent burst upon the mobile man was to procure a vehement expression of agreement . . . The whole thing was intensely instructive and interesting, but it was also to me, as it certainly would have been to you, very painful. Yet every minute of the interview convinced me more and more that his retention must have brought wider mischief."

In August Minto, after months of careful investigation and much anxious thought, took the first practical step in his reforms policy. He appointed a committee, consisting of Sir A. T. Arundel, Sir Denzil Ibbetson, Mr. Baker, and Mr. Erie Richards, with Mr. H. Risley as secretary, to consider the question, and himself wrote a minute for their guidance. He referred to paragraph 7 in the report of Sir Charles Aitchison's committee as detailing the interests which must be protected in any increase of representation; the interests, namely, of the hereditary nobility and landed classes, of the trading, professional, and agricultural classes, of the planting and commercial European community, and of stable and effective administration. The subjects he proposed for the committee's consideration were: (a) a Council of Princes, and, should this be impossible, whether they might be represented in the Viceroy's Legislative Council; (b) an Indian member of the Viceroy's Executive Council; (c) increased representation on the Legislative Council of the Viceroy and of local governments; and (d) prolongation of the Budget debate, and increased power of moving amendments.

The following is an extract from Minto's note to his Council when appointing the committee:--

"I feel sure my colleagues will agree with me that Indian affairs and the methods of Indian administration have never attracted more public attention in India and at home than at the present moment. The reasons for their doing so are not far to seek. The growth of education, which British rule has done so much to encourage, is bearing fruit. Important classes of the population are learning to realize their own position, to estimate for themselves their own intellectual capacities, and to compare their claims for an equality of citizenship with those of a ruling race, whilst the directing influences of political life at home are simultaneously in full accord with the advance of political thought in India.

"To what extent the people of India as a whole are as yet capable of serving in all branches of administration, to what extent they are individually entitled to a share hi the political representation of their country, to what extent it may be possible to weld together the traditional sympathies of many different races and different creeds, and to what extent the great hereditary rulers of native states should assist to direct imperial policy, are problems which the experience of future years can alone gradually solve.

"But we, the Government of India, cannot shut our eyes to present conditions. The political atmosphere is full of change, questions are before us which we cannot afford to ignore, and which we must attempt to answer: and to me it would appear all-important that the initiative should emanate from us; that the Government of India should not be put in the position of appearing to have its hands forced by agitation in this country, or by pressure from home; that we should be the first to recognize surrounding conditions, and to place before His Majesty's Government the opinions which personal experience and a close touch with the every-day life of India entitle us to hold."

The committee sat through an entire month, and during its session Minto's letters to Mr. Morley showed that his views were hardening fast about the native member of the Viceroy's Council. He had come to think it a step not only desirable but essential. The committee's report, when completed, was circulated to the other members of Council, with a note from the Viceroy dealing especially with the question of a native member, of which two out of the four signatories to the report were in favour. Minto recognized that he must proceed slowly, and the opposition which he expected to be most formidable was that of Kitchener. For the time the Secretary of State was too actively engaged in the parliamentary struggles of his Government, in connection mainly with education and the powers of the House of Lords, to give his undivided attention to India. His private letters were discursive and wholly delightful--speculations on the dullness of a Viceroy's life according to Dufferin and Lytton: a description of a tea-party at Wimbledon for the Gaekwar of Baroda, and of a visit to Lord Roberts: an explanation, accompanied by a gift of his Life of Gladstone ("When you are done with it, pray add my book to the kinematographs, brocades, Martinis, and other appropriate presents to Kabul"), of the "frightful school" of financial churlishness in which he had been reared: and a recommendation that, should the House of Lords be abolished, Minto should succeed him on his return from India as member for the Montrose Burghs. The Secretary of State was in excellent spirits:--

"I am perfectly fascinated by that idea of yours, of you and me taking a walk together on your frontier. But then I have misgivings--when I think of the possible effect upon your mind of the teaching of your new friends at Kashmir, and their maxims upon the 'political convenience' of 'the quiet removal to another world of a troublesome colleague.' What a temptation to rid yourself of an importunate economist once for all! Your description of the enchantments of Kashmir brings the wonder of them well before me, and makes me half jealous of you in my own trade of man of letters."

VII

The Mohammedan population of India has always been a problem by itself, different in kind from that of the other races. The sixty-two millions of the followers of Islam had, with a few exceptions, hitherto taken little part in political life, and their leaders had held aloof from the National Congress. Their loyalty to the British Raj had been beyond criticism, but, owing to their insistence upon a system of education which was essentially religious, they found themselves outstripped by the Hindus in the securing of public posts, and were beginning to smart under a sense of inferiority. The partition of Bengal had been to their benefit, but the fate of Sir Bampfylde Fuller, whom they regarded as their special champion, had roused anxiety, and there was a danger that their young men might fall a prey to the peripatetic agitator. Minto, like the Secretary of State, had a liking for the Mohammedan, and the wiser heads in the body decided that the best preventive to unrest was to seek an interview with the Viceroy and state their grievances. The deputation was received at Simla on 1st October, and the address, bearing the signatures of every class of the Moslem community, was presented by the Aga Khan. Never before had so representative a body voiced Mohammedan views, and the address was notably moderate and dignified. It pointed out that the position of Moslems "should be commensurate not merely with their numerical strength but also with their political importance and the value of the contribution which they made to the defence of the Empire." Accepting, without great enthusiasm, the setting up of representative institutions, it claimed that provision should be made for the election of Mohammedans by purely Mohammedan electorates.

Minto replied in a speech which was one of the most sagacious and tactful that he ever made. He realized that no reforms would work which did not carry with them the assent of this great community, and that the moment had come for a clear statement of his policy. The following passage was accepted as a charter of Islamic rights:--

"The pith of your address, as I understand it, is a claim that, in any system of representation, whether it affects a municipality, a district board, or a legislative council, in which it is proposed to introduce or to increase the electoral organization, the Mohammedan community should be represented as a body. You point out that in many cases electoral bodies as now constituted cannot be expected to return a Mohammedan candidate, and that, if by chance they did so, it could only be at the sacrifice of such a candidate's views to those of a majority opposed to his own community, whom he would in no way represent; and you justly claim that your position should be estimated not merely on your numerical strength but in respect to the political importance of your community and the service that it has rendered to the Empire. I am entirely in accord with you. Please do not misunderstand me; I make no attempt to indicate by what means the communities can be obtained, but I am as firmly convinced as I believe you to be, that any electoral representation in India would be doomed to mischievous failure which aimed at granting a personal enfranchisement regardless of the beliefs and traditions of the communities composing the population of this continent."

There was far more in his speech than the formal pledge; there was an accent of friendliness and sincerity which deeply impressed his hearers. "Your address," Mr. Morley wrote, "was admirable alike in spirit, in its choice of topics, and in the handling," and he added that its gravity and steady dignity were thoroughly appreciated at home. After the interview the delegates had tea in the garden, and the old Prime Minister of Patiala said to

Lady Minto, "A hundred years ago Lord Minto came and saved our state. We cannot forget the gratitude we owe to his family. Now God has sent his descendant not only to help Patiala but to save India, and our hearts are full of thankfulness." The language of hyperbole was not without reason. The speech undoubtedly prevented the ranks of sedition from being swollen by Moslem recruits, an inestimable advantage in the day of trouble which was dawning.

The Mohammedan deputation having been received, the Viceroy departed on a lengthy tour. He went first to Quetta, where he held a durbar of Baluchi chiefs and enjoyed a day's hunting over remarkable country, a network of ridges, blind ditches, and old irrigation works. Then by way of Rawal Pindi he reached Kashmir, proceeding to Srinagar up the Jhelum in a lordly house-boat. "It was amusing," Lady Minto's diary notes, "to see the Viceroy trying to take a little exercise by walking along the bank. He was surrounded by a concourse of people. His dignity demanded a huge escort in front, soldiers bringing up the rear, policemen to the right and left of him, scouts on ahead, and skirmishers surveying the country on either side. Had we been marching through an enemy's country it would have been impossible to take more drastic precautions." In Kashmir the Mintos were royally entertained, and, later in Poonch, among other forms of sport had a day's bear-shooting, when the bag was thirty-one bears, of which Lady Minto accounted for five. Here is an extract from her Kashmir diary:--

"At Dachigan Camp two thousand were accommodated, including the Maharaja's band of eighty musicians, and the beaters numbered six thousand. We were told to expect bear, deer, and barasingh, but the forest was nearly devoid of game. Owing to the disturbing noises of this vast imported multitude the wild animals had all migrated over the mountains into Tibet. I was fortunate, however, in killing a large brown bear, and the next day Rolly shot the only barasingh in the beat. The return of the party was a curious sight. They alighted from the tongas at the gates, where the pipes and drums awaited them, playing a suitable Scottish air for the return of the successful sportsmen. Rolly and the Maharaja slowly advanced, accompanied by the band, and followed by a huge retinue, and preceded by an army of men carrying torches. It seems at five o'clock the Maharaja heard there was to be another beat, and became terribly fussy lest the Viceroy should be out in the dark. Orders were sent to all the neighbouring villages that men carrying torches must line the road, and with some of the coolies sent from the camp this was accomplished. The Maharaja drove to the foot of the mountain himself to see that all was faithfully carried out, and sure enough, as if by magic, for eight solid miles a thick avenue of coolies held flaming torches to illumine the Viceroy on his way. . . .

"It was amusing to see old Dandy's departure from camp, lying at his ease on the soft mattress of a specially-made wooden bedstead, which was carried by four coolies with four relief men, and one man in a red uniform, fully armed, and holding a sword at the salute, walking beside him to ensure that he should not fall out. The coolies speak respectfully of the Viceroy's dog as 'Dandy Sahib,' who accepts their homage and seems quite aware of his own importance."

The next visit was paid to Bikanir, where they had some marvellous sport with the sand-grouse. In the brief space of this Memoir it is impossible to do justice to the splendid hospitality extended to the Viceroy and his family by the Princes of India. For many of them Minto felt the warmest regard, they looked to him constantly for counsel, and in the native states perhaps his happiest hours of recreation were spent.

On 26th November his younger son, Esmond, arrived from England, and accompanied him for the rest of the tour. At Nabha the old Raja went up to the little boy, who could hardly be seen under an enormous sun hat, and bent low so as to look in his face. Then he said in Punjabi, "Your father is kind to the Phulkian misl (confederation), because God, the Immortal, has caused the noble spirit of his ancestor, who saved their forefathers, to pass into him. You must never forget this, and must be kind to my grandchildren as your father is to me. My sword is yours." He put out his sword for Esmond to touch. Then came Patiala, and then Delhi, where Minto dined with the 18th Sikhs, and was conveyed to the barracks in a motor-car, the property of some Raja. "It meandered about all over the road, and finally charged a lamp-post, nearly demolishing the whole party." On inquiry it was discovered that the Raja had not allowed his accomplished chauffeur to drive "not thinking his station in life to be adequate; so the Viceroy's life was entrusted to his principal sirdar, who knew nothing about motor-cars."

So closed the first year of Minto's Viceroyalty. He could look back on it with a modest comfort, for his health had stood the strain of incessant work--no small feat for a man of sixty--and he had established the best relations with the civil service, the native princes, and large classes of the Indian people. Sir Arthur Godley, the permanent under-secretary at the India Office, summed up the year in a kindly Christmas message:--

"You came into office at a time of unusual difficulty, and at the end of twelve months you can not only say like Sieyes, J'ai vécu, but you can look round upon a greatly improved state of things, and look back upon some thoroughly good pieces of work. And the prospect before you is, I hope and believe, a satisfactory one. Not the least of your achievements is that of having established thoroughly satisfactory relations with the Secretary of State. I can assure you (so far as I can judge) you have completely won his confidence, and (what is not so easy to win by correspondence alone) his friendship."

CHAPTER TEN

VICEROY OF INDIA, 1907-8

The first month of 1907 was given up to functions and gaieties, for it was the month of Lady Minto's Fête in Calcutta for her Nursing Association and local hospitals, and it saw the advent from the north of the ruler of Afghanistan. Of the Fête let it be recorded that it was a conspicuous success, the most comprehensive fancy fair which India had ever seen, perfectly organized in all details, and productive of no less a sum in net profits than £25,000. Side by side with the anxieties of this gigantic tamasha the Vicereine had to face with the Viceroy the entertainment of the Amir Habibullah, on whose visit hung grave issues for India's foreign policy. The great Durbar was held at Agra, where the Amir arrived on 9th January in a deluge of rain--which he fortunately considered a good omen. The Viceroy and the commander-in-Chief were there to meet him, and a large concourse of guests, English and native. The Amir's camp was superbly equipped. Huge silver poles support the great Durbar shamiana, where about a dozen gorgeous silver chairs are arranged in a circle. There is a large empty room with prayer carpets, where his devotions will be said. His bed is a silver four-poster with gold and silver embroideries instead of sheets, and his bath is a large inlaid marble tombstone with an iron pedestal beside it, on which a man stands and pours water over him. His other toilet requisites are all encased in plush and embroideries. On his dressing-table is a golden case full of scents--one bottle containing the pure extract of attar of roses.

Then began a succession of garden parties, dinners, and receptions, and a Grand Chapter of the Indian orders of knighthood, when the Amir was invested by the Viceroy with the Grand Cross of the Bath. It was a scene of impressive splendour as he walked in procession with the Viceroy and the Princes through the Dwan-i-kas to the Jasmine Hall, with its priceless traceries and carvings, which in other days had witnessed the glories of the Mogul dynasty. He was--after much anxious discussion--addressed as "His Majesty" and given a salute of thirty-one guns. He proved to be a short, thick-set gentleman, cheerful, voluble, strong-headed, with a passion for novelties, most friendly and susceptible, and obviously of a stout heart and a quick intelligence. He wore English clothes, except for a small astrakhan cap, adorned with a diamond sun, and occasionally put himself into knickerbockers and Norfolk jacket. He was deeply impressed by the review which he witnessed of 32,000 Indian troops, and rated his sirdars for making him believe that the Afghan army outweighed the combined forces of India and Russia. "And the whole army of India, I now learn, is but a fraction of the total military strength of the British Empire, and the whole army of the British Empire, I further find, is one of the smallest among the armies of the world's Great Powers. What! Have you naught to say? Look to it, I shall require your answer."

There was high comedy in the visit. The Amir lost his heart to so many ladies of diverse types that it was difficult to say whom he most admired.

"Lord Kitchener entertained the Amir at dinner last night," says Lady Minto's diary, "and it seems to have been a great success. He became most hilarious, drank three bottles of soda-water and a tub of plain water, and the effect could not have been more invigorating had the liquid been wine. He led Lord Kitchener to a sofa and said, 'You my friend, I your friend. Now we joke.' Lord Kitchener had the greatest difficulty in getting rid of him towards midnight."

He delivered various homilies on total abstinence, and a surprising address at Aligarh College on the need of religious education, but he resolutely declined to mention politics. Here is a picture by Lady Minto of his appearance at the State Ball in Calcutta:--

"He had never seen dancing in his life, and I was terrified that he was going to ask me to teach him. We sat together on the dais in the ballroom discussing old Persian sayings, from which many of our proverbs are derived. There happened to be an eclipse of the moon, and the Amir gallantly said, 'The moon in our country is masculine, and he even hides his face to-night so that your ball may have no rival.' Later at supper I told him that it was our custom to put our knife and fork together if we had finished and wanted our plate removed. He said, 'You tell, I learn!' . . . He said, 'Please you tell me I been heavy guest or light guest?' Of course I said, 'You've been a light guest;' whereupon he added, 'Then I come and stay with you next year, not official. I come as your friend for a long time.' With a sickly smile I told him that we should look forward to that pleasure, privately praying that the Government will never allow the experiment to be repeated oftener than once in five years."

The Amir purchased enormous quantities of goods at the Calcutta Fête; he gave largesse to any one who took his fancy; he did his best to arrange a marriage for Lord Kitchener, whose celibacy was a constant grief to him; and he departed at long last in tears, having found the rivers of Damascus more attractive than his own scanty waters of Israel. In his farewell speech he gave a promise which he loyally kept throughout the anxious days of the Great War: "Before I came to India we called ourselves friends; now I find myself in such a position that our friendship, which was like a plant before, is now like a big tree. I have gained much experience in India, and from that experience I hope to benefit my country in future. Let me say that at no time will Afghanistan pass from the friendship of India. So long as the Indian Empire desires to keep her friendship, so long will Afghanistan and Britain remain friends."

Lady Minto, 1907

Melancholy telegrams and letters were dispatched to the Viceroy from every haltingplace on his return journey, and he crossed the frontier in utter dolefulness. "He drew Sir Henry M'Mahon aside, put on his motoring goggles to hide the tears that were coursing down his face, and was too overcome to say one word. He finally jumped on to his horse, spurred him into a gallop, and disappeared through the mountain passes towards his barbaric kingdom."

The visit was not perhaps to the advantage of Habibullah; the fleshpots of the West were much too attractive to him, he fell out of conceit with his own people, and the way was prepared for the fate which befell him twelve years later. But from the point of view of Indian policy it was an unequivocal triumph, for relations of cordial friendship had been established which made it possible to tide over the difficulties of the agreement with Russia, now approaching completion. The British Government warmly congratulated Minto on the success of the visit, and two extracts from the correspondence of the Viceroy and the Secretary of State may be quoted to show that the burden of it was not light and that this was appreciated in Whitehall. On 6th February Minto wrote:--

"The Amir is still with us. I am afraid these words can hardly convey what they mean to me. Lady Minto and I are at the last stages of exhaustion. He fills up one's every spare moment. He came down to Barrackpore on Sunday for luncheon, after which I hoped for an afternoon to myself, but could not leave him. He then got involved in a game of croquet with my daughters, and finally remained till dark. He dined at the Frasers', and sang a Persian love song to Lady Fraser to his own accompaniment on the piano, and has shot clay pigeons with me, though for international reasons I thought it wise to divest the amusement of the conditions of a match! The worst of it is he won't go away, and now, though every one was sworn to secrecy, he has discovered that our State Ball is on Friday, and insists on remaining for that. A horrible rumour reached us this evening that he wants to stay for the races on Saturday, but I have told M'Mahon that he absolutely must insist on his leaving, as His Majesty's ships are specially awaiting his arrival at Bombay, and there is a naval programme there which he cannot neglect. He is simply irrepressible, more like a boy out of school than anything else. Not a word of affairs of state. . . . I only pray that the joys of Calcutta may not have entirely unsettled him! The responsibility of another such visit would really be more than I could bear, and I hear with apprehension that his sirdars say that there is no doubt there will now be an excellent motor-road from Kabul to Peshawar! I am in great hopes, however, that the attractions of Western life may suggest a visit to you in London rather than to me!"

To which Mr. Morley replied with an incursion into realpolitik:--

"I felt the horrible force of your opening words, 'The Amir is still with us.' Ah, well, il faut souffrir pour être beau, and Viceroys cannot have bright feathers in their caps without prodigious doses of boredom. I am glad His Majesty has at last taken himself off, and without one single bit of new engagement on our part. If, as I most confidently expect, he gets knocked on the head some fine morning by his brother or some other near relative, we are not bound to put him back on his shaky gadi, or, rather I should say, to avenge his deposition therefrom. One great spring of mischief in these high politics is to suppose that the situation of to-day is to be the situation of tomorrow. If I were Lord Chesterfield, writing to a son whom I meant to be a statesman, I should say to him, 'Remember that in the great high latitudes of policy all is fluid, elastic, mutable; the friend to-day, the foe to-morrow; the ally and confederate against the enemy, suddenly his confederate against you; Russia or France or Germany or America, one sort of Power this year, quite another sort, and in deeply changed relations to you, the year after!' Excuse this preachment, and be sure not to suspect any 'application,' such as your Scotch preachers are fond of."

II

During the first months of 1907 the discussion of reform was approaching its culmination--the embodiment of the Viceroy's proposals in an official dispatch. The Arundel committee had reported, and the suggestion as to a native member met with no support from the Viceroy's Council, with one solitary exception, its chief opponents being Lord Kitchener and Sir Denzil Ibbetson. Minto's own view on the matter was unshaken ("In accepting an Indian member of Council we should at once admit the immediate right of a native to share in the highest executive administration of the country "), but he was ready to look at the question from every side, to admit the difficulties with the British public, and to put before Mr. Morley the arguments urged against it in

India. It was a strong measure to push the proposal in the face of all his colleagues but one, but he was prepared to face it. He told Mr. Morley so on 27th February:--

"The reasons against it as stated in the notes of members of Council are generally very narrow, based almost entirely on the assumption that it is impossible to trust a native in a position of great responsibility, and that the appointment of a native member is merely a concession to Congress agitation. The truth is, that by far the most important factor we have to deal with in the political life of India is not impossible Congress ambitions, but the growing strength of an educated class, which is perfectly loyal and moderate in its views, but which, I think, quite justly considers itself entitled to a greater share in the government of India. I believe that we shall derive the greatest assistance from this class if we recognize its existence, and that, if we do not, we shall drive it into the arms of Congress leaders."

On 21st March Minto, much encouraged by a deputation from Hindus and Mohammedans, who were anxious to combine in putting an end to the unrest,* sent off the dispatch: "I do not believe that any dispatch fraught with greater difficulties and greater possibilities has ever left India." The contents were kept a close secret, but some hint of them got abroad, and Minto recognized that sooner or later, whatever happened, the native member proposal would be known, and his own share in it.

* Footnote: He wrote to Mr. Morley: "Of all the wonderful things that have happened since I was in India, this, to my mind, was the most wonderful. . . . The burden of it was that they are most anxious to put an end to unrest and bad feeling, and that they propose to organize associations throughout the country with a view to inducing Mohammedans and Hindus to work together for the control of their respective communities. . . . It was simply marvellous, with the troubles and anxieties of a few months ago still fresh in one's memory, to see the 'King of Bengal' sitting on my sofa with his Mohammedan opponents, asking for my assistance to moderate the evil passions of the Bengali, and inveighing agamst the extravagances of Bepin Chandra Pal. I hope you will forgive me a little feeling of exultation at the confidence expressed to me by these representatives of hostile camps, and their declaration of faith in you and Mr. Hare and myself."

"I think," he wrote to Mr. Morley on 17th April, "that Anglo-India would be divided into two camps, agreeing and disagreeing with me, and that I should be violently attacked by the latter both here and at home. If he is appointed, the attacks will, I believe, die down, and gradually disappear; if he is not appointed, we shall have a tremendous revival of agitation, in which moderate natives will join and with which many Anglo-Indians will sympathize. It will be generally known throughout India that the Viceroy (and it will be assumed, I am sure, that your sympathies run in the same direction) and reasonable British opinion as well as native have given way to the clamour of a bureaucracy largely influenced by concern for their own interests. We shall have a row either way, but in the case of the appointment of a native member it would emanate from the official world alone, and would, in my opinion, gradually subside."

On 5th June Minto wrote that he had never been anxious to escape from criticism, and was "quite ready to stand the shot."

The Secretary of State, as he admitted in a later letter of 31st October, was less bold. The King's Speech at the opening of Parliament had hinted at Indian reform, and he clamoured from January till April for the Viceroy's dispatch. When he got it he was inclined to take alarm at the opposition of the Viceroy's Council, and the certain repercussion at home. "I have known," he had written on 24th January, "some slippery places in my ill-spent political days, but I declare I do not recall one when any step, both in reaching a conclusion and in the process of making it known, needs more wary deliberation." He foresaw that his own Council would be unanimous against the native member; ex-Viceroys like Lord Elgin and Lord Lansdowne were hostile, as was an ex-Indian Secretary, Sir Henry Fowler, who, however, according to Mr. Morley, was "not happily constituted for swimming, or even floating, in deep waters "; there was the whole host of retired Anglo-Indians, and the wary and untiring opposition of Lord Curzon to be reckoned with. Even Lord Ripon was against the scheme on its merits. Mr. Morley was better at dealing with recalcitrants in the ranks of his own party, the rump of Indian sympathizers in the House of Commons whom he despised, than with an opposition of which he knew little and which he vaguely respected. His own views in the abstract were Minto's, but he was only half-persuaded himself of the wisdom at the moment of the step, and he failed to persuade the Cabinet, who had always at the back of their minds the agitation which followed the notorious Ilbert Bill. In the Budget debate in the first week of June the Secretary of State did not mention the subject, but announced that the time had now come when he might safely nominate one, or even two Indian members to his own Council. These appointments followed in August.

Meantime, by the fantastic irony of events, while reforms matured anarchy and disorder raised their heads. The area was the Punjab, always a dangerous neighbourhood because of the virile and warlike qualities of the Sikh people, who formed a substantial part of the Indian army. There was rioting in Lahore in April and at Rawal Pindi in May--serious rioting which had obviously been skilfully organized. Something was due to the anti-British propaganda of Bengali agitators, something to the recent plague and the wild suspicions which always accompany such a visitation, and much to the unwise handling by the local Government of the canal colonies. Undoubtedly the native army was being tampered with, and in India a little flicker may in a day be a prairie fire. As Lord Kitchener said, "My officers tell me it is all right, but they said the same thing in the Mutiny days till they were shot by their own men." Sir Denzil

Ibbetson, as Lieutenant-Governor, asked for special precautions to meet a special danger. There was some difference at first in the Viceroy's Council, but summary measures were undertaken. Under an old regulation of 1818 the two chief agitators, Lala Lajpat Rai and Ajit Singh, were arrested and deported without trial. An ordinance was also issued (The Regulation of Meetings Ordinance, 1907) prohibiting the holding of seditious meetings in the provinces of the Punjab and Eastern Bengal. These were strong measures for a Liberal Secretary of State, but Mr. Morley rose gallantly to the occasion, accepted the need for them, and loyally defended the Government of India in Parliament. He had in many letters shown a curious restiveness under the very suggestion of the charge that he might be averse from using the strong hand when the situation demanded it. He felt that to be a suspicion which followed naturally upon his political record, and he was determined to give it the lie. He desired to make concessions to the Indian people, and was the more zealous, therefore, to show that he also stood for law and order. "If we can hatch some plan and policy," he wrote, "for half a generation, that will be something; and if for a whole generation, that would be better. Only I am bent, as you assuredly are, on doing nothing to loosen the bolts."

The instancy and vigour of the action of the Government of India had a miraculous effect in allaying the Punjab unrest. But more effective than anything else was Minto's behaviour in connection with the Chenab colony, suspicion of the Government's attitude as to which had been a prime cause of the trouble. In the administration of this colony, peopled by 1,200,000 souls, the Punjab Government had introduced certain measures which the colonists regarded, and with justice, as a departure from the pledges on which the settlement had been formed. The bill, passed by the Punjab Legislative Council, was now up for the Viceroy's assent; it was admittedly an imperfect measure, it was notoriously unpopular, and to Minto it seemed a clear breach of faith. But he was told, if he disallowed it, that at a critical time he would lessen the prestige of the local government in the eyes of the people. This was never the kind of plea that appealed to Minto's mind. If it was an unjust bill, he told an inquirer, he would not consider the feelings of fifty Punjab governments. "I hate the argument," he wrote to Mr. Morley, "that to refuse to sanction what we know to be wrong is a surrender to agitation and an indication of weakness. It is far weaker, to my mind, to persist in a wrong course for fear of being thought weak." So he disallowed the bill, with the most fortunate consequences. The trouble among the colonies disappeared, and the Viceroy acquired in the eyes of the natives the repute of a just and beneficent divinity. It is needless to say that in his action he had Mr. Morley's fullest support. Lord Kitchener, too, was in favour of the course followed, and Minto's only qualm was that it might seem to cast a slight upon Sir Denzil Ibbetson, a most courageous and competent administrator, who was leaving the Punjab fatally stricken with disease.

During these months the relations with the Secretary of State were cordial, though on occasions a little delicate. Mr. Morley's letters were always full of urbanity and reason, but his telegrams, if there should be any trouble brewing in Parliament, were sometimes petulant and exasperating. His extreme sensitiveness was now apparent to Minto, who laboured to avoid any matter of offence, but sudden storms would blow up, as on the question of Mr. Morley's private correspondence with Kitchener, where an odd misunderstanding arose when Minto thought that he was interpreting Mr. Morley's own expressed wishes. Lady Minto was in England at the time, and had some interesting talks at the India Office. "I don't suppose," the Secretary of State told her, "that any Viceroy has had such a weight of responsibility on his shoulders since India was taken over by the Crown." He felt to the full the comedy of a situation in which a Tory Viceroy on a matter of reform was bolder than a Liberal Minister.

"Lady Minto," he wrote, "told me the other day that I had said that you were a stronger Radical than I am; or else that I was the Whig and you were the Radical, or something of that sort. I daresay I did in good humour talk in that vein, at my own expense, not yours. If I may seem over-cautious to you, 'tis only because I do not know the Indian ground, and I hate to drive quick in the dark. You are at close quarters and see things with your own eyes, and this gives you, rightly gives you, confidence in the region of political expansion. At least be certain that, in object and temper, I am in entire sympathy with you, even if in detail I may now and then differ. You remember old Carlyle's saying of himself and another--'We walked away westward, from seeing Mill at the East India House, talking of all manner of things, except in opinion not disagreeing!' About India I don't know that you and I disagree even in opinion."

In April Minto went into camp at Dehra Dun and elsewhere, and early in May was settled again at Simla. Those summer months, when the Punjab danger was gone, were a time of constant busyness but of comparative peace. Minto had exerted himself to encourage independence among officials, so that they should write what they believed to be true and not what they assumed that the Viceroy wished to hear. His work was bearing fruit in a widespread sense of confidence throughout the hierarchy, and the candour which confidence inspires. Small annoyances were not absent. A section of the English press had constituted itself the passionate apologist of Lord Curzon--which was well enough; but this came to involve a subtle disparagement of his successor, which was merely foolish. Servants of the Crown are not rival beauties, so that the praise of one involves the discrediting of the other. Few people had less vanity than Minto, but any honest man must chafe under misrepresentation. There were difficulties, too, about some of Lord Curzon's enterprises--the Delhi memorial, for instance, which was to commemorate the famous Durbar, and which had got into dire confusion, and the proposed memorial to Clive, with which Minto fully sympathized, but which he saw danger in connecting with the field of Plassey in the then state of feeling in Bengal. He had little leisure for amusement, but at the Horse Show in June he rode his horse "Waitress" and had a toss over a wall--a thing which can never have happened to a Viceroy before. Lady Minto returned from England in July, and Sir Pertab Singh came on a visit in August to reassure Minto about the condition of India. "People know Viceroy," he said; "he soldier, he two-hand man, he make people happy; everyone trust two-hand man. Civilian, he only one-hand man." Under the heaviest press of duties Minto never lost his humour or even his boyishness of temper. He could always see the ridiculous in pompous occasions, and enter into the escapades of his staff, and gossip of sport past, present, or to come, and laugh at the preposterous letter bag of a Viceroy--proposals from unknown Bengalis for the hand of one of his daughters, and requests for gifts to be repaid by the blessing of God, "Whom your Excellency greatly resembles."

During the summer the negotiations for an Anglo-Russian Convention came to a head. The pourparlers between Sir Arthur Nicolson and M. Isvolsky had begun early in 1906, and the first draft of the Convention was telegraphed to India in May 1907. Within these dates there had been a lengthy correspondence between the Viceroy and the Secretary of State, in which the former emphasized especially two points--the absolute necessity of safeguarding the status quo in the Persian Gulf, and the desirability of carrying the ruler of Afghanistan with them. "It is most important," he wrote in June 1906, "to remember that the present position has been agreed between the Amir and ourselves, and that we are not entitled to cancel it without his consent." Minto had little confidence in the decencies of Russian diplomacy and the assurances of St. Petersburg, and he foresaw that the agreement would leave northern Persia a happy hunting-ground for Russian intrigue. More, too, than Mr. Morley, he felt distaste for the whole tradition of the Tsarist government. But it was not his business to criticize the foreign policy of His Majesty's advisers, though he would have assented to many of the criticisms which Lord Curzon made on the Convention in the House of Lords, and, the Gulf position being secured, he was only concerned with the Afghanistan problem.

The possibility of an agreement as to Central Asia between Russia and Japan, which was apparent early in 1907, hastened the steps of the British negotiators, and during the summer there was a continuous and somewhat hectic correspondence between Simla and Whitehall. Minto had to work strenuously to prevent the British Cabinet from ruining utterly the future relations of India and Afghanistan. One instance may be selected. The Cabinet had accepted the following provision: "Should any change occur in the political status of Afghanistan, the two Governments will enter into a friendly interchange of views on the subject." The clause, away from the context of Article II., of which it was to form a part, looked innocent enough, but Minto saw that it might be a fruitful parent of mischief. In order to secure from Russia no more than a repetition of her pledge that Afghanistan was outside the sphere of her influence, we were to bind ourselves to do what we had never dreamed of before--to consult her whenever a change in the political status occurred. Such a change might mean anything. If the Amir sent a batch of officials to India to be trained in revenue work, or asked for a Royal Engineer officer to advise on the fortifying of Kabul, these requests might be reasonably construed as a change in the political status. Moreover, even without any action on the Amir's part, Russia could herself at any time force an alteration in the political status, and so bring the whole question of Britain's relations with Afghanistan into the melting-pot. Minto's protest had its effect, and the objectionable clause was dropped.

The Viceroy failed, however, to induce the Government to consult the Amir before concluding the negotiations. Mr. Morley felt the difficulty, but his colleagues were obdurate; candour with the Amir would prevent the speedy execution of a diplomatic coup on which they had set their hearts. On 2nd August he wrote: "It came to this at last-a choice between accepting the drawbacks and losing the Convention, Of course any one can see that the relations between us and the Amir were never so good as they are at this moment. Nothing can mend them. On the other hand, it is inevitable that the Convention between us and Russia should make him suspicious and uneasy. The notion of his two neighbours 'exchanging views' about annexing and occupying him will naturally have a very ugly look of Partition in his eyes. . . . If the Convention goes on--as in spite of all its drawbacks I am bound to hope that it will--I would ask you to encourage yourself in the delicate diplomacy that we shall in that case impose on you with the Amir. . . . Certainly, if you do not succeed in managing your Kabul friend, the results of the whole proceeding will be disastrous." On 31st August the Secretary of State telegraphed that the Convention had been signed, and on 10th September the part relating to Afghanistan was communicated to the Amir. Minto wrote that he was pleased with the arrangement, and hoped that the Amir would assent, but repeated that he did not believe that it would enable India to reduce her military budget. Months of weary procrastination and obstruction on the part of Kabul were to prove the soundness of his forebodings.

The trouble in the Punjab was allayed for the present, but there was ugly evidence of disquiet elsewhere. The tour in the Madras Presidency of the Bengali agitator, Bepin Chandra Pal, led to a series of riots, and in the autumn his doings in Calcutta resulted in his going to prison for six months. Throughout the autumn and early winter the capital city was in a disturbed state, seditious meetings were frequent, the police were stoned, and in the beginning of December an attempt was made to murder Sir Andrew Fraser, the Lieutenant-Governor. The circular of the British Cabinet on the proposed reforms had arrived in India, and had been communicated to the local governments for their observations, but side by side with the discussion of reform there rose for consideration the necessity of further steps for the preservation of order. Lord Kitchener, whose term of office had been extended by Mr. Morley, was anxious for an improved Press Act, and the subject was discussed in many letters between the Viceroy and the Secretary of State: both disliked the policy on general grounds, but the former was daily growing more convinced of its inevitability. In November the Seditious Meetings Bill was passed (superseding the recent Regulations of Meetings Ordinance), and Minto made a speech in the Legislative Council in which he frankly denned his policy. "The bill is aimed at the inauguration of dangerous sedition, not at political reform, not at the freedom of speech of the people of India. . . . Far from wishing to check the growth of political thought, I have hoped that with proper guidance Indian capacity and Indian patriotism might earn for its people a greater share in the government of their country. . . . We may repress sedition, we mil repress it with a strong hand, but the restlessness of new-born and advancing thought we cannot repress. We must be prepared to meet it with help and guidance, we must seek for its causes." This speech earned the commendation of Mr. Gokhale, who had opposed the bill. "I liked it," he told Dunlop Smith, "though I cannot agree with it. There was a true ring about it." The passing of the Act involved the release of the Punjab deportees. "I have not a shadow of doubt," Minto wrote on 5th November, "that we must release them, and that the sooner we do so the better." So, in spite of the forebodings of the timid, released they were at Lahore on 18th November.

The correspondence of these months with Mr. Morley shows the Secretary of State preserving an air of philosophy under anxieties which he was unwilling to confess and a growing exasperation at the denseness of mankind. "I am not very clever at egg-dances, as my old Chief was," he wrote, "but I'll try my best; and I know that in you, who are the person most directly involved, I shall have a judge who will make allowances. . . . Radical supporters will be critical, and Tory opponents will scent an inconsistency between deporting Lajpat and my old fighting of Balfour for locking up William O'Brien. I shall not, however, waste much time about that. I have always said that Strafford would have made a far better business of Ireland than Cromwell did. . . ." A month before he had written: "I fancy you are of a good temperament for troublous times, and I believe that I am not bad;" but his philosophy was not always proof against vexation, and so we have this cri du coeur:--

"I am so very glad that my lot was cast in the nineteenth century, and not the twentieth! When a man has that sort of feel, 'tis a sign that he should take in his sail, and drift peaceably into harbour. You will understand this highly figurative conclusion."

In July he was getting very weary, not only of the Radical independents in the House of Commons ("I have often thought that a man of Cotton's stamp would like nothing less than such a pacification of India as you are seeking--so perverse and wrong-headed is the vain creature's whole line "), but even of the Indian moderates like Mr. Gokhale. "I am the best friend they have got in England . . . yet they seize the first chance that offers to declare me as much their enemy as Curzon!" Yet, though the letters show now and then the brittle patience of a man approaching seventy, the main impression they leave is of a marvellous vitality. He sends Minto not only his reflections on life and statesmanship, but news of every kind, including a startling view of the German Emperor--which he called a "golden impression"--that "he does really desire and intend peace." At the close of August, when he had appointed the two Indian members* of his Council and was looking forward to a Swiss holiday, he again toyed with the notion of a visit to India. "I have sometimes played with the idea of a scamper to India. . . . How glorious it would be! But my shagreen skin (you know Balzac's Peau de Chagrin?) is rapidly sinking to a sadly diminutive scrap, and I am above all things a homebird. Yet I would honestly give up a moderate bit of my talisman skin if I could have a week's talk at Simla with you." Minto's letters are confined, as a rule, strictly to business, but once he follows the example of the Secretary of State and gives an excerpt from his philosophy of life:--

"It is important to choose the right opportunity for the battle. Of course in many things one must fight and chance the consequences, but sometimes one is more sure to win if one can afford to wait. There is an old racing motto, of which I used to be very fond and which I have always thought well adapted to the race of life:

'Wait in front'--which, being interpreted, means, Do not make too much running, but always be in the place from which you can win when you want to."

* Mr. Krishna Gobinda Gupta of the Indian Civil Service, a Hindu, and Mr. Saiyid Husain Bllgrami, a Mohammedan who had been a member of the Viceroy's Legislative Council.

In November the Mintos paid a visit to the Nizam at Hyderabad, and proceeded thence to Madras. Then they crossed the Bay of Bengal to Rangoon, and after a pleasant but fatiguing tour in Burma were back in Calcutta for Christmas. One of the duties of a Viceroy is that of public entertainer, and he is never without his guests, for any visitor of note has to be bidden to Government House, and the Mintos, having many relations and having accumulated up and down the world an infinity of friends, entertained more extensively than most of their predecessors. Minto's modesty made him willing to learn from any man, and his placid good sense and friendliness made a success of even difficult meetings. A case in point was the tour of the socialist leader, Mr. Keir Hardie, in 1907. He talked beyond question a good deal of nonsense, but mischiefmakers perverted what he said, until he became a bogey of the first order to both England and India. Minto took a juster view and invited him to the Viceregal Lodge. "Keir Hardie," he wrote to Sir Arthur Bigge, "was much better than he was painted. I rather liked him, as I think every one at Simla did who met him. He is simply a crank, and his sayings were very much exaggerated. He was most anxious to see people entirely opposed to his views, and he saw many." To Mr. Morley he wrote: "He said nothing that I could in the least find fault with. He impressed me as a warm-hearted enthusiast, who had come out here with preconceived opinions. He was quite prepared to admit the difficulties of the present position. . . . Though much of this (his criticism) is entirely wrongheaded, there are grains of truth." "What a singular world," Mr. Morley replied. "A talk with Scindia one day and then with Keir Hardie the day after! The last event fills one with a queer exquisite sort of satisfaction; and I think if you had been here while the Keir Hardie storm was at its height (I did not quite escape the force of the gale myself), you would relish the notion of a 'cordial interview with the Viceroy' as keenly as I do. The King heartily approved of your seeing him."

III

In December 1907 a decentralization commission had begun work in India, and in the beginning of 1908 it was plain that trouble would ensue. The commission had been the result of a suggestion of Minto's made early in 1907 as an alternative to Mr. Morley's dangerous proposal of a parliamentary inquiry into Indian affairs. It soon became a pet scheme of the Secretary of State, and he took a keen interest in its composition, selecting various chairmen who failed him one after the other, and finally appointing Mr. (now Sir) Charles Hobhouse. Mr. Hobhouse did not turn out to be the most fortunate of choices. He contrived to offend many of the officials with whom he came into contact, he disregarded the terms of his inquiry and proposed to report on the most delicate and secret matters completely outside his scope, and he finally came into conflict with the Viceroy himself. One evening about 9 p.m. he sent in eighty-six questions, which he asked the Viceroy to consider before noon next day; when told that this was impossible, and that he was in the range of his inquiries exceeding his powers, he demanded a private luncheon with the Viceroy to discuss the question, which was incompatible with viceregal etiquette. Minto wrote to Mr. Morley on 3rd January an account of the deadlock. He did not think that the Government of India should be itself examined on any of the great questions of administration, but should keep clear so that it might be able to give an independent opinion upon the report when completed. Above all, it was impossible to have the commission visiting and interrogating the native states, whose internal relations were a delicate matter and depended mainly upon personal intercourse between the ruling princes and the Viceroy. On 9th January he wrote that the chairman of the commission "is apparently under the impression that some superior power to that of the Government of India has been delegated to him," and he went on to suggest a principle of which Mr. Morley cordially approved: "Indian policy should generally depend upon an exchange of views between the Secretary of State and the Viceroy. There must be a policy for India as a whole approved by His Majesty's Government, and I can see nothing except confusion of ideas if the Secretary of State should be advised by the heads of a number of local governments, in whom generally little reliance can be placed in reference to questions of imperial magnitude."

The worst difficulty was the matter of the native states. Minto refused, rightly, to let the commission visit these states, since its purpose would have been misunderstood, and it would have led to endless perplexities; so it was arranged that, so far as that subject was concerned, the chairman should examine the head of the Foreign department in Calcutta and political officers belonging to any native state he cared to name. Unhappily Mr. Hobhouse misunderstood or forgot the arrangement, went to Rajputana apparently on a private tour, and while there called for confidential reports on a variety of subjects, alleging--or so the officials understood him--that he had a secret commission from Mr. Morley to examine into these matters. The Viceroy promptly forbade the officials to furnish a line of information or Mr. Hobhouse to ask for it. Allowances must be made for the difficulties of the commission; they had "sun-dried bureaucrats" on the brain, and, being on the look-out for secretiveness naturally found it; their task could not be a very easy or popular one, though the Viceroy and the Government of India did everything to facilitate it. But the chairman was unhappily chosen, for his ability and energy were not mellowed by the necessary tact. The Secretary of State was the last man to suffer his name to be taken in vain. Even before the Rajputana incident he had written: "I am in some despair about a certain commission that in a doubtful hour I launched upon you. From many quarters I have the same story of want of tact, and of excessive brusqueness. I can only plead that I did my utmost to warn him, and in every letter I have harped upon the same tune." On the matter of a "secret mission" he was flat in his denial. On 12th March he wrote: "The trouble Hobhouse is giving us really is almost exasperating. The 'secret mission' is wholly unintelligible. Why, I told him fifty times that you were to decide everything in this region. It is as absurd as his talk about my 'delegating' the powers of a Secretary of State to him." The commission was brought to a close with some celerity, and presently Mr. Hobhouse was promoted from the India Office to the Treasury.

The second daughter, Ruby, had become engaged to Lord Cromer's eldest son, and in February Lady Minto went home for the wedding. Before she left she had the felicity of seeing her youngest daughter, Violet, win the Calcutta Ladies' Steeplechase at Tollygunge.

"I took up my position," she wrote in her diary, "in a long stretch of country where we could see four of the wall jumps, feeling too sick with fear to speak. Rolly was equally wretched. It was an awful moment seeing them crash past us. One lady fell at the first wall; Rolly saw a heap on the ground with fair hair, and for one horrid moment thought it was Violet. She was wonderfully calm, not a bit nervous, and holding her horse well together. . . . After seeing them pass we galloped back to the winning post. It was a tricky course with turns, the slippery ground making it much more dangerous. Fortunately the suspense was short-lived. We had hardly got into position before Violet sailed round the corner, leading by several lengths, looking round with the savoir faire of an old jockey to see what she had in hand, as if she had been riding races all her life. She cleared the last fence beautifully and won easily. . . . Violet's first remark after the race was, 'Why wasn't I a boy?' For my peace of mind I am too thankful she wasn't."

Lady Minto left just as the long-expected war broke out on the North-West frontier. The frontier policy of India had been laid down in Lord George Hamilton's dispatch of January 1898, during Lord Elgin's viceroyalty, and had been accepted by Lord Elgin's successors. Its aim was limited liability, and it was based on two main principles--that the military force should be concentrated so as to command the strategical points of the border, and that Government interference with the tribes should be limited so as to avoid the extension of administrative control over independent tribal territory. In consequence most of the regular troops were withdrawn inside the border, Chitral and Malakand being among the few transborder stations occupied, while the tribal valleys, like the Khyber, Kurram, Tochi, and Zhob, were held by local militia corps commanded by British officers. The position could not in the nature of things be satisfactory. The tribal levies were often incompetent, one tribe after another grew restless or took to raiding, punitive expeditions followed, there was a burning of huts and crops, the British retired, and a little later it all began again. The policy had no promise of finality, and the men whose business it was to hold the frontier were inclined to the belief that the strip of no-man's-land lying between India and Afghanistan should be brought directly under British control. The Amir, talking to a British officer, once said, "Till the British frontier reaches the frontier of Afghanistan we never can have peace. So long as these tribes have not been subdued by the British there will be trouble and intrigue." The whole question indeed bristled with difficulties. There was on the one side the natural desire of the British Government not to enlarge its territorial responsibilities; and there was on the other side the exasperation of the frontier officials with a system which did not get rid of responsibility but gave no real guarantee of protection. Minto's view was that a modified occupation was necessary. He wrote to Mr. Morley on October 16, 1907:--

"There need be no necessity for taking the country in the sense of forcing upon it British administration, collection of revenues, etc. We could simply hold it by the creation of one or two roads, or rather by the improvement of the existing roads by means of tribal labour . . . and the establishment of a few advanced posts, leaving the tribes as heretofore to carry on their own tribal administration, as we have done in the Swat valley and other districts. Why should we have a nest of cut-throats at our doors when all our experience has taught us that the mere evidence of British strength means not only safety to ourselves but happiness and prosperity to the districts we have pacified? . . . Putting aside the loss of life and property consequent upon perpetual frontier outrages, the pacification of Waziristan would, in the long run, be far less expensive than a succession of expeditions. I hope when an occasion does arise to resort to force that all this may be borne in mind."

On January 29, 1908, he wrote again:--

"I think perhaps you misunderstand me. I doubt very much if any one who thinks at all would wish to increase our landed property purely for the sake of adding to our possessions. But an examination of our frontier history would, I should say, undoubtedly prove that when we have assumed control of tribal districts comparative civilization and peace have been the result. . . . The examples that come to my mind are Baluchistan, the Kurram valley, the Swat valley, and the tribal country on this side of the Malakand, in which latter district the chief request of the jirga which met me was for an improved railway service! I believe, too, that the responsibility and expense these districts entailed upon us before they came under our control was probably far greater than that which exists at the present day. . . . The state of affairs on our frontier is becoming simply disreputable. We cannot afford any longer to disregard the safety of our own subjects. We shall have to fight, and, of course, we are sure to win. But in doing so are we to spend lives and money and throw aside what we may gain, with the knowledge that in a few years' time we shall have to repeat the same expenditure, which our frontier experience has told us we can so well avoid?"

Mr. Morley was not convinced, but as the last letter was being penned part of the writer's forecast was coming true. On the night of 28th January the Zakka Khel tribe of the Afridi race made a most daring raid on Peshawar. This was the culmination of a long series of outrages, and it was decided to send an expedition into their country, the Bazar valley. A force, consisting of two brigades under the command of Sir James Willcocks, crossed the border on 15th February. Mr. Morley's telegraphed instructions were explicit: "Orders are that the end in view is strictly limited to the punishment of the Zakka Khels, and neither immediately nor ultimately, directly nor indirectly, will there be occupation of tribal territory." The expedition was entirely successful, and, having taken order with the tribes, it withdrew on 29th February. It was a delicate business, for the Zakka Khels had to be isolated from the other Afridis, and there was an ugly attempt of various mullahs on the Afghan side to raise a jehad. It was plain that Habibullah could not control his subjects, for presently came an attack by an Afghan lashkar at Landi Kotal, which was easily beaten off. Also the trouble spread to the Mohmands, who in April assumed an attitude so threatening that Sir James Willcocks had to re-concentrate his field force and read them a sharp lesson. By the middle of May the frontier was quiet again; but anxiety remained, for the springs of the mischief had been in Afghanistan, and the Amir had wrapped himself in mystery and vouchsafed no communication about the Anglo-Russian Convention or anything else. It was fortunate that the year before the Viceroy had at any rate established with him a strong personal friendship.

The campaigns were brilliantly conducted, and the inflammable elements on the frontier, which might have blazed into a formidable war, were skilfully damped down. Mr. Morley followed the details with acute interest, and perhaps with a little nervousness, and its conclusion was to his mind a relief, and also a source of pardonable pride. The philosopher for once had been in command of troops, for the war had been fought under his explicit instructions. The generals were his generals. To Sir James Willcocks he wrote: "I must congratulate you on having carried out my orders so efficiently."

"I follow the military doings with lively interest, and we have people in the office who know the ground. So, by the way, does Winston Churchill, who was there with Bindon Blood. Winston is, next to poor Chamberlain, the most alive politician I have ever come across. . . . They make other folk seem like mere amateurs, flâneurs. . . ."

On 4th March:--

"We Indians are all in good spirits here just now at the end of the Zakka, and at its being a good end; and our gratification is shared to the full by all the rest of the world. I think the policy of His Majesty's Government has been amply justified in the result; and the military part of the work has evidently been done to perfection. For this I cannot but feel that we owe Lord K. a special debt. I don't suppose that he had any taste for our policy of prompt and peremptory withdrawal, and yet he manifestly (and as I learn from letters) threw himself into the execution of it with as much care, skill, and energy, as if he had thought it the best policy in the world. That's the true soldier."

In reply Minto wrote: "K. is the very essence of caution as regards the frontier. I know no one more anxious to avoid punitive expeditions, possibly no doubt because he knows that with the vastly improved armaments of the tribes a frontier war on a big scale would be a very serious affair." And he added this picturesque note:--

"By far the most striking characteristic of the expedition has been its political management by Roos-Keppel. . . . His personal friendship with the very men against whom he was fighting is the most attractive part of the story. Though his own Khyber Rifles are full of Zakkas, they insisted on accompanying him to fight their own fathers and sons and blow up their paternal mansions, and I am told the first thing the Zakka jirga said to him when they saw him was, 'Sahib, did we put up a good fight?' to which he answered, 'I wouldn't have shaken hands with you unless you had!' He is unhappy about Dadai, who was the most powerful Zakka leader against us, and is supposed to have been mortally wounded. He wrote Roos-Keppel a very nice letter from his death-bed, saying how sorry he was for all that had occurred, and that he fully realized the mistake he had made in relying upon assistance from Kabul. Mooltan, too, the other great Zakka leader . . . is also a great friend of Roos-Keppel's, and at one time stayed with him as his guest for three months. He was leader of the famous attack on Peshawar the other day, and wrote to Roos-Keppel afterwards saying he hoped he was not annoyed at what he had done!"

This honeymoon atmosphere between the India Office and Calcutta was fortunate, for there were matters pending on which both Minto and Kitchener were directly at variance with the Secretary of State. Mr. Morley considered that the Anglo-Russian Convention should be followed by a decreased military budget for India; both Viceroy and Commander-in-Chief asked, most pertinently, in what respect the Convention strengthened India's security or enabled her to relax her defensive vigilance. Another point of difference was the policy to be pursued as to southern Persia and the Gulf. Mr. Morley was inclined to criticize Minto's view of the place as the glacis of the Indian fortress; he questioned the appropriateness of the whole metaphor, and he was disposed to deny India's right to a view on the larger questions of foreign policy. "China, Persia, Turkey, Russia, France, Germany," he wrote, "I have never been able to understand, and never shall understand, what advantages the Government of India have for comprehending the play of all these factors in the great game of Empire. On the contrary, the Government of India is by no means the Man on the Spot. That, I say again, is just what the Government of India is not." To such outbursts, which must seem a little beside the mark, Minto replied by stating patiently in many letters the common sense of the case. It was not a matter for extreme dogmas on either side.

"It is not the appearance of German armies that we have to fear, it is the growth of German influence and its effect on Eastern nationalities. Given paramount German influence in Turkey, Asia Minor, Mesopotamia, and southern Persia, our position in India would be seriously threatened. . . . I don't see how Indian interests in Persia and the Gulf can be handed over entirely to home administration, for if this were done, putting aside political matters, any military expenditure in Persia or naval expenditure in the Gulf could not fairly be charged to India. And yet we know that, as a matter of fact, in the case of difficulties arising in Persia it would be upon Indian troops that His Majesty's Government would be obliged to rely. I don't think you can separate Indian interests from the commerce of the Gulf, or the strategical position in Persia from the possible necessity of Indian military assistance."

In April the resignation of Sir Henry Campbell-Bannerman involved a reconstruction of the Cabinet; Mr. Asquith became Prime Minister and Mr. Morley went to the House of Lords, because, as he told Mr. Asquith, "though my eye is not dim nor my natural force abated, I have had a pretty industrious life, and I shall do my work all the better for the comparative leisure of the other place." To Minto he wrote on 15th April:--

"My inclination, almost to the last, was to bolt from public life altogether, for I have a decent library of books still unread, and in my brain a page or two still unwritten. Before the present Government comes to an end, the hand of time will in any case have brought the zest for either reading or writing down near to zero, or beyond. I suppose, however, one should do the business that lies to one's hand."

The new adventure seemed to have raised the spirits of one who never wanted for courage, and who behind a staid exterior preserved a boyish liking for enterprise. A week later he wrote:--

"I have been swamped with correspondence about my grand glorification, winding up with a fuss with a bearish squire in my native Lancashire, who swears I have no right to take the name of his manor as a tag to my own surname. His argument is that his family were there in 1600, 'when there were no Morleys and no Radicals.' . . . I daresay I'll let the bear have his way. . . . As if it mattered to a man with no children who is within a few months of the Psalmist's allotted span! All I hope is to be alive as long as I live--if you understand that; and at present I don't feel otherwise than alive!"

The summer of 1908 was marked by a recrudescence of barbarous outrages, of which the attempts to murder Sir Andrew Fraser and the district magistrate of Dacca in the previous year had been a foretaste. On the night of 30th April a bomb, intended for Mr. Kingsford, a former Chief Presidency Magistrate of Calcutta, was thrown into a carriage in which two Englishwomen were returning from the Club at Muzaffarpur, and both ladies died of their injuries. A secret murder society, operating in Calcutta and Midnapur, was revealed, connected with the notorious Maniktolla Gardens, and bomb factories were discovered in various quarters. In July there were ugly disturbances in Bombay consequent upon the prosecution of Tilak for sedition, and riots at Pandharpur and Nagpur. In September an approver was shot dead by two of the Muzaffarpur prisoners in the chief prison in Calcutta. In November there was another attempt to murder Sir Andrew Fraser, and a native inspector of police was shot in a Calcutta street. It soon became clear that there was a wide network of secret anarchist societies, whose members, mostly of the student class, were inflamed by a scurrilous press, and directed in their crimes by subtle and unwearied leaders.

Minto took the alarming development with fortitude and good sense. "I am determined," he said in the Legislative Council on 8th June, "that no anarchist crimes will for an instant deter me from endeavouring to meet as best I can the political aspirations of honest reformers, and I ask the people of India, and all who have the future welfare of this country at heart, to unite in the support of law and order, and to join in one common effort to eradicate a cowardly conspiracy from our midst." But if he refused to be panicky, he was resolved not to be supine. He was responsible for the lives of many millions of quiet folk, and for the maintenance of order and law, and he was determined to apply the exact measures needed to meet the situation-- no more and no less. He did not ask for a "free hand," he realized that he must carry the Secretary of State with him in all his new measures; but it was his duty to be frank with the British Government and make them realize the truth, even at the cost of giving offence to minds which loved to wrap ugly facts in soft phrases. The measures which Minto enforced may be briefly set down. The English Explosives Act was passed in June as an Indian statute. The Indian Criminal Law Amendment Act, passed in December, provided a summary procedure for the trial of seditious conspiracies, and gave power to suppress associations formed for unlawful acts. The executive Government was empowered to declare an association unlawful, and there was no appeal against its decision. The Press Act of 1908, dealing with newspapers which published incitements to murder and violence, did not create new offences but provided a more drastic procedure, a better machinery for getting at the real culprit, and severer penalties. The Prevention of Seditious Meetings Act of 1907 already gave the Government power to "proclaim" an area and prohibit public meetings within it. The old Regulation of 1818, which permitted the Government to place persons under detention without trial, was put into use, and nine Bengali agitators were clapped into jail in December with excellent results for the peace of the realm. This was perhaps the most criticized of the measures, but it was on the same plane as the British power of suspending the Habeas Corpus Act, and was made necessary because witnesses were being terrorized and dared not go into court.

Such measures were a hard trial for the Secretary of State, and on the whole he faced the facts with courage and reasonableness. The legality of a lawyer is as nothing to the legality of a Whig statesman, and Lord Morley had to strive--not with critics in Parliament, of whom he was habitually contemptuous--but with the prepossessions and traditions of a lifetime. He may have drawn comfort (for he loved to have philosophic authority on his side) from the words of his master Mill, who had written, "A people like the Hindus, who are more disposed to shelter a criminal than to apprehend him . . . who are revolted by an execution but not shocked by an assassination, require that the public authorities should be armed with much sterner powers of repression than elsewhere." It was Lord Morley himself who suggested the application of the Explosives Act to India, and it was enormously to his credit that he accepted the arrest of the nine ringleaders in December. He was unable to resist Minto's resolute and moderate good sense, his clemency which was not changed by difficulties, and his firmness which was not clouded by hysteria. But the Secretary of State had to overcome his ingrained distrust of a bureaucracy, which he believed to be always contemptuous of law and clamorous for the violent hand.

"We cannot carry on upon the old maxims. This is not to say that we are to watch the evildoers with folded arms, waiting to see what the devil will send us. You will tell me what you think is needed. . . . I trust, and fully believe, that you will not judge me to be callous, sitting comfortably in an armchair at Whitehall while bombs are scattering violent death in India."

On 21st May he wrote:--

"I am much with you, or rather you are much with me, in these pretty anxious days. . . . I daresay, however, that you are of the temperament of Thiers. 'In public things, take everything seriously, nothing tragically.' When I began life I was rather the other way, scenting tragedy before there was any need; time and experience have brought me round. Whether I should keep as cool if bombs were flying I don't know."

But sometimes his anxieties got the better of his philosophy. He was alarmed at the sentence of twelve months for the Bombay stone-throwers--he seems to have regarded them as only mischievous urchins--and he was quick to take offence at any phrase in Minto's letters which was capable of being construed into a defence of arbitrary government. There is an illuminating passage in his letter of 17th June:--

"This notion of the 'free hand' is really against both letter and spirit of law and constitution. It cannot be; and let me assure you, on my word of honour as a student of our political history, that nobody would have been more opposed to it than that excellent ancestor and official predecessor of yours, Gilbert Elliot, the friend and disciple of Burke and one of the leaders against the greatest of our Governor-Generals. . . . I have amused myself by turning to Burke's correspondence, and in a letter to Gilbert Elliot I found this: 'No politician can make a situation. His skill consists in his well-playing the game dealt to him by fortune, and following the indications given him by nature, times, and circumstances' (including H. of C. and the British Demos). This sage reflection by one of the greatest of men needs not to be quoted to you, for it is exactly in the vein of your own political temper.

"Oh, but I must hold up my hands at your hint of 'Prerogative'! What a shock to all the Greys, Elliots, Russells, and other grand Whig shades, discussing over and over in the Elysian Fields the foundations of the happy and glorious Constitution of Great Britain! But then you say that on this 'I feel that I am getting into deep water, and would rather sit upon the bank.' My temperature had been slowly rising, but at this good-natured doubt it instantly fell to normal, and I thought how, if you and I had been conducting the controversy with face answering to face--you as Tory, I as the good orthodox Whig--we should have pushed our chairs back and gone forth laughing for a saunter in the garden."

"If reforms do not save the Raj nothing else will," Lord Morley had written, and Minto had replied with spirit that he utterly disagreed. "The Raj will not disappear in India as long as the British race remains what it is, because we shall fight for the Raj as hard as we have ever fought if it comes to fighting, and we shall win as we have always done. My great object is that it shall not come to that." Accordingly the Viceroy pressed on with the reform scheme now being incubated at leisure by the local governments. In this work the Secretary of State most loyally and fruitfully co-operated, and, though the proposals came from India and the details were all worked out there, the scheme may fairly be regarded as preeminently the work of these two men. On 1st November there fell the fiftieth anniversary of Queen Victoria's proclamation of 1858, and it was decided to make this the occasion of a message from the King to the people of India, foreshadowing the reform proposals. Minto was resolved that it should also touch on another matter which lay very near his heart--the abolition of the military disabilities of the Indian gentleman. By law an Indian might, if he were a member of the Indian civil service, become lieutenant-governor of a province, he could hold the highest position on the bench, and there was no legal objection to his being Governor of Bombay or Madras, but whatever his value as a soldier he could not rise above a very inferior rank. Minto was well aware that at first few Indians might be found qualified for responsible commands, but, as he argued in reply to Lord Kitchener's objection, that was not the point. "We want to remove the disability for promotion to such posts which now exists. We can deal with the appointments to them according to the merits of the individuals when the time comes." In November, too, the Secretary of State at last consented to his proposal for a native member of Council.

On 1st October the Viceroy sent home the fateful dispatch giving the considered scheme of the Government of India. Lord Morley appointed a small expert committee to report on the proposals, and in a dispatch of 27th November sanctioned the scheme, subject to certain slight modifications. Meantime, on 1st November, Minto, in a great durbar at Jodhpur, had delivered the message of the King. Lady Minto's diary describes the scene in that ancient city set amid the deserts:--

"It was exactly as if we had gone back at least five centuries. The entire route was lined on each side with the Thakurs and their retinues, each band having their distinctive pugrees. On either side of the road there were caparisoned horses with marvellous trappings, long flowing draperies covering their heads, richly embroidered with gold and silver, all wearing the thick gold bracelet above the right knee, pawing the ground and arching their necks as they are taught to do; elephants completely covered with velvet embroideries and massive silver ornaments; camels galore, some carrying antediluvian guns which look as if they could never have done much execution; mounted men covered from head to foot with chain armour, wearing the identical suits of mail used in battle at the time of the early Mogul Emperors."

In this romantic setting the Viceroy read the words of the King-Emperor, repeating and enlarging the charter of 1858. The time had come when the principle of representative institutions must be prudently extended, and the measures to ensure this would soon be made known. "For the military guardianship of my Indian Dominion I recognize the valour and fidelity of my Indian troops, and at the New Year I have ordered that opportunity should be taken to show in substantial form this my high appreciation of their martial instincts, their splendid discipline, and their faithful readiness of service."

In December the reform scheme, the details of which will be discussed in the next chapter, was made public both in England and India. There was little criticism, and much approval in both countries. The "native member," the supposed bone of contention, was universally accepted. Only the scheme for "electoral colleges," which had been inserted at home, was disquieting to the Mohammedans. "I hope," Minto had written to Lord Morley on 30th November, "I am not overweening in my feeling that we are about to share in the triumph of a great work. There may be no visible triumph at first, and there will be any amount of criticism, but I believe that thinking India will realize that much has been gained. Notwithstanding all my warnings as to possible further trouble, perhaps I am more sanguine than you are. Instinct seems to tell me that we are nearing the turn of the tide." So the year 1908, which had been dark enough at times, ended with a brighter horizon. A vicious outbreak of anarchist crime had been promptly checked, miscreants had been laid by the heels, and Tilak, the cleverest agitator in India, had been transported for six years. A great scheme of reform had been happily passed into law. The anxiety about Afghanistan's attitude towards the Convention with Russia had been protracted till September, to Lord Morley's intense annoyance, but it was allayed during that month by the receipt of a friendly letter from the Amir, and wholly dispelled in October when M. Isvolsky visited England. In spite of unceasing work Minto had kept his health, and his private life had been happy as ever. His youngest daughter had become engaged to Lord Lansdowne's second son, Lord Charles Fitzmaurice, and in November Melgund and Lady Eileen arrived from England. Even in the most harassing times Minto's correspondence never fails in a sense of the humour of life. He describes for the benefit of Lord Morley his visit to Scindia, when the Maharani sang Scots songs to him from behind the purdah, and he joined in the choruses. "It was really all too curious--the more so when I think that less than a hundred years ago my grandfather, General Sir Thomas Hislop, finally defeated the Mahratta army under Holkar at the battle of Medhipore, not so very far from here, and that here was

I, his grandson, singing songs with Scindia's wife!" Nor was the Secretary of State slow to reply in kind. He regrets that he did not remain in the House of Commons to deal as "'chief goose-herd'" with what he described as "the honest Liberal Fools and the baser sort of Unionist ditto." "An under-secretary cannot put the fear of God into their silly hearts, as the Secretary of State can at least try to do. However, I am up aloft, and there I am happy to stop; at the same time I have told Asquith that there is to be no playing with India to please the geese." In a delightful letter on 10th December he complains that he has a black dog on his back, which "makes me think of the Psalmist at his worst, or Job, Chapter III.," and which might be explained by an influenza cold. "To cook up a powerful and impressive oration, one half for coercion and t'other half against it, in the midst of cough, quinine, and blankets, is no joke, I can assure you. Ah, well, as I think I'm always saying to you:--

"'Be the day short or be the day long, At length it ringeth to Evensong.'

"A jingle that comforts me, I hardly know why, for Time is bringing me into pretty close sight and sound of the last Evensong of all. Time recalls the Times newspaper--" and then follows press gossip, which never failed to amuse him.

But loyal and helpful as he was in all great matters, and warm as were the feelings of the two men for each other, the Secretary of State did much to increase the Viceroy's load. The India Office was swathed in red tape and slow in movement, and it was excessively curious about trivialities--a free passage to a widow or a pension to some minor official. In September Minto protested strongly against this habit; already a member of the Hobhouse commission had told Lord Morley that the first object for decentralization was the India Office. But the Secretary of State himself was not free from the same fault, and he harassed the Viceroy with constant telegrams about matters with which he had no real concern, forgetting the words of Mill, at whose lamp he said he had kindled his "modest rushlight"--"The executive Government of India must be seated in India itself." Lord Morley had not the gift of quickly acquiring information on unfamiliar topics; he remained oddly ignorant of the details of Indian conditions, and to the end made suggestions which were occasionally so beside the mark as to be comic. That would have been a small matter if he had not wished to direct actively parts of the administrative machine himself, a task for which he had neither the right kind of experience nor the right kind of talent. Constantly he wanted to use his fine brain as ineptly as the man who sets a race-horse to the plough. This habit doubled the Viceroy's work, and it is impossible to read the telegraphic correspondence between Simla and Whitehall without regarding much of it as a sheer waste of time and energy. There was often material for a quarrel. Lord Morley was jealous of the correspondence of Minto or any high Indian official except with himself, and when Minto hinted at the extension of the same principle to Lord Morley's correspondence with Lord Kitchener he was seriously hurt. When an Indian official went to England he was shepherded by the Secretary of State from any contact with Foreign Office or War Office. Few Ministers of the Crown have been so unyieldingly despotic in the lesser matters of conduct. His sense of personal dignity, too, was easily offended; his vanity, otherwise an innocent and attractive thing, could suddenly become peevish; a casual careless phrase in the letter of an overworked man became the occasion for a homily. The truth seems to have been that in 1908 he was beginning to feel his seventy years, and that the outrages in India and the inevitable measures that followed so offended his sense of decency and his lifelong traditions, that they preyed upon his mind and unsettled his temper. His letters were invariably courteous, his telegrams, reflecting his momentary moods, were often petulant and unjust. Minto set himself the difficult task of refusing to be ruffled and replying always considerately and calmly, and to his lasting honour he succeeded.

But it wore him down. He was not the man to complain in public or private; but in an occasional letter to his wife or to an old friend like Sir Arthur Bigge there is a hint that he found it hard to soothe the sensitiveness and allay the suspicions of a Secretary of State who did not readily understand the etiquette of a service, and was apt to accept, as veracious, preposterous gossip from private letters, and demand of an overworked Viceroy immediate inquiry and explanation. It was his business to allow for Lord Morley's temperament as part of the problem he had to meet, and in reading the correspondence it is pleasant to note how Minto's knowledge of human nature and his real affection for the Secretary of State taught him the best way of handling his colleague. He overstates a point that Lord Morley may have the satisfaction of whittling it down; he insinuates in successive letters a policy till presently it returns from Whitehall as Lord Morley's own proposal; he patiently crumbles a prejudice against some official till Lord Morley becomes the advocate of his merits.

Such a result would never have been obtained but for the solid foundation of liking and respect between the two men. The compensations were great, for there would suddenly come from Lord Morley such an outflow of kindliness that a less sensitive heart than Minto's would have been touched. The Viceroy hints that the Secretary of State takes perhaps too detailed an interest in the affairs of India, and the latter replies that he read the words with a friendly smile. "My only excuse is that I have to aid you in your battle." There is a slight difference of opinion, and Lord Morley writes: "We are placed in positions where the points of view of Whitehall and Simla are necessarily different, but what I can say . . . is that you and I have entire confidence in one another's aims and sense of public duty." On October 30, 1908, he writes again: "We have now had all but three years of it, and considering the difference in our experience of life and the world, and the difference in the political schools to which we belong (or think we belong), and the intrinsic delicacy of our official relations, our avoidance of reefs and snags has been rather creditable all round. When 11th December comes--the anniversary of my taking the seals--I feel as if I could compose a very fine Te Deum duet, in which you shall take one part if you will, and I the other." And the last day of December brought the Viceroy this New Year message: "Believe that I am very heartily your well-wisher for 1909, and as many more years as you care to have. At least you leave off at the end of 1908 in a position that must gratify all your friends, including Morley of B." Exasperation could not endure for long with a nature so essentially warm and gracious, and--in its considered moods--so magnanimous. In talking with Lady Minto on her visit to England Lord Morley paid the finest tribute which perhaps Secretary of State ever paid to Viceroy. "I am swimming," he said, "in a popular tide through victories which are not my own."

CHAPTER ELEVEN

VICEROY OF INDIA, 1909-10

JANUARY was filled with preparations for Lady Violet's marriage to Lord Charles Fitzmaurice, which was celebrated in Calcutta Cathedral on the 20th. "Scindia, Sir Pertab Singh, and Cooch Behar," Minto wrote to Lord Morley, "were all in the church--the ecclesiastics not being the least shocked by their presence." Wedding gifts were offered from every quarter, and though their acceptance was forbidden by the etiquette of the Viceroy's office, the feeling which prompted their offer was gratefully recognized. One such present, which was purchased by Lady Minto, was a posteen offered by an Afghan trader with the following letter: "As Vicereine of India, and we humble savages of the wilds of Afghanistan having heard that your honoured daughter, Lady Violet Elliot, will to-morrow become, by the grace of the Great Allah, Lady Fitzmaurice, the husband which to-morrow will be the second son of that great noble and benefactor of our land, the Marquis of Lansdowne. On such news reaching us, we thought we could do no better than pay homage to thee, good Ladyship, and to the great Viceroy, Lord Minto, and to thy gracious daughter, Lady Violet, by coming and offering, as our poor means will allow, something that will prove our loyalty to thy Great Family and to the invincible British Raj." Lord Kitchener proposed the health of the bride, and the cake was cut with his sword. "Lady Violet," he said, "has won more hearts than that of Lord Charles, and I feel sure there are none present who do not deeply and sincerely regret her departure from amongst us. For that we hold Lord Charles responsible, but considering his temptation, I think we must forgive him."

The year 1909 had for its chief work the final perfecting and establishing of the new reforms. The scheme received in India an almost unanimous welcome, and Mr. Gokhale in the Budget debate in March declared that the Viceroy and Lord Morley between them had saved India from drifting "towards what cannot be described by any other name than chaos." In the early months of the year the Secretary of State was engaged in piloting the necessary bill through Parliament, a task which he performed with remarkable skill and with a certain humorous enjoyment.

"Balfour spoke in his usual pleasant and effective way for a short half-hour, mainly occupied with an interesting analysis of the conditions that are required to make representative government a success, ending in the conclusion that India satisfies none of these conditions. . . . He vouched me as undoubtedly agreeing with him as to Indian unfitness for representative institutions; and he was quite right. With the bill and the scheme he hardly dealt at all, and his criticism was purely superficial. It reminded me of what Gibbon said about Voltaire 'casting a keen and lively glance over the surface of history.' On the whole, sitting perched up over the clock in the Peers' Gallery, I felt as if I were listening to a band of disembodied ghosts--so far off did they all seem from the hard realities and perplexities with which we have been grappling all these long months. Though it would never do for me to say so, I must secretly admit that the thing compared very poorly with the strength and knowledge of the debates on the bill in the House of Lords. I found also, when the dinner hour arrived, that I had already, in less than a twelvemonth, acquired one inexorable propensity of every selfrespecting peer; I adjourned; and after a modest meal at the Club, instead of returning to hear more speeches, I went home to bed, where I did not dream of Mackarness, Cotton, and other excellent men. Some day it will be your turn to listen to an Indian debate from the same perch; for I dare not suppose that we have finally settled the business. I will not ask you to send me an account down in the Elysian Fields, where I shall then be wandering at my ease."

The inevitable criticism of the bill in the British Parliament and press had its repercussion in India, and the doubts were chiefly about the native member of the Viceroy's Council. It had been decided to offer the appointment as legal member to Mr. Sinha, the Bengal Advocate-General, who, greatly to his credit, was willing to sacrifice his very large private income at the Calcutta Bar. King Edward was seriously concerned at the whole proposal, and in a talk to Lord Morley, while admitting that there was no alternative against a unanimous Cabinet, remonstrated vigorously about the whole proceeding. Minto wrote to the King on 4th March in the hope of removing certain misconceptions:--

"The Viceroy was inclined when he first came to India to argue with certain of his colleagues on his Executive Council that an Indian member should be added to their number and a seat provided for him by statute. The Viceroy has, however, since come to the conclusion that an Indian member, occupying a seat created by statute, would be an admission of the necessity for racial representation, which would create rival claims for such seat amongst the many nationalities, religions, and castes of India. Moreover, a seat held on racial qualifications would, it appeared to the Viceroy, indicate a disregard for the special qualities which should entitle an individual to hold such a seat, viz., professional ability, administrative experience, and social standing. . . . From the Viceroy's point of view, therefore, the point involved is the question whether, if an Indian gentleman is possessed of the above qualifications, he should be debarred because of his race from holding an appointment for which he may be exceptionally suited. The Viceroy thinks he can no longer in justice be so debarred, and that racial disability should be removed."

The step required no statutory authority, and on 24th March the press contained the news of Mr. Sinha's appointment. At the accomplished fact criticism died away. "The Times" Lord Morley wrote, "shakes its head a little . . . they shed tears over the fact that Sinha has not some score of the rarest political virtues in any world-- courage, patience, tact, foresight, penetration, breadth of view, habit of authority, and Heaven knows what else--

just as if all those noble qualities were inherent in any third-rate lawyer that I could have fished out of Lincoln's Inn, or even as if they are to be found in all the members of the Executive Council as it stands to-day!"

The new member did his work most competently, though he often sighed for his unofficial days, and at various times alarmed the Viceroy by showing a strong inclination to return to them. The notion that his appointment would give offence to the ruling chiefs was dramatically disposed of when in September Scindia came to Simla, and of his own accord made it his first business to call on Mr. Sinha. "Times have changed," Minto wrote. "How long will it take 'Indicus olim' to recognize the fact?" As to Mr. Sinha's attitude to British rule, it is sufficient to record a saying of his in conversation with Lady Minto: "If the English left India in a body, we should have to telegraph to Aden and get them to return as fast as they could, for in a couple of days India would be in chaos."

The Reform bill was passed into law on 25th May, and, since much had been left to be effected by regulations, the Government of India had to frame these and send them home early in July. Lord Morley appointed a committee to consider them ("I can at least promise you that it shall not be illuminated by the shining presence of Lord Macdonnell"), and the Viceroy in Council brought the Act into operation as from 15th November. It is unnecessary here to give more than a general sketch of the main provisions. The total strength of the various legislative councils was raised from 124 to 331, and the number of elected members from 39 to 135, a majority of non-official members being introduced in every legislative council except that of the Viceroy. Power was given to members to move resolutions on matters of general public interest, to discuss the annual budgets more freely, and to put supplementary questions. We have already seen the appointment of an Indian member to the Viceroy's Executive Council; the members of the Executive Councils of Madras and Bombay were increased, and power was given to appoint an Indian member of each, while it was also made possible for the Viceroy, with the assent of the Secretary of State, to create an executive council in any other province.

The method of election of non-official members to the various legislative councils was complex, since it was desired to ensure an adequate representation of the professional classes, the landholders, the Mohammedan population, and the European and Indian commercial communities. In a country such as India a simple plebiscitary system was obviously out of the question. These interests could be represented only by means of separate electorates or by nomination. The main difficulty concerned the Mohammedans, as to whom a vigorous controversy raged all summer both in India and in Britain. The Government of India's plan, following upon Minto's pledge to the Moslem deputation on October 1, 1906, was to give the Mohammedans separate electorates, supplemented to the full extent of their legitimate claims by further representation through mixed electorates, or by nomination where they failed to obtain a fair share of the elective seats. Minto desired to prevent the followers of Islam from becoming a rigid enclave, divorced from the rest of Indian life. But unfortunately during the discussion of the bill in Parliament the Secretary of State suggested as the best solution mixed electoral colleges based on proportional representation. This proposal, which seemed to entrust Mohammedan interests wholly to mixed electorates, and to abandon the principle of communal representation, was stoutly opposed by Indian Moslems, and by Mr. Ameer Ali and the Aga Khan in London. The Mohammedan leaders put their claims too high, but eventually they were induced to agree to what was virtually the Viceroy's scheme, receiving a minimum of six members in the Viceroy's Legislative Council--five elected by purely Mohammedan electorates, one nominated, and possible additions from the mixed electorates. There were many deputations received and interviews granted in Whitehall and Simla, and Lord Morley seems, in spite of his tenderness for Islam, to have grown very weary of Islam's spokesmen. It was delicate ground, for, as he wrote, "We have to take care that in picking up the Mussulman we don't drop our Hindu parcels." "I have agreed," he told Minto, "to receive the sons of the Crescent next week. I wish the Prophet himself was coming! There are not many historical figures whom I should be better pleased to summon up from Paradise, or wherever he now abides."

The Viceroy and the Secretary of State had been at one in every major detail of the reforms. They were at one, too, in the perspective with which they regarded them, though Lord Morley may have placed the main emphasis on the increase of elected representatives in the legislatures, and Minto on the executive partisanship of which the first step was the admission of natives to the executive councils. Neither thought that the scheme would be a final settlement; both believed that it was "that just measure of change required to meet what was reasonable in the current demands." The words of the Secretary of State in the letter of 2nd April would have been willingly subscribed to by the Viceroy:--

"It may be that the notion of co-operation between foreigners and alien subjects is a dream. Very likely. Then the alternative is pure Repression and the Naked Sword. But that is as dangerous and uncertain as Conciliation, be that as bad as Balfour thinks, because it is impossible that the Native Army can for ever escape contagion. And railways and telegraphs put new and formidable implements in the hands of even the civil population, if they break into mutiny. Our Liberal expedients may fail. The Tory experiment of grudging and half-and-half concessions is sure . . . to end in dangerous impotence. The only chance, be it a good chance or a bad chance, is to do our best to make English rulers friends with Indian leaders, and at the same time to do our best to train them in habits of political responsibility."

But there was one question on which at no time the two men saw fully eye to eye. This was the matter of the deportations. Lord Morley, though he had assented to the strong measures of the previous winter, was never enamoured of them, and he was perpetually haunted by doubts as to their advisability--doubts which it pleased certain young Conservatives in the House of Commons to increase in their search for cause of offence against the Government. The question arose on the political disqualification of deportees for which Minto argued. The mere right of veto in the Viceroy after election seemed to him to be attended with the gravest disadvantages, and he proposed a general disqualification, with the right of the Viceroy to permit candidature in special cases. Minto stated his views, as he felt it his duty to do, with vigour and frankness:--

"What is our main duty? Surely it is, in the first place, to govern India with due regard to the welfare and peace of its population--not to attempt, irrespective of those interests, to conform with principles which the political training of years may have rendered dear to the people of England, but which are totally unadapted to the conditions we have now to deal with in this country. . . . It is such guidance of the Government of India by a Parliament totally ignorant of local conditions which, if it is to represent a generally accepted principle in our administration of India, is, I must regretfully say, in my opinion certain to prove disastrous. . . . Political disqualification in England, and in India just awakening to political life and governed largely by the mere prestige of British authority, cannot be judged by the same standard. A released political prisoner who becomes a member of Parliament in no way threatens the safety of the constitution, but the election of Lajpat Rai to the Viceroy's Legislative Council would set India in a blaze. . . . . We must not forget . . . that our councils will be comparatively small, and that the introduction into them of a stormy petrel would have a very different effect to a similar introduction into the historic atmosphere of the House of Commons."

The matter was finally settled by permitting the Viceroy by regulation to give to himself and the local governments the power to prevent the nomination of any irreconcilable--which was, of course, a more stringent precaution than the disqualification of deportees as such. On a second point the controversy was still warmer. Lord Morley, not unnaturally, wished to signalize the completion of the Reform scheme by some notable act of clemency. "The continued detention of the deportees," he telegraphed on 21st October, "makes a mockery of the language we are going to use about reform. It makes a thoroughly self-contradictory situation." He therefore wished to announce their release simultaneously with the publication of the regulations. The Secretary of State was being much badgered on the matter, and he wished to get rid of so embarrassing a burden.

"A very clever Tory lawyer, F. E. Smith," he wrote to the Viceroy in May, "the rising hope of his party and not at all a bad fellow, has joined the hunt. . . . You will understand that I have no notion whatever of giving way, whatever happens, unless you see a chance of releasing some or all of the detenus one of these days. . . . The mischief to India of a long stream of nagging questions and attacks, especially if even a handful of Tories join my knot of critics, rather perturbs me. . . . F. E. Smith said to a friend of mine, 'I would not object to deportation in an emergency if the man who imposed it was an English country gentleman.' 'But then,' was my answer, 'what else is Lord Minto?' . . . Don't be offended if I say boldly that, if I were Governor-General to-day, I would make up my mind to have an amnesty on the day when the new Councils Act comes into force. As you know, I could argue the other way if I liked, but I have an instinct that this is the way that would redound most to the credit and honour for courage acquired by you already."

Minto had long ago come to the conclusion that the deportees must be released as soon as the reforms were in operation. But he was resolutely opposed to their release till the elections were over, and so strongly did he feel on the matter that at one moment, when it seemed likely that he might be overruled, he took the strong step of asking that the protest of the Government of India should be made public. His argument, which ultimately convinced Lord Morley, seems difficult to resist:--

"One of the great hopes of our Reform scheme was to 'rally the Moderates.' Surely it would not be wise to turn loose those firebrands into the political arena just at the very moment when we are hoping that the reasonable and stable characters in Indian society will come forward and range themselves on our side, and on the side of constitutional progress. It seems to me that, if we were to do this, we should indeed be creating a 'self-contradictory situation,' in that, having withdrawn the deportees from political life for nine months or so while nothing was going on, we should be liberating them at the very moment when the whole country will be in the turmoil of a general election, and when we are trying for the first time to work out an entirely novel electoral machinery!"*

(* Footnote: The following telegrams may be quoted:--

Secretary of State to Viceroy.

"31st October 1909.

"Regarding the deportees--I earnestly hope that I am not to understand that you reject the unanimous suggestion of the Cabinet. Such a result would be most grave, and I am sure you will consider the situation with a full sense of responsibility, as I sincerely try to do."

Viceroy to Secretary of State.

"2nd November 1909.

"Your telegram of 31st October. I have always recognized the great importance of our agreement in all matters, and also know the many considerations you have to deal with at home, but the Viceroy and Government of India are answerable to you for the immediate administration of India, and are bound to state their views to you as to the safety or otherwise of action affecting that administration. I have already told you that the decision of my Council against release is unanimous, and is supported by the strong opinions of Lieutenant-Governors. My telegram of 22nd October explains our reasons. I cannot state position more clearly than in last part of my private telegram to you of 31st October, the following portion of which I venture to quote, namely:--

"'The question is whether the deportees can be released with due regard to the internal peace of India. My Council have twice decided that they cannot now be so released, in which Lieutenant-Governors concerned absolutely agree. We shall be heartily glad to release them when we know that conditions will allow of it, but I must say distinctly that to release them on either of the dates you name would be full of unjustifiable risk, and would be entirely contrary to the reasons for which they were deported--namely, that their freedom endangered the peace of the country.'

"I have most carefully considered the situation, and can only say, with a full knowledge of conditions throughout the whole of India, that the Viceroy and

Government of India would be betraying the trust imposed upon them by His Majesty's Government if they now expressed themselves otherwise than in my telegram of 22nd October. If His Majesty's Government decides upon the opposite course, the Viceroy and Government of India must accept their instructions, but they could not be held responsible for the results: and, putting aside the renewal of agitation, I feel bound to tell you that, from an Indian point of view, I cannot conceive at the present moment anything more dangerous than that disregard should be had to the matured opinions of the Government of India and local Governments.")

The period during which the reforms were approaching their consummation was ironically marked by anarchy and outrage. In February the public prosecutor in the Alipore case was murdered; in the early summer secret criminal societies were discovered in Gwalior, the Deccan, and Eastern Bengal; and on 1st July there was perpetrated the hideous murder of Sir William Curzon Wyllie and Dr. Lalkaka at the Imperial Institute in London. The murderer, Dingra, belonged to a most respectable Punjab family, one of whom had written a book which he had dedicated to the Viceroy. There were constant dacoities in Bengal, committed by young Hindus in order to swell the revolutionary funds, and there was disquieting evidence that the mischief might spread from the Bengali student class to the more virile races of the north. Finally, on 21st December, Mr. Jackson, the collector of Nasik in the Deccan, was shot dead by a young Brahmin at a farewell theatrical performance given in his honour. The Nasik case compelled the Government to postpone the return of the deportees and to prepare more stringent measures of precaution. Minto kept his head amid these embarrassments. "I hope," he wrote to Lord Morley, "that public opinion won't take the unreasonable view that the deeds of a few anarchists are proof of the doubtful loyalty of all India. Of this I am absolutely certain, that if it had not been for our recognition of Indian political ambitions, we should now have had ranged against us a mass of discontent composed not only of extremists, but of those who are now our most loyal supporters."

He had himself a share of the attention of the criminals. On 13th November, while on a visit to Ahmedabad, two bombs were thrown at the carriage in which he and Lady Minto were driving. They failed to explode, but one subsequently went off in the hands of a water-carrier who picked it up, causing serious injuries. Both the Viceroy and his wife took the affair with the utmost coolness and courage. Lady Minto in her journal merely records that the day was her birthday and that bombs were an odd kind of birthday present. Minto, writing a short account of it to Lord Morley, prefaced his letter by saying that he was too overworked to send him more than scraps of news, and ended with a mild grumble at the discomfort which attempts on a man's life entailed:--

"Imagine our portentous precautions! Last night we proceeded solemnly to that awful ordeal, a State Banquet. After being seated some time and no food appearing, various high officials sallied forth to investigate the causes of delay and found two sentries with fixed bayonets standing over the soup, which they refused to admit without a pass!"

Lord Morley wrote:--

"In spite of your magnanimous refusal to attach any political significance to the bombs, one cannot but feel that the miscreants who planned the outrage were animated by politics, if one can give the name of politics to such folly and wickedness. Anyhow it was fine and truly generous of you to say that you stoutly resisted the idea that it represented anything like the heart of the general Indian population. This is one of the utterances that will stick, and will cause your name to be held in honour. Lord Roberts was here the day after, and I read him your first telegram. He said, 'Ah, Minto is an intrepid fellow! He hasn't a nerve in him!' This would be rather an awkward thing for you from the anatomical and physiological point of view; but I knew what he meant!"

II

The year 1909 deprived the Viceroy of two fellowworkers whom he deeply valued. His private secretary, Sir James Dunlop Smith, whose great Indian experience, unfailing loyalty, and tireless industry had been of incalculable service, was appointed to follow Sir W. Curzon Wyllie at the India Office. In August Lord Kitchener ceased to be Commander-in-Chief, and was succeeded by Sir O'Moore Creagh. It was an open secret that Kitchener would have liked to be the next Viceroy; he was made a Field-Marshal and accepted the offer of the Malta command which was pressed on him, but he obtained permission after his long Indian service to indulge himself with a preliminary holiday in the Far East. His relations with Minto had been always those of the most cordial friendship, and the fact is the more remarkable when it is remembered that Minto was himself a soldier and in no way disposed to accept the Commander-in-Chief's views on army questions without a searching examination of his own. "In military matters," he wrote to Lord Morley, "I am not quite the same as other Viceroys have been, or are likely to be in the future. For many years I served as a soldier in various capacities all over the world, have seen much active service, and much of other armies besides our own, and this not only from the love of adventure, for I worked hard at the more intellectual requirements of a military career. Consequently the comprehension of military organization and administration comes very naturally to me, and military policy in India is a matter on which I shall always hold decided views of my own, no matter what my Commander-in-Chief may think!" In August he wrote: "I shall miss K. very much, for he has supported me most loyally always, and I look upon him as a real friend. We have differed--as, of course, we must occasionally--over certain things, but I have always found him very open to conviction. He is such a different man to what the outside public suppose him to be. In my humble opinion you could not select for the gadi a more reliable occupant." Minto had laboured to interpret Kitchener to the Secretary of State, and had met with some success, but on the question of the Viceroyalty he found him adamant. "I should not much care," wrote Lord Morley, "to be Secretary of State if he were Governor-General, and what is more, my dear Viceroy, I don't mean to be." To Lord Morley Kitchener was only a competent and stiff-necked soldier; perhaps it was impossible except for those who worked closely with him to realize that his political sagacity and prescience were more notable than even his talents for tactics or strategy.

Lord Kitchener's departure was not unattended with sensation. His farewell speech at Simla proved to be largely an adaptation of Lord Curzon's farewell speech at the Byculla Club in 1905. Parallel columns in the Times showed a damaging identity both in matter and style. There had been no such case of plagiarism since Disraeli cribbed from Thiers his panegyrics on the Duke of Wellington, and the situation was made piquant by the fact that copier and copied were old and unreconciled antagonists. Minto's letter to Lord Morley explains the affair as far as explanation was possible. Sir Beauchamp Duff had been in the habit of helping Kitchener with his speeches.

"At first I thought the similarity might be mere coincidence--but such a possibility vanishes when one sees the passages side by side. The best explanation I have heard--and I have good reason to think it the true one--is that K. merely told Duff that he would find some good points in Curzon's speech, but I am firmly convinced that K. never intended that he should use it as he did, and never had any idea that he had done so. But then, as I say--how is Duff's performance to be accounted for? Of course there are ill-natured explanations beneath contempt. The supposition that it was irony on K.'s part has also gone the rounds here--sheer impossible nonsense. . . . K. is a very bad speaker--hates having even to say a few words--always reads his speeches, and read the one in question particularly badly. . . . I am very sorry about it all. It is lucky for K. that he is on the high seas!"

The arduousness of the Viceroy's life did not decrease as the months went by. In October he wrote to Lord Morley: "I have been in India almost four years now, and during that time I have not had one single free day to myself. Even on the few occasions I have been away in camp, I have never had a day without official work. One must be strong and well to start early in the morning, go through long tiring hours in the sun, and come back to one's tent to find it full of files and official telegrams and work till midnight or the small hours of the morning. But so it is, and I am thankful to say, so far, I am fit and well." The relief in such a life was the shifting of base--the move from Calcutta to Simla, and the journeys to distant provinces.

The visit to Lahore in April was a great success. The Viceregal party on elephants entered the narrow streets of the old city, where every house was decorated with embroideries and mottoes, including the remarkable couplet:--

"Eipon, Minto, Morley, England's greatest three, India sing their praises till eternity."

"The wonderful part," Minto wrote to Lord Morley, "was that our route lay through the very heart of the old city, through streets no Viceroy had ever before been allowed to pass. It had not been considered safe. . . . Nothing but friendly enthusiasm the whole way. I confess it was all very encouraging. Yet it is an inflammable population, a much more dangerous population in reality than in Bengal."

Later in the same month the Mintos went tiger-shooting in the vicinity of Dehra Dun, and while waiting mounted on elephants while the jungle was being beaten out, encountered an appalling thunderstorm. "The air seemed full of electricity," says Lady Minto's journal; "the noise was deafening, and besides the forks of flame flashes of light seemed to break out in all directions. . . . We all agreed that, as long as the Viceroy held on to his rifle, the rest of the party were in duty bound to follow suit. Rolly declared that he would have given a thousand pounds to get rid of it, but his izzat forbade his taking such a course."

That summer Minto and his wife had an encounter with a mad dog, and had to undergo the Pasteur treatment, which has a most depressing effect upon the system. Happily both had equable nerves, but the twenty-one days of suspense were a nightmare to the staff. During the autumn there was an extended tour among the Rajput states, and at Udaipur on 6th November Minto delivered an important speech on the subject of the native states and the ruling princes. The loyalty of the latter had been questioned in irresponsible quarters in Britain, but their behaviour during the outbreak of anarchy in the past two years had given the lie to the calumny. The Viceroy now took occasion to define the policy of Britain--the more necessary now that democratic reform was on the eve of being introduced in British India. At Gwalior in 1899 Lord Curzon had announced that he considered the native chiefs as "his colleagues and partners in the administration." But such colleagueship might involve an unwelcome and unworkable responsibility, and an attempt to enforce uniformity in administration. It was not possible to turn a ruling class, sensitive about their prerogatives and status, into a picturesque kind of lieutenant-governor or commissioner. Minto accordingly emphasized their internal independence, as far as it was consistent with the interests of India and the British Empire, and the need of elasticity and variety in their relations with the Raj. He had no belief in a world steamrollered out into a uniform flatness to please a certain type of official mind.

"I have made it a rule to avoid as far as possible the issue of general instructions, and have endeavoured to deal with questions as they arose with reference to existing treaties, the merits of each case, local conditions, antecedent circumstances, and the particular stage of development, feudal and constitutional, of individual principalities. . . . I have always been opposed to anything like pressure on Durbars with a view to introducing British methods of administration--I have preferred that reform should emanate from the Durbars themselves, and grow up in harmony with the traditions of the State. It is easy to overestimate the value of administrative efficiency."

The colleagueship of the Viceroy and the Secretary of State remained during the year close and friendly, though not without occasions of vigorous dispute. There was the old trouble of private correspondence by subordinates without the cognizance of the superior, and in the case of a flagrant breach of etiquette by one member of the Viceroy's Council the Secretary of State seemed scarcely to appreciate the Viceroy's indignation. Minto, too, was harassed at times by Lord Morley's thirst for what he felt to be irrelevant information, and, as we have seen, the matter of the deportees involved much cabled argument. But the mutual regard of the two men is shown in the correspondence by their inclination to discuss with each other matters of moment not strictly pertinent to their offices. Minto laments that in a time of strain and constant watchfulness he has no leisure for private reflection. "It makes me sad to think how little time there has been to read or study the many mysteries of India--it has been a life of every-day action--certainly learning much as one goes along, but realizing all the more how terribly ignorant one is of many things." He comments on the land clauses of Mr. Lloyd George's famous Budget, and mentions that at Minto he had, out of a gross rent-roll of £5,600, net receipts of £83, which he hoped would still be available to entertain the Secretary of State when he visited the Borders. Lord Morley replied with his impressions of the German Emperor as "Mars commis-voyageur." "He is a consummately interesting figure all the same, with just that streak of Crackedness which is perhaps essential to the interesting. As for Bagman, don't suppose I think it a term of reproach: just the opposite. The soldier is a fine fellow; the diplomatist is indispensable; but the alert and thrifty Bagman, making money, accumulating it, employing it, he's the foundation of a strong State! I much suspect that this will revolt you!" He draws an amusing picture of Indian humbug in Surendra Nath Banerji. "He nearly made me cascade with gross compliments--their Guru, a Great Man, then (by noble crescendo) the greatest Man since ATthbar! I hope he'll balance the little account between us two by swearing that you are far greater than Aurungzebe. After this nauseating dose, he went straight off to a meeting presided over by Cotton, and listened with silent composure to an orator denouncing me as no less of an oppressor and tyrant than the Tsar of Russia!"

There are graver moments, too. He transcribes, to comfort Minto in his difficulties with a disloyal colleague, a wise passage from Mr. Gladstone:--

"The imperious nature of the subjects, their weight and form, demanding the entire strength of a man and all his faculties, leave him no residue, at least for the time, to apply to self-regard; no more than there is for a swimmer, swimming for his life. He must, too, in retrospect feel himself to be so very small in comparison with the themes and interests of which he has to think."

He was beginning, in spite of all his vitality, to feel the burden of his years, and wondered sometimes whether he would ever have a talk with his correspondent face to face. "I am rather jaded, and I have a birthday of terribly high figure next month. I had promised myself a rest as soon as ever I got free of Reforms and Deportees. Unhappily I am not quite my own master for three or four weeks to come. They insist that I denounce the House of Lords to their noble faces-- a pastime that would have given me lively satisfaction once, and I should have produced an hour's oration with the utmost ease. So I shall have to revive my memory of Pym, Hampden, Eliot, and King Charles. Then I'm bidden to Windsor for four days--very agreeable always, only not rest like my library." The shadow of a general election, too, hung over him, and a possible change of

Government. "The men named by the Cabinet-makers for this office are Percy, Midleton, and Milner. If it should be the last, I do believe you will sometimes sigh with a passing breath for the meek individual who now subscribes himself."

III

The Nasik murder in December 1909 had created throughout all India a sense of insecurity, and on January 24,1910, it was followed by a no less startling crime, when the Mohammedan police officer who had been mainly instrumental in unravelling the Bengal murder plots was shot dead in the very precincts of the Calcutta High Court. It was an ill-omened prologue to the opening of the reformed Legislative Council. Some comfort was to be drawn from the replies of the ruling princes of India, whom Minto had officially consulted on the question of the growth of sedition. Their responses, published on the 21st, were a splendid manifesto of loyalty, and a promise of vigorous co-operation in whatever policy of repression the Government of India proposed.

Lord Minto addressing the First Meeting of the new Legislative Council, Government House, Calcutta, 1910

It was clear that that Government must arm itself with further powers, for, as Minto wrote on 6th January, "we want above all things to convince the public, both Indian and European, that we are determined to do all in our power to protect the safety of individuals and to uphold the credit of British administration. We can afford no delay in doing so. We may have another assassination at any moment." That other assassination came on the day preceding the opening of the new Council.

It was a season of tense anxiety, in which only the Viceroy seems to have wholly kept his head. "The worst of it," he wrote, "is that the meaning of outrages is so enormously exaggerated at home. I wish the British public would understand that the troubles we have to deal with do not mean the possibility of rebellion." He was very averse to further deportations, for he believed that he had adequate machinery to deal with the crisis-- the Criminal Amendment Act and the ordinary processes of law. "Speaking frankly," he wrote later, "there was at one time a very decided slackness on the part of local governments in respect to prosecutions for sedition. They were much more inclined to advise deportation and throw the responsibility on the Government of India and the Secretary of State, and there was a tendency to complain of the weakness of our legal machinery, the truth being that it was often ample, but that its application was neglected. I have done all I can to insist on every use being made of the ordinary law and to discourage demands for exceptional procedure." But in January he was doubtful whether the Criminal Amendment Act would be sufficient. "The difficulty is that the European Calcutta population is so unnerved that, if things go wrong, it may be necessary to restore confidence by immediate deportation. I do not like saying this sort of thing at all, but that's how it is." There was a proposal for martial law, made by the Commander-in-Chief, which Minto vetoed, and which Lord Morley said made his hair stand on end. The Viceroy decided to ask the support of the new Council for an enlarged Press Act--for one main source of the mischief lay in press incitation--and at the same time to seek the earliest favourable occasion for the release of the nine Bengalis deported in December 1908. Lord Morley had been pressing for their release in a tone which was not far from peevish, and with arguments which, however justifiable by formal logic, were strangely remote from reality. No doubt it seemed an anomaly that men, whose release had been determined upon, should continue in confinement because of fresh murders in which they had no complicity, but such anomalies are of the essence of practical administration. "If this indefinite detention," the Secretary of State wrote, "until the Day of Judgment (if that be thought necessary) is what you mean by deportation, then I do not expect to find myself able to sanction any more of it, nor the continuance of this." The argument was purely academic; the facts were that murders had been committed which had spread consternation in India, that reforms were about to be put into practical effect which involved in many eyes a slackening of the reins of British government, and that any day fresh deportations might become inevitable. To release deportees at the moment without any new safeguards would have been a "gesture" wholly contrary to the logic of facts, and a potent stimulus to the prevalent anxiety.

On 25th January, in the old-world Council Room at Calcutta, with the portraits of Warren Hastings, Wellesley, Cornwallis, and the first Lord Minto looking down upon him, the Viceroy opened the new Legislative Council. "He began his speech," Lady Minto wrote, "amid profound silence; you might have heard a pin drop. He spoke gradually with more and more emphasis, and when he announced that whether for good or ill he alone was responsible for the reforms, his strength and determination quite carried his audience with him, and at last they broke out into an enthusiastic burst of applause, a thing hitherto unheard of in the Council Chamber." He traced the reasons for the reforms, and the various steps in their progress, which showed that they had sprung from the initiative of the Government of India. "It is important that my colleagues and the Indian public should know the history, the early history, of the reforms which have now been sanctioned by Parliament. They had their genesis in a note of my own addressed to my colleagues in August 1906--nearly three and a half years ago. It was based entirely on the views I had myself formed of the position of affairs in India. It was due to no suggestions from home: whether it was good or bad, I am entirely responsible for it." Then he turned to the assassinations. "I had hoped to open this new Council under an unclouded political sky. No man has longed more earnestly than I have to allow bygones to be bygones, and to commence a new administrative era with a clean slate. The course of recent events has cancelled the realization of those hopes, and I can but assert that the first duty of every Government is to maintain the observance of the law--to provide for the present, and as far as it can for the future, welfare of the populations committed to its charge--to rule, and, if need be, to rule with a strong hand." These were almost the words of his great-grandfather: "No man of honour at the head of a Government will ever compromise with revolt." He concluded on a more hopeful note:--

"I do not for an instant admit that the necessity of ruthlessly eradicating a great evil from our midst should throw more than a passing shadow over the general political situation in India. I believe that situation to be better than it was five years ago. We must not allow immediate dangers to blind us to the evidence of future promise. I believe that the broadening of political representation has saved India from far greater troubles than those we have now to face. I am convinced that the enlargement of our administrative machinery has enormously strengthened the hands of the Viceroy and the Government of India, and has brought factors to our aid which would otherwise have had no sympathy with us. I believe above all that the fellow-services of British and Indian administrators under a supreme British Government is the key to the future political happiness of this country."

The behaviour of the new Council was such as to justify the hopes of the reformers. On 9th February the new Press Act was passed, which compelled the publisher or printer of a newspaper to give security for good behaviour, and laid down that, in the event of the paper publishing prohibited matter, the security might be forfeited, and, on the second offence, the plant itself. An editor was free to publish what he pleased, as in England, but he did it at his own risk; in England that risk took the form of liability to damages or imprisonment, in India of the forfeiture of property. Mr. Gokhale, though he criticized certain details, accepted the measure, only two members differed from the main principle, and the bill passed the Council without a division.

That same day the Viceroy issued orders for the release of the Bengal deportees. The loyal co-operation of the new Council gave him the cue which he had long sought. In a note which he sent to a colleague who criticized his decision occur these sentences: "That advice (to his Council on the subject of release) was given without any reference whatever, either by letter or telegram, to the Secretary of State. I did not even forewarn him of the possibility of release. I acted entirely on my own responsibility, and I was especially anxious to do so in order to avoid any appearance of any documentary suggestion that the Government of India had acted under pressure. As far as I am concerned, the advice I gave my Council was based entirely on what I considered best for India, independently of any influence in England." But he went on to point out that at any moment there might arise an agitation in Parliament for release, to which the British Government might be compelled to bow, and that it would be disastrous for the strength of future Governments of India if they were dictated to from home on a matter of internal administration owing to the exigencies of party politics.

There was much criticism of the action in India, and more in Britain, by those who accused Minto of being, in the phrase of Tacitus, "suarum legum auctor ac subversor," of passing a repressive measure with one hand and giving a licence to notorious agitators with the other. The defence is obvious: it was manifestly unjust to keep men in captivity indefinitely because of new crimes which they had not committed, and the loyal action of the Legislative Council made their release both desirable and safe. But Minto's note which has just been quoted did not please the Secretary of State, who read him a grave homily for imagining that he or any member of the Cabinet had ever urged the release of the deportees from any other motive than strict justice. Minto gently replied that they seemed to be at cross-purposes, and that he had been answering a specific accusation, which, if believed, would have done mischief, and not criticizing the Secretary of State. He might have added that for four years Lord Morley had been emphasizing the fact that the House of Commons governed India, and that that House must consequently be humoured. But indeed the question of deportations and prosecutions was becoming an obsession with Lord Morley, and he ceased to judge things with his wonted acumen. During the early summer he discovered a tenderness for Arabindo Ghose, perhaps the most dangerous man in India, and hoped that the Bengal Government would not secure a conviction against him, and he appeared to hanker after some spectacular exercise of the "clemency of the Crown" in the shape of an amnesty in the ancient Oriental fashion. In June Minto was compelled to speak with great frankness:--

"I can only say that under existing conditions it is an impossibility. The old Oriental monarchs exercised their clemency in different circumstances to those of the present day. Their jurisdiction was summary--they had no House of Commons to answer to-they took life freely as it suited them, they released as they liked, and imprisoned as they liked without any question. No one is a greater believer than I am in the elements of sentiment and imagination, but their influence cuts both ways. It may bring grateful tears to the eyes of the effeminate Bengali, or it may shock the spirited traditions and the warlike imagination of more manly races. The great factor, as far as I have been able to judge, in the success of Indian rulers has been strong personality represented by sympathy and power, but sympathy and power must work together hand in hand."

IV

In April the Mintos went by way of Agra, Delhi, and Dehra Dun to the North-West Frontier, and visited Peiwar Kotal and the Kurram valley, the scene of the

Viceroy's old campaign with Roberts. On this trip occurred the incident which has been narrated elsewhere.*

* Footnote: See Chapter Three: "While riding through the village he met a tall bearded Pathan about whose appearance there was something familiar . . . . "

In the first week of May came the news of King Edward's death. Behind the stately memorial services there was evidence of a sincere national mourning throughout India. Thirty of the accused in the Nasik case were anxious to send a message of sympathy to Queen Alexandra, and were surprised when the prison authorities forbade it. There was a great Hindu demonstration on the Maidan at Calcutta, when the Maharaja of Darbhunga pronounced a eulogy on the dead monarch. "After all that has passed," Minto wrote to the Secretary of State, "I am sure you will think the manifestation of feeling most remarkable--Surendra Nath Banerji, Bhupendra Nath Basu, and Moti Lai Ghose on bended knees before a picture of the King-Emperor! What an emotional people! And yet the fact that they are so ought to give us a master-key to many of the secrets of governing them." Lord Morley's note is worth quotation:--

"He (King Edward), had just the character that Englishmen at any rate thoroughly understand, thoroughly like, and make any quantity of allowance for. It was odd how he had managed to combine regal dignity with bonhomie, and regard for form with entire absence of spurious pomp. As I told you, I had an audience just a week before he died, and the topic was one on which we did not take the same view. He was very much in earnest, but not for an instant did he cease to be kindly, considerate, genial, nor did he press with an atom of anything like overweening insistence. Well, he is gone. The Queen Alexandra took me to see him yesterday, and he lay as if in natural peaceful slumber, his face transfigured by the hand of kind Death into an image of what was best in him, or in any other great Prince. I had known him off and on in various relations since he was a boy at Oxford, where I was; and it was moving to see him lying there, after the curtain had fallen and the play come to an end. The part he had played was generous and high."

Meantime Lord Kitchener had arrived in London after an absence of eight years, and had been enthusiastically received. When he had his first interview with the King and was created a Field-Marshal, he left his baton in the hall of Buckingham Palace, and was in a great state till he discovered its whereabouts. The advent of Kitchener meant that the appointment of Minto's successor could not long be delayed. Lord Morley records his impression of the distinguished soldier:--

"I was a good deal astonished, for I had expected a silent, stiff, moody fellow; behold I could hardly get a word in, and he hammered away loud and strong with manly gestures and high tones. He used the warmest language, as to which I was in no need of such emphasis, about yourself; it was very agreeable to hear, you may be certain. He has the poorest opinion possible of your Council, not as an institution, but of its present members. He talked about the Partition of Bengal in a way that rather made me open my eyes; for, although he hardly went so far as to favour reversal, he was persuaded that we must do something in bringing the people of the two severed portions into some species of unity. We got on well enough--he and I--for nothing was said about his going to India. At night he dined alone with Haldane, and then he expressed his firm expectations with perfect frankness, and even a sort of vehemence. Haldane told him that the decision would be mine; whatever my decision might be, the Prime Minister would back it (though, by the way, I hear that the Prime Minister personally would be much better pleased if the lot fell upon K.). To-day I had an audience in high quarters and found the atmosphere almost torrid!"

Minto, as we have already seen, had hoped for Kitchener as his successor, his only doubts being as to his shyness, his brusqueness, and the want of a wife. Mr. Asquith was in favour of the appointment, but Lord Morley was adamant on the ground that at that juncture a military Viceroy would be fatal. "My own mind has been clear enough for a long time, that Lord K., while he would be no bad Viceroy, and indeed from his marked personality and his fame might be an extremely good one, still would produce an impression that might easily set back the clock that you and I have with no ordinary labour and pains successfully wound up." To this argument Minto reluctantly assented. There was much gossip, the names of Lord Selborne, the Master of Elibank, Sir George Murray, and others being tossed about by rumour. Late in June the appointment was announced of Sir Charles Hardinge, the permanent under-secretary at the Foreign Office. On 16th June Minto wrote:--

"I cannot but feel that I am only now commencing to gain an insight into many things, and that no successor could start where I leave off. In many ways he will have to begin the game over again. But I hope the great principles for which we have fought so hard are safe. As far as I can judge, Hardinge's appointment is excellent. I hardly know him myself, but he has a record, and his family connection with India will stand him in good stead, for the stories of British administration of old days are cherished here. Lady Hardinge, too, will, I know, play a great part in a world where a lady leader has great and growing opportunities for good."

Lord Morley early in the year had told Minto of his intention to leave the India Office simultaneously with Minto's relinquishment of the Viceroyalty, and there were signs throughout the summer that the Secretary of State was beginning to bow under the burden of his work. A tartness appeared in a correspondence previously so urbane, and phrases like "grave displeasure" and "painful inadequacy" became frequent. Vexatious little incidents arose to make a rift in the harmony. There was the complaint of Mr. Ramsay Macdonald that on his Indian visit he had been shadowed and his letters tampered with; complaints decisively answered by the production of the instructions to the police that there was to be no sort of surveillance, and by the explanation that in the mail-bags in the hot weather sealing-wax was apt to melt. A more difficult matter arose in connection with the question of a new Education department. For this it was decided to appoint a member of Council from the Indian civil service, and it was therefore possible to appoint a man from home, as Lord Morley desired, to the vacant department of Commerce and Industry. He selected Mr. (afterwards Sir William) Clark, who had been Mr. Lloyd George's secretary, and was thought well of by the future Lord Inchcape. Against Mr. Clark personally there was no word to say, but to Minto it appeared that he scarcely met the requirements of the office. "The commercial world in India," he wrote, "wants, quite justifiably, to have an experienced representative on the Viceroy's Council, and it will not admit that a young official from Whitehall can be in touch with its interests. Moreover, from the Viceroy's point of view, there are even stronger reasons against such an appointment, as what he needs to assist him is not merely departmental experience, but a wide knowledge of India and its requirements. If he does not find this assistance he must assert himself and rule alone, or with the help of an inner circle of his Council, and that is not what is wanted. The Viceroy does not want a pupil, but an adviser." But Lord Morley's obstinacy (it was his own word) had been aroused by the newspaper clamour against Mr. Clark and what he described as the "unreasonable pretensions of the I.C.S.," and, though shaken for a moment by the Viceroy's disapproval, he persisted in the appointment.

But the most serious difference between India and Whitehall was the work of Mr. Edwin Montagu, the under-secretary for India, who, in his Budget speech in the beginning of August, had this passage:--

"The relations of the Viceroy to the Secretary of State are intimate and responsible. The act of Parliament says 'that the Secretary of State in Council shall superintend, direct, and control all acts, operations, and concerns which in any way relate to or concern the Government and revenues of India, and all grants of salaries, gratuities or allowances, and all other payments and charges whatever out of or on the revenues of India.' It will be seen how wide, how far-reaching, and how complete these powers are. Lord Morley and his Council, working through the agency of Lord Minto, have accomplished much. . . ."

The last sentence roused a storm of criticism in India, for it asserted unequivocally that the Viceroy was merely an agent of the Secretary of State, and the Government of India a registry office. The doctrine was bad alike in constitutional law and in constitutional practice. The supreme authority of the Secretary of State was beyond doubt, but, both by statute and custom, that authority had been limited to certain definite functions.

Mr. Montagu was unfortunate in his statutory citations. His quotation was from the Act of 1833, but section 39 of the same Act provided that "the superintendence, direction, and control of the whole civil and military government of all the said territories and revenues in India shall be and is hereby vested in a Governor-General and Councillors to be styled 'The Governor-General of India in Council." The Act which Mr. Montagu quoted described the powers of the old Board of Control, which were transferred to the Secretary of State by the Government of India Act of 1858. That Act in section 3 declared that the Secretary of State should have and perform the powers and duties which might have been held and performed by the Company and the Board of Control. What these were has been described by an authority whom Lord Morley was bound to respect. The Board of Control, said Mill, "is not so much an executive as a deliberative body. The executive government of India is, and must be, seated in India itself." It is clear from the Act that, while the Secretary of State had full ultimate powers of supervision, their exercise was contemplated as the exception and not as the rule. As for the accepted practice, the reader may consult Chapter V. of Sir John Strachey's great book on India. In such a case the letter of a statute is less authoritative than that customary law which has grown up out of urgent practical needs. The Viceroy was the visible ruler to millions who had never heard of the Secretary of State. To reduce him to the level of a docile agent was to strike at the root of British prestige.

Lord Morley apologized for Mr. Montagu's manner as "not felicitous," but he adhered to the substance of the doctrine. Minto contented himself with a good-humoured protest, for he did not wish to mar his last weeks with a quarrel; but he regarded the matter as one of the first importance, and, had the incident occurred earlier in his term of office, he would undoubtedly have fought the fight to a finish. His views are best gathered from his personal letters to Sir Arthur Bigge (Lord Stamfordham), from one of which (July 5,1910) a long quotation is justified:--

"What is important is the constant insistence by the S. of S. on his sole right to appoint members of Council, together with perpetual interference with the details of administration in India. By statute the members of Council are appointed by the King--and there is no mention of recommendation by either S. of S. or Viceroy. I had much correspondence about this when I first came out--my argument being that, whilst quite recognizing the S. of S. as the King's constitutional adviser, it seemed to me reasonable to assume that it was intended that the Viceroy should be consulted as to appointments to his own Council which concerned him more than any one else, and that great weight should at any rate be given to his objections.M., on the other hand, arrogates to himself complete independence, and I am bound to say that the appointments he has made off his own bat have been most unfortunate. I have constantly felt that I must depend upon myself alone with the exception of one or two advisers I had managed to secure, and that those sent me were not only useless but mischievous. As to lieutenant-governors, they are appointed by the King on the recommendation of the Viceroy, and consequently have always been considered as the Viceroy's appointments; but though I have succeeded in maintaining them as such, it has been after any amount of useless correspondence and often of useless objections. Besides the damage done to Indian authority by interference of this sort at home, the door is thrown open to wire-pulling in England by the friends of candidates for appointments, and the Viceroy is bound to feel that his advice is handicapped by that of personally interested and unqualified persons.

"It seems to me that, as regards these high appointments made by the King, the position of the Viceroy is so peculiar, as being answerable for the safety and good administration of India, and that the authority of the King-Emperor is so direct towards India itself, that the King would be fully and constitutionally justified, when such appointments are submitted to him, in asking for the Viceroy's opinion and in being largely influenced by it in his decision. As long as I am here I cannot feel justified in writing to the King about one of his own Ministers. I must serve H.M.'s Government straightforwardly, but if I had been going to stay longer I should have felt bound to ask that the position of the S. of S. towards the G. of I. should be considered. No one except those who have been behind the scenes here knows what the interference has been about every little thing. I used to imagine that the S. of S. aimed only at directing great principles of Indian policy, and that the administration of the country rested with the Government of India, but there has been interference in everything. It only results in intense worry for the Viceroy, for, do what he will, the S. of S. cannot administer India. . . . As a matter of fact, I believe I have gained my point hi everything since I have been here, but it has generally been by not losing my temper when I should have been thoroughly justified in doing so--sometimes by not answering--often by asserting myself in the most courteous language--and often by humouring the peculiar personality with whom I had to deal. Ever since I have been in India it has seemed to me of vital importance to run the ship as best I could, regardless of the inexcusable troubles hurled at me from home. . . . So I have been determined to sit tight, to say what I wanted, and to get it, without raising the personal question on my own behalf--and so far I know I have won the game--and there are only a few months more. But for the sake of the future of India things must not be allowed to go on as they are."

Lord Morley's conception of his office was in the truest sense despotic--a despotism but little tempered by lip service to a Parliament which he believed he could manage. He was prepared to accept a friendly Viceroy as a junior colleague, but with these two began and ended the government of India. With Minto personally he would deal, but he jibbed at the "Governor-General in Council," and he always tended to ignore the existence both of his own Council and of the Viceroy's. With little talent for practical administration, and with an imperfect sense of those arcana imperii which are more potent than the text of statutes, he attempted by fits and starts the task of direct government, and only Minto's stalwart resistance prevented disaster. But the method he followed had inevitably a malign effect upon the efficiency of the Indian Government. His policy was in the strictest sense retrograde, a relapse into bureaucratic and personal rule. His denial to the Viceroy's Council of a voice in foreign policy led India to take too narrow a view of her imperial responsibilities; his substitution of private communications to the Viceroy for official correspondence weakened the prestige and energy of her executive officers. As has been well said, Lord Morley narrowed India's institutions at the top while broadening them at the bottom; in the Great War she suffered the penalty of this impossible regimen, and the report of the Mesopotamia Commission is the best comment on its unwisdom.

The series of letters to Minto which Lord Morley has printed in the second volume of his Reminiscences is a contribution to English epistolary literature which will not soon be forgotten. But it is an anthology, not the full text, and its humour and kindliness, its blend of wise saws and modern instances, its occasional pedagogic tone as if instructing a promising pupil, do not give the reader a fair conception of the relations between the two men. Some of Lord Morley's sagest passages are, when read in conjunction with Minto's letters which occasioned them, curiously beside the point; often his arguments are captious, the result of a misunderstanding; often they are pleas which in practice he was compelled to abandon. An innocent suggestion that England did not readily understand Indian conditions would elicit a spirited defence of the plenary inspiration of the English people, but in a month's time the Secretary of State would be repeating the Viceroy's suggestion as his own considered opinion. Minto complains of parliamentary ignorance, Lord Morley replies that no King Canute can restrain the ocean, Minto rejoins that "we nowadays know of some most effective sea-walls," and presently the Secretary of State himself adopts the attitude of a haughty Canute towards the tides of ill-informed popular opinion. In reading the full correspondence the impression grows that it was the Viceroy who from start to finish had the more consistent and considered view of Indian problems, and that by tact and patience he invariably got his way with the Secretary of State. It is difficult for a man whose chief equipment is a wide reading in the history and philosophy of politics and a long experience of party strife to keep an even keel in the yeasty seas of foreign administration, for the aphorisms of philosophy may be useless, since they can be summoned to support either of two opposite practical policies. Minto's arguments are often met to begin with by opposition, buttressed by stately citations from the past; but in the end they are accepted and come forth eventually as the ukase of the Secretary of State, dressed in all the purple and gold of the literary graces.

It is necessary to make this clear, for Lord Morley's publication of one side of a correspondence may well leave a false impression. It is necessary, too, to remember that this correspondence was not always the friendly docile affair which the letters in the Reminiscences would lead one to believe. There was much stiff and strenuous argument, and much plain speaking. But it is no less necessary to emphasize the deep underlying friendliness, the fundamental respect, sympathy, even affection of the two men for each other. As Minto's term of office drew to its close he communicates to Lord Morley his feelings as freely as he would to a brother. Though he is tired out, he hates the idea of leaving his work before it is completed.

"I wish I could found a dynasty," he writes. He longs to be back among his own hills, and he finds comfort in the Simla landscape. "I was reared in the mountains and the mist, and have suffered from mountain madness all my life. Peaks, passes, and glaciers have a fascination for me. I never saw anything so gorgeous as the view of the snows here yesterday morning--a whole range of peaks towering one above another against the brightness of blue skies and a dark foreground of hills and pinewoods. You must never think I don't share in your passion for hills and mist." And again: "You tell me when I come home I may find myself in the turmoil of a Tibetan debate. No, nothing will draw me into the political arena, not even the suffragettes! I shall go straight off to my own Borderland and bury my head in the heather." He talks, too, with the utmost frankness about party questions at home. He deplores the decadence of the Parliamentary system, and pleads for "some sort of federation in the United Kingdom." Again, "Though I am enrolled in the ranks of the present Opposition, I often feel that in many ways my inclinations are much more in accord with the views of your side of the House. Yet I suppose in many matters I am diametrically opposed to them. I am afraid I am possessed of that infirmity--a 'cross-bench mind.'" Of Lord Spencer he writes: "I was a rabid anti-Home Ruler, knowing nothing whatever at all about it--and now, still knowing nothing at all about it, am half inclined to think that you and he were right." Lord Morley had written of the same statesman: "If ever there was a man to go bear-hunting with, it was he; and if ever I am engaged in shooting tigers, I bargain that you accompany me;" and Minto replied: "You don't realize how refreshing your words are. If we go tiger-hunting together, it must, I am afraid, be after some political tiger in the Westminster jungle. There seems to be a large preserve of them in that district."

In October the two colleagues took leave in their letters of their high offices and of each other. "I suppose," Lord Morley writes, "this will very likely be my last letter to you; and somebody says that to do anything for the last time has always an element of the sorrowful in it. Well, we have had plenty of stiff campaigning together, and it is a comfort, and no discredit to either of us, that we have got to the end of it without any bones broken, or other mischief. There was opportunity enough, if we had not been too sensible. . . . About the time when you get this, you will know by wire that your famous prediction, that you and I should quit Indian government at the same hour, has come true. . . . I think five years of arduous work are a justification for retirement. And I shall have a short span for serene musing on my own virtues. After all, a short span will be quite long enough for so meagre a topic." A week later Minto wrote his farewell:--

"As I look back upon the years that have passed, I must say, if you will allow me, that few people, as far as I can judge, could have differed so little upon big questions of policy and principle as you and I have. In fact, I really think we have hardly differed at all. About questions of actual administration, or rather of the interpretation of executive authority as it should be wielded at a distance from a supreme Government, I know we do hold different views, and, when we have done so, I have always told you my opinions and the reason for them. We have certainly been through very stormy times together, and after all it is the risks and dangers that strengthen comradeship. No one knows as well as I do how much India owes to the fact of your having been Secretary of State through all this period of development, and I hope you will never think that I have not truly realized the generous support you have so often given me at very critical moments, or that I have not appreciated the peculiar difficulties which have surrounded you at home, and from which I have been spared."

CHAPTER TWELVE

VICEROY OF INDIA: DEPARTURE

THE positive achievements of Minto's Viceroyalty may be read by those who seek them in the many volumes of the departmental reports of the Government of India. They include a thousand matters which can only be mentioned in such a memoir as this--matters of administrative and financial reform, such as the reorganization of the railway and education departments; policies of great social import, like the new and vigorous attempt to grapple with the scourge of malaria and the plague; questions of India's foreign relations, such as the effort to obtain just treatment for Indians in South Africa, the controversy with the home Government over the Convention with Russia, and Minto's far-sighted representations as to the Bagdad railway, Mesopotamia, and southern Persia. Like all Viceroys, he had a frontier problem to grapple with, and a little frontier war. On the vexed matter of the "open" and the "closed" frontier, he took up, as we have seen, the attitude of a practical soldier, and his contribution to a discussion which is still unconcluded has not been excelled in wisdom; for, while he was as averse as Lord Morley to territorial extension, he held that the strip of border no-man's-land instead of being a security was a constant peril, unless British influence was brought to bear on it and it was within reason opened up to civilizing and pacifying influences. The strategy of frontier defence could only be complicated by a terra incognita in which unknown mischief might at any moment blow up like a sandstorm in the desert. One temporary safeguard he provided, for he made of the Amir of Afghanistan an attached friend. In military affairs generally, his technical knowledge rendered him an efficient coadjutor to Lord Kitchener in carrying out the changes of machinery made at the beginning of his term of office. For the Indian army he had a deep admiration and care; he laboured, as we have seen, to give Indian gentlemen the right of serving the British Crown on equal terms with the British-born, and the last dispatch he sent home was on this matter.

But it is customary to judge a Viceroy by those parts of his work which constitute a new departure in policy, which are not merely "carrying-on" but initiation. On this view Minto had to his credit two notable achievements. The first was that into a fevered and disturbed India he introduced by the sheer force of his personality a new harmony and confidence. The official hierarchy, the educated classes, the ruling chiefs, were all, in 1905, in a state of discomfort and discontent. Their nerves had been frayed by startling changes; often their feelings had been wounded by blunders in tact, by a dictatorial tone insulting to their pride, by the left-handedness of an able man whose delicacy of perception was not equal to his earnestness of purpose. On this side Minto was able to realize the hope which he had expressed before leaving England of "giving the horse a rest in its gallops." His personality alone, apart from his acts, was soothing and engaging. He was both trusted and liked by his officials, for they realized that he asked only for candour and honest service, and had no vanity to be offended by plain dealing; that he was loyalty itself, and would never leave a colleague in the lurch. The educated Indian recognized in him one who believed in the fundamental good sense of the Indian people, and who was warmly sympathetic towards all that was honourable and reasonable in Indian arms. Though he passed more repressive laws and acted more absolutely than any Viceroy since Canning, he did not lose the confidence even of the classes most opposed to his measures. Lastly, his relations with the ruling chiefs were cordial and straightforward, as of one gentleman to others. They understood him as he understood them. He showed a scrupulous regard for their rights and dignities, and a wise appreciation of their difficulties. By his speech at Udaipur he dispelled the last remnants of their distrust of the Government of India, which had been growing up during the previous regime, and by his personal relations he made of them devoted allies and friends.*

* The Begum of Bhopal, on receiving a letter written by the Viceroy himself, was so elated that she ordered her troopa to parade with the letter held at the saluting point, while twenty-one guns were fired in its honour.

This aspect of his constructive work--and there is no greater constructive task than to create confidence out of distrust--was primarily a triumph of character. There were not wanting critics who complained that he reigned but did not govern, because he refused to turn his office into a fussy satrapy, based upon constant personal interference. There were critics who saw in his avoidance of pedantry and his love of sport the proof of a secondrate mind. "What can you expect," one of these was reported to have asked, "when they send out as Viceroy of India a pleasant-spoken gentleman who jumps hedges?" The critic was blind to the spell which, since the world began, has been exercised by honesty, kindness, and simplicity. Minto's was not a subtle character, for it was built on broad and simple lines, but his qualities were those which men at the bottom of their hearts prize most, and he had a rare power of communicating them. Good breeding is happily not uncommon, but Minto's was of that rare type which the French call politesse du coeur. He was friendly to everybody, because he liked everybody; and he could judge men shrewdly because he had learned the ways of human nature not only in an office but on the turf, in the hunting field, in many wars, and in much travelling in strange countries. Old Ayub Khan, the victor of Maiwand, who had been given an interview, declared: "The Viceroy rained gentlemanliness upon me." Sir George Roos-Keppel wrote: "If I had a son I would ask you to let him come and stay for a month at Minto in order to show him what a perfect English gentleman should be." Bhupendra Nath Basu, who might be considered an unprejudiced witness, said, "The Viceroy has the power of drawing out the best side of a man, because he makes them feel affection for him." To the long-descended chiefs he was one whose every taste and quality they whole-heartedly understood. They respected him as a fine horseman and a bold shikari, and after his sedentary predecessors rejoiced in a Viceroy who galloped on to the parade ground; they admired the unhesitating courage which made him treat an attempt at assassination as a trifle and take the risk of driving through narrow streets to show his trust in the people. Old Sir Pertab, after his fashion, put it all down to good family. "Viceroy has good pedigree. Why for sending man no pedigree? I not buying horse no pedigree, not buying dog no pedigree, not buying buffalo no pedigree, why for man no pedigree?" But lest ruling chiefs should be held to be biased, we may quote from Mrs. Besant's words when in September 1910 Minto visited the Hindu college at Benares:--

"It will help you to understand the real nature of the Viceroy if I tell you what happened. . . . When he got into the carriage at the station surrounded by guards, it went at a gallop through Calcutta streets. Reaching Government House, he asked why such a strange pace was adopted. The answer was, 'Your Excellency, there is danger in the streets.' 'Is that the way to meet danger, as if you were running away from it?' 'Your Excellency, we removed the Indian guards and replaced them with Scots.' 'Take the Scots away and put on my Indian guards. If we do not trust Indians, how can we hope Indians will trust us?' This when Calcutta was seething with excitement, and he was not alone, but with his wife and children. He tried to draw the two nations together in spite of the difficulties. He inherited many sad traditions, and the wave of life sweeping over India showed itself in many objectionable forms. He rightly struck down violence, but did not refuse the gift of self-government. He has done what few would do in the midst of danger and criticism. He kept a straight course. Flawless justice and perfect courage laid the foundations of self-government within the Empire. Of his own initiative, taking full responsibility, he set free the deportees. A man so strong, far-seeing, and quiet, who makes no boast, says little, does much, is the best type of English gentleman."

On the eve of his departure a high official wrote to him: "May I add a humble tribute to your healing power. India cried aloud for a healer, and there is not a man in the British Empire who could have healed India as you have done." "Healing" is the appropriate word to describe the influence of his character. In spite of the tumult of events he had succeeded in giving the horse a rest in its gallops, for he exercised a balancing and moderating power, sweetened the acerbities of life, and calmed anxieties. He radiated a simple kindliness, and accepted criticism, misunderstanding, and set-backs with a smiling face and an unshaken heart. Lord Canning in his troubled years of office declared that he had become "a moral rhinoceros as regards the world at large." Minto had the same proof armour, woven not of callousness but of simplicity. It is an idle task to compare one Viceroy with another, for there is little uniformity of conditions. Minto did not belong to the school of those who come to India with certain preconceived policies, or those who have far-reaching ideals wedded to lively personal ambitions--a combination which is apt to induce hurry and violence. If we seek a parallel in temperament it will be found in his own great-grandfather, or in some figure like Lord Mayo, whom he resembled in his geniality, his love of sport, and his invincible sangfroid. For the successful administrator the intellectuel is not needed, nor the egoist; a Viceroy should possess the kind of ability required of a Viceroy, and what this is some sentences of Mr. Rivett-Carnac's, speaking of Lord Mayo, will show. "Your clever man is not what is wanted. Such a one will probably be full of fads, and will rub every one up the wrong way in his desire to assert himself and make himself important, and in doing so will overlook the necessity of keeping the Government machine working steadily and quietly. If you employ a very clever man, the effect will be somewhat the same, as I have seen it described, as using a sharp pen-knife in cutting the leaves of your book. The very sharp blade will run off the line and commence to cut out curves on its own accord, independent of direction. What is wanted for the purpose is in the nature of a good, solid, sound paper-knife, which, working steadily through the folds of the pages, will do its work honestly and neatly."

But, if we put Minto's gifts of character as the basis of that constructive work which consisted in bringing a spirit of harmony out of discord, we must set beside them the other achievement which was based upon vigorous powers of mind. He had to face a great emergency and devise a remedy to meet it. The questions of the reforms and the handling of sedition were really one. He had to diagnose a widespread unrest, check with a firm hand its purely mischievous elements, and relieve what was worthy and reasonable. He framed a scheme from his own diagnosis, and that scheme was put into effect; the reforms were primarily his work, and to him must belong whatever merit or demerit history may assign to them. There can be no denying that they met the immediate crisis. Minto did not believe in the possibility of a universally contented India. The land would continue in travail, for West and East were drawing close together, and in their meeting lay endless possibilities of strife. His task was to legislate for the present and the immediate future; all beyond that was in the lap of the gods. The reforms fulfilled the purpose for which they were framed. They satisfied the immediate ambition of educated Indians, they checked the influence of the professional politicians, and for a little they drowned nationalism in provincial and local sentiment. But they did not abolish all the causes of unrest, and in India no system of the kind could hope for permanence. The old secret anarchy remained, weakened but alive, and there was the eternal difficulty--that education had created, and was creating, a class far larger than the opportunities of employing it.

In the reforms there were obvious points of danger. An immovable executive and an irresponsible legislature do not, according to the teaching of political philosophy and the lessons of history, make for harmony. The appointment to high executive posts of Indians of one race or creed, would, in a land of racial and religious rivalry, antagonize those of another race and creed. These objections were considered at the time and dismissed, for, however weighty they might be, they were not final, and certain risks must be taken in all constitution-making. Minto had no wish to add a Brahmin bureaucracy to an English; his aim was simply to remove a barrier to capacity which he felt to be insulting, and so to pave the way for the co-operation of the best brains of the two races. The reforms, again, must be read in conjunction with his policy towards the ruling princes, and with his settled determination to stamp out cruelty and crime. He was aware of the dark worships of the Hindu pantheon, which might blaze into a sudden madness--the fires smouldering beneath the lava crust. But he believed, too, in the common-sense and decency of the great masses of the Indian people, and while prepared for the worst he sought to give encouragement to the best.

All constitutional experiments must in one sense sooner or later fail. If they are organic things they must be outgrown and superseded. It is probably true to say that even before the outbreak of the Great War, which produced a chemical change so that no constituent was left unaltered, the reforms were in need of revision--the more as they were not accompanied by that firmness and consistency in executive government which Minto had postulated. Both Viceroy and Secretary of State deprecated too long a view in such a matter; sufficient unto them the day, and the day after to-morrow. Could the two men now look back from those Elysian Fields which were always in Lord Morley's mind, and see the course of India, in what light would they regard their efforts? To Minto there would be certain grounds for satisfaction. He would rejoice at the great achievement of India in the War, and in the fact that at last to Indians had been opened British commissions in the King's army. He would not be surprised at the continuance of the North-West frontier problem, for he had never believed that Britain's policy there gave any chance of a final settlement. But both men would be puzzled, and a little perturbed at the dyarchy of the Montagu-Chelmsford scheme, and somewhat sceptical of its continuance. We can imagine Lord Morley quoting some high phrase of Burke's about "great varieties of untried being," and shrugging his shoulders. Both would admit--since they constantly admitted it to each other--that reform in India had no fixed limits, and that the Great War with its loud promises of self-determination, accepted literally by many peoples who had no self to determine, made some bold advance inevitable. The ironic spirit of The Dynasts has brooded so long over the modern world that we have ceased to marvel at paradoxes, but a paradox the two would most certainly consider the present government of India. Representative government they believed in, but to both responsible government, even a truncated version of it, would be a startling thought, for each conceived of India, in Mill's words, as "a kingly government, free from the control, though strengthened by the support, of representative institutions." Minto would be the first to recover from his surprise; for, since he did not trouble greatly about theories, a theoretic revolution would shock him the less.

About India he held the same view as he held about the British Empire, that progress must come mainly by executive co-operation, and for that reason he regarded the addition of native members to the councils as the most potent of the reforms. But it was always his habit to face facts, and, had he read in the facts the need for a long stride forward in India's education in the responsibilities of government, he would not have shrunk from it. It is significant that in one of his last letters to Lord Morley he declared his view that the future problems of India would be fiscal and economic, matters directly concerning the livelihood of her people, and that in these native opinion must have a controlling voice. He would have assented to any change which promised a real advance in opportunities for political education, though he might have had qualms about a system which invited constant deadlocks, and therefore the revival of the reserved dictatorship of the Government.

But there was one proviso which he would have made, and in which Lord Morley would have solemnly joined. He realized that the real demand in India was not for irrelevant slices of the British constitution. The Indian moderate asked not for democracy, but for Indianization, the extremist for "national" independence, and though the first could in large measure be granted, the second was on the facts impossible. In a land so remote from true integration the only national government must be British government. The status of an autonomous dominion for all India was, in India's interest, inconceivable. If one may judge from his letters, he would have gone far in the direction of provincial autonomy where there was a homogeneous race to be dealt with, but he would never have surrendered the right to interfere and the duty to oversee. "Blow hot or blow cold as you please," the Nizam once said to Sir Harcourt Butler, "but never forget your strength." "I am bent," the Secretary of State told the Viceroy, "on doing nothing to loosen the bolts." We have seen that when Lord Morley had said in a moment of fatigue that, if reform could not save India, nothing would, Minto had replied trenchantly that India would not be lost, reform or no, for in the last resort Britain would fight for her and win. This was the fundamental principle of both men--that the immense bulk of the Indian people cared not a straw for politics, but depended for their very lives on the continuance of British authority, and that any talk of giving up India was a mischievous treason to national honour, to civilization, and to the world's peace. Always, or at all events for any period within the forecast of the human mind, Britain must be responsible for that Indian Empire which she had created out of conflicting creeds and races, and retain in the last resort the power of enforcing her commands. This robust faith was held by Minto and Lord Morley alike; without it Indian reforms would have seemed to them no more than a drifting towards the cataract.

As a summary of Minto's viceroyalty a memorandum may be quoted which Sir Harcourt

Butler, the most devoted of his lieutenants, wrote towards the close of 1919:--

"To a captivating grace of manner and unerring tact he added a peculiar gift of putting one at ease. He was interested in and courteous and considerate to all. He drew the best out of men because he looked for the good in them. There was nothing forced in this. It seemed natural to him. Nothing mean or petty could live near him for any length of time.

"He will long be remembered as the joint author of a scheme of reforms for internal India, and as the originator of a new policy and spirit in the relations between the Government of India and native states. Nothing new is popular in an intensely conservative country like India. Both reforms were criticized at the time for going too far, and later for not going far enough. Both were inspired by deep and sincere appreciation of the changes at work in India. No one now questions the wisdom of Lord Minto's policy towards native states. It has been adopted and developed by his successors. As regards the joint reforms, I said publicly at Meerut on July 15, 1918, and repeat here:--

"'You have been told that the Minto-Morley reforms were doomed to failure and have failed. With all respect to those who hold this view, I must say that this is not my experience as vice-president of the Imperial Legislative Council, as Lieutenant-Governor of Burma, and as Lieutenant-Governor of the United Provinces. In my experience, and this was the expressed opinion of Lord Hardinge, the Minto-Morley reforms have been successful. They have been a valuable training to Indian politicians and have prepared them for another forward move. The executive government has been far more influenced by the discussions in Council than is popularly imagined, and the debates have been maintained at a really high level. Occasionally time has been wasted. Occasionally feeling has run high. Of what assembly cannot this be said? I was led to believe that in our Legislative Council I should find a spirit of opposition and hostility to Government. I have found, on the contrary, a responsive and reasonable spirit. Indeed, I go so far as to say that it is the very success of the Minto-Morley reforms that makes me most hopeful in regard to the future course of reform.'

"This also I may say. As a reformer Lord Minto showed not once but on many occasions high courage, patience, and clearness of vision. He was as absolutely straight in his public as in his private life. He took large-minded and generous views of things. He met formidable difficulties with a rare sense of duty. 'If I resign, following the action of my predecessor,' he once said to me, 'the office of Viceroy will be lowered for ever.' He never hesitated to do what he thought the right thing. . . .

"Working under him I was struck by his sagacity and sense of justice. He reminded me of an elephant, which will not tread on rotten ground. Once he had harvested the facts of the case in his mind his judgment was seldom wrong. There was no limit to the trouble that he would take to master facts when any question of justice was concerned. Again, more than any one under whom I have served, he had the gift of seeing 'the other fellow's point of view.' 'Think how that letter will read at the other end,' he often used to say in correcting the abruptness of official communications. He was a great sportsman, and up to the last he admired a spirit of adventure. He used to quote some lines on the spirit of adventure written by my uncle (Arthur Butler) at a time when people wrote to the press about the dangers of mountaineering. He always supported frontier officers or officers in distant places who took reasonable risks.

"Looking back on Lord Minto as statesman, administrator, gentleman, sportsman, man of the world, and constant kind friend, I can truly say of him:--

"'He was a man, take him for all in all, I shall not look upon his like again.'"

II

As the time of leave-taking approached there were hourly proofs of the regret of every class in the community. The rotation of Viceroys has always been a puzzle to the Indian native, who looks for permanence in his rulers. Said one tiny heir to a native state: "Why is the Lat Sahib going to leave us? Is it because he wants the Gods to let him live on a great stone horse in the Maidan like the other Lat Sahibs? The great Queen asked the Gods to let her come to India too, and she sits and watches over them from a chair." One Indian tradesman journeyed from Hyderabad to say farewell, announcing that the "Viceroy has sprinkled water on the people after the fire which he found." The Maharaja of Darbhunga, the greatest of the Bengal zemindars, Lady Minto's diary records, "As he was leaving the room, flung himself on his knees, removed his cap, and begged Rolly to bless him."

In October Simla saw a succession of farewell dinners--a Scots dinner on the 11th, and on the 14th a banquet at the United Service Club, where Minto took occasion to review the years of his Viceroyalty. It was almost the best of his speeches, because it contained not only a just summary of his work, but his whole political creed and philosophy of life. One passage may well become a part of the unwritten manual of British administrative wisdom, worthy to rank with Dalhousie's famous saying that "to fear God and to fear nothing else is the first principle even of worldly success."

"The public, especially the public at home, not fully acquainted with Indian difficulties, has, perhaps not unnaturally, been unable to distinguish between the utterly different problems and risks that have confronted us. The necessity for dealing with reasonable hopes has been lost sight of, while every outrage that has occurred has been taken as indicative of the general state of India. And throughout its time of trouble every action of the

Government has been subjected to microscopic examination, to a running fire of newspaper criticism, to questions in Parliament, to the advice of travellers who have returned home to write books on India after a few weeks' sojourn in the country--while sensational headlines have helped to fire the imagination of the man in the street, who in his turn has cried out for 'strong measures,' regardless of the meaning of his words, and for a 'strong man' to enforce them. Gentlemen, I have heard a good deal of 'strong men' in my time, and I can only say that my experience in all our anxious days in India has taught me that the strongest man is he who is not afraid of being called weak."

It was the last occasion when he would meet the representatives of the public services, and he could not leave his old colleagues without emotion.

"I have told you my story--I have told it to you who have been my fellow-workers and comrades in troublous times, who have helped me to steer the ship through many dangerous straits--the men of the great services which have built up the British Raj. We may perhaps at times have thought differently as to the course to be steered--it could not be otherwise--but you have stood behind me loyally, and I thank you. I leave India knowing full well that you will perpetuate the great traditions of British rule--perhaps with few opportunities of much public applause, but with the inestimable satisfaction that you are doing your duty."

On 16th November Minto held his last review in Calcutta, and told General Mahon that "it had revived the memories of service in the field in the years gone by and the wish that it would all come over again." That night there was a banquet at the Turf Club, when Minto recalled his early racing career in a speech which has already been quoted,* and two days later a great dinner at the Calcutta Club, when Mr. Sinha proposed his health and he replied by pleading for the abolition of a foolish race barrier in ordinary social relations: "National and racial differences of thought and ways of life there must be, but a good fellow is a good fellow all the world over."

* See Chapter 2: ". . . . your welcome and your farewell to a fellow-sportsman. . . ." On the 21st the guns announced the arrival of the new Viceroy, and two days later, a little after noon, the Mintos left Calcutta. I take the description of the scene from Lady Minto's journal:--

"I tried to feel as stony as possible, but tearful eyes, the pressure of the hand, and a 'God bless you' are enough to upset one. A great many Indian friends came to bid us farewell--the Maharajas of Gwalior, Kashmir, Bikanir, Benares, Jodpur, Kurupam, Gidhour, Burdwar, Darbhunga, Vizianagram, the Prince of Arcot, and crowds more whose names I can't cope with. By 12:15 the halls were packed, and Rolly and I took twenty minutes, literally fighting our way through the people. I can never describe the enthusiasm. . . . At last we reached the top of the marble steps, and walked for the last time over the red carpet between the two lines of the splendid Bodyguard. The Hardinges stood at the foot of the steps, and we both bade them a most cordial farewell . . . and I made them each a curtsey and wished them good luck. He seemed quite overcome, and it really was a moving sight, the enormous escort and a guard of honour, and the steps thronged by this wonderful concourse of people. . . . Scindia and Bikanir pressed our hands in both their own, but they couldn't speak. We passed through the gates where the band was stationed playing 'Auld Lang Syne.' . . . As we drove through the streets packed with spectators, cheer after cheer rang out, and occasionally I caught sight of a face I knew at some window or on a balcony. Howrah Bridge was beautifully decorated with palms, as was also the railway station; a few officials met us there, and I found my carriage a bower of flowers. Amid cheers we steamed slowly out of the station, and sat down with a sigh of relief, but with very mixed feelings of sorrow and gladness. A wonderful chapter in our lives is ended. The guns boomed out our departure, and announced the installation of the new Viceroy."

They arrived at Bombay on the afternoon of the 25th, and after a final reception by the native community at Convocation Hall, where Mr. Gokhale proposed their healths, they drove to the Apollo Bundur. There stood Sir Pertab Singh, with tears rolling down his cheeks, and speechless with emotion. At sunset they embarked in the R.I.M. steamer Dufferin, and moved away from the shores of India.

"The evening was a gorgeous one. The sky was a deep orange, and the glow was reflected on the sea. The dark spires and buildings of Bombay stood out in sharp relief. Then came the twilight, and along the coast the lights blazed out in a myriad twinkling eyes, turning the darkened mass into a city of fire. A great calm pervaded the atmosphere, and we sat on in the ever-increasing gloom till the beacons of flame from the revolving lighthouses faded away like stars in the heavens. Nature seemed to understand our mood, and I could not have wished to bid a more perfect farewell to the shores of India. The East has cast her magic spell around us, and nothing can ever fascinate me quite in the same way again."

In every such leave-taking there must be both solemnity and sadness. Of the latter the smallest part was the laying down of great office and becoming again one of the crowd, for, as Walter Savage Landor has written, "external power can affect those only who have none intrinsically." But there was the parting with old friends, the unlacing of armour, the sense that a great epoch in one's life was over. There was the bidding farewell to a staff of which any Viceroy might have been proud, a staff perfect in its official capacity, and working harmoniously, unselfishly, and devotedly for the success of the regime. Yet mingled with regrets was that knowledge of a thing well completed which is the highest of mortal pleasures. Lady Minto had been the organizer of great enterprises of charity and social welfare; she had, in the words of the Aga Khan, "humanized the homes of which she had been for five years the chatelaine;" she had made warm friends in every class and province; and she had been to her husband a constant source of wisdom and sympathy.* Minto himself left India with his work honoured by all competent to judge, and, though he had had his troubles with the Government at home, he could not complain of neglect and frustration--unlike Dalhousie who, crippled, heart-broken, and dying, limped on board a wretched cockle-boat of six hundred tons, which was all that England could spare for one of the greatest of her servants. He left with the priceless boon of a quiet mind. Patient and deliberate in arriving at a conclusion, he had no regrets for a single decision. He told his wife, as the Bombay lights sank astern, that, had he those five years to live again, he would do nothing differently, that he wished no single act undone, no single word unspoken.

(* A verse or two may be quoted of a poem addressed to Lady Minto which appeared in the Empire in February 1910:--

Lady, yon at your husband's side for years An Empire's burden like a queen have borne, You have found smiles for them that joy, and tears For them that mourn.

You, when the assassin's deadly aim had failed, No sign of terror to our eyes displayed; And in your task at danger never quailed, Regal and unafraid. . . .

We have no stars nor jewels to bestow, Nor honours that shall make your name to live; But what of love and gratitude we owe, That we can give.

A people whom your care has helped shall be For ever mindful of a noble name, And in their hearts enthroned by memory Shall live your fame!)

When the Mintos reached Port Said, they found there, to their delight, Lord Kitchener, who had travelled in haste from Smyrna to meet them. At Dover they were met by Dunlop Smith, and at Victoria by Sir Arthur Bigge, Lord Morley, Lord Crewe, Lord Roberts, and a great concourse of family and friends. Minto was greeted on his arrival by a letter from the Lord Mayor of London offering him the freedom of the City. Four days later they both lunched at Buckingham Palace, and Minto was invested with the Order of the Garter.

He was eager to get back to his Border home, which in all his Indian years had been rarely absent from his thoughts. There was no heather in mid-December to bury his head in, but he had a wish to complete the circuit of his journey where his great-grandfather had failed.* Among the papers of the first Lord Minto there is a pathetic bundle, containing the plans for his homecoming; over this his widow had written the words "Poor fools!" The fates were kinder to his descendant. At Hawick there was a guard of honour from the King's Own Scottish Borderers and the Lothians and Border Horse, and the provost and town council were on the platform. Denholm, the little village at the park gates, was ablaze with lights and decorations, and in a procession, accompanied by flaring torches and pipers, the party moved up the long avenue to Minto House, where the oldest tenant presented an address and he heard again the well-loved Border speech. Above the doorway were the words "Safe in," a phrase from his own kindly pastoral world. The far-wandering Ulysses had come back to Ithaca.

* See Introductory: ". . . . he died on the first stage of that happy northward journey of which for seven years he had dreamed. . . . "

CHAPTER THIRTEEN

CONCLUSION

IT has always been the fashion for a British proconsul on his return home to give a public account of his stewardship, and in this case the occasion selected was the presentation of the freedom of the City of London. On February 23, 1911, the ceremony took place in the presence of many friends and colleagues, such as Lord Crewe, Lord Morley, Lord Midleton, Lord Cromer, Lord Lansdowne, Lord Strathcona, Mr. Asquith, and Mr. Austen Chamberlain. Minto in his speech carefully avoided matters of contention, but in his sketch of his years of office he reiterated the principles which he had followed--the need in India of "separating the sheep from the goats," of following a dual policy of administrative reform and the enforcement of disciplinary law. He thought it right to emphasize the necessity for an elastic administration on the part of Britain in the new era which was beginning.

"It is an era in which I firmly believe the Government of India--in India--will continue to grow in strength, in response to Indian sympathy and support. But it is an era also in which its relations with the central Government of the Empire will require to be directed with a very light hand. The Government of India is, of course, entirely subservient to the Secretary of State, and must be so in respect to the recognition of political principles and the inauguration of broad lines of policy.

But the daily administration of the Government of the country can only be carried on efficiently and safely by those to whom long and anxious experience has given some insight into the complex and mysterious surroundings of the people committed to their charge. India cannot be safely governed from home. Any attempt so to govern it in these days of rapid communication, when collusion between political parties in India and political parties in England is not difficult, and when consequently the Government of India may be harassed by political influences to which it should never be exposed, can only end in disaster. No one admires more than I do the generous impulses of the people of England in respect to the just government of their fellow-subjects, of whatever race, in every part of the Empire; but Western modes of treatment are not necessarily applicable to Eastern grievances. No Viceroy, however eloquent he may be with his pen, can portray to the Secretary of State thousands of miles away the picture which lies before him. He can, perhaps, describe its rugged outlines, but the ever-changing lights and shades, which must so often influence his instant action, he cannot reproduce. He and his Council can alone be safely entrusted with the daily conduct of affairs in the vast territories they are appointed to administer."

At the luncheon which followed Lord Morley paid a final tribute to his colleague. "Lord Minto could reflect with confidence that he had left behind him in India high esteem, large general regard, and warm good-will. The great feudatories and native princes had found in him a genial, sincere, and unaffected good-will. The Mohammedans respected and liked him. The Hindus respected and liked him. The political leaders, though neither Lord Minto nor the Secretary of State agreed in all they desired, had perfect confidence in his constancy and good faith. The Civil Service, not always averse from criticism, admired his courage, patience, and unruffled equanimity. He really got on consummately well with everybody with whom he had commerce, from the Amir in the fastnesses of Afghanistan down to the imperious autocrat who for the moment was Secretary of State in the fastnesses of Whitehall. Having come back from the banks of the Ganges, he found on the banks of the Thames a cordial appreciation and generous recognition of his fulfilment of a great national duty. His predecessor, Lord Curzon, a man of powerful mind and eloquent tongue, had said that a man who could bring together the hearts of sundered peoples was a greater benefactor than the conqueror of kingdoms. Lord Minto was entitled to that praise." The same evening he wrote to his friend: "I cannot go to rest to-night without a word of congratulation. It ends a chapter in the day's fine ceremony that is infinitely to your honour and credit, and I have a right to use language of this sort, because I do really know all the difficulties with which you have had to contend, and which you have so manfully overcome. I shall always be proud of your kind words about me. We have had a great campaign together, and I believe more than ever to-day, when you have been in my visual eye, that we have been good comrades and shall remain good friends. May you and Lady Minto have long and unclouded days."

The days were not destined to be long. Minto was now a man of sixty-five, and with his marvellous constitution and his vigorous habits might well have looked forward to a hale old age. But his labours in India had worn down even his iron strength, and taken a score of years from his life. After the Mansion House ceremony he went for three weeks to Corsica, and visited the house in Bastia where the first Lord Minto had lived in 1794. Lady Minto describes in her letters the high rooms and windows overlooking the sea, and the garden full of orange blossom. "The whole place to our imagination seemed peopled with Sir Gilbert, Lady Elliot, Nelson, Hood, and Jervis. It was wonderful to feel that after all these years Lord Minto's descendant should have discovered this remote house and should be gazing at the same objects that had been so familiar to his great-grandfather.... We called on the descendant of Pozzo di Borgo, Sir Gilbert's old friend, and saw the full-length picture of his ancestor, a smaller replica of which hangs at Minto. The present Pozzo told us that the name of Elliot was still remembered in Corsica." After that came spring in the Borders, a happy and peaceful season, in which the only noteworthy event was the presentation of the freedom of the City of Edinburgh in April.

The season in London was a succession of dinners, private and official. At the dinner of the Central Asian Society Minto declared his belief that Indian industries were entitled to a reasonable protection, a speech which alarmed both Lord Morley and Mr. Austen Chamberlain. "Morley afraid for free trade," the journal notes, "Austen apprehensive for Manchester--yet both admitting that I had spoken the truth." At the Asquiths' he met Louis Botha, whom he described as "most manly and attractive." The Mounted Infantry dinner gave him the keenest pleasure, for his old hobby was still close to his heart. "The toast of my health was enthusiastically welcomed, and things were said which I treasure more than I can say, and shall never forget. It took me back to the old days, and I longed to have them over again." He presided at the Newspaper Fund dinner, when Lord Kitchener, who was not prone to the dithyrambic, gave eloquent expression to his affection:--

"Lord Minto needs no words of praise from me to strengthen his position in the hearts of his countrymen, for I venture to say that there are few living men whose services to the Empire have been greater and more valuable than those of the subject of my toast. Two great countries can bear testimony to his administrative genius, his modesty, his industry, and, above all, to his knowledge of human nature and his warm sympathy with all those various races it has fallen to his lot to rule. It is to these qualities that the great success of his government in such different surroundings as Canada and India has been mainly due. But if I was asked what quality above all others I would ascribe to Lord Minto, it is that of pluck; not mere physical pluck, although of that he has shown innumerable proofs, but the greater quality of moral pluck. There comes always to a public man a time when the right course is not the most popular course; in such cases I have never known or heard of Lord Minto weighing popularity in the scale against what he has considered right and just: and I venture to say that this quality is one without which no man can achieve true greatness as an administrator. . . .

"I can speak with perhaps more intimate knowledge of his career as a soldier, as we more than once served in the same campaign. I feel sure that, had he stuck to military life, he would have attained the highest honours my profession could give him, though perhaps not such a distinguished position as he now holds. Lord Minto in his military career was thorough and no medal hunter or seeker after a soldier's bubble reputation; and the medals he wears were always won in the hardest and most arduous services in each campaign. . . .

"During his tenure of office as Governor-General of Canada and Viceroy of India the world closely followed his policy, and as one who was nearly associated with him in India, and perhaps to a certain extent behind the veil, I can only say that my admiration of his able statesmanship in somewhat difficult times was unbounded. Few Viceroys have been able to impress so favourably the Princes of India, and in his sympathetic treatment of the natives, as well as of the officers and men of the Indian Army, he obtained and retained the affectionate regard and esteem of the whole country."

In June Minto received the honorary degree of Doctor of Laws at Cambridge, his first visit to those precincts since he had taken his bachelor's degree in racing kit forty-five years before. At the Coronation in that month he was one of the four peers who held the panoply over the King. In July he saw Eton win the Ladies' Plate at Henley in record time, with his younger son Esmond as cox, and a week later was in command of the veterans in the review at Holyrood during the Royal visit. It was the year of the acrimonious debates on the Parliament Bill, and in August the measure reached the House of Lords, when Lord Crewe announced that, should it be defeated, the King had given the Prime Minister his promise to create as many new peers as might be necessary to pass it into law. Minto, little as he liked the bill, liked the alternative still less, and having no taste for melodramatic intransigence, voted with the Government--a proceeding which brought him a deluge of letters, half of which described him as a traitor and half as a patriot.

The autumn and winter were spent at Minto, broken by a visit to Eton in December to unveil a portrait of Lord Roberts. He was settling down into the routine of a country gentleman--shooting, an occasional day with hounds, dinners at the Jed Forest Club, the management of his estates--and was induced to accept the convenership of the county of Roxburgh. But the peace of Minto was impaired by an enormous correspondence with friends in India, for an ex-Viceroy cannot divest himself of matters which for five years have monopolized his life. With the vagaries of home politics he was not greatly troubled, but Indian policy deeply concerned him. He was alarmed at the proposal to reverse the partition of Bengal, he distrusted the wisdom of moving the capital to Delhi, and, above all, he felt that the association of these steps with the coming visit of the King-Emperor to India was to put upon the Sovereign the direct responsibility for a dubious scheme. In February 1912 he went to London for the Indian debate in the House of Lords, where he supported Lord Curzon in his criticism of the Delhi move. His speech was in a high degree tactful and wise, and earned general commendation as that of a man who spoke only from a sense of duty and with none of the vanity which has sometimes made ex-Viceroys critical of the doings of their successors.

Minto had been elected Lord Rector of Edinburgh University, defeating Lord Crewe, and in January 1912 he was the guest of honour at a University dinner. The election gave him peculiar pleasure, for if the Borders were the cradle, Edinburgh had been the nursery of his forbears. In March he was elected to the Athenaeum Club under Rule II. "I don't think," his brother Arthur wrote, "I have ever seen so much unanimity at an election." Meantime, in February, "Cat" Richardson had died. Minto saw him just before the end, and his journal records his sense of loss.

"My oldest friend gone. I cannot say what a wrench it is--the link with so many recollections, and with a life which seems now to have belonged to another world. We had been friends ever since we went to Cambridge. A change seems to have come over my world, and it is not the same now he has gone out of it. He was a splendid fellow, by far the best and most polished rider I ever saw, and not only very excellent at all games, but possessed of brilliant natural ability. . . . In any line of life he might have taken up he would have held a foremost place among his fellow-men."

In the summer he was much in London, and a good deal at a house he had taken on the river near Windsor. The autumn at Minto was restful--parties of Indian and military friends, much shooting and hunting, and the modest cares of the estate. No man who has been blessed with a sound body will admit readily that its forces can fail, and as late as March 1913 we find hunting notes in the diary like this: "I got a most abominable toss. I hope I am not losing my power of gripping. Certainly it was a detestable place, and I was at the top of the hunt. . . ." But presently it became clear that his ill-health was no trivial thing, that his strenuous Indian years were inexorably demanding their price. The journal grows scrappier, and it is only the passing of a friend that moves him to an entry. Such was Lord Wolseley's death in March--"By far our greatest soldier; and perhaps the greatest service which he has rendered to this country has been the example of his own personality." The last sentence would be a not inappropriate epitaph for the writer himself.

We need not linger over the year during which his body was dying of its wounds, for to those who knew his eager vitality it is hard to think of Minto on a sick-bed.* From April 1913 he was continuously unwell. He recovered to some extent, and in the autumn was able to welcome a few friends at Minto. But with the opening of 1914 he became gravely ill, and on the first day of March the end came. Since a death in battle was denied him, it was the passing that he would have chosen, for he drew his last breath in his ancient home with his family around him. When he received his last Communion he said, "I have tried to be loyal to my God and my King," and his dying words were faltered messages of love to the wife and children who had so warmed and lit his house of life. * Footnote: Minto in his illness often referred to some lines by Professor Blaokie, which he declared contained his confession of faith:--

"Creeds and Confessions! High Church or the Low I cannot say; but you would vastly please us, If with some pointed Scripture you could show To which of these belonged the Saviour Jesus? I think to all or none: not curious creeds Or ordered forms of churchly rule He taught, But soul of love that blossomed into deeds With human good and human blessing fraught. On me nor Priest, nor Presbyter, nor Pope, Bishop nor Dean may stamp a party name; But Jesus, with His largely human scope, The service of my human life may claim. Let prideful priests do battle about creeds, The Church is mine that does most Christlike deeds.

He was buried in the little churchyard of Minto, which looks towards the blue hills of Teviotdale. The press proclaimed the achievements of his public life, but it is by the simple, homely, often broken messages of condolence received by his wife that the magnitude of the affection he inspired may be judged. Lord Kitchener, always chary of superlatives, called him simply "the best, most gallant, and able administrator that England ever produced," and a brother-officer wrote: "I do not believe that any man ever passed away, or ever will do so, leaving more behind him who will from the very bottom of their hearts say 'Dear Minto.'" That is not how men commonly write of the esteemed and the successful; it is more like the lament of youth for youth.

Minto died on the very eve of the Great War. He was by training and taste a soldier, and that profession was always dearer to his heart than any other, but fate had sent him nothing but minor campaigns. It is sometimes given to a son to realize the ambition of the father, and the little boy whom we have seen in a great sun-helmet touching the proffered sword-hilt of the old Raja of Nabha and promising when he grew up to protect that state, was destined to a part in the sternest test of manhood which the world has known. Once, at Agra, the Begum of Bhopal took Esmond's hands in hers and told him that he would be a great lord sahib one day and do much for the British Empire. The prophecy came true, for he gave his all for his country, and in a brief time fulfilled the ends of life. At Eton he had coxed the Eight for three years, and had lived in the sunshine of that affection which young men give to one who combines infinite humour and high spirits with modesty and kindliness. On the outbreak of war he joined the Lothians and Border Horse, and presently, a boy scarcely out of his teens, he was in France as A.D.C. to General Geoffrey Fielding, then commanding the Guards Division. He could not endure to remain a staff officer, so in June 1916, during the Battle of the Somme, he joined the Scots Guards, and in October was gazetted to the second battalion.

There never was a happier soldier or one more clearly born to the trade of arms. His gallantry was remarkable even among gallant men, he was supremely competent in his work, and in the darkest days his debonair and gentle spirit made a light around him. Alike over his men and his brother-officers he cast a spell, which was far more than a mere infection of cheerfulness, for, as one wrote, he made other people ashamed of all that was ignoble. He was given some of the roughest material for his platoon, because the most troublesome old soldier became docile under his influence. His men made an idol of him, and would have followed him blindly to any hazard. When one of them went on leave his comrades used to commission him to bring back some little present for Esmond. Once, when volunteers were called for a raid, only a few came forward, till it became known that Esmond was to be in command, when the whole platoon volunteered and most of the company. "When the war is over and these Scotsmen return to their homes," an officer wrote, "they will tell their people of the wonderful boy who came to them in France, and who showed them what could be achieved by goodness."

Courage and devotion such as his could scarcely escape the nemesis which in those years overtook the flower of youth. The end came during the Third Battle of Ypres, when he was selected to command his company in the trenches. Shortly after midnight on August 6, 1917, there was an engagement between pickets, and while reconnoitring the situation Esmond was shot through the chest by a chance bullet. A little later he died in the clearing-station, peacefully and without pain. In a short space he had lived greatly, and had left an influence which will fructify in the lives of those who knew him long after the memory of the war is dim. The noble monument which commemorates him at Minto stands near the tall cross which marks his father's grave. It is the memorial of two soldiers fallen in arms that meets the dawn coming over Cheviot from the eastern seas.

A life of conspicuous public achievement, spent largely in the handling of great affairs, belongs even in its own day to history, and must be assessed by other canons than personal friendship. The statesman plays for high stakes, and is judged by a high tribunal. In the service of the State two notable types stand out, each with its share of merits and deficiencies. The first is the man of searching and introspective intellect, who has behind him the treasures of the world's culture. Such an one has studied and meditated upon the whole history of politics, he is steeped in good literature, his mind by constant application has become a tempered weapon, so that easily and competently it attacks whatever body of knowledge presents itself. A new problem to him has familiar elements, for it is related to kindred problems in the past, and he has in his memory large store of maxims and precedents. For certain matters of statecraft such a mind will be of superlative value--matters principally where exact science, whether legal, economic, or constitutional, is the prime factor. Imagination, too, and the balance which a wide culture gives, will rarely be absent. In politics the pure intellect has its own splendid functions which only folly will decry. But there is a danger that a man of this type, though he may be the parent of ideas which have an enduring power over humanity, will fail in the day-to-day business of government. He may live too much in the world of books and thought to learn the ways of the average man, so that he lacks the gift of personal leadership. He may speak a tongue, like Burke, too high and noble for the commonplace business he has to conduct; he may fall into the snare of intellectual arrogance and excessive subtlety, so that, like Shelburne or George Canning, his very brilliance breeds distrust; or he may be betrayed into an impractical idealism which beats its wings in the void. If he miss the human touch, his place is in the library and not in the council or the field, for, though he may move the future world by his thought, his personality will leave his contemporaries cold.

In the other type the human touch is the dominant gift. The second man will always be a leader, but he will lead by character and not by mind. He has a large masculine common sense, an accurate notion of what can be achieved in an imperfect world, a fine and equable temper, good humour, patience, and an honest opportunism. His very foibles will be a source of strength; his qualities and tastes will be exactly comprehended by everybody; he will be popular, because no one will feel in his presence the uncomfortable sense of intellectual inferiority. Lord Palmerston might be taken as an instance, but a better is Lord Althorp, who largely carried the Reform Act of 1832 by his popularity. That "most honest, frank, true, and stout-hearted of God's creatures," as Lord Jeffrey called him, had the foremost influence in political life of any man of his generation, and he won it not by great knowledge, for he had little, or by great dialectical powers, for he had none, but by the atmosphere of integrity, unselfishness, and humanity which he diffused around him. To such a leader England will always respond, for he has the characteristic virtues of her people. But he has also their characteristic faults. He is without a creed in the larger sense; he is incapable of the long view and the true perspective, for he has no appreciation of principles; and in complex matters he will be too simple and rough-and-ready to meet the needs of the case. He may serve his day well enough with hand-to-mouth expedients, but he will lay down no lasting foundation for posterity.

Such are the two extremes in talents and temperament. A just mixture is needed in the work of governing, but it is proper that the second should have the larger share. The right character is more essential than the right mind; or, to put it more exactly, the right disposition will succeed, even though the intellectual equipment be moderate, whereas high intellectual power, not conjoined with the requisite character, will assuredly fail. Minto, as we have seen, had the normal education of his class and no more; he had not, like Lord Morley, many chambers in his memory stored with theory and knowledge. But he had what was more important for his task, a strong natural intelligence, not easily befogged by subtleties, an intelligence which had a notable power of cutting clean to the root of a problem. He had a flair for the essential, which was in itself an intellectual gift, not indeed working by complex processes of ratiocination, but simply the result of a strong mind accustomed for long to exercise itself vigorously on practical affairs. We see it in Canada--his instant perception of the proper sphere of the Governor-General, his wise appreciation of the Alaskan tangle, his infallible constitutional probity. We see it in India--his diagnosis of the unrest, his understanding of the complex interplay of creeds and races, his instinct as to when to relax and when to tighten the rein, his doctrine of the true relation of Secretary of State and Viceroy. We see it in his view of the development of the British Empire--his ready assent to the principle of colonial nationalism, his early realization that the hope of the future lay not in legislative federation but in an executive alliance. We speak of a flair, but let us remember that such a flair is no blind instinct, no lucky guess, but the consequences of reasoning none the less close and cogent because it is not formally set out. He judged calmly and correctly because his powers of mind were strong, and in no way weakened by that theoretic distraction which often besets the professed intellectuel.

Such talents are inestimable in the business of life, and they are essentially the talents of the British people--the landowner, the merchant, the plain citizen; that is why we have always had so rich a reservoir to draw on for the administration of the country and the Empire. When raised to a high power, the result is some great achievement, like the settlement of Egypt and the union of South Africa. Both Cromer and Louis Botha had this gift for simplifying the complex, and by concentrating on the essential bringing order out of confusion. They, like Minto, made no pretensions to academic superiority; their principles were a sober deduction from facts, and their brilliance was revealed not in dazzling theories or glittering words but in the solid structure which they built. Their qualities of mind won them confidence, because they were always comprehensible, the qualities of the ordinary man on the heroic scale. Much the same may be said of Minto. He had the endowments of the best kind of country gentleman raised to a high power, and it may fairly be argued that in the art of government these endowments are the most valuable which the State can command for its service--the more valuable because they are not rare and exotic growths, but the staple of the national genius.

Character plays the major part in the life of action, and Minto's we have seen revealed in a variety of testing circumstances. A nature always modest, generous, and dutiful was broadened and toughened by his early life on the turf. The career of a gentleman-jockey has doubtless its drawbacks, but it is a school of certain indisputable virtues. A man starts on a level with others and has to strive without favour. He learns to take chances coolly, to cultivate steady nerves and the power of rapid decision; and he acquires in the process a rude stoicism. He meets human nature of every sort in the rough, and learns to judge his fellows by other standards than the conventional. Such a man may be a philistine but he will rarely be a fool, and Minto was preserved from the hardness and narrowness of the ordinary sportsman by his liberal education, the cultivated traditions of his family, and his perpetual interest in the arts of politics and war. Physically he was handsomely endowed by nature, for apart from great good looks he had perfect health and an amazing vitality, so that he was always eager for work and adventure. Nor had he any foibles or eccentricities of temper. He looked on the world cheerfully and sanely, wholly untormented by egotism, with a ready sense of humour--even of boyish fun, and also with the modest soldierly confidence of one who could forget himself in his task.

All who came in contact with him fell under the spell of his simple graciousness, for he could not have been discourteous had he tried. But those who saw much of him soon realized that his charm of manner was only the index of an inner graciousness of soul. This deeper charm sprang from two impressions which he left on all who had to deal with him. One was of unhesitating bravery. It was inconceivable that under any circumstances he should be afraid, or should hesitate to do what he believed to be right. The physical side was the least of it, for most men of his antecedents have that kind of courage; far rarer and more impressive was his moral fortitude. In Canada he could oppose all those whose esteem he most valued in a matter where an imperial officer and the local Government came into conflict; in India he could shape a course in direct opposition to the prejudices of his own military and sporting worlds, and choose in the pursuit of his duty to earn the imputation of weakness. The other impression was of a profound goodness--honour as hard as stone, and mercifulness as plain as bread. Deep in his nature lay an undogmatic religion, a simple trust in the wisdom and beneficence of God, and in the faith which he had learned in his childhood. It was a soldier's creed, unsullied by doubt, and it gave him both fearlessness and tenderness; though far enough from the rugged Calvinism of Dalhousie, it had the same moral inspiration. His assessment of values in life had the justness which comes only from a sense of what is temporal and what is eternal, and at the same time this clear-sightedness was mellowed always by his love of human nature. He judged himself by austere standards, but the rest of mankind with abundant charity.

Few men have had a happier and fuller life, which was indeed his due, for he had a supreme talent for living. An adventurous youth, a middle age of high distinction, a delightful family circle, innumerable attached friends, a temper which warmed the world around him--the gods gave their gifts in ample measure. Looking back upon his career, it is notable how little in essentials he changed. The man who smoked out a gambling den at Cambridge was the same man who put down his foot about the Punjab colonies. Nor did the boy in him ever pass, for at whatever age he had died he would have died young. He had indeed to the full the two strains which we have seen in his race--the speed and fire of the old Liddesdale Elliots and the practical sagacity and balance of the Whig lords of Minto. It is a combination that is characteristic of the Borders, which were never prone to a narrow fanaticism, and which rarely lost a certain genial tolerance and a gift for mirthfulness and the graces of life. Of this the greatest of Borderers, Sir Walter Scott, is an example, and Minto had something of the same central wisdom, combined with the same ready ear for the fife and clarion. The union makes for happiness and for achievement, and is perhaps the best that can be found in the "difficult but not desperate" life of man.

"Blest are those Whose blood and judgment are so well commingled."

INDEX

ABDTJE RAHMAN Abercrombie, Sir Ralph (Lord Dunfermline) Afghan War, the Afghanistan Aga Khan, the Alaskan Question, the Ale, river Althorp, Lord Alverstone, Lord (Sir Richard Webster) Arabi Ardagh, Sir John Argyll, Duke of Armour, Mr. Justice Arundel, Sir A. T. Ashburnham, Harriet Lady Astley, Sir J. Asquith, Mr. H. H. Aylesworth, Mr. A. B.

BALFOUR, Earl of (Mr. A. J. Balfour) Baroda, the Gaekwar of Bartholomew the Englishman Batoche Behawalpur Bentinck, Lord George Bentinck, Lord William Beresford, Lord Charles Beresford, Lord Marcus Beresford, Lord William Besant, Mrs. Annie Bhopal, the Begum of Bigge, Sir Arthur (see Lord Stamfordham) Bikanir Birkenhead, Earl of (Mr. F. E. Smith) Blood, Sir Bindon Boorde, Andrew Borden, Sir Frederick Borden, Sir Robert Border Mounted Rifles, the Borders, the Scottish Borthwick, Sir Algernon (Lord Glenesk) Botha, General Louis Bourassa, Mr., Brodrick, Mr. St. John (see Midleton, Earl of) Bryce, Lord Bucoleuch, family of Buccleuch Hunt, the Burke, Edmund Burnaby, Colonel Fred Butler, Rev. Arthur G. Butler, Sir Harcourt Butler, Dr. Montagu

CAMBRIDGE Campbell-Bannerman, Sir Henry Canada (see under Minto, 4th Earl of) Canning, Lord Cannon, Joe Cannon, tom Carlist Army, the Cavagnari, Sir Louis Chamberlain, Mr. Austen Chamberlain, Mr.

Joseph Chermside, Sir Herbert Churchill, Mr. Winston Clark, Sir William Cleveland, President Colley, Sir George Commune, the Paris Corlett, Mr. John Corsica Creagh, Sir O'Moore Cromer, 1st Earl of Curzon, 1st Marquis (Mr. George Nathaniel Curzon)

DALHOUSIE, 1st Marquis of Dane, Sir Louis Darbhunga, Maharaja of Dawnay, Lewis Disraeli, Mr. (Earl of Beaconsfield) Doughty, Dr. A. S. Douglas, Lord Francis Drummond, Major-General Laurence, Duff, Sir Beauchamp Dufferin, 1st Marquis of Dumont, Gabriel Dundonald, 12th Earl of Durham, Lord

EDE, George Edward VII., H.M. King Egyptian Campaign, the (1882) Elliot family, origin of Elliot, Arthur Elliot, Lady Eileen (Lady Francis Scott) Elliot, Esmond Elliot, Lieut.-Colonel Fitzwilliam Elliot, Gavin, of Midlem Mill Elliot, Gilbert, of Stobs Elliot, Sir Gilbert, 1st Baronet Elliot, Sir Gilbert, 2nd Baronet Elliot, Sir Gilbert, 3rd Baronet Elliot, Sir Gilbert, 4th Baronet (see Minto, 1st Earl of) Elliot, Sir Henry Elliot, Hugh (the Ambassador) Elliot, Mr. Hugh Elliot, Lady Ruby (Countess of Cromer) Elliot, Lady Violet (Lady Violet Astor) Eton

FISHER, Mr. Sydney, Forbes, Archibald Fraser, Sir Andrew French Canadians, the Fuller, Sir Bampfylde

GALLIFET, General George V., H.M. King Gladstone, W. E., Godley, Sir Arthur (Lord Kilbraeken) Gokhale, Mr. Gordon, General Charles Graham,

Captain Harry Grand National, the Grandin, Bishop Grenfell, Francis Grey, Albert, 4th Earl Grey, General Charles Grey, Henry, 3rd Earl Grey, Viscount (Sir Edward Grey) Guards, the Scots

HABIBULLAH Haldane, Viscount Hamilton, Lord George Hardinge of Penshurst, Lord Hardy, Mr. Thomas Hartopp, Captain Hastings, Warren Heathfield, Lord Henley Herschell, Lord Hislop, Lady Hislop, Lieut.-General Sir Thomas Hobhouse, Sir Charles Home Rule, Irish Hope, Sir Edward Hutton, Lieut.-General Sir Edward

IBBETSON, Sir Deuzil Indians in Canada, the

JAMESON, Sir Starr Jameson Raid, the Jersey, 7th Earl of Jette, Sir Louis Jind Jodhpur

KASHMIR Keir-Hardie, Mr. King, Mr. W. Mackenzie Kitchener, F.-M. Earl Kruger, President

LAHORE Lansdowne, 6th Marquis of Lariston Laurier, Sir Wilfrid Legard, Cecil Lesley, Bishop Liddesdale Limber Lloyd George, Mr. Loch, Lord Lodge, Mr. Henry Cabot Lonsdale, 5th Earl of Lyons, Lord Lyttelton, Mr. Alfred

MACDONALD, Sir John Macdonald, Mr. Ramsay Macdonnell, Lord Machell, Captain M'Kinley, President M'Mahon, Sir Henry Manners, Lord Maude, Sir Stanley Mayo, 6th Earl of Melgund, Lord (see Minto, 4th and

5th Earls of) Methuen, F.-M. Lord Middleton, General Midleton, 1st Earl of Mill, John Stuart Mills, General Nelson Milner, Lord Minto, 1st Earl of Minto, 2nd Earl of Minto, 3rd Earl of Minto, Gilbert John, 4th Earl of, birth and childhood; Eton; Cambridge; gazetted to Scots Guards; his steeplechasing career; in Paris during Commune; visits Carlist Army; work with Border Mounted Rifles; candidatures for Parliament; Russo-Turkish War; in Afghan War; life in London; in South Africa with Roberts; death of his mother; the Egyptian campaign; marriage; Military Secretary in Canada; in Riel Rebellion; sporting reminiscences; succession to earldom; life at Minto; appointed Governor-General of Canada; work for Canadian Defence; Canadian contingent for South Africa; the Hutton affair; the Dundonald affair; views on Imperial union; the Alaskan difficulty; visit to the Yukon; society and sport in Canada; work for Canadian Records; departure from Canada; summary of Governor-Generalship; appointed Viceroy of India; arrival in India; relations with Lord Kitchener; the partition of Bengal; exception of the Reform scheme; visit to North-West Frontier; speech to Mohammedan delegation; visit to Kashmir; reception of Amir of Afghanistan; the Punjab colonies question; the Anglo-Russian Convention; visit to Madras and Burma; the Hobhouse commission; the Zakka Khel rising; measures to deal with Indian unrest; the Jodhpur Durbar; the Reform Bill passed; the deportations; the opening of the new Legislative Council; last visit to North-West frontier; Mr. Montagu's speech; summary of Viceroyalty; departure from India; receives the Garter;

Mansion House speech; the Parliament Bill; Lord Rector of Edinburgh University; death; character and achievements Minto, 5th Earl of Minto, Mary Countess of Minto, Nina Countess of Minto House, Moncreiff, Lord Montagu, Mr. Edwin Montagu-Chelmsford scheme, the Morley of Blackburn, 1st Viscount (Mr. John Morley) Mountaineering Mounted Infantry, the (see also under Volunteers) Mulock, Sir William Muzaffarpur murders, the

NABHA Nicolson, Sir Arthur (Lord Carnock) Nizam of Hyderabad, the North-West frontier of India, the Norton, Mrs.

OSBOBNE, Mr. John (n.)

PALMERSTON, Lord Parkin, Sir George Patiala Pole-Carew, Lieut.-General Sir R. Police, the Canadian North-West Mounted Pozzo di Borgo Primrose, Sir Henry

RED RIVER Expedition, the Rhodes, Cecil Riarden, Sergeant Richardson, John Maunsell Riel Rebellion, the Ripon, 1st Marquis of Roberts, F.-M. Earl (Sir Frederick Roberts) Robinson, Sir Hercules (Lord Rosmead) Roosevelt, President Roos-Keppel, Sir George Root, Mr. Elihu Rosebery, Lord Russell, Lord John Russia Russo-Turkish War the

SALISBURY, Lord Saunderson, Colonel Scindia, Maharaja Scot of Satchels Scott, Mr. F. W. Scott, Sir

Walter Seddon, Mr. Richard Seeley, Sir John Singh, Sir Pertab Sinha, Lord Smith, F. E. (see Birkenhead, Earl of) Smith, Goldwin Smith, Sir James Dunlop South Africa South African War, the Southwell, Rev. H. Q. Spencer, Lady Sarah Stamfordham, Lord Stewart, F.-M. Sir Donald Stobs, family of Strachey, Sir John Strathcona, Lord Stuart, Lady Louisa Sudan Expedition, the (1884)

TASHI LAMA, the Tarte, Mr. Israel Teviot, river Thompson, Sir John Tongsa Penlop, the Townshend, Charles Turner, Senator

VICTORIA, H.M. Queen Volunteers, the

WALKEB, Horace War correspondents, position of War, the Great Warre, Dr. Webster, Richard (see Alverstone, Lord) Wellesley, Marquis Wellington, Duke of Willcocks, General Sir James Wolseley, 1st Viscount (Sir Garnet Wolseley) Wood, Sir Evelyn Woodford, F.-M. Sir Alexander Wyllie, Sir W. Curzon

YUKON question, the

ZAKKA KHEL rising, the

www.ingramcontent.com/pod-product-compliance
Lightning Source LLC
Chambersburg PA
CBHW032008220426
43664CB00006B/176